THE KING'S PARDON
FOR HOMICIDE
BEFORE A.D. 1307

THE KING'S PARDON
FOR HOMICIDE

BEFORE A.D. 1307

BY

NAOMI D. HURNARD

M.A., D.PHIL.

OXFORD
AT THE CLARENDON PRESS
1969

Oxford University Press, Ely House, London W. 1

GLASGOW NEW YORK TORONTO MELBOURNE WELLINGTON
CAPE TOWN SALISBURY IBADAN NAIROBI LUSAKA ADDIS ABABA
BOMBAY CALCUTTA MADRAS KARACHI LAHORE DACCA
KUALA LUMPUR SINGAPORE HONG KONG TOKYO

PRINTED IN GREAT BRITAIN

because they failed to secure or even to seek pardon. Paradoxically, the prerogative which enabled the king to show excessive leniency to the guilty tended to perpetuate an extraordinarily harsh method of treating the innocent, the involuntary slayers, those involved in fatal accidents or who slew in defence of life, honour, or property. With few exceptions these people could not be acquitted by the courts; together with infant and mentally deranged killers they needed the king's pardon. This requirement was grotesquely strict. In the year 1249, for example, Katherine Passeavant, aged four, was imprisoned in the abbot of St. Albans' gaol because in opening a door she had accidentally pushed a younger child into a vessel full of hot water in consequence of which it had died soon after; her father showed this matter to the king, who ordered the sheriff to deliver her 'quia rex totum sibi perdonavit'.[1] Had she been brought before his justices they would no doubt have recommended mercy, as they did for many adult slayers by mischance, but many people who found themselves in this situation and could afford to pay something for it sought clemency at once. Some did so even when it was not strictly necessary, either because they did not realize this, or because they did not care to bank on the court's recognizing it.

Since pardon was a matter of grace there was uncertainty as to both the need for it and the prospect of its being conceded. A deplorable result of this uncertainty, coupled with ignorance and superstitious fear, was the frequency of panic flight after fatal accidents or even sudden death from natural causes. People who were not responsible in any way whatever sometimes fled and such persons—*meticulosi* is Bracton's word for them—might obtain pardon though they did not really need it. Those who had contributed in some way to a death yet qualified for pardon were likely to flee and might never apply for it, so being outlawed and suffering punishment in this form. For example, two men sat down together on a bench which collapsed under their combined weight; one came down on top of the other and his knife, slipping from its sheath, gave him a fatal cut; the survivor fled, and the justices in eyre in 1272 ordered that he should be outlawed.[2] No evidence has been

---

[1] *Close Rolls, 1247–51*, 189.
[2] J.I. 1/238, m. 57[d]. (Except when otherwise stated all MSS. quoted are in the Public Record Office.)

CONTENTS

INTRODUCTION

THE power of pardon is regarded as 'indispensable to the wise administration of penal justice'.[1] This power may be used in various ways. It is not restricted to remitting or commuting a sentence passed in court but may also avert trial, staying prosecution. It can be used in exceptional cases to correct error in the courts, but it may also be a regular feature of penal justice, as it was until very recently in the form of the Home Secretary's recommendation of reprieve for those of unsound mind but not found insane according to the over-strict M'Naghten rules. Such a power may be abused; it can be perverted by political expediency, personal favour, or the whim of an absolute ruler. Even its regular exercise, intended to provide a responsible method for determining the fate of offenders who are thought not to deserve the normal penalties for their actions, may be criticized for substituting administrative discretion for judicial decision, uncertainty for predictability of punishment. In medieval England the king's prerogative of mercy, however worthy in conception, was certainly used to excess. It was scarcely ever available to those condemned to death in error, but in other respects it was grossly over-employed. Criminals were pardoned before trial from motives which were unrelated to the circumstances of their crimes, with no suggestion of extenuation, and in complete disregard of the need to maintain the deterrent force of prospective punishment. The main motive for this was military necessity: recruits could be enlisted by the promise of pardon. But even before Edward I adopted this disastrous expedient it may be suspected that a great many criminals were pardoned for equally irrelevant reasons. In this regard Henry III was too responsive to pressure, whether of a religious, personal, or social nature.

Yet, while pardons were granted to far too many criminals who did not deserve to escape punishment, they were also granted to large numbers who thoroughly deserved clemency, who should not, indeed, have stood in any need of it. Worse still, others who should not have needed it were punished

[1] *Kenny's Outlines of Criminal Law*, 19th ed. Par. 784.

found that he ever obtained pardon. Thus the harsh treatment of accidental slaying was aggravated still further by the tendency to flee in panic and so incur outlawry. For slayers in self-defence flight might be only prudent since absence of felonious intent was less obvious in such cases and their fate if they appeared in court was more problematical. At least it was wise to secure pardon without awaiting trial. Even justification for slaying, as when a felon was killed resisting arrest, might be difficult to establish and in cases of this sort, too, pardon was sometimes obtained as a precaution. Altogether, a great many pardons were secured by slayers who had not appeared in court. Many of them would have been recommended to the king's grace had they appeared there, a few might even have been acquitted, some found guilty. By going straight to the king they gave him the opportunity to exercise the prerogative at his discretion, uninfluenced by judicial opinions, and such appeals to his grace made it harder to achieve any definition of the types of homicide which needed and deserved it. Thus uncertainty and mistrust created a vicious circle, delaying the establishment and public recognition of a norm, the absence of which increased the anxiety and hardship suffered by many individuals. Basically, official policy was not quite so severe as a cursory reading of the enrolled pardons would suggest, but even when allowance is made for the unintended repercussions of the system of pardoning its deliberate application to killing by mischance or in self-defence seems indefensible.

The flight of many killers who deserved pardon led eventually to a worsening of the position of those who did not flee. Provided they had at no point withdrawn on account of the death, the slayers who secured pardon in the thirteenth century were not normally punished in any way, though they suffered some inconvenience and incurred some expense. But flight was an offence in itself, whatever the crime with which the fugitive expected to be charged, and the regular penalty for it was forfeiture of chattels. Since a great many slayers fled before securing pardon a great many were punished in this way, but still it was recognized that the punishment was not for the actual slaying. The situation changed when the justices ceased to inquire whether the slayer who had been or was about to be pardoned had fled, and ordered the confiscation of his chattels regardless of this important distinction. As a result of this it came to be supposed that some measure of culpability attached to all these cases. In the time of Henry VIII, while it was thought proper for those who had slain in self-defence in a chance medley to be punished by forfeiture of chattels, even though they had not fled, there was doubt whether those who killed robbers, murderers, and burglars in defence of life and property ought so to be punished. A statute of 1532 settled this 'question and ambiguity' in favour of those who had killed such evildoers in self-defence.[1] In theory other types of pardonable homicide continued to entail forfeiture and this was taken to imply that they deserved some punishment. Thus Blackstone distinguished three kinds of homicide: justifiable, excusable, and felonious. 'The first', he said, 'has no share of guilt at all; the second very little', but its very name 'imports some fault, some error, or omission: so trivial, however, that the law excuses it from the guilt of felony, though in strictness it judges it deserving of some little degree of punishment.'[2] However, by his day there was a revolt against this view and Sir Michael Foster, writing in mid-eighteenth century, reveals how he and other justices were already allowing juries to bring in verdicts of not guilty, so averting both the need to apply for pardon and the liability to forfeiture. They had, he claimed, 'to say the worst, deviated from ancient practice in favour of innocence'.[3] On the strength of Foster's remarks, Sir J. F. Stephen concluded that 'The law upon this subject may thus be considered as having fallen into desuetude in the course of the eighteenth century', and he went on to summarize the statute of 1828, 'which provides that no punishment or forfeiture shall be incurred by any person who shall kill another by misfortune, or in his own defence, or in any other manner without felony'.[4]

This particularly obnoxious aspect of the treatment of excusable slaying, with its implication of some degree of guilt, was a comparatively late development. In the period dealt with here, the king did not consider that every homicide he pardoned

---

[1] 24 Henry VIII, cap. 5.

[2] *Commentaries*, iv, cap. 14. The term 'excusable' will be used here to denote homicides which needed but deserved pardon, but its use must not be taken to imply that excusable homicides had always 'imported some fault'.

[3] *Crown Cases*, 288. Forfeiture on account of flight continued, however: 'Flight, it is well known, at this day induceth a forfeiture of goods, though the party should be wholly acquitted of the fact.' Ibid. 286.

[4] *History of the Criminal Law of England*, iii. 76–7.

merited punishment. However, this did not mean that pardon entirely averted punishment; sometimes it only commuted it. Moreover, there was a remarkable limitation on his pardons: they nearly always contained the stipulation that the grantee should stand to right, stand trial, if prosecuted by the victim's associates, and for a time they contained also the stipulation that alternatively he should make peace with them, in other words, pay them some agreed sum as reparations. The pardons did not, then, purport to give protection against punishment as the result of prosecution by revengeful kinsmen of the slain. The reason for this limitation and its effects in practice present problems of some interest. The other proviso, that of making peace with the kin, is of interest from another point of view. It was the last vestige in England, for many centuries, of the ancient notion that compensation ought to be paid for slaying. Some type of emendation might well be thought appropriate for excusable killing when punishment was not. It is significant that in parts of the Continent compensation in the form of wergild continued to be payable, not only for killing in self-defence or by mischance, but even for manslaughter until the seventeenth century and in a few places in theory even later.[1] The early and total disappearance of wergild in England left a gap which this proviso in the pardons made some attempt to fill. But it was only a feeble attempt, since it provided no legal machinery for enforcing its implementation. It was soon found to be of no practical value and was dropped from the pardons; once this had happened even the notion that the bereaved family had a moral right to some form of compensation was soon obliterated. It was, indeed, a serious additional count against the system of pardoning that it failed to preserve their legal right to it; not until the nineteenth century were they even enabled to sue for damages by a civil action. Thus the medieval system was impartial in its harshness, bearing heavily on both the excusable slayer and the family of the slain.

No theory has yet been put forward to explain in detail how and why this peculiar if long-lived method of dealing with homicide by mischance and in self-defence was adopted, though legal historians have touched upon it in passing. The issue was at one time obscured by the belief that excusable slaying had always incurred the punishment of forfeiture of chattels. In

---

[1] See B. S. Phillpotts, *Kindred and Clan*, 96, 124–5, 156, 168.

this belief, some writers connected the treatment of excusable slaying with the Anglo-Saxon system, supposing that the penalty derived from the ancient fixed wite or some other ancient payment. Thus Blackstone suggested that the penalty was the continuation of forfeiture 'by way of fine or wergild: which was probably disposed of . . . *in pios usus*, according to the humane superstition of the times, for the benefit of his soul who was thus suddenly sent to his account, with all his imperfections on his head'.[1] Blackstone misconceived the nature of wergild, which was really reparation to the bereaved family, not a penalty. He then went on to confuse both wergild and wite with deodand, the animal or inanimate object which had occasioned an accidental death and was indeed supposed to be dedicated to some religious use, though it came to be appropriated by the king. To connect these payments with the later punishment was inadmissible; two of them were not penalties at all and there was no continuity between the third, the wites, and the much later forfeiture of chattels of pardoned slayers who had not fled. But although Blackstone's notions on the subject were hazy, the general idea of some connection between the system of wergild and wite and the treatment of excusable homicide remained attractive. Foster challenged the belief that the pardoned homicide's chattels had all along been forfeit regardless of the question of his flight, yet he also suggested some such connection.[2] Stephen was well aware of the danger of arguing from the forfeiture, but was inclined to follow him in this. 'It is, I think, by no means improbable that (as Foster suggested) this method of treating homicide in self-defence, or by accident, as matters requiring a pardon and possibly involving some forfeiture (though the evidence as to this in cases where there was no flight is not clear) may have been the last remnant of the old system of bot and wite . . .'.[3] Thus despite the realization that there was a weak or even a missing link in the chain, these writers were reluctant to abandon the theory that the severity of the treatment of such homicide harked back in some way to Anglo-Saxon customs.

Maitland took the opposite view. It was not continuity with the old system but its complete disappearance that must account for the 'monstrous' treatment of slaying in self-defence and by accident.

[1] Loc. cit.   [2] Op. cit. 287.   [3] Op. cit. iii. 40.

We do not say that the law of England was ever committed to the dogma that he who slays by misadventure must be put to death. We take the truth to be this:—Far into the twelfth century the main theory of the law still was that an intentional homicide could be paid for by *wer* and *wite*; but there were exceptions which devoured the rule, and, under cover of charges of felony, *guet-apens* and breach of the king's peace, intentional homicide became an unemendable crime to be punished with death or mutilation. What to do with cases of misadventure, the law did not see. In the past many or all of them had given occasion for a *wer*, if not for a *wite* or a blood-feud. There was nothing for it but 'mercy'; the king himself must decide in each case whether life and limb shall be spared. Meanwhile the law of *wer*, being no longer applicable if there was felony, perished for lack of sustenance, and the *parentes occisi* were reduced to getting what they could by threats of an appeal.[1]

Similarly with killing in self-defence. The system of pardoning in these cases was, then, a *pis aller* and a thoroughly bad one at that. All that Maitland can say in palliation is that the system was not confined to England. In France also 'far on into modern times the king's *lettres de grâce* were granted to those who had slain a man *per infortunium vel se defendendo*. We are not dealing with an insular peculiarity.'[2]

The contrast with the older rules is certainly striking. Anglo-Saxon legislation had tackled the problem of differing degrees of liability and shown itself sensitive to the finest distinctions. If it had paid great attention to claims for compensation it had not overlooked the need for penalties in some cases, and it had recognized that there might be neither culpability nor such negligence as to render the slayer liable to compensate the dead man's relatives. This is seen already in Alfred's law concerning spear-carrying.[3] A spear might be carried in a dangerous or negligent way; it might not only be carried at a dangerous angle but deliberately used to wound someone; it might be carried safely. If someone was slain by it intentionally then both wergild and wite must be paid. If death was due to negligence it involved the payment of wergild alone, that is the slayer must pay compensation but incurred no penalty. If the death was not attributable to the spear-bearer's negligence but was entirely accidental or due to the victim's own jay-walking, no

[1] *Hist. Eng. Law*, ii. 483.   [2] Ibid. 484.   [3] Cap. 36.

emendation need be paid at all. The later system would not entrust the courts with the task of drawing distinctions such as these; it was now left to the king's own discretion to remit punishment and to extra-judicial action by the bereaved relatives to extort reparations if he did so. It is, of course, impossible to say how far the Anglo-Saxon laws were in fact effective, and even if some attempt was made to put them into operation the system they envisaged was very far from being a sophisticated one; yet in contrast with its clumsy and inhuman successor it showed some refinement and rationality. Yet in spite of the contrast between the two systems of dealing with homicide other than murder and the loss of much that was valuable in the older system, the change may have been less cataclysmic than Maitland supposed. The gesture, even if it was no more than that, of requiring peace to be made with the family when the king pardoned a slayer, itself hints at some wish to preserve, or appear to be preserving, elements of the ancient law. Those writers who found some continuity between the two systems may have had the right instinct, although other evidence than theirs will have to be adduced to establish it.

The first object of this study is to discover how the medieval system of pardoning took shape, especially why pardon was normally limited to the king's own suit and why slayers by accident and in self-defence came to require it. The second is to examine the way in which the system operated in the thirteenth century, and its effects both on the people most directly concerned and also on the general public, whose security was liable to be reduced by excessive clemency to murderers and professional criminals. It will be considered chiefly from three points of view, that of the killers, the victim's kin, and the king. The attitude of the latter was complex and liable to contortion, for not only was he the guardian of public order as well as the dispenser of mercy and equity, but also in this last role he wielded a prerogative which he was likely to guard jealously against interference and encroachment. His interpretation of his duty and his exploitation of his power would prove decisive for the other groups affected by his pardons.

I

THE ORIGIN OF THE
MEDIEVAL SYSTEM OF PARDONING

THE king's authority to grant pardon goes back to the Anglo-Saxon period. It was one aspect of a more general power to determine what punishment should be imposed for a particular category of offences and to remit or commute the prescribed penalty in individual cases. It might be assumed that there would be very little scope for such discretion and very little chance of its proving acceptable in a society based on kindred and seigneurial rights, which entailed the payment of a fixed wergild and manbot for homicide and bot for all sorts of injuries. Yet public penalties were inflicted from an early time, and although only pecuniary ones, the wites, were compatible with payment of compensation some offences were recognized as calling for corporal punishment. Nor were these more heinous offences only ones which directly affected the king as an individual rather than as ruler and lawgiver, and punishments decreed by him were by no means insignificant or merely subsidiary to wergild and bot. The growth of the royal prerogative of mercy may have been somewhat retarded because the need for it was limited, but it always had some scope, and this steadily widened as penalties became more stringent.

Late in the seventh century Wihtred of Kent decreed that when a thief was taken with the stolen goods on him the king should choose between capital punishment or slavery overseas or ransom by the culprit's wergild.[1] By the end of the Anglo-Saxon period the unemendable crimes included murder, that is secret and so presumably premeditated killing, plotting against king or lord, acts of violence in the army, assaults upon houses, arson, obvious theft, harbouring an excommunicate or outlaw, coining, fighting in the king's court; the perpetrator of most if not all of these deeds was liable to lose his life,[2] but the king's

---

[1] Cap. 26.
[2] IV Ethelred, 5, 3 and 4; 7, 1; II Cnut, 56; 57; 59; 61; 64; 66, 1.

power to mitigate the punishment was frequently emphasized. Wihtred had reserved to himself the choice between the various penalties for thieves, and it is not inconceivable that he actually determined them in individual cases; in a small kingdom like Kent this would not have been impracticable. In an England which was coming to be united it was not feasible to leave the choice of punishment to the king in quite this way, and the laws came instead to lay down one penalty, but if this was capital add that he might commute it. The culprit could now, it seems, take the initiative in asking the king to do so. In the time of Athelstan, the Londoners' ordinance decreed the death penalty for slaying in vengeance for the killing of a thief 'unless the king is willing to pardon him'.[1] A little later Edmund issued his famous code attempting to reduce blood feuds by restricting liability to vendetta, when satisfaction was not forthcoming, to the actual culprit; anyone who took vengeance on a member of his family instead was to incur the hostility of the king and all his friends. In the course of this ordinance he declared 'concerning mundbryce and hamsocn, that anyone who commits it after this is to forfeit all that he owns, and it is to be for the king to decide whether he may preserve his life'.[2] This reference to the power reserved to him to commute the capital sentence is particularly noteworthy because it occurs in such an important and innovatory assertion of royal authority. The policy of strengthening public sanctions against acts of violence was to continue to be associated with references to the discretionary power. The prerogative of pardon gained in significance not only because enactments of this kind greatly increased the opportunities to exercise it, but also because the king recognized the wisdom of tempering any new severity by drawing attention to the possibility of mitigation in approved cases. Discretion in the imposition of penalties was not, however, always reserved to the king himself. In some instances it resided in the court, or in the bishop who sat in it.[3]

Thus by the end of the Anglo-Saxon period not only was there considerable scope for clemency but there was also a deliberate policy which involved it. This was true to some extent also in the early part of the period, but it is unlikely that

---

[1] VI Athelstan, 1, 5; cf. 1, 4.   [2] II Edmund, 6.
[3] See, e.g., F. L. Attenborough, *Laws of the Earliest English Kings*, Appendix I, and Cnut's Proclamation of 1020, cl. 11.

the king would often wish to commute the capital sentence so long as this was reserved for crimes which were particularly heinous in their nature and in which guilt was demonstrable to a very high degree of probability. Thus the king's mercy may have been invoked less often on the grounds that a given case was being treated with undue harshness, than on some extraneous pretext, or through the intercession of an influential lord or ecclesiastic. The protection of the church could be obtained in another way by the criminal's taking sanctuary. There are many references to this in the laws, and it may well have been the most important single means of securing mitigation of the prescribed penalties. For although the kings were zealous to make sanctuary really inviolable and safeguard the sanctuary-seeker from being slain in revenge for his crime, yet its effect was not to free him from all punishment whatever, or reduce it, as in the Middle Ages, to abjuration of the realm. While protected against vendetta and generally against loss of life or limb he might still receive some punishment. Accordingly the degree of protection given by sanctuary was regulated by royal legislation and in individual cases, also, the king's discretionary power might be invoked and the fate of the sanctuary-seeker might still lie in his hands. For example, Ethelred reserved to the king power to commute the punishment on one who had sought sanctuary himself after violating it by slaying in church:

And if ever henceforth any man so violates the sanctuary of God's Church that he commits homicide within the church walls, that then is beyond compensation ... unless it happen that he escapes from there and reaches so important a sanctuary that the king grants him his life on that account, in return for full compensation both to God and to men.[1]

Edgar may earlier have tried to make the protection afforded by it depend on the king's consent in individual cases of theft and treason.[2] Thus the king was closely concerned in the fate of sanctuary-seekers and his clemency may thereby have acquired an additional religious tinge, though no doubt it had been associated with Christian charity ever since the conversion.

[1] VIII Ethelred, 1, 1.
[2] III Edgar, 7, 3. The wording of this clause is vaguer and it is not altogether certain that it applied to sanctuary. Only one MS. refers to the king's allowing the culprits' lives to be preserved.

As the extension and intensification of punishments in the
tenth and eleventh centuries gave more general scope for it, the
king continued to respect the claims of the injured individual
or family to reparation. These were necessarily extinguished
when capital punishment was imposed, but they revived when
it was remitted or commuted for a pecuniary penalty. For
example, the king could grant a general amnesty, but in so
doing he would be careful of these claims; thus Athelstan pardoned all thefts committed within a certain period, but on condition that the thieves confessed their crimes before a set date
and also made amends.[1] It was a matter of policy, then, to
temper the severity of new penal legislation to the benefit of
both offender and victim by showing mercy to the former in
certain cases but with the stipulation that reparation must be
made to the latter. This applied also to sanctuary-seekers. In
the clauses quoted and probably throughout they were liable
to make amends to the injured. 'If anyone', said Ine, in cap. 5,
'is liable to the death penalty and he reaches a church, he is to
retain his life and to compensate as the law directs him.' Alfred
remitted half the penalty to the man who took sanctuary 'on
account of any crime which has not been discovered, and there
confesses himself in God's name', and, apparently, also required
the culprit who had reached sanctuary to pay compensation, for
if he handed over his weapons to his foes, they were 'to keep
him for 30 days, and send notice about him to his kinsmen',
in order, it seems, that the latter might produce the first
instalment of the money required to compensate those he had
injured.[2]

Homicide was one of the crimes punishment for which might
be remitted, but there may have been less frequent occasion to
seek clemency for this than for some others. Presumably the
general rule that the pardoned offender must make reparation
applied. If the king remitted capital punishment for murder,
then the victim's family would have the right to wergild, and
if the slaying was in any case emendable, the king's remission
of the wite would not affect wergild. When purely accidental
slaying was concerned there would be no wite to remit. There
might still be a question as to liability to pay wergild as this
depended on there having been some negligence, but this was
a matter for the court. The king might exhort his subjects to

[1] III Athelstan, 3.   [2] Alfred, cap. 5, 3, 4.

moderate their claims but would not apparently interfere with them. Edgar decreed that 'there is to be such remission in the compensation as is justifiable before God and supportable in the State',[1] and Ethelred that 'he who is an involuntary agent in his misdeeds should always be entitled to clemency and to better terms',[2] but both seem to have been referring to decisions and agreements reached in court, not imposed by the king.

Before the Norman Conquest, then, it appears that the king's clemency sometimes amounted to pardon in the sense that punishment was remitted altogether, though compensation was not affected, but that it was often confined to commuting a sentence of death or mutilation to a pecuniary penalty. Outright pardon is seldom mentioned in the laws, but that does not necessarily imply that it was infrequent in practice, especially in the later period when the lengthening list of unemendable offences gave more opportunity for it. At this period, especially, a deliberate policy can be discerned of emphasizing the king's authority to commute or remit a newly decreed and more severe penalty. Throughout, whether he was acting judicially in choosing between alternative punishments, or remitting punishment of his grace or in recognition of sanctuary, his decision apparently related only to the penalty and did not diminish any right of the injured parties to compensation; such rights seem, indeed, to have been reinstated whenever punishment in life or limb, which would have obliterated them, was remitted.

The same trends can be seen after the Conquest, but it was some time before the use of the prerogative became very frequent and pardons assumed the form which was to endure for so long. The need for this new departure did not arise immediately. The penal policy of the Norman kings was not at first so severe as might have been expected in the circumstances of the Conquest, and the wergild system was allowed to linger on for a while. Indeed, it has even been thought that the Normans at first, far from intensifying punishment, actually reduced it. William the Conqueror is supposed to have substituted mutilation for capital punishment, but it is far from certain that he did so.[3] In any case, mutilation would in practice often prove

---

[1] III Edgar, 1, 2. [2] VI Ethelred, 52, 1; cf. II Cnut, 68.

[3] See *E.H.R.*, 1949, 312, n. 2; H. G. Richardson and G. O. Sayles, *Law and Legislation*, 47. The statement in the Articles ascribed to the Conqueror may be a

fatal, and if William ever did issue such a decree the risk of undergoing its penalties must have been a powerful incentive to seek mitigation. William Rufus is said to have shown leniency towards thieves, but Henry I certainly did not shrink from the infliction of capital punishment, though he employed other forms as well.[1] By the middle of his reign, the sending out of justices *ad omnia placita* in addition to the appointment of resident local justiciars, very much concerned with pleas of the Crown, would suggest that important steps had been taken to curb and punish acts of violence. The *Leges Henrici Primi*, compiled at this time (1114–18, according to Liebermann), stress the reservation of many pleas to the king's justice. Yet they suggest that punishments had not yet been greatly extended. The situation appears to have been both complex and ill defined. A great deal seems to have rested in the discretion of king or justiciar. The system of amercement was in use, but had not entirely superseded wites calculated according to ancient tariffs or at the sum of the culprit's own wergild. To be in the king's mercy meant liability to loss of life, limb, or property, but with every hope of redemption by an amount of money fixed in each case. Thus a rather vague threat of capital punishment, mutilation, or total forfeiture now hung over a miscellaneous assortment of offences and the tendency was to substitute this threat for predetermined penalties. Even for theft the capital sentence might be commuted by the king to a money penalty.[2] Only for treason to a lord does the compiler state categorically that there can be no commuting of the sentence of the most agonizing death, though he repeats Cnut's rule that murder and other serious crimes are unemendable.[3] Unless it was aggravated by such circumstances as felony or breach of the king's hand-given peace, open homicide was still emendable, the amount of the fine being determined by the culprit's wergild. This did not necessarily mean that he was liable only to a money penalty and not to make amends towards his victim's

garbled rendering of earlier prohibitions of the death penalty 'pro parvo delicto' (V Ethelred, 3; VI Ethelred, 10; II Cnut, 2, 1), or an unwarranted generalization from the customs of Winchester, for there the savage mutilations which William was said to have substituted for it do seem to have taken its place. See J.I. 1/778, mm. 59, 59d; cf. *Close Rolls*, *1247–51*, 173. J.I. 1/40, m. 30 shows that mutilation was also inflicted in Wallingford in the thirteenth century on the strength of its grant of the customs of Winchester.   [1] See *E.H.R.*, 1949, 312, n. 2.

[2] *Leges Henrici Primi*, 13.   [3] Ibid. 75, 1; 12, 1a.

family by paying the latter's wergild to them. Although he does not say so in this context, later on the compiler represents the ancient system as still in operation, and devotes many clauses to elaborating its rules. Not only is the matter of wergild for slaying by misadventure considered in some detail (cl. 90), but it is made clear that it is not restricted to such cases. There is a special section on the payments for the slaying of slaves and servants, and much is said of the actual tariff and the liability of associates to contribute to the wergild and the order in which payments must be made.[1] However, much of this material may really have been of antiquarian rather than practical interest.

As Maitland remarked, the system as formulated here must have been too cumbersome often to be workable in practice:

> The tariff however is now very cumbrous. In the simplest case there is the *wer* of the slain, varying with his rank, to be paid to his kin; there is *manbot* to be paid to his lord, . . . there is the *wite* to be paid to the king or some lord who has regalia. But in all probability the offender will have run up a yet heavier bill by breaking some *grith*; the owner of a house will claim a *grithbrice*, the owner of the soken will claim *fyhtwite* or *blodwite*; happy will it be for our man-slayer if he has committed neither *hamsocn* nor *forsteal*.[2]

Failure to meet the bill 'exposes the slayer to the vengeance of the slain man's kin'.[3] The system of emendation was thus in a precarious state because it had been stretched too far. It was in no shape to survive when official policy was directed towards superseding it by punishments, whether in life and limb, as of far greater deterrent force, or by amercements which, their amount being incalculable beforehand, had perhaps some deterrent effect, and which in any event diverted more of the financial proceeds from the injured parties' pockets to the royal fisc. The compiler of the *Leges Edwardi Confessoris* took little interest in wergilds. He did not ignore the subject altogether, but his references to it were made in passing and do not suggest that it was of much practical importance at the time when he was writing, probably a little later than the compilation of the *Leges Henrici Primi*.

The wergild system does not appear to have been the target

---

[1] Especially in clauses 69–71, 75–9.   [2] *Hist. Eng. Law*, ii. 458.

[3] It is possible that the courts were allowing compromises in these cases, some smaller payment being agreed in lieu of wergild, but no direct evidence of such a practice has been found.

of open and direct attack. No decree is known to have abolished it outright, and probably it was reduced by indirect methods, especially the extension of the king's special peace, for once this became continuous and all-pervasive every culpable homicide was automatically rendered unemendable by wergild and wite. The date when this occurred is not known. At the very beginning of his reign Henry I had decreed firm peace throughout his realm, but it has been shown that his purpose in this was not to make the king's peace in the technical sense universal.[1] Both the *Leges Henrici Primi* and the *Leges Edwardi Confessoris* indicate that the king's special protection had been extended. The latter, indeed, place very great emphasis upon it, and list so many occasions, places, and persons as coming within it that there can have been little difficulty in making out that almost any slaying was in breach of it. If this evidence is reliable, the king's peace had not been declared universal when these compilations were made, yet its different varieties must already have been coalescing to form an almost continuous whole and the process may have been completed by the end of the reign. Henry II seems to have felt no hesitation in claiming universality for his peace. In 1166, for example, the Assize of Clarendon ignored completely any possible distinction between killings that were and were not breaches of it. By Glanvill's time, any assault could be placed outside the competence of the local courts by the assertion that it was a breach of the king's peace.[2] At the end of the twelfth century, when plea rolls begin to be available, every appeal of homicide had to allege that the killing had been in breach of the king's peace. It also had to allege that it had been committed *nequiter*, i.e. that it was felonious, and the notion of felony had probably been making some contribution also to the practice of treating all culpable homicide as unemendable, but the history of this term is even more obscure. The *Leges Henrici Primi* used it on several occasions but in such a way that it may still have stood for treason to a lord rather than iniquity in general. Eventually, the term came to be used in a general way to denote that a crime was a heinous one and as such merited capital punishment. These two conceptions were, then, available as weapons in any onslaught upon what remained of the old system of emendation for culpable homicide. Late in the reign of Henry I it seems to

[1] By L. Riess, *E.H.R.*, 1926, 328.   [2] Glanvill, *De Legibus*, Lib. i. 2.

have been near to, if it had not already reached, vanishing point; thus it is uncertain how much Henry I had left for Henry II to do, or how much the civil war under Stephen made it necessary to do again. Henry II's determination to suppress crime does not need to be emphasized, and there can be little doubt that wergild for culpable homicide, if it did survive into his reign, was eliminated in its first decade.

It was not only the slayers who regretted its disappearance. Many bereaved relatives still hankered after it when the circumstances of the slaying were not too much of an affront to the honour of the family; they were not so vindictive as always to prefer to see retribution inflicted rather than accept some form of pecuniary atonement. No doubt there were many homicides of such a shameful nature that the anger of the victim's relatives would not be assuaged until they had seen condign punishment inflicted by the order of the court, failing which they might still be tempted to take vengeance on the culprit themselves. It is possible that at the time of the Danish invasions there had been some increase in vendettas and this may point to some turning against the practice of accepting compensation. Since that time, however, the number of unemendable crimes had so multiplied that there was little need to fear that the courts would be over-lenient. The only type of culpable homicide which could still be paid for by wergild and wite in the early years of the twelfth century was slaying in a fight or medley, and that without any aggravating circumstances. In a warlike society public opinion tends to condone fighting, and slaying in the course of it, even if illegal, is not regarded as a shameful crime. While such a spirit prevailed this type of homicide could properly be atoned for by wer with the addition of wite as token of its unlawfulness, and it would not be dishonourable for the relatives to accept the wergild. For over another century in England there is plenty of evidence for the payment and acceptance of compensation for homicide either out of court or, with the king's licence, in court, and on the Continent the wergild system itself continued to operate much longer. It is highly improbable that there was some short-lived access of vindictiveness, peculiar to England, which led to the concerted and voluntary relinquishing of their ancient right by bereaved relatives. It would have been optimistic to expect even their reluctant acquiescence in the policy which was fast threatening to deprive them of it. In fact, there is evidence to show that in the campaign against crime Henry II at least was confronted with a good deal of obstruction from his subjects. Measures had to be taken to hold those entitled to appeal to their duty of bringing a capital charge.

The vigilance of Henry and his justices in dealing with recalcitrant appellors has left many traces on his pipe rolls. It was an offence to withdraw an appeal once it had been launched, or to compromise it without permission. Appellors were being amerced for failure to prosecute their appeals quite early in the reign. In 1166 William FitzRobert owed 100 shillings 'quia defic. de appellatione sua de morte sororis sue in murdro' and two other men owed a mark each 'pro defectu appellationis sue'.[1] Default means failure to prosecute; failure to prove the charge by winning the judicial combat would be 'recreantisa', and three other entries on the pipe roll of this year mention this by name, the fine in each case being the 60 shillings laid down for this by William the Conqueror.[2] But there are even clearer cases on the roll for 1168: 'Adam de Triwa red. comp. de 1.m. pro appellatione sua remissa'; 'Serlo parmentarius redd. Comp. de dim. m. pro appellatione quam fec. & postea dimisit.'[3] These two appeals were probably not for homicide as the sums due were comparatively small, but in the following year a woman owed 20 shillings 'quia retraxit se de Appellatione mortis viri sui'.[4] It is evident that many appeals were not followed up, but it is impossible to judge how many related to homicide. Many appeals were settled out of court, and by the end of the reign there is evidence that it was an offence to help to bring about such a concord.[5] Probably other settlements were negotiated without an appeal even being begun in the county court, for the slayer could be blackmailed by the mere threat of appeal as well as by its being actually started there. Settlements of this kind were not in themselves illegal and failure to appeal could not be treated as an offence in itself, however irritating this negative reaction to his policy might be to the king. Thus the pipe rolls can supply no information as to the

[1] *Pipe Roll, 12 Henry II*, 46, 49, 76.
[2] Ibid. 20, 69, 85; Liebermann, *Gesetze der Angelsachsen*, i. 484.
[3] *Pipe Roll, 14 Henry II*, 165, 167.
[4] Ibid., *15 Henry II*, 114. There are several other entries for default of appeal on this roll; see pp. 6, 29, 59, 139, 147.
[5] Ibid., *31 Henry II*, 230.

number of potential appellors who abstained from appealing and came to terms with the slayers of their kinsmen. While the authorities could not impose any penalty on them, however, they could and did show some hostility towards them. Henry II's attitude can only be inferred, but the early plea rolls show that his successors' justices looked askance at persons who failed to appeal when they were in a position to do so. Things could be made extremely nasty for them, especially if they had been present at the slaying and could put forward no adequate explanation of their own survival; such persons tended to be regarded and condemned as accomplices.[1] Failure to appeal was thus a risky course, but in a great many cases no appellor came forward and in some, at least, compensation had probably been obtained.

The measures taken to discourage the withdrawal and un-authorized compromising of appeals indicate very clearly that the policy of stepping up punishment at the expense of repara-tions met with opposition. It is likely that this was already happening under Henry I. The extension of the king's peace was making it ever harder for the relatives of slain men to secure compensation, yet they might see no good reason for their being deprived of it just because the slaying had occurred on, say, the king's highway rather than elsewhere. When some arbitrary and recent extension looked like robbing them of it, they would already be tempted either to prosecute but minimize the gravity of the case by keeping silent over this circumstance, or to refrain from prosecuting in court, seeking to extort as much as possible from the slayer by extra-judicial means. The cumbrousness of the old system of wergild, bot, and wite had probably long been encouraging the practice of negotiating peace out of court, and this tendency would now be accelerated. Whatever measures the government took to make things awkward for those who should have appealed and did not, or who did not prosecute their appeal to its conclusion, there was special need to supple-ment this method of prosecution.

The intensification of sanctions against crime thus made it necessary for the king to concern himself more and more with ensuring that criminals were brought to trial. Punishment was the end result of a process which could not safely be left to

---

[1] e.g. *Curia Regis Rolls*, xii, no. 1172; cf. *Select Pleas of the Crown*, Seld. Soc. i, no. 197.

the injured party or next of kin to initiate when private prosecu-
tors no longer stood to gain financially, but even before this
there had been need for public prosecution in some circumstances and the machinery was already at hand in the jury of
presentment. By means of this the new policy could be made
effective and appellors could be kept up to scratch or justice
done despite their all too frequent default. From the turn of
the century surviving eyre rolls reveal how this was achieved.
If the next of kin attempted to conceal the slaying altogether,
with the idea of negotiating a settlement, then, of course, it was
the business of the jurors to frustrate this attempt by presenting the slaying and perhaps suggesting his complicity in it.
If the relatives did not conceal the slaying but tried to minimize
the slayer's culpability and claim damages, their appeals would
be quashed and the court would ask for the jurors' account of
it, so ensuring that the matter was investigated and treated as
a possible case of felonious killing; while if an appeal had been
begun before the local serjeant or coroner or in the county
court but was not prosecuted before the itinerant justices, the
jurors would present not only the slaying itself but also the dis-
continuation of the appeal, with the consequences for the defaulting appellor which have already been noticed. Finally, if
an appeal of felony was prosecuted at the eyre but was quashed
for some technical defect in it or the disqualification of the
appellor, then, too, the jurors would give their account of the
matter and the suspect would be arraigned and tried at the suit
of the king.

The supersession of the wergild system and the increasing
threat of capital punishment or mutilation invited the extended
use of the prerogative of mercy, but it was the fact that the
king's policy was not universally supported by those entitled
to appeal, and the consequent increase in prosecution at his
own suit in place of theirs, that gave it a new form, that which
was to characterize the great mass of pardons for centuries to
come.

Although conditions were not ripe for this mutation until
a considerable time after the Norman Conquest and the king's
clemency was extended in much the same way as it had been
before, there seems to have been some development here too.
A more definite demarcation appeared between the royal
prerogative of pardon and the discretion which could still

be left to the courts to mitigate or adjust penalties in certain circumstances. At first, perhaps, the king's own clemency was chiefly exercised in those cases which placed the criminal 'in his mercy', and thus there may still have been few occasions for outright pardoning. But as the power to impose a pecuniary penalty in lieu of more severe punishment was shared by the king's justices, at any rate for crimes of the sort which were not regarded as the most serious, to be in the king's mercy came to mean liability to 'amercement' by his justices, to being sentenced to pay an amount fixed *ad hoc*, but probably calculated with some regard to the culprit's capacity to pay as well as to the gravity of his crime. Those guilty of the most serious crimes would still require the actual exercise of the king's own authority, and this would now be more likely to take the form of pardon, though this itself might have to be bought.

It is easy to point to the financial advantages accruing to the royal fisc from amercement and pardon and regard them as the motive both for threatening sterner penalties and then varying them in individual cases. But the danger of ascribing too much to the king's mercenary instincts has recently, and rightly, been stressed.[1] The paramount aim of Henry I and his great minister, Roger of Salisbury, was the maintenance of good law and good order, and in relying on discretionary powers to avoid undue rigidity in their new rules they were following the traditional policy of Saxon and Danish kings. Greed may have stretched discretion too far on occasion, but it did not dictate the retention of such powers. The policy of coupling mercy with sterner measures for the repression of crime was a conscious one. Its merits were recognized by Henry's advisers. This is revealed by the compiler of the *Leges Henrici Primi*, in a passage which follows the section on the pleas of the Crown, and that 'de placitis ecclesie pertinentibus ad regem'. The reservation of certain pleas to the king is justified in cl. 10, 1: they are retained 'commoda pacis ac securitatis institucione', and in cl. 11, 16ᵃ this is elaborated: 'unde pro multa malorum infestacione commoda pacis dispensacione prouisum est, ut grauiora placita magisque punienda soli iusticie uel misericordie principis addicantur, ut uenia petentibus et pena peccantibus habundancius habeatur'. The advantage of reserving the graver pleas to the king's hearing is that it makes discretion possible in these cases; more

---

[1] e.g. by H. G. Richardson and G. O. Sayles, *Governance of Medieval England*, 181.

severe penalties can be laid down provided there is a chance of grace for those who seek it. The compiler may have been thinking of the system of amercement when he stressed the opportunity the reservation gave for clemency, but by this time it seems to have been a routine matter for the justices to dispense it in this form and the expression 'venia petentibus' suggests the loftier conception of the king's own grace. This may be extended to those who seek it, apparently including those who seek him out and beg for mercy as well as those who are brought to trial. The whole range of his clemency towards offenders is suggested, and with it the principle that it by no means detracts from his regal authority. Rather, the king's position is displayed as being enhanced not only by the assertion of his right to impose such punishments as he deems fit in individual cases, but also by his condescension to those who throw themselves on his mercy. In the context—the king's responsibility for punishing offences against the church—some theological borrowing is natural enough,[1] and it contributes to the suggestion of his godlike attributes, his power to punish linked with his prerogative of mercy. In this clause, then, the quality of mercy is exalted, but at the same time its use is shown to be particularly appropriate in conjunction with the introduction of sterner measures against crime.

The compiler does not go into much detail over the occasions when actual pardon might be sought, but he takes it for granted that this was something to be expected in cases even of murder, for in the section (cl. 92, 7) dealing with the murder fine he states: 'Et licet malefactor regem requirat, ut uitam et membra recipiat, nichilominus murdrum soluatur . . . '. His concern here is to insist that the district which has failed to produce the murderer of a Frenchman must pay the murder fine even though his identity is revealed and capital punishment may be commuted as a result of his seeking out the king. It is implied that the king may vary or perhaps waive the penalty for a crime which is too serious normally to fall into the category of placing the criminal in his mercy, but it does not follow that this was a common use of his powers. As the compiler is not here concerned with the treatment of the murderer but with the liability of others to pay the communal murder fine he does not

---

[1] Cf. Romans v. 20: 'Lex autem subintravit ut abundaret delictum; ubi autem abundavit delictum, superabundavit gratia.'

give any indication of the effects of a successful approach to the king beyond the saving of life and limb; whether any other penalty will be substituted and if so what it is likely to be are not divulged. The *Leges Edwardi Confessoris*, however, insist that a pardoned murderer must abjure the realm,[1] and it seems unlikely that the other compiler thought of the reprieved murderer going scot free.

The evidence of the *Leges Edwardi Confessoris* points to a considerable use of the royal pardons. One of the compiler's interests was the nature of royal authority, and one aspect of this which he stressed most emphatically was the king's pardon. He was at pains to distinguish two types of pardon. One seems to have been more casual and part of the prerogative due to the king's royal dignity rather than representing any particular development of his policy in criminal matters. 'Habet etiam rex aliam potestatem misericordie super captiuos, quod, ubicunque uenerit in ciuitatem, uel burgum uel uillam uel etiam in uiam, si captiuus ibi fuerit, potest eum soluere a captione' (cl. 18, 1). This power to release prisoners was proper to kingship, and the compiler's words conjure up a picture of the royal progress through the country, graced with the passing gesture of clemency. But the other type of pardon, and the one which first attracted his attention, was that granted to those who sought out the king:

Tamen si aliquis forisfactus requisierit misericordiam eius, timore mortis uel membrorum pro forefacto suo, potest ei condonare, si placet, lege sue dignitatis. Et ipse cui fecerit misericordiam, faciat rectum cui prius forisfecerat, in quantum poterit complere, et inueniat fideiussores de pace et legalitate tenenda. Quodsi non poterit, exulabitur a patria (Cl. 18).

By the autumn of 1130 the new type of pardon had been introduced. This clause certainly does not describe it accurately, but it is possible that some rumour of it had reached the compiler and that he gave a characteristically garbled version of it. His evident interest in the subject of pardons may be attributable to this new development. On the other hand it is possible that he wrote shortly prior to 1130 and before it had occurred, but at a time when pardons of the older type were already becoming more frequent.

[1] Cl. 18, 2.

The new type of pardon appears on the pipe roll of 1130, where, under the heading *Nova Placita and Novae Conventiones*, it is recorded that 'Willelmus filius Rogeri de ponte Alerici debet ii marcas auri ut habeat pacem de morte Willelmi del Rotur. Et siquis eum apellauerit defend. se legali lege.'[1] The novelty here lies in the fact that the homicide is not fully assured of remission or commutation of punishment for his crime. He is given peace in respect of it by the king, but is still liable to be appealed and has to undertake to answer the appeal in court. The implication is that if his defence fails he will be punished despite the pardon. Thus the new pardon is drastically limited in scope. It gives no protection against prosecution by the victim's kinsmen, or his feudal lord or man. The victim's associates are no longer fobbed off with mere emendation, though no doubt they may accept it if they choose; their right to appeal is safeguarded, and if the appeal succeeds the appropriate punishment will presumably follow unmitigated by the pardon. Since appeal is not affected, it is evident that prosecution of another kind is remitted here, and this must be prosecution at the suit of the king. This kind of prosecution is entirely remitted: it is not simply a matter of commuting the penalty which would follow on conviction. Thus the king is content entirely to abandon his prosecution of the homicide on receipt of two marks of gold, but will refrain from intervening in any way if he is appealed.

At first sight this new type of pardon may appear incompatible with the situation which, it has been suggested, held at this time: the backwardness of the relatives in appealing and the king's anxiety to secure prosecution. The stipulation that the grantee stand to right if appealed would seem to point to a different situation altogether. It looks more like a concession to the vindictiveness of his subjects than a stage in the development of the king's own policy. Far from resenting his severity towards the type of killing which till recently had been emendable, it appears that it was the exceptional case of leniency to which they objected, either because they tended to be peculiarly vindictive at this time, or because public opinion was in advance of royal policy in its concern with public order, demanding the consistent application of effective sanctions against acts of violence, so that even individuals might place this general good

[1] p. 102.

before private profit. Yet it is highly unlikely that such motives were prevalent or that they could have affected Henry I's policy had they been so. And, indeed, further consideration of the terms of the pardon shows that they do not really imply any such general demand for the infliction of punishment. The pardon was a triangular affair, the concern of the king, the killer, and potential appellors among the victim's kin. The king who granted it must have approved its terms and the grantee who paid for it found them acceptable, and both must have taken into account the probable attitude of the relatives. There must have been some possibility of an appeal or the king would have had no reason to insert the proviso, but the possibility must have been remote or the pardon would have been worthless to the grantee. If the proviso had been included because the vic- tims' relatives were normally vindictive and public opinion clamoured for retribution there would have been no market for such pardons. Since one was worth buying—at the con- siderable price of two gold marks—it follows that the continuing liability to appeal did not perturb the purchaser. His victim's associates were by no means likely to press a charge involving life or limb. On the contrary, it was prosecution of such a charge at the king's suit which was now the most imminent threat and which he was anxious to buy off. It was just because appeal was unlikely that the king's suit was so threatening, and thus the pardon which remitted it alone was well worth obtaining. William FitzRoger's pardon fits into—indeed it presupposes— the situation in which prosecution at the king's suit was fast encroaching on the private appeal.

Nor need it be doubted that this pardon was an example of a new type deliberately introduced by the king. There are other entries concerning grants of 'peace for homicide' on this pipe roll;[1] this expression suggests that they too were remissions of the king's suit even though they do not mention the proviso of standing trial if appealed, for this by no means implies that it was not included in the actual grants. But even if FitzRoger's was in fact the only pardon of this type on this roll, it cannot be dismissed as a solitary, atypical pardon, drawn up specially to meet the case in which one individual found himself. The proviso of standing to right was to be included in the great majority of pardons for many centuries. It would be remarkable

[1] pp. 75, 156.

enough if a single pardon in the reign of Henry I contained it for some quite distinct reason, one which had no connection with its prevalence later on. But it would be straining coincidence still further to suppose that a unique case in the time of Henry I chanced to occur in the very year of the one and only surviving pipe roll of his reign, and to involve a deferred payment which meant that it figured on that roll. Henry I appears, then, to have adopted a new form of pardon in or shortly before 1130. In this his clemency was restricted to his own suit, leaving the grantee liable to prosecution by the victim's relatives or feudal associates, and to the full punishment if the appeal succeeded. The fact that this type of pardon was worth buying indicates that prosecution at the king's suit was now greatly to be feared in some circumstances, and suggests that the balance between it and private appeal had shifted to a significant degree. If the function of many of the royal pardons was from now on to be remission of his suit it looks as though some decisive move had just been made in the attempt to repress crime, a move in which the king realized he would have to rely more than ever on communal presentment since he could not count on the co-operation of those entitled to appeal when no financial profit would accrue to them. The move which was most likely to meet with such special obstruction was that which gave the final push to the already tottering wergild structure. William Fitz-Roger's pardon provides a possible clue to the moment when the remains of the antique system were brought tumbling.

No evidence has been found to show whether Stephen continued to use the formula found in William FitzRoger's pardon. Henry II did issue pardons of this type, both for homicide and other crimes. The pipe roll of 1166 records that 'Serlo de Turlauestona deb. x m. ut habeat dir̄oñē (disrationationem) suam si appellatus fuerit ab aliquo de morte cujusdam unde retatus est.'[1] Apparently, he had been presented and was now obtaining remission of the king's suit and the promise that he should be tried only on appeal. Remission of the king's suit on condition of standing to right in a case of homicide may be implied also in the entry, 'Robertus de Eya redd. comp. de xliii s. et vi d. ut habeat liberam legem in curia regis si appelletur de morte Osberti de Lindesia',[2] but there is a much clearer indication of the proviso of standing to right in a pardon for

_____
[1] *Pipe Roll, 12 Henry II*, 57.   [2] Ibid., *23 Henry II*, 39.

rape.[1] The evidence of the pipe roll is, of course, incomplete since it relates only to pardons which were not paid for immediately, and it is not until the charters themselves begin to be enrolled that their approximate frequency and their wording can be discovered. John's surviving patent rolls reveal that only a small proportion of the pardons granted featured on the pipe rolls; his father's grants may thus have been quite numerous. There is a very late piece of evidence for one of them in a letter of 1267 which relates that one Mael 'forfeited his lands by the felony he did in killing a man in malice in the time of Henry II; and that the said Henry II pardoned the said Mael his suit for the said death and restored to him his lands which had been taken into his hands on that account'.[2] To speak of a pardon of the king's suit at this date undoubtedly implied continuing liability to appeal, and if the wording can be accepted as an accurate summary of the pardon it shows that it was of the same type as FitzRoger's.

The author of Glanvill's treatise does not discuss at length the scope of the king's authority to reprieve or pardon, but what he does say is suggestive. In dealing with the crimes of killing the king and other treason in Lib. xiv. i, he distinguishes between prosecution when there is 'accusator certus' and when 'fama solummodo publica accusat'. In the latter event, if the suspect is convicted of a capital crime, 'ex regiae dispensationis beneficio tam vitae quam membrorum suorum euis pendet iudicium, sicuti in ceteris placitis de felonia'. The king's discretion to commute the death sentence seems here to be restricted to criminals prosecuted at his suit. In an earlier passage the compiler had remarked in passing on the effect of the king's pardon for outlawry.

Cum quis uero per legem terre fuerit utlagatus et postmodum beneficio principis paci restitutus, non poterit ea ratione hereditatem si quam habuerit ille uel heredes sui uersus dominum suum nisi ex misericordia ipsius domini et beneficio recuperare. Forisfactum enim et utlagariam solet dominus rex damnatis remittere, nec tamen aliena iura ideo querit infringere.[3]

[1] Ibid., 28 Henry II, 19: 'ut habeat redditus suos et catalla sua ut tamen sit ad rectum in Curia Regis si quis voluerit loqui adversus eum de puella quam dicitur violasse in custodia sua'. Since the property had been taken into the king's hand the case must already have been presented.

[2] Cal. Pat. Rolls, 1266–72, 53.

[3] Lib. vii. 17.

This passage occurs in a chapter on escheat and it would have been irrelevant to mention the rights of the victims of the crime, but if the general principle stated here was respected the remission of outlawry would leave these unaffected also. It is probable, then, that Henry II normally safeguarded the right of the injured party or the relatives of the slain to prosecute a capital charge when he pardoned outlawry or remitted his own suit against a criminal. John and his successors certainly did so.

It has been seen that the reason for this was not concession to the general vindictiveness of potential appellors and the question accordingly arises of the motive for this self-imposed limitation on the prerogative of pardon. There were several possible reasons for it and all may have been taken into account. Once it is recognized that this type of pardon was not introduced in order to mitigate the severity of the existing penal laws, but to facilitate the introduction of yet sterner measures, then it becomes apparent that there was every reason to try to ensure that pardon did not provoke acts of violence. Although the victim's relatives were unlikely to object to it when he had been slain in extenuating circumstances, there was still some possibility of their not concurring with the king's view of the slaying and, if they were debarred from prosecuting an appeal, of their seeking to be avenged on the slayer or even his kin. This risk alone made it desirable to conserve their right of appeal. But, secondly, there was the consideration of the continuing utility of appeals and the importance of not seeming hostile to them. The king's dominant policy was the suppression of crime. If he was hampered in this policy by some obstruction from those entitled to appeal and was driven to rely more on communal presentment, this would not imply that he wished to check proper appeals. On the contrary, he would naturally wish to enlist the maximum co-operation of appellors. The last thing he wanted was for them to be discouraged by the suspicion that he would pardon the appellee unconditionally and their efforts at helping in the repression of crime would be frustrated. Accordingly, he emphasized their duty to appeal, drawing attention to their ancient right, even recognizing its primacy when remitting his own suit. Again, although he was still sometimes ready to mitigate his treatment of criminals, the mitigation was now rather more grudging and affected only one of the two routes by which they might be brought to trial.

It would nullify his main policy if he were too generous. The intensification of public prosecution and punishment could be pressed to its limits only so long as the prerogative of mercy provided a safeguard against undue severity in particular cases, but there was need for a safeguard also against misplaced leniency in the use of the prerogative. The proviso that the pardoned man must stand to right afforded this. Since, in general, the injured or the next of kin were unlikely to be over-vindictive, this second safeguard should prove effective only in appropriate cases, those in which the crime really did call for the most stringent punishment. To put it at the lowest, the proviso would serve to check undue optimism on the part of those who meditated such crime and who believed they might be able to beguile or bribe the king into granting pardon; they would have to calculate also with the chances of appeal, and so the deterrent effect of the king's overall policy would not be undermined by his own excessive clemency or venality. It must be doubted whether the king himself appreciated the possible value of this proviso in offsetting the effects of his abuse of the prerogative, but his ministers may have done so. Finally, the stipulation of standing to right may have been thought useful because it might enable an appellor, by bringing and then compromising an appeal, to secure some reparation rather than bring down punishment on the slayer's head; it might reassure people that the elimination of wergild was intended to modify and not entirely to abolish the right to compensation.

The early pipe roll entries relating to pardon do not mention the proviso of making peace with the victim or his kin. It is possible that the actual pardons already did so, but even if it was not mentioned explicitly this alternative was probably understood. It has been noted that it was the traditional policy to require compensation to be paid when the king remitted punishment for homicide; the compiler of the *Leges Edwardi Confessoris* regarded it as a rule.[1] There is no reason to suppose that royal policy at any time in the twelfth century diverged from this tradition. The king was probably prepared all along to countenance the payment of compensation when he himself had decided against punishment. This attitude appears very clearly in relation to concords made after an appeal had actually been begun. Although Henry II waged a campaign against the

[1] See above, p. 15.

withdrawal of appeals without his or his justiciar's permission, he and his successors did not necessarily show themselves reluctant to grant such permission. While there were many unlicensed concords there were also a good many licensed ones. The concord was the ideal solution of a civil action;[1] the courts preferred to act as arbiters and bring the parties to terms, so avoiding the invidious task of deciding entirely in favour of one party and against the other. Something of the same sentiment may not have been entirely absent in criminal trials—long ago, so Maitland thought, it had been at the root of the wergild system itself.[2] The king's justices, whether in the *Curia Regis* or on eyre, had authority to license concords in appeals of breach of his peace. It is not clear whether they ever had it in relation to appeals of felonious homicide, but if so they soon lost it. The king monopolized the power to allow concords in such cases, perhaps because he had found or feared that his justices would be too much inclined to encourage them, as they did in civil cases, and would be too lenient if this power was entrusted to them. Nevertheless, his own use of it shows that he was not entirely opposed to compromise and the payment of damages even when a capital appeal had been brought. The appellors themselves would be unlikely to be amenable to negotiation unless there were mitigating circumstances and so some ground also for his clemency. The licences for concords were, in short, the counterparts of pardons, obtainable when an appeal was being actively prosecuted, whereas pardons were likely to be granted when there was as yet no appeal, or in ignorance that one had been launched. Both reveal the king's readiness to retain something from the ancient law of wergild, subject, however, to its ceasing to be a matter of law and becoming entirely dependent on his grace.

Pardons of his suit for homicide had, then, a logical place in the general measures for repressing crime. They were the concomitant of a policy of severity, by which the king envisaged penalties which would be effective deterrents. Since he was somewhat ahead of public opinion in this regard, or at least of the views of a good many bereaved relatives, the policy met with some obstruction, and it became necessary to rely increasingly on public prosecution. At the same time it was only politic

---

[1] As emphasized by R. C. Van Caenegem, *Royal Writs*, Selden Soc. lxxvii. 42.
[2] *Hist. Eng. Law*, i. 47–8.

to maintain the traditional practice of tempering the threat of greater severity; this could be done by holding out the prospect of remission of his suit to the slayer as well as a chance to get compensation to the victim's kin. This prospect made it feasible for the king to cast his net more widely than the contemporary attitude to violence warranted, so that all types of culpable homicide became punishable in life and limb. In fact, the net was cast wider still to embrace homicides which deserved no punishment whatever.

It is obvious that this royal policy of superseding the wergild system by liability to punishment in life or limb for all culpable homicide could not be successful without some measures affecting the payment of compensation for homicide in self-defence or by mischance also. The king was forcing the pace and could not count on appeals being made in cases which public opinion was still inclined to regard as emendable. If they could not obtain compensation in court for these types of culpable homicide, the victim's relatives would be tempted to treat them as killing in self-defence or mischance, so long as by so doing they could obtain wergild or some other payment awarded or sanctioned by the court. Thus the whole scheme might be wrecked if it was left to them to decide which homicides were culpable and which were not. Even presenting juries might not be entirely reliable on this point; if they were permitted to keep silent over excusable killing their sympathy either with the slayer or with the relatives' desire for compensation might lead them to conceal homicides which they should have included in their presentments. It was in any case a delicate matter to discriminate between killing in self-defence and killing culpably in open fight. The obvious solution to these difficulties was to require the presentment of all homicides whatever, so that all could be investigated, and any excuse established to the satisfaction of the king himself or his justices. Until they had undergone this screening, all cases of killing in self-defence or by accident must be treated as potentially culpable. They could not safely be accorded different treatment, treatment on their individual merits, until these had been convincingly established. Almost inevitably, therefore, these types of homicide were drawn into the system.

By the thirteenth century all homicides (apart from execution on the order of a competent court) had to be presented at the eyre, not only culpable, accidental, and homicides in self-defence, but also those which were justifiable or perpetrated by persons of diminished responsibility. Moreover, sudden deaths from natural causes had to be reported, and suicides and all accidental deaths, even if nobody apart from the victim was believed to have been involved. In these last cases there was likely to be profit to the king in the shape of chattels or deodand, but he could look for no profit in some of the others. Thus the main reason for requiring that all these matters should be investigated and reported must have been to ensure that all felonious homicides were brought to light. How early this rule was established is not known. It may well have preceded the introduction of the inquest into sudden death, held by serjeant or coroner by way of an immediate, preliminary investigation. On the other hand, both the preliminary investigation of all these cases and insistence on their inclusion in the presentments at the eyre may have commenced together, as complementary facets of the royal policy. Unfortunately, it is not known when inquests, or even less formal inquiries by local serjeants, started; nor is it known whether all these types of death were investigated from the beginning. It is not impossible that the Benjamin who kept the pleas of the Crown in Norfolk in 1130 and who was elsewhere described as a king's serjeant was already doing this work.[1] Inquiries were being held in the time of Henry II. There is evidence of the serjeants making some form of preliminary investigation into murder in 1168, when one was amerced for not reporting to the sheriff the proof of Englishry made before him,[2] and entries relating to the chattels of a suicide and of drowned and slain persons are also suggestive of investigation into all types of sudden death.[3]

There can be little doubt, then, that excusable homicide had to be investigated locally and presented at the eyre at latest in the time of Henry II. Indeed, what looks like an abortive attempt to gloss over a killing because it was not regarded as felonious is recorded in an entry on the pipe roll of 1176: 'Osbertus de Stirchlega redd. comp. de ii m. quia interfuit ubi excusatio de morte Iohannis facta est . . . Warinus de Burwarleg'

---

[1] *Pipe Roll, 31 Henry I*, 91; *Sir Christopher Hatton's Book of Seals*, ed. L. C. Lloyd and D. M. Stenton, no. 407.
[2] *Pipe Roll, 14 Henry II*, 164.
[3] Ibid., *18 Henry II*, 108, 8; *15 Henry II*, 148; *20 Henry II*, 104.

redd. comp. de ii m. pro eodem.'[1] This points the need for exhaustive investigation of these cases. Not only might a seeming accident have been cunningly contrived, in the hope that both the victim's relatives and the authorities would fail to suspect a malicious and premeditated killing, but there was also the secondary danger that the victim's relatives would connive in an attempt to pass off culpable homicide as accidental in the hope of securing compensation, and that the neighbourhood would conceal the matter in sympathy. It was perfectly reasonable, therefore, and indeed in the interests of law and order it was necessary, that accidental and still more alleged killing in self-defence should be presented at the eyre.

While these cases obviously had to be thoroughly investigated it is less obvious why the king should have reserved to himself the decision to remit his suit. Yet he may well have done so from an early period, although evidence of this is lacking until the time of John. The justices' impotence to dismiss such cases is well brought out in one from 1203, when they had to refer to the king the slaying in self-defence of a man who had himself just killed five others in a fit of madness.[2] Again, in 1212, it was recorded that 'Roger of Stainton was arrested because in throwing a stone he by misadventure killed a girl. And it is testified that this was not by felony. And this was shown to the king, and the king moved by pity pardoned him the death.'[3] It need not be doubted that such cases had had throughout to be referred to him by the justices. The motives for this stringency can only be inferred. The extension of the notion of felony could not reasonably be and clearly was not stretched to the point of including slayings by accident and in self-defence. There was no question of prosecution for felony at the king's suit once their nature was established, nor does it appear that any lesser degree of culpability attached to them. This is indicated by the fact that the justices took the initiative in referring them to the king. It was not left to the prisoners to throw themselves on his mercy, as in the case of those who had killed culpably. Excusable slayers were admitted to deserve it, and not to merit even some

---

[1] Ibid., *22 Henry II*, 57. But *excusatio* here may possibly mean acquittal rather than justification or excuse, and the offence may have been that a local or private court had dealt with a plea of the Crown which exceeded its competence, rather than concealing the case because it was excusable.

[2] *Select Pleas of the Crown*, Selden Soc. i, no. 70.

[3] Ibid., no. 114.

small punishment. One reason for the king's reservation to himself of the decision to remit his suit was probably his desire to emphasize his determination that these slayings should be efficiently screened. He was unwilling to entrust the task entirely even to his own justices, in view, perhaps, of the lack of support his policy received in some quarters. Secondly, there was the problem of definition. It was by no means easy to determine which homicides were excusable; this problem was not to be fully solved for centuries. Short of attempting the forbidding task of defining all acceptable excuses in advance, there was nothing for it but to require that individual cases should be referred to him.

But there was another consideration which could be held to rule out acquittal. To have allowed this would have been to ignore and nullify the relatives' claim to compensation, which was admittedly valid in these cases. Remission of the king's suit purported to respect and safeguard it, so that pardons of this kind would appear particularly well suited to them. There is some reason to think that this factor was actually taken into account by the king or his ministers when it was decided to include non-felonious homicide in the system of pardoning, for some discrimination was shown in delimiting the category of excusable homicide, a highly significant distinction being made between justifiable slaying on the one hand and slaying in self-defence or by mischance on the other. Justifiable homicide, such as the slaying of a thief or returned outlaw who resisted arrest, had to be presented to the itinerant justices, but provided the justification was fully established the justices had power to acquit. Now, at no time, as far as the Anglo-Saxon laws show, had wergild been due to the kin of a slain thief. The laws had much to say on this topic; the relatives of the thief were apt to take vengeance on the slayer or his family and legislation was directed against this practice, which was entirely unwarranted.[1] Probably it was prevalent simply because no wergild was legally due and so their wrath was not bought off in that way. The *Leges Henrici Primi* continued to stress that various kinds of justifiable homicide did not give rise to wergild.[2] Thus the exclusion of this type of killing from the general rule that there must be pardon for non-culpable slaying shows that the new system here followed the pattern of the old.

[1] II Athelstan, 6, 2; VI Athelstan, 1, 5.   [2] Cl. 87, 6ª.

Moreover, this pattern can be discerned underlying other cases which did require but merited pardon, for these coincided closely with those which had still given rise to wergild in the Norman period, so far as they can be discovered.

The compiler of the *Leges Henrici Primi* was extremely strict in dealing with liability for accidental slaying. He reiterated 'Qui inscienter peccat, scienter emendet'.[1] Wer had to be paid for accidental shooting at play,[2] spurring or beating a horse so that it struck someone fatally,[3] overlaying a child entrusted to one's care.[4] But he emphasized the need to take all the circumstances into account, and made some attempt to draw the line: if a man falls from a tree or from some mechanical device on to another so that the latter is injured or killed, and he can prove that his fall was unavoidable, then he is not responsible. But if anyone is so obstinate and unreasonable as to presume to demand vengeance or wer, this person may, if he wishes, climb up and fall in the same way on to the defendant—the classical *reductio ad absurdum* of the notion of absolute liability.[5] In the thirteenth century the belief that tree-climbers were not to blame for the accidents they caused survived and pardon was seldom thought necessary, but most other types of accidental slayers were still held accountable for the death, and so needed the king's pardon.

The treatment of infant homicides is particularly significant. For much of the thirteenth century not only did child slayers require pardon, but their pardons might even be conditional on standing to right or making peace. According to *Leges Henrici Primi*, cl. 70, 15, slaying by an infant had to be settled for by the full wergild payment. The inclusion of children in the system of pardoning is thus a carry-over—a particularly deplorable one—from the wergild system. Naturally, slaying by young children was nearly always accidental, and it might have been thought safe enough to omit such accidents from the scheme had it not been for the ancient notion of the child's, or his parents', liability to make reparation. The treatment of homicidal maniacs is not made clear in the lawbooks. The compiler of the *Leges Henrici Primi* included Alfred's rule that the father of a deaf-mute must make amends for his misdeeds,[6] and then went on to say 'Insanos et eiusmodi maleficos debent

---

[1] Cl. 88, 6a; cl. 90, 11a.   [2] Cl. 88, 6.   [3] Cl. 90, 11c.
[4] Cl. 88, 7.   [5] Cl. 90, 6b, 7, 7a.   [6] Cl. 78, 6, quoting Alfred, 14.

parentes sui misericorditer custodire', but it is not certain that
he meant to imply that the family had the same responsibility
for paying compensation for their misdeeds, though this may
well be intended.[1]

Killing in self-defence against a deliberate and aggravated
assault had not given rise to a right to wergild, for a man forfeited his wergild by his own crime or attempted crime.[2] Killing
at a feast or drinking party had given rise to it;[3] sometimes
such killing may have been necessary in self-defence, but it
looks as though the participant in a fight could not evade his
liability on these grounds. Fighting in the king's court had been
a serious crime and slaying in the course of it, even in self-
defence, had had to be emended.[4] It cannot be determined how
closely the types of self-defence which had involved payment
of wergild coincided with those which later called for pardon.
The difficulty of distinguishing this sort of homicide from culpable homicide in open fight meant in any case that very careful
investigation was needed and there was special reason here to
withhold the power of acquittal apart from concern for the
claims of the victim's kin. The retrospective consideration is
likely to have counted for more in determining the manner of
treating accidental slaying and slaying by children and maniacs,
who might possibly not have been thought to require the king's
own pardoning of his suit had it not been for his wish to show
some respect for the ancient family right to compensation.

While the system of pardoning was severe to the excusable
slayer it was possible, then, to argue that this severity was necessary, not only to prevent felonious homicide being passed off as
unintentional, but also to salvage something of the rights of the
victim's relatives. It may be attributable partly to consideration
for them, or at least to a politic tendency to carry over into the
new system as much of the old as was compatible with the
determination to suppress crime. The wergild system may, in
this sense, help to account for the creation of the class of
excusable homicide, that which deserved but needed pardon.
It appears, therefore, that this severe method of dealing with
excusable homicide was not a mere *pis aller*. It was not adopted
without reason and even some measure of justification. Although
the king did not himself hold consistently to the course of

[1] Cf. N. Walker, *Crime and Insanity in England*, i. 15–16.
[2] *Leges Henrici Primi*, 87, 6.   [3] Ibid. 87, 9.   [4] Ibid. 80, 7[b].

inflicting exemplary punishment for intentional homicide this was his dominant policy, and it entailed the elimination of wergilds at a time when the relatives of some of the slain would have welcomed compensation. He could not count on their co-operation and was, perhaps, doubtful even how far he could rely on those who shared in the administration of justice; so long as he was forcing the pace in this way, it was desirable for him to reserve to himself the decision to pardon his suit even if a homicide had been committed by mischance or in self-defence. This emphasized the principle that every one who was in any way responsible for a death was answerable to him until the absence of criminal intent was fully established; it also made it possible to insist that the slayer was answerable to his victim's relatives as well, whether they sought compensation or to see him punished. It might, of course, have been claimed further that the excusable homicide's need of pardon helped to drive home the notion that unnecessary force ought not to be used in self-defence, so contributing to a higher conception of law and order and setting a standard of self-restraint, and that it was a warning against negligence of any kind that might lead to a fatal accident. But whether these broader principles helped from the start to determine the treatment of excusable homicide cannot be ascertained in the absence of any statement of policy.

The severity of this treatment is explicable once it is seen in its original context. The whole system of pardoning homicide on condition of making peace with the victim's family or stand-ing to right was intended to subserve not to subvert a stricter penal system. It made it possible to decree punishment in life or limb, and presently capital punishment alone, for all types of culpable homicide, by supplying a method of mitigating this severity in individual cases in which it still seemed inappropriate, as, for example, when there were extenuating circumstances or some special occasion for clemency. Excusable homicide was included, not because there was any intention of actually punish-ing it in any way, but because its inclusion was necessary to make the system watertight, and probably also with an eye to the claims of the relatives, for compensation was an age-long right which it was not intended to do away with altogether. The system of pardoning was apparently meant to strike a fair balance between the needs of public order, the slayer's deserts and the rights of the victim's kin; but to say this is not to claim that it was defensible as it worked out in practice. Good intentions were particularly likely to fail of practical achievement in so complex a balance as this. One or two interests could too easily be subordinated to the third, or all three sacrificed through unwillingness to face up to their mutual incompatibility. Moreover, it was a serious danger that the operation of the system rested in the king's discretion. This in itself involved uncertainty, mistrust, and misunderstanding. The king himself was not always concerned to maintain the balance. The original objectives might come to be forgotten or disregarded, and in his view his discretionary powers always transcended them. The practical application of the system was controlled in the last resort only by the dictates of the king's conscience; there could be no definitive legal rules governing it, and for this reason it is peculiarly difficult to generalize about it. Indeed, lack of material makes it impossible to judge how far the system worked in the twelfth century. Royal writs and charters of pardon, together with the considerable body of extant judicial records, make it feasible to attempt to trace its working in the thirteenth, though at points it remains obscure, and if some norms can be discovered all too many deviations from them must be noted. This examination of the application of the system at this period will deal first with the position of the slayer, secondly with that of the victim's relatives, thirdly with that of the king as wielder of the prerogative of mercy, and finally with its effect on that law and order of which he was the guardian.

II

PROCEDURE

SINCE pardoning homicides was a royal prerogative there could be no hard and fast rules as to the manner in which clemency should be sought and bestowed. Various procedures could be adopted on the initiative of various persons to bring cases to the king's attention, but apart from certain stages in the business, especially the final publication of the pardons, there was no set procedure in the strict legal sense. Often, the applicants or their friends had to select their own line of approach, and the king's response might be informal. But in the course of the thirteenth century formalities tended to increase and the business of obtaining pardon became more complex, though at the same time it was coming also to be rather better understood. Throwing oneself on the king's mercy was neither as simple nor as safe as it might sound, and even those with every claim to it might find that the process of securing pardon proved too uncertain or too expensive, whilst some were so daunted by these difficulties that they did not attempt it at all. People who had slain unintentionally found themselves suddenly thrust into a dangerous situation and their reaction to it was often one of panic. The deliberate killer, especially if he was a person of some social standing and wealth, might appraise the chances of securing pardon more coolly and have a much better notion of how to set about it, but neither might consider it prudent to surrender. The reaction of the slayer to his predicament helped to determine the manner in which his case could best be brought before the king.

The problem of how to set about obtaining pardon varied, then, according to the position of the applicants. Some had been arrested and were in prison pending trial when they sought pardon. Other prisoners awaited their trial or were released on bail and duly surrendered for it, hoping to secure pardon on the record of the court and virtual recommendation of the justices. The majority of applicants were fugitives from justice and many of these were already outlawed. A fair number of homicides took sanctuary; one or two applied for pardon whilst there, others after they had abjured the realm, though not necessarily quitted it. The main differences in procedure, however, depended on whether or no the slayer appeared in court; both the fugitive and the prisoner who sought pardon before trial had to take the initiative, or their friends had to do so. The prisoner who came before the justices had, especially at first, to take a smaller part in obtaining it.

The outlaws and those who had abjured were in the most difficult situation. An outlaw could not safely approach the king in person and plead for pardon, although he might surrender, if he dared, to prison and petition him from there. Someone who had abjured the realm would also be taking a grave risk if he returned in order to beg for clemency in person. A royal visit to France might afford an opportunity to do this without risk, but such opportunities were few. Before the exile could legitimately return to England or the outlaw safely show himself in districts where he was known he must be armed with a pardon covering his outlawry or abjuration. However, it was not necessary for him to obtain two consecutive pardons, the first merely for outlawry or abjuration, the second for the crime for which he had fled. Normally one pardon covered both, though there were occasional circumstances in which outlawry or abjuration alone was pardoned or annulled. For example, outlawry might be annulled because it had not been carried out in due form, and this annulment would not, of course, prejudice future prosecution for the original crime. One reason—not an uncommon one—for pardoning outlawry alone was the discovery that the supposed victim was still alive; since there had in fact been no homicide the question of prosecution for it could not now arise, and so there was no need to remit the king's suit. Generally, however, pardon was needed for both the slaying and the outlawry and one and the same charter of pardon covered both. In theory, no doubt, it was proper for it to specify both, but in practice, until near the end of the thirteenth century, little attention was paid to this point. A pardon might be cancelled because it referred ambiguously to outlawry for homicide, and a new one drawn up pardoning the death and the outlawry for it,[1] but few

---

[1] e.g. *Cal. Pat. Rolls,* 1232–47, 340.

grantees were perturbed by the ambiguity and for a long time
the normal formula was that the king pardoned 'outlawry for
homicide', not 'homicide and outlawry'. The courts accepted
this as remitting the king's suit for the actual death,[1] and
although there were occasional variations, this was the accepted
formula until 1254; in the course of that year while the king
was in Gascony 'pardon for the death and any consequent
outlawry' was current, and this gradually became the most
usual.[2] Sometimes a more positive phrase was used: 'homicide
and his consequent outlawry'; but from 1266 on this became
rare, and the vague 'if any' was preferred. This suggests that
many fugitives obtained pardon without knowing whether
they had been outlawed or not. The officials who drew up the
letters patent did not insist on being definitely certified as to
this, and ceased even to inquire about it, being content to
refer to hypothetical outlawry even in charters to those who
were well enough aware that they were outlaws. The king's
readiness to grant pardon seems not to have been affected by
the fact of flight and outlawry,[3] and his justices were unlikely
to quibble over the wording of his pardons, however ambiguous.
But towards the end of the reign of Edward I a stricter policy
was attempted and some outlaws were pardoned their outlawry only, being required to surrender for trial.

Since outlaws were in no situation to apply directly to the
king they had to rely on some intermediary and it is apparent
that many of them were able to find someone to act for them.
This is not altogether a matter for surprise since many outlaws remained in England and did not lose contact with
their families and neighbours. Some settled successfully and

[1] e.g. J.I. 1/872, m. 35ᵈ records that Walter de Midelton was outlawed at the
suit of Robert de Norle's widow and that the king pardoned him for the death by
his letters patent. The latter, according to the enrolment, pardoned him 'his
outlawry for the death of Robert . . .' (*Cal. Pat. Rolls, 1247–58,* 163). A pardon
enrolled in the same terms, ibid. 91, was said at the eyre to have granted peace
for the death, i.e. whatever pertained to the king (J.I. 1/300ᶜ, m. 24). The *Calendar
of Patent Rolls* generally indicates the formula correctly but occasionally omits one
section which the enrolment did include. It is also occasionally inexact, e.g. as to
the reference to outlawry if any or outlawry for the death.
[2] John had sometimes pardoned 'outlawry if any'; e.g. *Rot. Litt. Pat.* i. 11.
[3] But a pardon might be granted provided that the grantee had not been outlawed; cf. *Cal. Pat. Rolls, 1247–58,* 353. This was a case in which a large number of
men had been appealed but alleged that the appeal had been withdrawn. The
eyre roll shows that this was not true (J.I. 1/1109, m. 7). The proviso may have
been due to doubt as to how far the appeal had gone.

undetected under new names in new localities. Those who went abroad could find new friends there or at any rate settle down and earn a sufficient livelihood to be able to hire agents. Still, for many life must have been precarious and they would have no such resources; their only hope would lie in the action taken by their friends on their behalf. But the latter ran a considerable risk in communicating with them, laying themselves open to the very serious charge of harbouring outlaws if they permitted them to enter their houses. One man, for example, was indicted, fled, and was himself placed in exigent simply because he had made contact several times with an outlaw.[1] In spite of these risks, relatives and friends were often prepared to take the necessary steps to obtain pardon, if they could afford to and understood the procedure, though the records seldom reveal their activities. In one case of outlawry for killing by misadventure it emerges that John de Bethun arranged a fine of 20 marks for the pardon, but his friendliness did not extend to undertaking any responsibility for its payment; the sheriff had to find four other men to act as pledges for it.[2] Unless the outlaw was the protégé of someone at court it is generally impossible to discover how the problem of approaching the king was tackled, but in a few cases his wife or another relative appears as a petitioner for his pardon.[3]

Homicides who had been arrested and were still in prison could obviously not approach the king in person. Their friends,

---

[1] *Close Rolls, 1237–42*, 180. But the king instructed the justices to revoke the order to exact.

[2] Ibid., *1247–51*, 454; cf. *Cal. Pat. Rolls, 1247–58*, 97.

[3] A glimpse of the efforts made on behalf of one fugitive is provided by a charge brought against the man who eventually came to his aid. John Bene had killed William Pyk by mischance with a knife; he was arrested, but released on bail; as he failed to appear before the justices in 1293 he was placed in exigent (*Cal. Close Rolls, 1288–96*, 160; J.I. 1/1098, m. 31ᵈ). A second inquisition was ordered in 1300 to discover if he had killed him by accident (*Cal. Chancery Warrants*, 124), and on a favourable verdict he was pardoned next year (*Cal. Pat. Rolls, 1292–1301*, 569). There can be little doubt that the knifing had in fact been accidental and that John's default at the eyre and delay in getting pardon were due to his lack of knowledge of the proper procedure. Eventually a helper was found for him, one John Bullock. The latter was arrested and charged at a gaol delivery with having covenanted with a felon, John Bene, that he would obtain peace for him at the price of 13s. 3d. John Bullock denied the charge and the jury found that John Bene's sister, Matilda, had made a covenant with Bullock to get the king's peace for him, for 40s.; John Bullock without committing any felony had taken 13s. 3d. of the 40s. for this reason and no other. On this verdict he was acquitted (J.I. 3/74, ii, m. 6.), but if he had himself made contact with Bene he might have incurred some punishment.

or possibly friendly officials, would have to act for them, though the very fact that they had let themselves be arrested might tell in their favour. Those who had been arrested and had obtained bail could petition him in person, but it was probably usual to find someone to act as a go-between. Some requests for pardon seem to have been made to the king orally, perhaps by a member of the household or by a noble patron or churchman,[1] sometimes possibly by the homicide in person throwing himself on the king's clemency. But a written petition could be handed in and this was the best way of ensuring accuracy in the wording of the charter of pardon.[2]

Once the slayer or his envoy or patron made contact with the king some inducement had to be put forward to persuade him to show clemency. What inducements were effective in the early period is altogether obscure. John granted a considerable number of pardons, but the enrolments normally fail to indicate how the cases were brought to his attention and on what grounds his leniency was forthcoming. Sometimes it was bought outright, but the recorded proffers were generally too low to have constituted any great inducement. The sums recorded on John's pipe rolls suggest that 5 to 10 marks was the normal range.[3] Amounts of this order were paid even by excusable killers for their pardons, and it is doubtful whether a murderer could have secured clemency at this price. Some other consideration may have weighed with the king, influence perhaps, as well as excuse or extenuating circumstances, when he accepted these proffers. Very much larger sums, up to £100, might be promised and these may readily be regarded as buying off prosecution for felonious killing.[4] A few of John's pardons were stated to have been granted at the request of an influential person or royal servant, such as Faukes de Bréauté,[5] and pressures of this kind continued to be exerted.

In the early part of the thirteenth century the king sometimes pardoned a homicide but did not entirely remit punishment. He might insist on abjuration of the realm.[6] He might

---

[1] e.g. *Cal. Pat. Rolls, 1247–58*, 533.

[2] A petition authenticated by privy seal might be sent to Chancery as warrant for the charter; see S.C. 8/53, no. 2612; *Cal. Pat. Rolls, 1301–7*, 20.

[3] Cf. *Pipe Roll, 3 John*, 73; *4 John*, 91, 136; *6 John*, 216; *Rot. de Oblatis*, 226.

[4] Ibid. 37.   [5] *Rot. Litt. Pat.* i. 114.

[6] Though John having required this might then revoke the condition. See ibid. 145, 146.

also pardon but with the stipulation that the slayer enter a
monastery or proceed to the Holy Land. The idea here seems
to have been that he should expiate the slaying by some kind
of religious penance rather than secular punishment. The slayer
himself may have been anxious to do so, having repented his
crime, or being overcome with remorse and horror at having
slain even by mischance, but it does not generally appear in
these cases whether this form of pardon was suggested by the
king or by the applicant or his friends.[1] It is likely that the
notion of expiation lingered on and it may account for some
later pardons stipulating that the grantee should go on crusade or pilgrimage.[2] Edward I, himself a crusader, pardoned
William de Dun, who refused to put himself on the country
for harbouring a son accused of homicide, 'provided that the
said William leave the realm within forty days, and go to the
Holy Land, to remain there until he has special licence to
return',[3] and this sounds as though it was the king's idea, not
William's. An applicant for pardon might offer some purely
secular service. Hugh de Tywe obtained release from prison
in 1248 on finding security for payment of a fine of £100 and
for his brother's going on the king's service to Gascony.[4] This
sort of inducement was not to become common for many years,
but from 1294 onwards Edward I granted pardons all too
readily to those who undertook to fight in his wars.

Under Henry III, the man who had killed in felony might
try to bluff the authorities into treating his deed as excusable
homicide. Otherwise his main hope of obtaining mercy probably lay in his having an influential position or influential
friends. The proffer of a large sum of money was not in itself
likely to succeed without some other pressure being brought to
bear. The majority of those who secured mercy from Henry III

---

[1] Alice de Nereford was probably responsible for suggesting the condition in
Henry III's pardon, granted on her intercession, to Roger de Panten that he
should enter the priory founded by her, for Roger's slaying had been found
accidental and in any case he had abjured the realm (see below, p. 77). He was
in no immediate danger and Henry would surely have been ready to pardon him
without this condition, but Alice may have been finding difficulty in recruiting
canons for her foundation.

[2] e.g. *Cal. Pat. Rolls, 1258–66*, 426.

[3] Ibid., *1281–92*, 194; cf. ibid. 247, for a similar pardon.

[4] *Excerpta è Rot. Finium*, ii. 39. He had killed the archdeacon of York. Cf. *Close
Rolls, 1247–51*, 85. However, his release was not tantamount to full pardon, for
he seems now to have abjured the realm; five years later he secured pardon for the
abjuration; see *Cal. Pat. Rolls, 1247–58*, 243.

claimed to have killed either justifiably or excusably, or not to have killed at all, having fled in panic or on account of a malicious charge. But the mere assertion of this was not likely to move the king to clemency: it must be substantiated either by credible testimony, or by the verdict of a jury. In course of time, the first hurdle to surmount was in fact to get the king to commission someone to hold an inquisition into the circumstances of the killing; sometimes the commission was appointed at the intercession of an influential protector but generally it could be bought and that at no exorbitant sum.

If the circumstances were so widely known that deception was out of the question, the king might consent to grant pardon on the information of various persons, without requiring a sworn inquisition. Thus in 1226 he pardoned a man who had been outlawed for theft when he had already surrendered to prison. The matter had been shown to the king 'a multis fide dignis', and the outlaw was said to be innocent 'per multos'. In view of this and of the county court's not having known of his surrender, Henry, asked by several magnates to act mercifully towards him, pardoned the outlawry and gave him firm peace.[1] He may for the moment have been content with the same sort of information and recommendation in cases of excusable homicide, but in 1230 one pardon was based on a verdict of killing by accident given 'per inquisitionem quam fieri fecimus',[2] and in the next year another accidental slaying was pardoned on the findings of a similar inquisition.[3] In 1232 there is a reference to a verdict which had been sent to the king, but it is not stated whether this was given at an inquisition *de odio et atia* or one into some alleged excuse.[4] In this year, too, a man who was actually in sanctuary was pardoned 'as it appears by inquisition that he killed . . . by misadventure'.[5] This inquisition must surely have been held by commissioners appointed *ad hoc*, since the verdict reached the king within the forty days allowed before abjuration or surrender. In 1233 a pardon was granted for outlawry for homicide 'as it happened by mischance'.[6] In spite of the absence of specific mention of an inquisition it may be inferred with some probability that one had been held in this case, though it may have been at the eyre or at a gaol delivery not before specially appointed

---

[1] *Pat. Rolls, 1225–32*, 36–7.   [2] Ibid. 393.   [3] Ibid. 456.
[4] Ibid. 512.   [5] *Cal. Pat. Rolls, 1232–47*, 2.   [6] Ibid. 19.

commissioners. For a year or two after this, pardons for excusable homicide tended to follow verdicts given at the eyre rather than before special commissioners, but there were two in 1235 based on an inquisition's finding of killing by mischance, and the second of these was quite clearly not held before itinerant justices, since order was given that the latter were not to hold a further inquest into the case.[1] It is evident that at this period the pardons, as enrolled, did not always specify the reason for clemency, since one granted, apparently, on the recommendation of itinerant justices omitted the considerations which led to their making it.[2] Thus it is likely that more pardons were granted in the 1230s as the result of verdicts of excusable slaying than appears from the enrolments, though perhaps the excuse was generally mischance, since it is only in the 1240s that evidence is forthcoming for special inquisitions into alleged slaying in self-defence.[3] It may be concluded that by about 1240 it was thought proper for the king to order an inquisition into the circumstances before granting pardon for excusable homicide unless a verdict had already been given before his justices, but that is not to say that he never acted more precipitately on information given to him by trustworthy persons or under pressure from influential friends of the culprit.[4]

---

[1] *Cal. Pat. Rolls, 1232–47*, 104, 109; cf. *Close Rolls, 1234–37*, 97. Another inquisition was ordered by the king in 1237 in a case of accidental death; ibid. 457.

[2] *Cal. Pat. Rolls, 1232–47*, 115. Significant evidence on this point comes from a pardon granted to Hugh le Kyeu in 1237 for his flight and outlawry for the death of Richard son of Alice (ibid. 194). There is no suggestion here of the slaying having been accidental; moreover the enrolment appears to have been inaccurate as well as much shortened, for Hugh's pardon was produced at the eyre by the hundred bailiff and it was for abjuration, not outlawry (J.I. 1/695, m. 24). According to the jurors, Richard had fallen by mischance from a cart and no one was to blame, but Hugh had been in the cart and had taken sanctuary and admitted his guilt and abjured. There can be little doubt that when the king granted the pardon the facts of the case had been available to him.

[3] e.g. *Cal. Pat. Rolls, 1232–47*, 468.

[4] e.g. ibid. 348. The sequence of inquisition and pardon might, indeed, be oddly reversed on the intervention of a really influential patron. In 1236 the king's sister, Eleanor, countess of Pembroke, showed the king that three of her men had found poachers in her park and in the ensuing struggle one of the latter had happened to be killed. Henry ordered the itinerant justices to inquire as to the truth of the matter and if the three men were found guilty, 'scire vos volumus quod ad instantiam dicte sororis nostre sectam que ad nos pertinet de morte predicta eis perdonavimus eo quod ille qui interfectus fuit in parcis malefactor extitit; ita tamen quod ipsi stent recto, si quis inde versus eos loqui voluerit' (*Close Rolls, 1234–37*, 257). Eleanor's assertion was obviously accepted implicitly, and the only point of the inquiry would seem to be to discover grounds for acquittal, making the pardon superfluous.

When the inquisition was held the slayer himself was unlikely to be present. He might still be a fugitive from justice,
and even if he was in prison he might not be brought before
the commissioners. Thus it was necessary for him to be represented by some friend or agent who could take further action
if the verdict was favourable. No evidence has been found to
show that this representative took any active part in the
proceedings, but on one occasion his presence was revealed.
This was in 1264, when justices holding assizes in Buckinghamshire were instructed to hold an inquisition into the slaying of
Hugh Shete by Ralph de Olneye, allegedly in self-defence. The
jury said that they had heard that Hugh had assaulted Ralph in
Northampton, trying to kill him with a hatchet; Ralph had
fled from him, running three times round a cart, but seeing
that he could not escape had struck him on the head with a
hatchet. The verdict, however, was not accepted as it showed
that the incident had occurred in another county. For this reason 'dictum est illi qui sequitur pro predicto Radulpho quod
perquirat breve directum vicecomiti Norhampt. de predicta
inquisicione facienda'.[1] Some of these agents at least are likely
to have been professionals, clerks or messengers familiar with
this type of business, for they showed considerable proficiency in
handling the applications for pardon, no doubt for a consideration.

The interval between the appointment of commissioners
and the sending of a writ to the sheriff to summon a jury to be
before them till the issue of the resultant pardon was not
generally unduly protracted. Sometimes, indeed, it was apparently so short that the accuracy of the dating of some of the
documents must be doubted.[2] Appointments of commissions

[1] J.I. 1/1197, mm. 4, 4^d. The second inquisition confirmed this verdict, and
Ralph was very soon pardoned; see *Cal. Pat. Rolls, 1258–66*, 339.

[2] e.g. on 28 May 1280 the sheriffs of London were ordered to have a jury before
two commissioners. The inquisition was held on 7 June and pardon ostensibly
granted next day (*Cal. Inquisitions Misc.* i, no. 2233; *Cal. Pat. Rolls, 1272–81*, 379).
This is just possible, since the king was at Westminster, but it would be rash to
accept the dates as exactly correct. Also in 1280, an inquisition was ordered on
8 September, from Carlisle. It was held at Newcastle upon Tyne on 15 September
and pardon was granted there on the same day, according to the patent rolls
(C. 145/38, no. 30; *Cal. Inquisitions Misc.* i, no. 2241, which gives the date of the
writ as 7 September; *Cal. Pat. Rolls, 1272–81*, 397). In this case it is reasonable to
suppose that the chancery officials dated the pardon to the day of the inquisition
rather than the day when the king approved it. However, as he was at Newcastle
for only a few days it is likely that the error, if there was one, was very small, and
it is evident that if the king was in the neighbourhood the whole business might be
handled with amazing dispatch.

to hold inquisitions are not always assigned to definite dates, but in spite of these difficulties it is possible to get a rough idea of the time involved in 228 cases, in which proceedings appear to have been fairly straightforward, and pardon was granted within a year of the appointment. It has been assumed that if it took longer than this then something had gone seriously wrong, or that the slayer was content for the time being with release on bail. Assigning these 228 pardons to three-monthly periods reveals that 129 of them were issued within three months of the order for the inquisition to be made; 52 were issued from 3 to 6 months after it, 30 from 6 to 9, and 17 from 9 to 12 months later. Thus in the great majority of these cases the business of ordering the inquisition, its being held, the verdict reported, and pardon granted was accomplished within 6 months, and in over half less than 3 months was required. Moreover, if the 129 pardons which took less than 3 months are subdivided it emerges that over half of these (69) were granted in less than 6 weeks, and of these 14 were apparently granted within a fortnight. It must be noticed, however, that the appointment of commissioners to hold the inquisition does not itself indicate the date when application was made to the king.

Proceedings were not always straightforward. The original appointment of commissioners might prove abortive and a second become necessary, though this need not mean long delay if it was due to the fact that the first commissioners were unable to act and the government therefore made a new appointment.[1] This was generally done within a month or two. In 6 cases of this kind the pardon itself was granted within 3 months of the first appointment, in 5 cases within 6 months, in 3 within 9 months, and in 2 within 12 months. It was only when things went by default and the applicant or his friends were driven to ask for another commission that the lapse of time was likely to be very great. On the other hand, it could take a

---

[1] e.g. *Cal. Pat. Rolls, 1258–66*, 680, 681, where a new commissioner was appointed within a fortnight. In the same year, 1266, Martin de Littlebury was appointed for one case early in February and Giles de Arginton for a different one on 10 March; both were superseded by two others, yet the inquisitions were held in time for pardon to be granted on 4 May (ibid. 656, 659, 661, 592, 593). Sometimes the second appointment seems to have been superfluous, for in another case one commissioner was appointed on 10 June and a new one on 22 June, but the pardon, issued on 23 July, was based on the verdict of an inquisition held by the first (ibid. 666, 667, 620).

considerable time for a mistake in the wording of the writ, especially a mistake as to the name of slayer or slain, to be rectified; it might not, perhaps, be noticed until an actual attempt was made to hold the inquisition.[1] There was sometimes great difficulty in doing so. Three commissioners were appointed to inquire whether Philip the Simple of Rowell killed Richard le Frannceys in self-defence, the first in November 1266, the second in August 1267, the third in July 1268.[2] The reason for this delay may have been that the commissioners failed to take any action, but it is possible that there was difficulty in raising a local jury because of a feud between the two families. Philip's pardon was granted in November 1268, but its protection was unavailing and he was slain by his victim's brother.[3]

Inquisitions and the resultant pardons were not to be had gratis. Especially where fugitives from justice were concerned, the king must have preferred cash down, but he sometimes accepted an offer of deferred payment and such proffers were entered, until the end of Henry's reign, on the fine rolls. Payment by instalments was allowed in some cases and the terms and dates were carefully recorded. The sum proffered to the king might cover various matters, particularly the holding of an inquisition as well as the pardon which was confidently expected to follow. Robert de Aula, for example, proffered 3 marks of gold for an inquisition as to slaying in self-defence 'et pro pace Regis habenda secundum tenorem predicte inquisicionis'; the verdict was indeed favourable and he was promptly pardoned 'pro predictis tribus marcis'.[4] Ralph del Elme proffered 10 marks for an inquisition as to whether he had slain by accident and for letters of pardon if the verdict was in the affirmative.[5]

[1] e.g. on 13 May 1266 a commissioner was appointed to inquire in Shropshire whether John son of Roger had killed William de Hineton in self-defence; 16 months later, on 10 September 1267 when the king was at Shrewsbury, another was appointed to inquire whether Roger son of John de Hoperton had killed William de Hinton in self-defence (ibid. 664; ibid., *1266–72*, 159). At least the final stages of this case were accelerated, for his pardon is assigned to 17 September (ibid. 109); no doubt the king's presence gave the opportunity to make a second application for an inquisition and to get this rushed through.

[2] Ibid. 124, 155, 288.

[3] Ibid. 304. See below, p. 308. The families were at enmity over a trespass, an action for which was being heard in 1269; see K.B. 26/193; m. 15[d].

[4] *Excerpta è Rot. Finium*, ii. 207; *Close Rolls, 1254–56*, 199; *Cal. Pat. Rolls, 1247–58*, 415, Cf. below, pp. 84, 255.

[5] *Excerpta è Rot. Finium*, ii. 477.

The inquisition was ordered,[1] but no pardon was enrolled for him, so perhaps he had been over-optimistic. Sometimes it seems that the original proffer was to cover the fee of the seal as well as the granting of pardon, or at least both payments were made together.[2] But the various payments might be quite separate. The fact that a slaying had already been clearly established by inquisition to have been accidental did not necessarily mean that no further fine had to be made.[3] A proved accidental slayer paid 20 marks for his pardon, even though it was granted at the instance of the countess of Devon.[4]

Apart from the expense still involved and possibly increased, the practice of appointing inquisitions into the circumstances made things simpler for those seeking pardon for homicides in self-defence or by accident. The mere appointment of an inquisition was less dependent on the king's readiness to show mercy. Provided a payment could be made or pledged it was probably largely a matter of routine, despite possible delays. Once the inquisition had been held its verdict was generally returned into Chancery, and it was then up to the Chancery officials to bring it to the notice of king or council.[5] Further formalities had to be gone through after the decision to grant pardon but these were not peculiar to those who applied for it before being brought to trial.

Whilst most slayers fled a fair number recovered their nerve and came back, and some stood their ground throughout. These people would be arrested; some, as has been seen, now got pardon, and a great many of them secured bail. Not all the latter surrendered when a judicial visitation was held, but still a good many homicides appeared in court confident of obtaining pardon after inquiry into their cases there. At first there was less need for them to take the initiative, but even for them the procedure of obtaining the letters patent became more complicated and involved some expense.

The only homicides who could hope to obtain mercy after appearing in court were those who had slain with excuse, including those who suffered from diminished responsibility.

---

[1] *Cal. Pat. Rolls, 1266–72*, 289.

[2] e.g. the proffers of John de Assewell and Alexander son of Giles; C. 60/53, m. 19.

[3] e.g. *Cal. Inquisitions Misc.* i, no. 2099; *Excerpta è Rot. Finium*, ii. 268. Cf. *Cal. Pat. Rolls, 1247–58*, 607.

[4] *Excerpta è Rot. Finium*, ii. 275; *Cal. Pat. Rolls, 1247–58*, 624.

[5] Cf. ibid., *1301–1307*, 313, 344.

These prisoners could expect to escape sentence and be recommended to mercy or given the opportunity to apply to the king for pardon. But once a prisoner had been convicted of felonious killing there was no right of appeal against sentence. If the king was near at hand he might possibly be persuaded to commute the penalty,[1] but generally there was scant opportunity for a reprieve, since the death sentence was carried out almost immediately. Only in the most exceptional circumstances would the justices order any postponement. Such circumstances arose in 1251, when the justices delivering Oxford gaol sentenced three men to be hanged for the death of Roger Bissop, but stayed the execution of two of them because the third now confessed that he alone was guilty, and that he had charged the others of complicity through spite. Other evidence was apparently heard confirming his confession, and the whole matter was brought to the notice of the king, who pardoned the other two and ordered their release from prison.[2] But a reprieve of this kind was entirely abnormal, and hardly possible if the prisoner was convicted on presentment. However, there was one class of convicted persons who could count on reprieve for a time: pregnant women were not executed; since their innocent children ought not to be slain, sentence was not carried out until after their birth. In the interval the mother might seek to get her conviction reversed or secure pardon. In 1228, for example, two women in this position obtained inquisitions into the slayings of which they had been convicted; the verdicts now were not guilty, and both were pardoned as a result.[3] Apart from these very exceptional cases, pardon after sentence was practically unknown. There were, however, a few cases in which pardon was granted not only after sentence but after its attempted execution, for the man or woman who had been hanged might be cut down too soon and survive, and it was usual to grant pardon when this happened.[4] But such survivors were mostly convicted

[1] This seems to have happened in 1226 when Henry III was only just coming of age and was perhaps eager to use his prerogative of mercy: John Herlisun, tried at the Tower for the death of Lambert de Legis, failed in his law, presumably the compurgation which was the Londoners' privilege, but the king granted him life and limb at the prayer of the women of the city, and he became a Hospitaller. See *Liber de Antiquis Legibus*, Camden Soc. 5.

[2] *Cal. Pat. Rolls, 1247–58*, 102.

[3] *Close Rolls, 1227–31*, 53. Cf. ibid., *1251–3*, 501; *Cal. Pat. Rolls, 1247–58*, 20.

[4] See below, p. 176.

thieves, not homicides. It is possible that some executioners deliberately bungled their job because they sympathized with the condemned person, either because they believed the sentence was unjust, or from partisanship.[1] Still these were freak events and there was in general no hope of pardon after conviction. Any grounds for pardon had to be put forward at an earlier stage of the proceedings.

The prisoner who had killed notoriously in self-defence or by accident should have run little risk of conviction. There were various ways in which the circumstances could be brought to the justices' attention. Unless appealed, he himself might mention them. If well advised he would plead not guilty; to start by admitting some degree of responsibility was pretty sure to prove fatal. But having asserted his innocence and put himself on the country he could safely mention the manner in which he was involved in the death, hoping that the jury would agree and absolve him from felony. Secondly, the jury of presentment might give a circumstantial account of the slaying or simply state that it was in self-defence or by accident. Thirdly, the jury on which the prisoner placed himself might give a verdict on these lines. Although they show that prisoners might mention some excuse, the eyre rolls do not suggest that they often did so. Normally, it seems, they relied on one or other type of jury being acquainted with the circumstances and including them in their presentment or verdict, but the defendant might think it prudent to proffer a sum of money for 'a good inquisition' at the eyre in order to make doubly sure that they were brought to the justices' notice.[2] The coroners' rolls might suggest some excuse and cause the justices to interrogate the jurors if they did not mention it, but this was not a very effective safeguard in practice. The prisoner could be convicted and executed because the justices had no knowledge that a case could be made out for clemency. The rolls give the impression that this very seldom happened, but it must be remembered that if the circumstances were concealed from the court there is little chance of their being accessible to the historian. There is one example of the execution of a man who had killed a felon as

---

[1] Deliberate use of a frayed rope seems very likely in a case in 1261, *Close Rolls, 1259–61*, 425.

[2] Robert de Feugers did this in a case of 'transferred intent' (J.I. 1/952, m. 43). Cf. *Close Rolls, 1242–7*, 544, and below, p. 99.

he fled, but this miscarriage of justice emerges only because others had been involved.[1]

If the justices were informed that there was good excuse and the case thus in their estimation called for pardon, the next step was to convey this to the king and get him to remit his suit. In the first half of the thirteenth century the reference of these cases to the king seems generally to have been made on their initiative, without entailing any immediate action by the prisoner or his friends. When the case was being tried in the *Curia Regis* the justices could consult the king orally, as seems to have been done when an accidental slaying was testified not to have been by felony, 'et monstratum fuit hoc domino Regi, et dominus Rex motus misericordia perdonavit ei mortem'.[2] When another slaying was pardoned by the king, 'audito infortunio ex literis S. de Sedgrave et sociorum suorum', it seems evident that the itinerant justices had written to him without any approach having first been made by the prisoner or his friends.[3] There were many cases, too, in which the justices were apparently uncertain if formal pardon was even necessary and decided to have consultation with the king about this. The prisoner obviously had to take no action in this event, though the outcome might be a charter of pardon for him. Often the king simply replied to the justices that he pardoned the slayer, or indeed merely instructed them,[4] or the sheriff if they had left the county, to release him.[5] No payment would be involved if no letters patent of pardon issued. Such discussion of his fate was carried on over the prisoner's head, and it was the justices' responsibility to evoke the royal clemency where need be, sometimes entirely free of charge. More often, the justices seem to have referred cases to the king in a way which was virtually a recommendation to mercy, and this would lead to a formal pardon, the chancery fees for which would have to be paid. But in such a case the prisoner does not appear to have had to fine with the king for it. The sums recorded on the fine rolls as promised for pardon for homicide were nearly all due from persons who had fled from justice, some being

[1] J.I. 1/786, mm. 2, 19ᵈ. Three of the others were pardoned; cf. *Cal. Pat. Rolls, 1272–81*, 158.
[2] *Select Pleas of the Crown*, Selden Soc. i, no. 114. For this case see above, p. 25.
[3] *Close Rolls, 1227–31*, 552; cf. ibid., *1234–37*, 340.
[4] As in the second case referred to in the preceding note.
[5] Ibid., *1237–42*, 258.

outlaws, or from prisoners and others awaiting trial. The fine rolls themselves do not reveal this, but the enrolled pardons in cases recorded there often show that a special inquisition had been held and had found some excuse, whilst in all the cases of this sort which have been identified on the eyre rolls it emerges that the pardon had been obtained before the session, not as a result of it.[1]

At first, then, the justices were responsible for bringing suitable cases to the king's notice and no doubt suggesting pardon. But this state of affairs did not last. By the time of Edward I the justices in eyre and also those of gaol delivery, on a verdict of slaying by mischance or in self-defence, had taken to remanding the prisoner in custody till he received the king's grace. The phrase 'ad gaolam ad expectandam gratiam', or merely 'ad gratiam', meant something rather different from consulting the king. It implied the justices' readiness to recommend clemency, but it did not, apparently, mean that they themselves would send off letters to this effect to the king;[2] the prisoner himself was now required to take some action. There is still nothing to suggest that he needed to fine with the king, but the application for pardon would itself entail some expenditure. His need to apply for the pardon is brought out particularly clearly in entries on the rolls of gaol delivery and oyer and terminer such as 'let him sue out pardon',[3] or in the decision 'let him be remitted to gaol and sue the king for grace',[4] and there is evidence to show that justices of gaol delivery at least were remanding in this way in the last years of Henry III.[5] Suing to the king for grace meant asking him to send for

---

[1] e.g. C. 60/50, m. 10: Thomas Wulmer proffered and paid in 20 gold shillings for a pardon for a homicide of which he had been appealed; J.I. 1/568, m. 1ᵈ shows that he had been appealed by his victim's widow, but that they had made a concord; he now produced his pardon before the itinerant justices.

[2] When justices of gaol delivery were moved by the prayers of his wife to take some action on behalf of Godfrey Tailor, who had killed in self-defence, they wrote not to the king, but to the Chancellor, asking him to use his good offices to secure pardon. The letter was delivered to the Chancellor by Godfrey's wife, but failed to achieve this, though he was granted bail (S.C. 1/22, no. 148; *Cal. Close Rolls, 1288–96*, 68). J.I. 1/653, m. 3ᵈ shows that he failed to surrender to his bail and was put in exigent.

[3] e.g. J.I. 3/74, ii. 11ᵈ: 'et interim sequatur versus dominum regem de gratia sua habenda'.

[4] *Cal. Chancery Warrants*, 146.

[5] According to a presentment at the eyre, a man had been arrested after killing another in a tavern and taken to the abbot of St. Osyth's prison; it had then been found by an inquisition before Laurence del Broke that he had killed in self-

the record of the case; on receipt of a writ of *certiorari* from him
the justices would send the record containing the verdict and
showing that they had indeed remanded *ad gratiam*.[1] It generally
sounds as though the king's writ was sent directly to the
justices, but this impression may be misleading; sometimes at
least it was sent to the prisoner and handed by him to them.[2]
The same procedure was apparently followed at the eyre though
the rolls do not reveal it so clearly. The king certainly sent to
the justices for the records of cases in which they had remanded
ad gratiam,[3] and this suggests that someone acting on behalf of
the prisoner had informed him of the remand. The record
itself was probably taken to him by the prisoner's agent.[4]
Moreover, it was occasionally returned to Parliament, and the
choice of petitioning the king in Parliament must have been
the prisoner's.[5] But while the prisoner had to take the initiative
there generally were people who could instruct and assist him
in this; at any rate if he was remanded at an eyre, he did

defence, for which reason he had been remanded to gaol until he obtained the
king's peace; this must have occurred at a delivery of the abbot's gaol. See J.I.
1/238, m. 51. Cf. below, p. 119, n. 4.

[1] As appears in the case of William under the Appelton remanded in 1305 to
await the king's grace for accidentally slaying his mother: 'ad sectam predicti
Willelmi', the king sent for the record (J.I. 1/676, m. 2); he pardoned him on the
strength of it (*Cal. Pat. Rolls, 1301–7*, 421).

[2] Hugh Virly was sent back to prison on a verdict that Henry de Scidaluys had
been killed by running on his knife, 'et sequatur versus dominum Regem de
gratia sua habenda etc.' The case is entered twice on the gaol delivery roll, and
the second version has the postscript: 'Et super hoc venit predictus Hugo et
protulit breve domini Regis' asking for the record (J.I. 3/69, mm. 5, 6). C. 47/83/2,
no. 30 consists of this writ and the record as returned to the king. Cf. J.I. 1/966,
m. 5[d], where the prisoner remitted 'ad exspectandam gratiam' came later 'et
tulit breve domini Regis ad recordari faciendum loquelam predictam coram
Rege, et ei mittitur etc.' The record sometimes concludes with a petition for mercy;
e.g. C. 47/79/9, no. 281, where an account of killing in self-defence is followed
by the prisoner's plea 'gratiam domini Regis sibi fieri in hoc casu si placet'.
Cf. C./47/55/6, no. 31.

[3] Several of these writs and the records returned in response to them survive
among the Chancery miscellanea.

[4] There is evidence for this in 1305 though not in a case from the eyre. An appeal
of homicide there had been, exceptionally, summoned to the court of Common
Pleas. The appellor failed to appear and in the following year a jury found that
Alan Tubyas, appealed as principal, had killed in self-defence, so he was remanded
ad gratiam. Later the king sent for the record and process which was delivered to
him by Simon de Hedersete 'qui sequitur pro predicto Alano' (C.P. 40/155, m. 79).
Simon who was thus acting for Alan while he was in prison was also one of the
mainpernors for two men who had been appealed with him. Pardon was granted
on the record (*Cal. Pat. Rolls, 1301–7*, 481).

[5] Cf. J.I. 1/1098, m. 47[d], quoted below, p. 111.

not necessarily have to rely on his own friends, who might be ignorant of the correct procedure. The handling of applications was too efficient on some occasions to have been the work of amateurs.

The Lancashire eyre which started in mid June 1292, produced a large number of cases for the king's mercy. His writs asking for the record to be sent to him have survived in many of them, and their dates are significant. One was dated as early as 24 June, another 4 July. But then on 13 July there were six and one on 14 July;[1] others were from 20 to 23 July. It seems clear that some applications reached him singly, but that one whole bunch came shortly before 13 July and another about a week later. This points to an organized system of transmitting the applications. The records were sent promptly in nearly all these cases, and pardons were granted on 20, 23 (2), 28 (5) July, but one not until 31 August.[2] In two cases no charter was enrolled although pardon is known to have been granted at this time and produced before the justices.[3] One pardon was dated exactly a week after the dispatch of the writ asking for the record, and one eight days later. Edward was on the Scottish border, but even so this shows creditable speed in dealing with these applications. Later in the same year, when the justices visited other counties in the north midlands and northwest, many prisoners remanded *ad gratiam* received their pardons in reasonable time and were also able to produce them before the end of the eyre. This suggests that there was a shuttle service of messengers between the place where the justices were in session and the king's court, the messengers being employed by the remanded prisoners to carry to the king their applications for pardon, to carry back the king's writs to the justices asking for the records, convey these to him, and finally take the engrossed and sealed letters patent to the prisoners. These messengers must have been official or semi-official. The unorganized efforts of the prisoners' friends could not have produced such uniform results, or results in so many cases so expeditiously. No doubt there was plenty of other work for them, especially in connection with civil pleas.

---

[1] C. 47/65/2, nos. 54–60; C. 47/65/3, nos. 61, 62, 63, 68; C. 47/65/4, no. 92. Cf. J.I. 1/409, mm. 6, 7ᵈ, 14ᵈ, 25, 27, 27ᵈ, 28.

[2] *Cal. Pat. Rolls, 1281–92*, 502, 503, 507.

[3] Those of Robert de Caterale, see below, p. 113, and Richard son of Adam de Neuton, see J.I. 1/409 m. 32ᵈ.

But the organization was not always so efficient, and may not always have been available, so that the process of securing pardon might take much longer. Even if the writ asking for the justices' record was obtained promptly the business of searching their rolls for the case, having it copied, and sent to the king could take some time. Occasionally there was a snag—variation in the names of applicant or victim, for example[1]—and the justices had to explain this when returning the record. And when, finally, this came to hand, the king and his council might be slow to deal with it. They might even require a second record if the first was deemed inadequate, either for some technical deficiency, or for obscurity in its substance. In a straight-forward case it might well be six or even eight weeks from the time the writ was sent for the record until the pardon was made out. In a good many cases the interval was much longer, but in these some special difficulty may have arisen.[2]

The organization seems to have operated when there were enough remands *ad gratiam* to make it worth while; if there were only one or two such cases at a particular session of the eyre it might not be available, or the prisoners might not get to know about it and receive no guidance as to the action which

[1] e.g. C. 47/86/31, no. 825, where the name of the victim's father was Henry, as the justices firmly pointed out, not Hugh as in the king's writ for the record. Whether because of this discrepancy or for some other cause, the slayer, W. de Steresby—who had been twelve years old when his arrow glanced off an apple-tree branch, flew over the garden wall and fatally struck Richard son of Henry— did not obtain pardon until fifteen years later, when he had earned it by serving in the Scottish war (*Cal. Pat. Rolls, 1301-7*, 175).

[2] A prisoner remanded to gaol to await the king's mercy might, if this was dilatory, try to hurry things up by sending a further petition for it. Among the surviving petitions is one from William de la Pyle, who had killed an unknown thief in self-defence (S.C. 8/309, no. 15411). This was the verdict at the eyre of Berkshire late in 1284, where Solomon of Rochester and his fellows remanded him to gaol 'quousque etc' (J.I. 1/46, m. 2). Possibly because of the seeming ambiguity of their decision (though this, of course, may be the fault only of the scribe), possibly because of some delay on the part of the king who was occupied with the Welsh at the time (but a woman who was remanded to await the king's grace at the same eyre was pardoned in November 1284; *Cal. Pat. Rolls, 1281-92*, 146), some months elapsed before his pardon was granted. From prison at Windsor Pyle petitioned Edward, 'pur deu, et pur le saluz de ses auncestres et de ses en-faunz' to send for the record of the rolls of the justices, and to show grace, since he would prefer death to the harsh imprisonment which he was suffering. This petition was endorsed: 'Rex concedit ei pacem'. Two pardons were enrolled, one on 12 May 1285, the other on 26 May (ibid. 164, 167). Possibly one was drafted in response to the petition whilst the other was already in the pipeline and would have reached him shortly even if he had not taken this action.

they should now take. At the eyre of Cornwall in 1284 a number
of homicides produced pardons obtained beforehand and were
given firm peace; there were very few who qualified for pardon
but still stood in need of it. One of these, Alice le Ster, who in
1272 at the age of six had accidentally caused a death, was
remanded to prison, but it was not until 1286 that she was
pardoned.[1] Another, Henry de Menhinak, was found to have
killed in self-defence and was similarly remanded, but in 1285
on the record of the eyre he secured release on bail, not pardon.
Nearly a year later he was pardoned on the same record.[2]
Neither of these prisoners seems to have had immediate help in
making application for pardon.

Henry de Menhinak was not the only prisoner who got bail
when he was in a position to secure pardon. Ignorance of the
best course to pursue may explain why some prisoners sought
only immediate release; others may have calculated that bail
would be cheaper and have been content with it for the time
being. It was rare for those remanded at an eyre to opt for bail,
but quite common at gaol deliveries. Some prisoners did not
grasp the fact that they would need to apply for pardon later
on and believed that bail would be sufficient. The confusion
over the action which they were intended to take is especially
well illustrated in a case from the time of Edward II. John
Patric was indicted at a gaol delivery for killing Richard le
Soudour, was found to have done so in self-defence, and remanded *ad gratiam*. At a later gaol delivery he claimed to have
been acquitted at the first, but the record was examined and
showed only the remand. It was stated that this had resulted
in a writ ordering bail. Now John claimed that 'Rex conferet
ei gratiam ex quo compertum fuit ut supra'. It was pointed
out that he ought to have sued out his pardon before and had
foolishly failed to do so. John asked what he should have done
when he had been delivered, and one of the justices replied:
'You should have sued out the king's charter, and since you
did not, we cannot tell whether the king was willing to grant it
to you or not, and so you must go to prison until you have the
king's charter.'[3]

---

[1] J.I. 1/111, m. 27; *Cal. Pat. Rolls, 1281–92*, 225. Cf. below, p. 155.

[2] *Cal. Pat. Rolls, 1281–92*, 216; J.I. 1/111, m. 36ᵈ; C. 47/52/3, no. 113; *Cal. Close Rolls, 1279–88*, 312.

[3] British Museum, MS. Harl. 453, f. 33; cf. J.I. 1/547ᴬ, m. 66.

While the choice between bail and pardon seems often to
have lain with the remanded prisoner himself, it is likely that
in some cases an application for pardon was made but the king
or his council decided not to accede to this plea, ordering release
on bail as a lesser concession. Justices of gaol delivery sometimes
remanded to prison 'donec sciatur de voluntate domini Regis'.
This may have suggested that they thought it was for him to
choose between bail and pardon. If so, his choice might be bail,[1]
or he might fail to reach a decision. In 1289 the king received
the record of a gaol delivery at Somerton showing that John de
Cory Revel had been returned to gaol 'donec dominus Rex de
ipso agat quod sibi placuerit'.[2] Edward was pleased to grant
bail,[3] but a few months later the record came before Parliament
and the reply to John's petition there was 'Habeat pacem
Domini Regis',[4] so that he seems only to have been playing for
time. This case may have presented some difficulty, but in others
it is very hard to see why the king should have hesitated to grant
pardon, yet a very definite recommendation to mercy might
be met only with the order for release on bail.[5]

The record of a gaol delivery which had resulted at first only
in bail might provide grounds for a subsequent pardon. There
would be no necessity for a second inquisition unless the
authorities had not been convinced by the verdict that pardon
was appropriate. If the killer who had thus been bailed
duly stood to right at the next eyre, the same record might
now be accepted as justifying remand *ad gratiam* without a
second verdict being taken. On one occasion, despite the fact
that the gaol delivery rolls had been searched and the case not

---

[1] e.g. C. 47/77/6, nos. 208, 218; *Cal. Close Rolls, 1288–96*, 424; cf. ibid., *1279–88*, 311.

[2] C. 47/77/10, no. 347.

[3] *Cal. Close Rolls, 1288–96*, 25.

[4] *Rot. Parl.* i. 64–5; C. 47/77/6, no. 226; *Cal. Pat. Rolls, 1281–92*, 365.

[5] e.g. C. 47/76/4, no. 140; *Cal. Close Rolls, 1272–79*, 433. In April and May
1282, when Edward was making hurried plans to deal with the Welsh rebellion,
he ordered that several remanded prisoners should be released on bail until Whit
Sunday, when they were to be before him at Worcester to hear his will (ibid.,
1279–88, 151–3). At Worcester all but one of them received pardon on grounds of
self-defence or misadventure (*Cal. Pat. Rolls, 1281–92*, 20, 22, 23). The exception
was a homicidal maniac who had attempted suicide; the king may well have
decided it would be prudent to leave him in charge of his pledges (*Cal. Close Rolls,
1279–88*, 151; C. 47/79, 10, no. 312). The initial grant of bail in the other cases
was probably due to lack of time to go into them adequately, and not to any
doubt that pardon was merited.

discovered there, the itinerant justices accepted the writ to the sheriff ordering bail as sufficient evidence: 'quod quidem breve supponit quod predictum Recordum alias missum fuit coram domino Rege, et quod predictus Rogerus occisus fuit per infortunuim et non per maliciam aut feloniam ipsius Ricardi excogitatam'. They accordingly remanded the prisoner, Richard de Penebrugge, and both the writ for bail and the record of the eyre were sent to the king, together with his writ asking for the record, endorsed with the statement that the record of the gaol delivery 'est penes dominum Regem', as the enclosed writ for bail shows.[1] The king now pardoned him.[2] But in a fair number of cases bail was not followed up by pardon, as far as can be discovered. The excusable homicide who had been released in this way might discover that there was no great need to incur additional expenditure by petitioning for pardon.

The number of cases in which neither bail nor pardon was ever granted, or at least recorded on the surviving rolls, for a prisoner remanded *ad gratiam* is small. As orders for release on bail were not always enrolled—and even some pardons were not enrolled—it cannot safely be asserted even in these cases that no action was taken. But the king could, of course, entirely reject the recommendation to mercy. He might consider that it was not merited. The likelihood of his disagreeing with the justices in this way will be considered later. It was a risk that could not be entirely discounted. There was also a possibility that the record might not be shown to the king. It was returnable to him or to the Chancellor, and one record at least appears to have been held up in Chancery until another was obtained and actually shown to him some three years later.[3]

---

[1] C. 47/76/3, no. 67; cf. J.I. 1/739, mm. 90, 92ᵈ; *Cal. Close Rolls, 1288–96*, 176.

[2] *Cal. Pat. Rolls, 1292–1301*, 7.

[3] In November 1296 Henry Tod of Alnmouth and Hugh son of Robert were charged at a gaol delivery with the death of William Bulhope. The jury found that William had been born in Scotland but had lived in England until the war broke out, when he withdrew to Scotland as the king's enemy; when he saw that the king of England had the upper hand, he returned to England as an enemy, and came to Alnmouth armed with two swords; Henry and Hugh met him and asked if he was loyal to the king of England and would submit to his peace; he refused to be in the peace and fealty of the king and drew his sword as an enemy and traitor, so they killed him. On this verdict they were remanded to prison 'ad voluntatem domini Regis'. Edward asked for the record on 25 June 1297 and it was sent, but he seems to have taken no action on it until 1300, when another copy of the same verdict was shown to him. This presumably had been obtained by

Once the king had decided to remit his suit his decision had to be conveyed to the persons concerned, not only the applicant, but if he were a prisoner his gaoler, and perhaps the justices before whom he had appeared or was about to appear. It has already been seen that the decision to pardon did not necessarily entail the issue of a charter, i.e. formal letters patent of pardon. In the years after Henry III's coming of age especially there is evidence suggesting that remission of his suit could be authorized by other means. If the itinerant justices or justices of gaol delivery recommended pardon it might be thought enough for the king to inform them, whether orally or by letter close, that he had pardoned the prisoner, and instruct them to deliver him from prison. In a number of cases such letters close are enrolled but no corresponding pardon appears on the patent rolls.[1] Allowance must, of course, be made for the fact that in some of these cases a formal pardon may have been issued but not enrolled,[2] but it is highly improbable that this explanation will cover all of them. Moreover, Henry sometimes told the justices or the sheriff not to place an absentee in exigent because he had pardoned him without, apparently, issuing formal letters patent.[3] In view of this extreme informality in granting pardon and informing the justices, it is not surprising to find that a grantee sometimes offered them a fine to have his pardon enrolled.[4] Incidentally, it emerges that it is by no means safe to rely on the patent rolls of this period to form an estimate of the total number of pardons for homicide. It is significant that

the prisoners' friends and the king may have felt that its authenticity should be checked, for on 10 October he ordered the Chancellor to have the prisoners delivered from prison, provided that the record which, so it was said, was already in Chancery, showed that they had killed William as the king's enemy and rebel, as was set forth more fully in the transcript shown to the king and which he enclosed. One copy is endorsed 'Concordatum est per consilium quod fiat', the other copy bears the note 'Istud recordum retornatum fuit coram Cancellario domini Regis anno xxv termino Pasche vel Pentecostis' (C. 81/22, no. 2162). They were granted pardon on 26 February 1301 (*Cal. Pat. Rolls, 1292–1301*, 576).

[1] e.g. *Close Rolls, 1227–31*, 206, 506–7, 552 (where there is no reference to delivery); (cf. 148, where the situation was rather more complicated); ibid., *1234–37*, 237, 340, 457; ibid., *1237–42*, 68, 258 (with no reference to delivery), 276–7. Cases of this kind were dwindling in the next decade but a few have been noticed in the 1250s.

[2] This appears from the case of Robert de Caterale; see pp. 48, 113.

[3] e.g. *Close Rolls, 1227–31*, 526 (J.I. 1/1043, m. 9^d shows that the justices had decided to have consultation on this case); *Close Rolls, 1231–4*, 83. Cf. the case of John de Fraxino, J.I. 1/318, m. 22; cf. *Close Rolls, 1242–7*, 491.

[4] e.g. J.I. 1/700, m. 2^d. The pardon is on *Cal. Pat. Rolls, 1232–47*, 382.

nearly all the cases where charters appear to have been thought
superfluous were homicides by mischance[1] and it seems evident
that less formality attended the king's clemency in such cases
than in homicide in self-defence which was far more likely to be
differently assessed by potential appellors. Indeed many, though
by no means all, were cases of one member of a family accidentally killing another. The formal pardon with its proviso of
standing to right or making peace with the relatives was less
necessary here.

The decision to issue a formal charter of pardon did not
necessarily ensure that the applicant would receive the document. Things could go wrong even at this stage. The first move
was for the king to instruct Chancery to draw it up. There was
a possibility that his warrant would not reach Chancery, but
this was very unlikely. Generally it was received there at once,
and the letters patent were soon drafted. They tended to be
given, as Maxwell-Lyte showed, either the date of the warrant,
or the date at which it was first dealt with there.[2] At this stage
the pardon might be entered on the patent roll, although it
had not yet been engrossed and sealed. Thus enrolment does
not prove that actual letters patent were ever engrossed, sealed,
and handed over. A prisoner might wait in vain for his agent
to return with his pardon. For example, John Harding was
pardoned in January 1282 on the record of a gaol delivery for
the accidental death of Robert Miller;[3] but in June he was
granted release on bail,[4] and at the eyre in 1288 he was again
remanded *ad gratiam*.[5] His pardon had not, then, reached him
after six years.

---

[1] *Close Rolls, 1234–7*, 418 appears to be an exception.
[2] *The Great Seal*, 243–4.   [3] *Cal. Pat. Rolls, 1281–92*, 9.
[4] *Cal. Close Rolls, 1279–88*, 159.
[5] J.I. 1/210, m. 38[d]. Cf. the case of William Fugergate. Robert Malet and his
fellows, delivering Hereford gaol, found that he had killed his brother, John, in
self-defence. The king was informed of this and in November 1291 sent for their
record, which stated that the killing had occurred in the course of a quarrel as they
were coming from an inn, and that as it had been in self-defence they had sent
him back to prison 'ad voluntatem domini Regis' (C. 47/61/3, no. 67). On the
strength of this, pardon was granted, also in November, and recorded on the patent roll (*Cal. Pat. Rolls, 1281–92*, 451). But the pardon seems not to have reached
William, for he was still in the prison when John Buteturt and others delivered
it early the following year. They also found that the killing had been in self-
defence, but this time, thinking perhaps that the pardon was on its way, William
was content to apply for bail, which the king ordered in March (*Cal. Close Rolls,
1288–96*, 222). At the eyre, shortly afterwards, he explained that he had been

The main reason for non-delivery of the pardon was no doubt
non-payment of the Chancery fees, amounting to 18*s.* 4*d.* At
one time the whole of this went to the Chancellor and his chief
officers. It was payable for pardons for homicide at least in the
1230s, probably much earlier.[1] Later, when the Chancellor
received a salary, the bulk of the fees went to the king, leaving
him only 2*s.* for each charter.[2] Payment was made after the
engrossment, usually in the Hanaper but sometimes in the
Wardrobe, the Keeper of which might tell the Keeper of the
Hanaper to hand over the charter which was ready in Chancery,
since he had sanctioned arrangements for the payment of the
fees. These might take the form of deduction from sums due
from the king to the grantee. Thus instructions were given
for the delivery of a pardon for forest offences in 1304:

Liverez a sire Owayn de Montgomeri la chartre de pardoun
faite pur lui qest en vostre garde, car du fiee qui appent au Roi
lauoms chargez sour ses gages et vous enferroms due allouance en
vostre aconte.[3]

The grantee was a king's clerk and had done service in
Scotland. Thus a convenient arrangement was made whereby
no money actually changed hands, but the king's share of the
Chancery fee was to be deducted from the wages due to the

---

bailed on the strength of the verdict in 1292, but made no reference to that of
1291. The justices in eyre remanded him to prison yet again, 'quousque dominus
Rex etc' (J.I. 1/302, m. 61^d). No second pardon has been found; it may be that
the first did now in fact arrive.

  [1] This is shown by the case of Gilbert le Brun, outlawed before 1238 for the death
of Ralph le Bret, whom he had killed as an escaped prisoner (J.I. 1/174, m. 36^d).
Gilbert obtained pardon for the outlawry, and the amount of his Chancery fee
for the pardon is revealed in an unexpected way. It was at this moment that Henry
III quarrelled with his Chancellor, Ralph Neville, and deprived him of the
custody of the great seal; it was restored to him in 1242-3 (see S. B. Chrimes,
Administrative History of Medieval England, 112) and in January 1244, less than a
month before Neville's death, the king ordered the sheriffs of various counties to
distrain his debtors to pay their debts before Easter; among these debtors was
Gilbert le Brun who owed 18*s.* 4*d.* 'pro litteris patentibus de utlagaria' (*Close
Rolls, 1242-47*, 235; cf. ibid., *1237-42*, 37). In 1236 Adam son of Reginald de
Wulvreton was pardoned for homicide and the patent roll notes that 'the Prior
of Wenloc for the writ of pardon owes 17*s.* 4*d.* at the Exchequer' (*Cal. Pat. Rolls,
1232-47*, 154). Probably this is a clerical error for 18*s.* 4*d.* and the prior was undertaking to pay the fee of the seal, but he may have proffered the smaller sum to
secure the grant of pardon.
  [2] See H. C. Maxwell-Lyte, op. cit. 332.
  [3] E. 101/211/3, no. 7; cf. *Cal. Pat. Rolls, 1301-7*, 260.

grantee. Familiarity with the ways of the court may explain
how Owen came to suggest this way out of his problem of
raising the sum required. Whether he had to pay the 2s. to the
Chancellor does not appear, but probably he was expected to
pay them, although the pardon was not to be withheld until he
had done so. Adam de Staneye obtained delivery of his pardon
for rape in 1306 by arranging with the king's Cofferer, Walter
de Bedewynd, that the fee should be charged against sums due
to him in the Wardrobe.[1] The sum involved was 18s. 4d. The
Hanaper was notified of this and its accounts record his payment, but only of 16s. 4d.; the remaining 2s. was presumably
paid to the Chancellor.[2] William de Thorntoft, Keeper of the
Hanaper at this time, seems to have been responsible for seeing
that instruments were not handed over until the fees were paid,
for he received instructions to hand over several pardons, the fees
for which were guaranteed by someone else. These orders show
that servants of the king were negotiating for payments for the
fees of the seal to be deducted from their wages, although they
were not themselves the beneficiaries. A grantee who could not
afford to make a cash payment would get a household clerk to
help him in this way, no doubt on promise of a somewhat larger
sum to be paid in future. Thus Thorntoft was told to deliver to
John de Flete charters of pardon for John de Weredale and
Thomas de Inde, charging the king's share of the fees of the
seal against Flete's wages.[3] The latter seems to have acted in a
general way as intermediary, since the charters were to be
handed to him as well as being paid for out of his wages. One
might expect to find that he had been instrumental in obtaining the grants of pardon to begin with, but both were
granted in return for service in Scotland, and Weredale's was at
the instance of Edward the king's son.[4] In other cases the fees
were to be deducted from the wages of a king's yeoman,[5] and
a squire of the household or an escheator (such as James de
Dalilegh) might make themselves responsible for them.[6]

[1] E. 101/211/5, no. 18.

[2] E. 101/211/4, m. 4; cf. Cal. Pat. Rolls, 1301–7, 418; J.I. 1/809, m. 11, where he
was said to have been pardoned.

[3] E. 101/211/2, no. 1.

[4] Cal. Pat. Rolls, 1301–7, 250. Weredale was pardoned for a homicide and
trespasses, Inde for a homicide, robberies, etc.

[5] E. 101/211/3, nos. 4 and 6.

[6] E. 101/211/2, nos. 22, 23. A more curious arrangement is that made with
the bailiff of Tyndale; the king owed him a certain amount for irons and nails

It was thus possible to get credit by indirect means and through the help of the king's servants for the fees of the seal and so get possession of the letters patent of pardon before paying out the 16s. 4d. which went to the king. But it is not altogether clear why it was necessary for some people to seek credit in this way, for the king would not exact the Chancery fee from anyone who really could not afford to pay it. He himself quite often ordered that the fee should be remitted; indeed some charters to men who had served in his wars expressly laid this down.[1] The reason in many cases may not have been the grantee's poverty; the king may have wished to give additional reward for good service, or to please the grantee's commanding officer or other patron. But quite apart from action by the king himself, the Chancellor, as Maxwell-Lyte observed, 'had discretionary power to remit or to reduce the fee'.[2] Nearly 300 pardons, mainly for homicide but including a few for other crimes and forest offences, are recorded on the roll of the Hanaper for 1305–6.[3] Half of these were paid for in full as far as the king's share was concerned. In some cases he obtained 18s. 4d. because the Chancellorship was vacant for a short period; it may be assumed that in others when the king got 16s. 4d. the Chancellor got his 2s. as well. But for half of these pardons the king's share was reduced or remitted entirely, and it may be doubted whether the Chancellor got anything. Total remission was very much more frequent than reduction, the ratio being nearly 4 : 1. Claims for remission and reduction were carefully examined. The applicant had to pledge his faith that he had no chattels, or that he could not raise more than his proffer. The

provided by him; from this were to be deducted the fees for three charters of pardon for men who had served in Scotland, William de la Forest, Robert le Filz William de Martindale, and Robert Chobbe of Slegill; E. 101/211/3, no. 10; cf. *Cal. Pat. Rolls, 1301–7,* 171, 180.

[1] e.g. in 1295 he ordered that letters of pardon should be made, quit of the fee of the seal, for William, Hugh le Croysier's son, who had killed Alan le Mouner as appeared by the record of Hugh de Cressingham and William de Ormesby (*Cal. Chancery Warrants,* 53). The case had been heard by them at the eyre shortly before when it had been reported that the two had wrestled together in a wrestling match and Alan, on account of being extremely drunk and being thrown by William, had vomited and 'incontinenter inde obiit' (J.I. 1/1098, m. 55; the actual record returned by the justices has survived in C. 202/C/6). The circumstances were such that the king might well have thought William deserved to get his pardon gratis, but this was not apparently the motive for remitting the fee, for the pardon was to be conditional on his finding security to stay in the king's service in Wales during the war. [2] Op. cit. 338.

[3] E. 101/211/1.

sums accepted varied greatly and appear to represent genuine capacity to pay. Even if he could manage only 2s. these were taken from him. One applicant could produce as much as 15s.;[1] it cannot have been easy for him to convince the Keeper of the Hanaper that he could not find the extra 1s. 4d. Occasionally, inability to pay was attested by some other official such as the king's Cofferer.[2] Whereas reduction of the fee was determined only by what the grantee could afford, total remission was regarded as an act of charity, although again the grantee must show that he could pay nothing; his charter was given to him 'pro deo quia affidavit quod nihil habuit in bonis'. In one case it was handed over gratis, on the instructions of the Keeper of the Wardrobe, at the instance of Mary the king's daughter, nun of Amesbury.[3]

The fact that some men did not secure remission of the fees although they could not or would not pay them at once indicates that the authorities were strict in their means test. A good many pardons were not handed over because of failure to pay these fees. Maxwell-Lyte quotes the case of John de Bonington, whose letters patent of pardon 'dated the 5th of November 1301, and sealed within the next fortnight, were not actually issued to him until 1305'.[4] Finally, there was also the scrivener's fee for engrossing the pardon to be taken into account. Failure to pay this may explain why some grantees failed at the last moment to obtain delivery of the document. A pardon to Mathew Pigot for homicide was ready for him to collect, but was never handed over. It bears the note, 'non solvit pro scriptura', which indicates non-payment of this final fee, and probably explains why it was not handed to him.[5] It is still among the Chancery files, together with some fifty other pardons of Edward I for homicide and various crimes, a continuing reminder of the fallibility of the system of pardoning.[6]

---

[1] E. 101/211/1, m. 7.   [2] E. 101/211/4, m. 4.   [3] Ibid., m. 7.

[4] Op. cit. 396–7. Cf. the case of John son of John le Whitesmith, a clerk, whose pardon was dated 29 July 1302 (*Cal. Pat. Rolls, 1301–7*, 50). Not only was it granted at this time; the letters patent were actually engrossed and sealed (E. 101/211/1, m. 7). Yet it was not until 1305–6 that John paid the Chancery fee and obtained possession of the charter (ibid.). He had been remanded at a gaol delivery, see J.I. 3/99, m. 7ᵈ, and finally produced his charter in court; see J.I. 1/966, m. 1.

[5] C. 202/H/5, no. 39.

[6] One or two of them may have been drafts only as they are unsealed and have no tag for the seal; e.g. nos. 2, 3, 37. In the fourteenth century there were so many unclaimed pardons in Chancery that the government ordered the destruction

There were other reasons why charters were not claimed and delivered. Some grants of pardon were apparently obtained for fugitives and outlaws by their friends before they had established contact with them. This is shown by the fact that a second pardon was sometimes granted for the same homicide. Daniel de Belewe, for example, was pardoned in 1264 at the instance of John de Pysing, the king's yeoman, and again in 1271, this time at the instance of Roger de Leyburn.[1] Even if he was aware that his friends were trying to get pardon for him, the fugitive might find it prudent to move on before they had succeeded, and so lose touch with them. The engrossed pardon might be handed over to his representative, yet never come into his possession. There was a special difficulty with joint pardons for two or more partners in crime; they might not each get a copy and this could prove fatal to some if they were not all brought to trial together.

The grantee's troubles were not over when he at last pocketed his charter. However informal the means by which the king's decision to pardon was sometimes reached and conveyed to those concerned, certain formalities attached to its publication from an early period. The returned outlaw in particular was in a dangerous situation until it was widely known that the king had sanctioned his return. Except in the border regions an outlaw might not, indeed, lawfully be executed out of hand by those who recognized him, but it was their duty to capture him and if he resisted arrest they could kill him with impunity— with no need even for the king's pardon for themselves. It would not be difficult for an enemy to provoke an affray which would give some backing to the plea of justifiable homicide because the victim was an outlaw resisting arrest, so that for the pardoned outlaw's own protection it was essential that his new status be well advertised. Even those with whom he lived were liable to the serious charge of harbouring an outlaw until this was done. Moreover, since pardons were nearly always conditional on standing to right it was necessary, if the proviso was meant seriously, for the opportunity to be given to appellors to make it effective. Accordingly, the person who secured letters

of hundreds of them. Those in C. 202/H/5 are a handful which escaped this destruction. Some were probably for criminals who enlisted in the army and who did not survive to claim them. Cf. Maxwell-Lyte, op. cit. 398–9.

[1] *Cal. Pat. Rolls, 1258–66*, 383; ibid., *1266–72*, 552.

patent of pardon was expected to get them proclaimed in court, and it was very much in his own interest to do this without delay. The first move seems to have been to show them to the sheriff,[1] who should then proclaim them in the county court, with an invitation, in accordance with the proviso, to anyone who now wished to prosecute to come forward. If no one did so, it could, at first, be announced by the sheriff that the pardoned man had the king's firm peace: he was no longer liable to prosecution for the slaying.

Proclamation of the pardon in court goes back at least to the time of John. At the eyre in Gloucestershire in 1221, Thomas Roscelin, who had been put in exigent at the preceding eyre after killing two women, was stated to have surrendered to King John two years after it, and the king, being moved to mercy, to have granted him peace. He had sent Thomas to the then sheriff 'et precepit quod hoc faceret clamari in comitatu suo, eo quod testatum fuit coram domino Rege quod predicte due femine latronisse fuerunt, et ipse supervenit ubi ipse voluerunt burgare quandam domum'.[2] In 1221 the justices thought it desirable to check up on this account, since the jurors, evidently speaking from long memory or hearsay, were uncertain whether Thomas really had had letters from the king, and whether the sheriff had acted on his own authority or on the king's order. They therefore decreed that Thomas should be taken. Later he was brought before them—in a litter as he was ill—and he gave half a mark to have an inquisition. The county court thereupon recorded that the king had pardoned him for the homicide, which had been in self-defence, and so he went quit. Thus although the itinerant justices were required to make sure that everything had been done correctly it was apparently sufficient, at this period, for the pardon to be proclaimed in the county court. In 1231 Henry pardoned a homicide and ordered the sheriff to have the letters patent read publicly there and to see to it that they were observed in the county.[3]

[1] See *Litt. Claus.* i. 426 (1220), where the sheriff of Lincs. was ordered to release on bail Jordan de Tid whose outlawry in the time of Richard I for slaying in the time of Henry II had now been pardoned (cf. *Pat. Rolls, 1216–25*, 200), but who was appealed by his victim's daughter, if this was the reason for his detention. The writ refers to his being pardoned 'per litteras nostras patentes quas tibi inde monstravit'. He obtained a second pardon in 1234, perhaps because the first had been issued during Henry III's minority; see *Cal. Pat. Rolls, 1232–47*, 69.

[2] *Pleas of the Crown for the County of Gloucester*, ed. F. W. Maitland, no. 362.

[3] *Pat. Rolls, 1225–32*, 437–8.

Orders of this kind continued to be given and even a hundred court was sometimes used for the proclamation, or at least the pardon was shown to the hundred bailiff.[1] Appearance at the eyre might be followed by the proclamation of peace in the county court. The king himself ordered this in 1248 in the case of Robert le Taillur, who had been outlawed for killing a man who was himself an outlaw, and then pardoned; Robert had later appeared before the itinerant justices and no one had come forward to prosecute him, so the sheriff was now ordered to give him firm peace.[2] This delay in making it irrevocable and the need to get the king himself to intervene were inconvenient to the grantee, and it must have become apparent that the respective duties of the county court and the itinerant justices needed to be more clearly defined. Proclamation in the county court might be somewhat prejudicial to would-be appellors, who might not have prior notice of it, but it was also liable to endanger the pardoned slayer himself if the existence of his pardon was inadequately publicized. On the other hand, proclamation only at the eyre would involve long delay in nearly all cases, although it would command the fullest publicity. It was finally decided that pardons must be shown at both assemblies, but that firm peace should be given at the eyre.

Production of the pardon in the county court continued to be important, if only as a preliminary. When the king pardoned a prisoner before his trial he still ordered the sheriff both to release him and to have the letters patent read and peace proclaimed and observed; pardons and peace for outlaws were to be published in the same way. There is little evidence for this being done, though there is reference to it in a case in 1280;[3] but early registers of writs contain the formula for these instructions to the sheriff, which suggests that the procedure was normal.[4] When the pardon was read out in the county court an appellor could come forward and announce his intention to prosecute an appeal, though this would have to be carried out later at the eyre. He might be given some encouragement to

---

[1] Hugh le Kyeu did not appear at the eyre in 1241, but the hundred bailiff produced his pardon, which was allowed by the justices; the jurors now confirmed that the death in question had been entirely accidental. Cf. above p. 38, n. 2.

[2] *Close Rolls, 1247–51*, 108; cf. *Cal. Pat. Rolls, 1232–47*, 435; *Lancs. Assize Rolls*, Record Soc. for Lancs. and Cheshire, xlvii. 101.

[3] J.I. 1/204, m. 50^d; see below, p. 64.

[4] e.g. British Museum, MS. Harl. 4351, f. 48; MS. Harl. 1608, f. 62.

withdraw, however, and if the county court could record that an appeal had thus been initiated and then withdrawn any attempt to renew it before the itinerant justices would be firmly quashed.[1] About the middle of the century it was established that all pardons must be proclaimed also by royal justices. This time the proclamation was final. The Northumberland eyre roll for 1256, for example, records that 'interrogatus est semel, bis, ter, si aliquis ex parentibus . . . vel aliquis alius velit sequi versus eum, modo veniant vel nunquam'.[2] After the three invitations to appeal firm peace was given irrevocably. In some later eyres the invitation seems to have been repeated at hourly intervals, or so the phrase 'ab hora prima usque ad horam nonam' suggests.[3] The peace once solemnly proclaimed after these invitations could not be disturbed, though an attempt was occasionally made to appeal in spite of it.[4]

There continued to be some confusion about procedure. People who had been pardoned might not realize that they had to appear at the eyre and the justices might have to order that they should be brought before them to show their pardons.[5] It was sometimes believed to be sufficient for a deputy to produce the charter of pardon and get it proclaimed in the absence of the grantee, and this was indeed allowed in some cases, but there could be doubt about its propriety. Moreover, there could easily be some confusion over the justices' decision, as there was in the case of Geoffrey de Rockingham, who obtained pardon in 1252 for the death of Philip le Escot.[6] He produced this pardon in the county court, but failed to appear at the next eyre in Rutland, and so the justices ordered that

[1] See J.I. 1/455, m. 7ᵈ; quoted below, p. 211.

[2] *Northumberland Assize Rolls*, Surtees Soc. lxxxviii. 98. A threefold proclamation seems to have been the rule earlier; cf. J.I. 1/174, m. 27ᵈ.

[3] e.g. J.I. 1/573, m. 81ᵈ; J.I. 1/736, mm. 46, 47.

[4] e.g. in 1280 Robert son of John appealed Alan de Beltoft of the slaying of his father, although Alan had been pardoned by Henry III, then appealed by John's widow, Emma, had thereupon gone quit before the justices, and so been given firm peace in accordance with his pardon. As a result of Robert's subsequent appeal in the county court Alan was imprisoned 'minus uuste [sic] et contra consuetudinem actenus optentam et usitatam in rengno nostro', as Edward I declared in ordering his release (J.I. 1/664, m. 39; cf. *Cal. Pat. Rolls, 1258–66*, 188, 254). In spite of this order Robert tried to prosecute his appeal at the eyre, but the justices acquitted Alan since he had been given firm peace at the last eyre when Emma withdrew hers, and 'pax illa tunc sibi concessa non esset firma si modo iterata [sic] respondisset de predicta morte' (J.I. 1/664, m. 39).

[5] e.g. J.I. 1/1109, m. 30ᵈ.

[6] *Cal. Pat. Rolls, 1247–58*, 140.

he be exacted; then, however, his brother-in-law showed his pardon to two of them; apparently they rescinded the order to exact, but the eyre clerks failed to take note of this; at any rate the county court now proceeded to outlaw him. It was not until 1260 that Geoffrey secured the annulment of his outlawry by the court *coram rege*.[1]

Geoffrey's troubles may have drawn attention to the need to clarify the procedure still further. It may be significant that the baronial Justiciar, Hugh Bigod, took the record of the county court at Oakham[2] and presided over the hearing *coram rege*. He took some interest in the business of pardoning and may have had ideas on the subject of its reform; though he had little opportunity to achieve this himself, his views may have had some influence on later practice. At any rate, the rolls of the eyre in 1268 show that by then the procedure of proclaiming pardons was well known and strictly followed. But it was not entirely restricted to the eyre. Later it also took place before other commissions such as oyer and terminer and gaol delivery, though this was not a very satisfactory arrangement as far as proper publicity and giving a genuine opportunity for appeal were concerned. The prisoner might appear at a gaol delivery in a different county from that in which the slaying had occurred; many slayers, for example, surrendered to Newgate Gaol.[3] However, in the next century, as the general eyre was obsolescent it was as well that peace could be given by these

[1] K.B. 26/168, m. 17ᵈ. He had made two earlier attempts to get the outlawry reversed. In 1254 Henry III had written from Gascony complaining that nothing had been done to implement an earlier order to amend this excess, and ordering that it should now be corrected or reason shown why not (*Cal. Pat. Rolls, 1247–58*, 360). From this letter it appears that Geoffrey had been in the king's service at the time of the eyre (cf. ibid. 231) and 'ignorant of the process'. In 1254 he was again pardoned, but his lands were none the less to escheat (ibid. 400) and in 1256 his estates were being handed over to his lords (*Close Rolls, 1254–56*, 271, 272). He had obtained bail for the homicide in October 1251 (ibid., *1247–51*, 512). Despite all these efforts he had been careless enough to lose his current pardon and had to get a new one on 21 November 1260 (*Cal. Pat. Rolls, 1258–66*, 129).

[2] See J.I. 1/1187, m. 15.

[3] Efforts were made to ensure that potential appellors knew that the pardon was to be proclaimed there. The sheriff of the county concerned would be instructed to announce solemnly that any one who wished to prosecute should come before the justices of gaol delivery at Newgate on a stated day. If the sheriff informed them that he had done so and no one then appeared the pardon would become effective. See J.I. 1/374, m. 77ᵈ (Kent). This procedure may have had some point in the home counties, but even there it was most unlikely that the invitation would be accepted.

commissions or the whole procedure would have tended to lapse. Peace could also be given all along, in the central King's Court,[1] but under Edward I the peace given there was often limited to his suit.[2]

Failure to appear before the justices was a serious matter. The pardoned homicide could be put in exigent and outlawed, as Geoffrey de Rokingham was. But generally the justices would hesitate to do this if they were aware of the pardon. An order to exact could be rescinded on evidence that the defaulter had received pardon,[3] and the justices might simply send for him if he was within reach and could produce it.[4] The preliminary proclamation in the county court would prove its worth in such cases. But many defaulters were outlawed. Some obtained a second pardon, covering this outlawry only, and stipulating surrender by a given date. After Geoffrey de Rokingham's unhappy experience it was exceptional for the pardon to be produced by proxy; nevertheless this could be done if there was a good excuse for the grantee's absence. In 1272 Henry III annulled the outlawry of a man who had earlier been pardoned and had then gone on the crusade; since he had had no friend to show his pardon to the justices they had placed him in exigent;[5] it is implied that in these circumstances production of the pardon by proxy could properly have been admitted. Absence overseas for less good cause was a more doubtful excuse, and in 1280 the justices decided to have consultation on the case of a pardoned man who had had peace proclaimed in the county court but failed to appear also at the eyre held while he was abroad.[6] Illness might be accepted as sufficient excuse,[7] or the king himself might authorize non-appearance.[8] In the 1290s the justices may have been rather stricter for a while, but later considerable lenience was shown to grantees

---

[1] Cf. K.B. 26/162, m. 36. In this case an appeal had just been withdrawn.
[2] e.g. K.B. 27/189, mm. 12, 50^d.
[3] e.g. J.I. 1/1109, m. 26^d; cf. *Cal. Pat. Rolls, 1247–58*, 422.
[4] e.g. J.I. 1/1098, m. 36^d; J.I. 1/1286, m. 51^d. The defaulter here had been pardoned on the verdict of a gaol delivery that he had killed in self-defence.
[5] *Cal. Pat. Rolls, 1266–72*, 616.   [6] J.I. 1/204, m. 50^d.
[7] J.I. 1/827, m. 33 (1286).
[8] e.g. Samson Foliot was pardoned in 1281 for the death of his son (*Cal. Pat. Rolls, 1272–81*, 441) and the king wrote to the justices informing them of the pardon and instructing them not to molest him. It was probably on the strength of this writ that they permitted his charter of pardon to be put forward in his absence by a knight, and proclaimed it in the usual way, announcing firm peace when no one came forward to prosecute (J.I. 1/1004, m. 85^d. Cf. below, p. 241).

who did not appear in person at sessions of oyer and terminer.[1] It is surprising to find that someone involved in the actual slaying could produce an absentee's charter and get it proclaimed and firm peace given, yet this was done by Robert Baynard in 1268.[2] Finally, it may be noted that the justices might allow some respite for the charter to be produced in court. It was prudent especially for a former outlaw to carry the pardon always on his person, as Bracton pointed out,[3] but a grantee might prefer to leave it in safe custody and if arrested without it would run some risk unless there was backing in court for his statement that he had received it. In one case the prisoner said that his charter was in his brother's keeping; the justices of gaol delivery in 1296 remanded him in custody and by the delivery of August 1297 he had got possession of it and produced it successfully.[4]

Proclamation of the pardon involved expenditure of both time and money. Probably it was expedient to get some official to advise on the correct procedure, for a small fee. At any rate by the time of Edward II the solemn proclamation partook of the nature of a ceremony with its appropriate scale of fees: a pair of gloves to every clerk, two shillings to the chief clerks, and two shillings to the marshals for proclaiming peace.[5] It meant also that there was an anxious waiting period before it was definitively settled that the homicide would not have to implement the condition of standing to right. There was little danger that the pardon itself would not be accepted, though the identity of the person named in it and the indicted prisoner sometimes had to be established because of variation in his name and description, surnames not yet being stabilized. The justices could not refuse to proclaim the pardon because of doubts about the way in which it had been obtained or the

[1] e.g. in 1306 the justices of oyer and terminer in Warwickshire accepted a pardon produced before them on behalf of a Hospitaller who was now overseas; they decided that nothing should be done about him at present nor should he be outlawed (J.I. 1/966, m. 1ᵈ). Similarly, in 1305 a friend produced the pardon of a man who had burgled a house and killed its owner, and on this occasion the pardon was proclaimed *in absentia*; at the same session another man who did not appear was not put in exigent as it was testified that he had a pardon (J.I. 1/1108, mm. 14, 12).

[2] J.I. 1/569ᴬ, m. 13ᵈ; *Cal. Pat. Rolls, 1258–66*, 267; ibid., *1266–72*, 230.

[3] *De Legibus*, f. 131ᵇ.   [4] J.I. 3/96, m. 34ᵈ.

[5] *Eyre of Kent*, Selden Soc., xxiv. 139. Details of the slaying in question, which was in self-defence, will be found in J.I. 3/26, ii, m. 7; cf. *Cal. Pat. Rolls, 1301–7*, 333.

merits of the case,[1] though they might think it desirable to get a jury to confirm the grounds on which it had been granted,[2] or check the circumstances against the records of earlier inquiries.[3] But the most they could do if they were dissatisfied was to punish those responsible for the error and fine the grantee; they could not refuse to give him firm peace. On the other hand, if they found something suspicious about the charter itself it was not impossible for them to postpone the proclamation, and in the meantime consult the king.[4]

Even after the formal proclamation of the king's peace the possibility remained that someone would attempt to reopen the case or there might be a dispute about forfeiture of property. The charter of pardon remained a valuable document for the rest of the grantee's life and might be of value to his heirs after his death. Thus it had to be guarded after the proclamation as well as prior to it, when the grantee's life literally depended on his being able to produce it in court. It was worth while getting a worn-out charter renewed and only prudent to get a lost one replaced;[5] the theft of his pardon was a particularly underhand way of injuring an enemy.[6]

The process of obtaining pardon and getting it finally proclaimed in court was complicated and might take months or

[1] Cf. below, p. 258.

[2] e.g. after Thomas le Tayllour had produced his pardon the jurors testified that he had hit the victim accidentally not meaning to kill him. The pardon was then proclaimed. It had been granted on grounds of self-defence. See J.I. 1/58, m. 20; *Cal. Pat. Rolls, 1247–58*, 533.

[3] e.g. J.I. 1/804, m. 76^d, where they checked the declaration in the pardon that the killing had been accidental with both the coroner's roll and the verdict of an inquisition held by the sheriff and the coroner before making the proclamation; cf. below, p. 284.

[4] The justices of gaol delivery at Northampton were puzzled when William Frere produced two charters, one dated 10 November 1303 pardoning him, for service in Scotland, the death of John son of Henry del Brok of Medeburne and robberies, etc., the other dated 1307 pardoning him the death of John de Meldeburn and William son of John de Stoke on condition he surrender to Northampton gaol. Because of the variation and doubtfulness of these charters they would not proceed to deliver him. A record of this decision was sent to the king and Edward II granted him a third pardon (C. 47/124/1, no. 1; *Cal. Pat. Rolls, 1301–7*, 171, 527; ibid., *1307–13*, 155–6).

[5] e.g. ibid., *1258–66*, 125, 129, 148 (under present seal); ibid., *1266–72*, 228.

[6] e.g. *Close Rolls, 1251–53*, 336, 504; *Cal. Pat. Rolls, 1247–58*, 226 (larceny); ibid., *1266–72*, 25. An attack on a clerk, Master Reginald de la Wade, in his home seems to have been made with the aim of beating him up and burning his pardon for homicide. See K.B. 26/177, m. 6; cf. *Cal. Pat. Rolls, 1258–66*, 335. He seems to have got another and produced it at the eyre; see J.I. 1/569^A, m. 32^d.

even years to complete. Help and advice were sometimes available, sometimes not. Some remanded prisoners failed to understand the possibility or the advantage of getting pardon and secured release on bail instead. If the applicant had a good conscience and had duly appeared in court he should have found little difficulty in getting it, yet he might find even the Chancery fees prohibitive and not be aware that they might be reduced. Things were naturally more difficult for the fugitive and outlaw, but so long as they were in contact with friends who were prepared to act for them the procedural problem was not really very much greater. It involved getting a special inquisition held if they could put forward some excuse. If they could not they would have to proffer considerable sums or find an influential friend at court. Even the excusable slayer had to pay for the inquisition and resultant charter, and in many cases poverty must have ruled out any application, whilst in a few it meant that pardon was granted but the formal charter never handed over. The cost involved in obtaining it and having it proclaimed was a grave defect in the system and meant that many people who fully deserved pardon were unable to take advantage of it. Apart from the purely procedural difficulties, aggravated at times by administrative inefficiency, there was the problem for the excusable slayer of convincing the king, the justices, or commissioners and juries of the validity of his excuse. The principles upon which homicide ranked as pardonable were not entirely clear. The justices themselves were inconsistent in interpreting them, and the vagaries of juries could be disconcerting. Thus if any assessment is to be made of the unintentional homicide's chances of securing pardon and of the degree of harshness with which he was treated, it is necessary to examine more closely the definitions of self-defence, mischance, and justification.

III

EXCUSABLE HOMICIDE

THE terms justifiable and excusable homicide were not used in the Middle Ages, though the notion of killing with justice was familiar and sometimes the circumstances were said to constitute *excusatio*. The terms are used here as a convenient means of distinguishing between slaying which was not felonious and did not even require pardon on the one side, and slaying which was not felonious but did require pardon on the other. Excusable slaying, defined in this way, included homicides by lunatics and infants, but these presented special problems and will be considered separately in a later chapter. The remaining types of excusable homicide were slaying in self-defence and by mischance, and these terms were freely used. Nevertheless, these categories were not strictly observed in practice. It was not always obvious whether or not pardon was needed; still less could it always be clear whether or not it was deserved. Since pardon was a matter of prerogative it was difficult for definitive rules to be formulated as to when it was appropriate. Yet the king's conscience was supposed to be guided by principles of equity, which amounts to saying that he, his advisers, and his justices should have been influenced by the concepts of natural law, or more practically, by such rulings as the works of Justinian and the canonists provided on these questions.

Unfortunately, while these authorities dealt to some extent with the distinctions between the different sorts of homicide and tried to measure varying degrees of culpability their distinctions were not drawn to meet the problems of the English penal system, and in particular the problem of pardoning excusable slaying. Civil Law absolved those who killed by accident or in self-defence from any guilt except in very special circumstances. Canon Law, on the other hand, set an extremely high standard, one much too severe to supply a suitable model for the secular authorities to adopt. It was concerned with divine forgiveness, not the king's pardon. Not every homicide was sinful, yet there was need to do penance for slaying not only if there had been intent but if there had been the very slightest degree of negligence. If there was any doubt on this point it was advisable, to be on the safe side, to do penance *ad cautelam*. Sometimes the penitent's own remorse and horror at his responsibility for a death, or even the slightest, perhaps an imaginary, contribution towards it, could only be allayed in this way. But what may have been an appropriate standard for tender consciences was totally unsuited to serve as a guide to the king in determining either criminal liability or the need for pardon. To make matters even worse, so far as its possible influence on secular practice went, Canon Law was concerned much more with homicidal clerks than with laymen. The great problem was to know whether killing someone rendered a clerk *irregularis*, whether one in lower orders was thereby debarred from promotion, or a priest incurred demotion: was the slaying such that he could no longer fitly minister at the altar? Scruples of this sort, while they helped to distinguish between fine points of motivation, degrees of self-control and of negligence, could not, in equity, be the basis for distinguishing between slayings which needed or did not need the king's pardon. Already in the twelfth century the study of Canon Law in England had made some of this material familiar, and the penitential literature which had a long history here was necessarily concerned with the problems of justifiable and excusable homicide. Bartholomew of Exeter's Penitential, composed probably between 1150 and 1170, enjoyed 'wide popularity',[1] and it included chapters entitled 'De homicidio non sponte commisso' and 'Non omnis qui occidit hominem homicidii reus est', which quoted some of the stock canonistic pronouncements. Well-known continental works were available, and in the next century use was to be made of those, for example, of Bernard of Pavia and of Raymond of Peñafort. At the same time the Civil Law was being taught and having a certain influence on various aspects of English legal procedure. Unsuitable as this sort of material was for this purpose, it provided a fund of learning on which the king and his justices could draw when exercising or recommending the exercise of the prerogative of pardon. One of the latter did so, if not in court at least in his own writings. Nearly all of what

[1] See A. Morey, *Bartholomew of Exeter*, 164, 174.

Bracton had to say about justifiable and excusable homicide was derived from either Civil or Canon Law, or both. His analysis of the different types of homicide on f. 120 and all but a few sentences of the following passage were copied, with slight verbal modifications, from Raymond of Peñafort's *Summa de Poenitentia* (or *de Casibus*) Lib. ii, tit. 1.[1] The sections on f. 136^b and f. 155 were derived from the works of Justinian. His struggle—and failure—to integrate these borrowings into his account of the laws of England illustrates not only their potential utility in rationalizing English procedure but also the limits of both their potential and actual influence.

Raymond de Peñafort, following Bernard of Pavia, divided homicide into two main types, spiritual and corporal, and subdivided the latter into two, verbal and factual, the first including ordering and counselling a slaying. Homicide *facto* was itself of four kinds, being committed justly, of necessity, by chance, or wilfully. It was by way of justice when a judge or his officer executed the criminal who had been justly condemned, but even this sort of homicide might be a mortal sin if the executioner acted from malevolence or enjoyed shedding human blood; the judge did not sin if he condemned the criminal from love of justice, nor did his officer in duly carrying out his order, but both sinned mortally if they did not observe the due course of the law. Killing of necessity was sinful if the necessity need not have arisen; if the slayer could have escaped without slaying he must do penance as for mortal sin. But if it was indeed unavoidable, and he slew without thought of hatred and in distress of mind to save himself and his property when there was no other way of escape, then he was not bound to do penance save *ad cautelam*. Homicide was committed by chance, for example, when a stone was thrown at a bird or otherwise and someone crossed its path and was unexpectedly struck and died, or when a tree was felled and crushed another person, and so on. In such cases the slayer's responsibility depended upon whether he was engaged on lawful business; it was unlawful if he hurled a stone towards a place where people were wont to pass by, or if he was trying to steal a horse or an ox and as he chased it someone was fatally struck by it. Even if his action was in itself lawful he was responsible if he had not taken every care. For example, if a master was

[1] See F. Schulz, *L.Q.R.* lxi. 286–92.

disciplining his pupil he must not have used excessive force; a man unloading a haywain, or felling his own tree, should have looked around and given warning, and that not too late or too low, but at the proper time and loudly, so that anyone there or approaching could look out for himself and get out of the way; otherwise they were responsible. Wilful homicide was always a mortal and frightful sin. There were certain types of homicide for which laymen might not be required to do penance but which still rendered clerks unfit for promotion to higher orders. Homicide of necessity, even if totally un-avoidable, had this effect, but accidental homicide in the course of a lawful action in which due care had been taken did not: the clerk who committed it should neither be demoted nor denied promotion on this account.

Raymond then went on to discuss some special types of homicide. Striking a pregnant woman so that she had a miscarriage or deliberately inducing abortion were, he decided, homicide so far as penance was concerned, and if the foetus had quickened causing its death rendered a clerk unfit for orders. Special problems arose also in relation to killing in brawls where it was not known who had given the fatal blow. He held that not only all those who had struck the victim but also those who had come with the will to kill him, and even those who had come with no desire to kill but nevertheless to give support to the slayers, were homicides 'quantum ad peccatum', though in differing degrees. A man was not free from the guilt of homicide if he failed to save another from death when he could have done so. Killing in jousting was homicide, for such play was noxious and illicit. Similarly with killing in duels. Finally, he discussed killing in war and in defence of life and property against aggression. Killing in immediate self-defence was not reprehensible, but any delay converted it into vengeance, which was. Moreover, self-defence must be proportionate to the danger: arms could be repelled with arms, but unarmed attack could not be, unless the aggressors were much stronger than the defenders and were levying war upon them. So with killing in defence of property.

There was much valuable material here for secular lawyers to ponder and Bracton evidently recognized this. He inserted the sections dealing with the different types of homicide and their subdivisions almost verbatim and summarized the rest, though omitting the statements concerning penance and the position of clerks as irrelevant to his purpose.[1] He included the passages on abortion and killing in a brawl, adding that anyone who held the victim 'malo animo' while others killed him was equally a homicide. He also included the statements about failure to save life and referred briefly to killing in war. But he gave a different definition of wilful homicide: it is committed 'ex certa scientia et in assultu praemeditato, ira vel odio vel causa lucri, nequiter et in felonia et contra pacem domini regis'; and he added a distinction between slaying in public and secretly, the latter circumstance constituting murder. The words 'ira vel odio vel causa lucri', were themselves another canonistic borrowing interpolated into the common-law phrases, a fact which reveals his wish to connect all these definitions with the work in hand, a treatise on the Laws of England. Yet this was as far as he ventured to go in linking the two systems, for much of this material was not assimilable by the latter. For references to penance and irregularity he could very profitably have substituted statements on the need for pardon if they could have been made to fit into this frame-work. Bracton showed discretion in abstaining from any such attempt. His readers could assume what they chose to be the bearing of this section on the problem of justifiable and excusable homicide. It was only in a later passage and very casually that he mentioned slaying in self-defence as an example of slaying *ex necessitate,* outlawry for which should readily be pardoned.[2]

Bracton's borrowings from Civil Law fitted into his general discussion little better. While Canon Law suggested a high degree of responsibility, Civil Law might have encouraged a far more liberal attitude to slaying with excuse or in extenuating circumstances. It did not regard slaying entirely by accident or in defence of oneself or one's relatives as punishable, though 'when death resulted from gross negligence, or the act was com-mitted in the heat of passion, the penalty was arbitrary and left to the discretion of the magistrate, who, in rendering judge-ment, was governed by the circumstances of each particular case.'[3] When a prisoner died as the result of an accident, his

---

[1] *De Legibus,* f. 120[b]. The passages from Raymond and Bracton are conveniently set out side by side by Schulz and also by H. G. Richardson in *Bracton, The Problem of his Text,* 126–31.   [2] *De Legibus,* f. 132[b].

[3] S. P. Scott, *The Civil Law,* xi. 67, n.

guard could obtain pardon,[1] but generally speaking there was no
need of it for unintentional slaying. However, the Lex Aquilia
(*Institutes*, Lib. iv, tit. 3) introduced the question of civil as
opposed to criminal responsibility, dealing with the question
of damages for killing another man's slave and, perhaps, his
child.[2] This could be extended to the notion of damages for
slaying any member of a family and thus might well have been
used to reinforce, or, in the 1250s, to revive the requirement of
making peace with the family of the slain. Bracton did not
raise this point but he did, when using this passage, refer to
the king's pardon.

Igitur qui latronem occiderit non tenetur, nocturnum vel
diurnum, si aliter periculum evadere non possit, tenetur tamen si
possit. Item non tenetur si per infortunium et non animo et voluntate
occidendi, nec dolus nec culpa eius inveniatur, de quo supra
dictum est, et de gratia principis cum eo mitius agitur hoc probato.[3]

It might be inferred from this that he was linking the question
of damages with pardon, but this is doubtful. His reference to
it was so brief that it remains possible that he used his authority
here without any theory of its having special relevance to the
practice of pardoning on condition of making peace. However,
he went on to make some points which could well be taken into
account by those who had to decide whether pardon was
requisite and, if so, merited. 'Item si quis unum percusserit et
occiderit cum alium percutere vellet in felonia, tenetur. Item
si cum levius credidit percussisse, gravius percusserit et occiderit, tenetur, Debet enim quilibet modum et mensuram adhibere
in suo facto.'

Earlier, in the section 'De homicidio per infortunium et
casuali', he had declared that slayers in this manner should
be absolved. He gave as examples: killing when hurling a
weapon at a wild beast, striking a comrade jokingly in play,
shooting from afar or throwing a stone, when playing ball
hitting an unseen barber's hand so that he cut his customer's
throat, and concluded in phrases taken from Civil Law that
for such killing,

non tamen occidendi animo, absolvi debet, quia crimen non contra-
hitur nisi voluntas nocendi intercedat. Et voluntas et propositum

[1] *Digest*, Lib. xlviii, tit. 3, § 14 (5).
[2] J. M. Kelly in 'The Meaning of the Lex Aquilia', *L.Q.R.* lxxx, 76–7, argues
that it included children in power. [3] *De Legibus*, f. 155.

distinguunt maleficia, et furtum non committitur sine affectu furandi. Et secundum quod dici poterit de infante et furioso, cum alterum innocentia consilii tueatur et alterum facti[1] infelicitas excuset. In maleficiis autem spectatur voluntas et non exitus, et nihil interest occidat quis an causam mortis praebeat.[2]

Here he does not even refer to the need for pardon, apposite though this would have been in the case of infant and insane killers as well as accidental ones. It was in fact only in the section on outlawry (f. 132[b]) that he dealt in any detail with the subject of pardon, and then only to insist, so far as slaying by mischance and in self-defence went, that it should be granted without difficulty, though elsewhere he mentioned the king's pardon for killing a thief when the slayer was not in danger.[3] Bracton, then, failed to make it clear how his quotations from Roman and Canon related to Common Law and the prerogative of mercy. He included this material, possibly with some idea that it might serve as a basis for reform, possibly merely because it provided him with some ready-made definitions of matters which were particularly ill defined in England.

There were some other sections of the Laws which he omitted in these passages but which might well have been laid under contribution, yet even so they would not have provided adequate and unambiguous guidance. At some points, of course, the two Laws disagreed, and when they were in agreement their example was not always to be commended, or was not clearly understood. Roman Law was concerned with provocation and defence against sexual assault, in which killing was lawful, while killing one's wife taken in adultery was to be lightly punished.[4] Both Laws placed great emphasis upon intention and a certain amount on negligence, some of the canonist illustrations of this being derived from Justinian. Neither gave much guidance as to the manner in which intention should be ascertained. One pointer, however, was the type of weapon employed: 'If the aggressor drew a sword and struck him with it, there is no doubt of his having done this with the intention of killing him. Where, however, during a quarrel, he struck him with a spike, or a brass vessel used in a bath, although the

---

[1] Bracton's source, *Digest*, Lib. xlviii, tit. 8, § 12 has *fati*, which is necessary to make sense here.

[2] f. 136[b]; cf. *Digest*, Lib. xlviii, tit. 8, §§ 1, 12, 14, 15; *Codex*, Lib. ix, tit. 16, § 1.

[3] f. 144[b].

[4] *Digest*, Lib. xlviii, tit. 8, § 1.

article employed was of metal, still the attack was not made with the intention of killing him . . .'.[1] Another was the nature and position of a blow: death from a kick could readily be regarded as involuntary;[2] if a blow was slight and fell on a part of the body where a light blow did not normally cause death, and expert medical evidence confirmed that a blow of such a kind was not lethal, then the clerk who delivered it need not be deposed.[3] There was an ambiguity, or at least a source of confusion, in the account of negligence borrowed by Bracton, mischance arising in the course of an illegal action, such as cattle-stealing, being treated in association with unlawful carelessness in performing an action which was lawful in itself. Both Laws were indulgent towards dangerous driving and riding and failed to give proper attention to negligence in fatal accidents arising therefrom, accepting inability to hold one's horses through illness or lack of skill as good excuse.[4] Canon Law dealt also with omission, such as failure to save life when this was possible, but this, though quoted by Bracton, could have little effect on secular law, although it was not, perhaps, entirely over-looked. These authorities, then, provided only an incomplete analysis of the concepts of provocation, intention, and negligence, relying rather on examples deriving ultimately from imperial or papal rulings given in individual cases. It was possible, but not always easy to draw out underlying principles and apply them to analogous situations. Some of their views, on the other hand, were matters of common sense and could have been adopted quite independently in England. A student of the Laws might conclude that the English treatment of excusable homicide was unduly harsh and be tempted to employ some of their distinctions in an attempt to mitigate that harshness to some degree, but they certainly did not provide a ready-made programme of reform. How far these principles and examples were accepted or had parallels in secular practice can emerge only from an examination of the king's writs concerning pardons and of the plea rolls and returns to inquisitions.

The early plea rolls do not supply much information as to the way in which the excusable nature of a homicide was

---

[1] Ibid. (S. P. Scott's translation).
[2] *Codex*, Lib. ix, tit. 16, § 5.   [3] *Decretals*, Lib. v, tit. 12, cap. 18.
[4] *Institutes*, Lib. iv, tit. 3; *Decretals*, Lib. v, tit. 12, cap. 13, 16.

expressed. The slayer's intention must always have been taken into account, but it might be indicated obliquely. To say that he had killed by chance was to imply that the killing had been involuntary, and to describe a killing as self-defence was to imply at least that it had not been planned in advance. But probably from the first rather more was needed to establish that the slayer was innocent of any criminal intent, this being excluded by the declaration that he had not acted feloniously. As early as 1212, in a case of accidental slaying, it was 'testified that this was not by felony',[1] and there is evidence that another accidental killing in the time of John was adjudged not to have been felony.[2] This, of course, said no more than the defendant had already said when pleading not guilty. It is likely that by now at least explicit exclusion of felony was generally required of the jurors, as well as some account of the circumstances. The judges, having heard the verdict, seem to have pressed the jurors on the absence of felony, unless they had already sworn to this. In time it would become more widely known that the verdict ought to include this point, but it was hardly enough in itself to show that pardon was deserved; the king's decision to grant it must have depended mainly on the details given in each case. Closer examination of the killer's state of mind, his motives and intentions came to be demanded, and by the 1230s the justices were eliciting the jurors' views on these matters. Thus in 1231 Reginald de Grendon was said at a gaol delivery to have thrown a stone, which by mischance hit Stephen de Putleston fatally on the head, 'non animo vel intentione ipsum interficiendi'.[3] In the same year, a presentment at the eyre stated that a man had thrown a staff at a plough-horse but hit his wife with the iron tip so that she died; he did this not 'aliquo odio vel atya sed per infortunium'.[4] This suggests that the jurors were aware that some statement of this sort was needed if the king was to be persuaded to act leniently, though their choice of terms in which to convey it was rather unfortunate. In an exactly similar case in 1236, the presenting jury said that the husband had not killed his wife 'sponte', but had meant to hit a horse.[5] In a case of the

---

[1] *Select Pleas of the Crown*, Seld. Soc. i, no. 114.
[2] J.I. 1/36, m. 4^d. This is the roll of the eyre in Berkshire in 1225, but the entry refers to the findings at the last eyre.   [3] *Close Rolls, 1227–31*, 507.
[4] J.I. 1/1043, m. 16^d.   [5] J.I. 1/775, m. 18.

justifiable slaying of an escaped prisoner in 1238 the jury testified
that some of the appellees were not guilty 'quia non venerunt
animo interficiendi ipsum . . . sed tantum capiendi ipsum'.[1]
Many of these terms are reminiscent of the passages from
penitentials and the works of canonists. But a little later verdicts
were using the formula 'non aliqua malicia vel felonia excogitata',[2] and sometimes the justices put the question, did
the slayer act 'aliquo insultu premeditato vel aliqua felonia?',[3]
thus reverting to more secular language to express much the
same concepts.

It is not clear whether the demand for the jurors' opinion on
the slayer's state of mind was made by the justices on their own
initiative, or whether they were acting in accordance with some
governmental directive. By this time special commissions to
hold inquisition into killing by mischance had appeared, and
the wording of the commissions required the same sort of
report. Indeed the first one recorded, in 1230, laboured this
aspect of the inquiry. The king, in the subsequent pardon,
stated that he had had an inquisition held 'utrum Rogerus
de Panten interfecisset Basiliam de Panten scienter et pru-
denter et per maliciam excogitatam, an invitus et per infortunium'; the inquisition had shown that 'ipse hoc non fecit
sciens et volens, immo invitus et per infortunium'.[4] The next
recorded pardon of this sort does not rehearse the wording
of the commission, but it does show that the inquisition had
found that the slaying had been 'per infortunium et non ex
malicia excogitata',[5] and it seems probable that this neater
formula had been included in the instructions to the commissioners. This formula, with *per maliciam* instead of *ex malicia*,
reappears in 1238.[6] It may well be, therefore, that the king had
introduced this sort of question in the special inquisitions and
had enjoined on his justices of eyre and gaol delivery to put it to
the juries which brought in verdicts of accidental slaying. On
the other hand, it may have been some of the justices who first

---

[1] J.I. 1/174, m. 36[d]. Later 'Non animo malignandi' also occurs (J.I. 1/998[A],
m. 40).

[2] e.g. J.I. 1/455, m. 7[d] (1247).

[3] J.I. 1/615, m. 8[d]; cf. m. 7.

[4] *Pat. Rolls, 1225-32*, 393; cf. above, p. 36, n. 1.

[5] *Pat. Rolls, 1225-32*, 456.

[6] *Close Rolls, 1237-42*, 68. On the same page is another pardon which uses the
same formula but does not state explicitly that there had been an inquisition.

put the question, or it may have been the result of a new policy adopted after discussion between the king, his immediate advisers, and his justices.

Special inquisitions into slaying in self-defence appear later than those into accidents. This may point to the king's feeling some reluctance to grant pardon on these verdicts, where the assessment of the slayer's responsibility was a more delicate operation. At first if the slayer was in prison he may have preferred to grant bail, rather than pardon, when an inquisition found self-defence,[1] though in 1245 he pardoned an outlaw on such a verdict.[2] The instructions to the commissioners were probably the same, or much the same, whether bail or pardon was to result from a favourable verdict. In the 1240s the term felony was apparently added to the question as to malice aforethought, whether the inquisition leading to bail was into slaying by mischance or in self-defence,[3] and felony soon appeared also when pardon was to be granted on the verdict.

Some writs ordering inquisitions were of a different type, detailing the alleged circumstances of the slaying in question, evidently using information supplied in a petition on behalf of the slayer. There is an example of this type from 1262, when the king wrote to the sheriff of Sussex that he was informed that William son of Simon de Hemsted 'killed David le Tanur, an outlaw, in the act of attacking the house and household of his father . . . and that he did so in self-defence.' The sheriff was instructed to inquire whether this was true and also where David had been outlawed.[4] Inquisitions of this kind were generally ordered by writs beginning 'Ex parte . . . nobis est ostensum' or 'Quia ex relatu quorumdam intelleximus', though they might simply ask whether the facts were as set forth in them. But even in writs of this type some attempt was made to include the phrases employed in the other. Thus one ordered an inquiry 'utrum H. . . . ludens ad pilum cum D. . . . vulnus casualiter recepit . . . an per feloniam et maliciam . . . nec ne, et si casualiter ludendo qualiter et quo modo et si per feloniam et maliciam ipsius D. per quam feloniam et quam

---

[1] As he did in 1244, when he ordered that Michael Geruvel should be released on bail to appear before the justices 'ut pleniorem inde faciant inquisitionem' (*Close Rolls, 1242–7*, 210).   [2] *Cal. Pat. Rolls, 1232–47*, 468.
[3] *Close Rolls, 1242–7*, 53, 145, 210, 491.
[4] *Cal. Inquisitions Misc.* i, no. 2111. William was duly pardoned; cf. *Cal. Pat. Rolls, 1258–66*, 15.

maliciam . . .'[1]. *Ex parte* writs were employed especially when it was hoped to show that the slaying had been justifiable. Since there was no term in general use to denote this, the writ would in any case have to descend to some detail, asking, for example, if the victim had been killed as a thief refusing to surrender. There was little need for details of this sort when the slaying could easily be subsumed in one or other of the familiar classes of mischance and self-defence. Accordingly, most of the writs did no more than indicate that the slaying was asserted to have been in self-defence or by mischance and order the commissioners to inquire whether this was so or whether there had been felony and malice aforethought, etc. The questions which the commissioners were instructed to put to the jury provided a convenient vehicle for transmitting the king's views on what, in general terms, would constitute sufficient grounds for pardon, provided the circumstances in individual cases did not appear to conflict with the jurors' estimate of their merits. It will be worth while, therefore, to examine the development of these formulas. Unfortunately, this is a rather complicated undertaking, since they were influenced by other factors as well, particularly the wording of other types of writ. As just noted, one and the same formula might be used in different types of inquisition, and different types of inquisition might lead to pardon. The inquisitions which are relevant here are those which were held with a view to pardon and those which were held with a view to bail, including those *de odio et atia*. These were by now used mainly for obtaining bail, but this was not their only function and because it overlapped them the writ *de odio et atia* had considerable influence on the other types. It will be necessary, therefore, briefly to summarize its history; a more detailed examination of it will be found in Appendix I.

The writ *de odio et atia* was used originally to challenge the *bona fides* of an appeal of felony, sometimes of homicide, more often of robbery or breach of the peace. It was hoped that the inquisition would bring in a verdict that the appeal was malicious and the appellee not guilty. It was at first produced in the course of the trial, not beforehand. But already under John an inquisition *de odio et atia* was sometimes obtained by an imprisoned appellee as a way of securing release on bail pending trial. The abolition of the ordeal in 1215 meant that trial by

[1] C. 145/38, no. 30.

jury was no longer a privilege which had to be bought as an alternative to ordeal, though it might still be necessary to pay for it as an alternative to trial by battle. However, by now exceptions to appeals were innumerable and generally successful, so that battle could nearly always be avoided without this expense. Thus there was now little occasion for the use of the inquisition *de odio et atia* in the course of the trial, and its use by prisoners seeking release on bail came to predominate. Since bail could be obtained without the king's own grant by prisoners accused of other crimes, this meant that it came to be used mainly by those accused of homicide.

Under Henry III the writ was already being obtained by prisoners whoever was responsible for their situation, an appellor or a presenting jury, for it was not difficult to suggest that a malicious individual had misled the jury, or even that the whole body of jurors was acting out of malice against an unpopular local figure. A great many charges against minor officials, especially reeves, were alleged to have been brought when those subject to their petty tyranny saw an opportunity as presenting jurors of getting their own back. As time went on and the number of appeals declined, the great majority of writs *de odio et atia* came in fact to be directed against presenting juries and individuals who had influenced them. But the persons imprisoned for homicide on such biased presentment were likely to claim to be in no way responsible for the slayings laid at their door; it would seem difficult to claim that a presentment was malicious because an avowed slaying had been in self-defence or by mischance; it was, after all, the duty of the jurors to include these cases in their indictments along with felonious homicides. However, this difficulty, if it was ever recognized, did not for long deter indicted prisoners from obtaining the writ even though they admitted having slain excusably. The number who did this was not large. The surprising thing is that anyone chose this course at all when he could have obtained an inquisition into the circumstances, on the strength of which the king could fairly have been expected to pardon him. The explanation may be simple misunderstanding of the correct course. A man who suddenly found himself in prison because he had had the misfortune unintentionally to cause a death might not be so familiar with the means of applying to the king for clemency as some more experienced offenders were.

He might be aware of the existence of the writ *de odio et atia* and yet not appreciate that its proper function was limited, hoping that it could lead to pardon, not merely to release on bail. And in fact, the prisoner who was in a position to seek pardon might prove not to have made a serious mistake in obtaining a writ *de odio et atia*: there was a chance that it would serve his purpose, however improper this use of it was in theory. Many juries at special inquisitions were unaware of or indifferent to the proper uses of the writ *de odio et atia*. When they believed that the prisoner had been responsible for the death, but not of felony or malice aforethought, they tended to assume that this was the issue put to them, blandly taking the *odium* and *atia* in question to relate to the culprit's state of mind up to the time of the slaying, not to the accusers' motives for accusing him. Whether this was always done through genuine misunderstanding or was sometimes a deliberate and ingenious way of transforming the wrong type of inquisition into the right type to render maximum assistance to the prisoner it would be difficult to say.[1] Under Edward I there are enough instances of this misinterpretation of their terms of reference to suggest that, however irregular, it was officially winked at, and throughout the reign pardons were in fact granted on the strength of these twisted verdicts. Thus it was not altogether a mistake to regard the writ *de odio et atia* as a means of obtaining pardon, though it was certainly not the normal, or, indeed, the correct means.[2]

If the writ could plausibly be interpreted in this way it was because the terms *odium* and *atia* bore a tempting resemblance to the felony and malice aforethought of the writs for inquisitions into allegedly excusable homicide. This resemblance set up a strong mutual attraction between the two types, and at times they even coalesced. At one point Henry III showed himself

---

[1] Even in inquisitions leading to bail the question about hatred and malice could be misunderstood in this way: in 1227 an inquisition found that a man throwing a staff at a plough-ox which was not keeping straight struck his son who was at the plough and 'per infortunium tale interfecit et non per odium vel athiam'; Henry accepted the verdict and ordered bail (*Rot. Litt. Claus.* ii. 198). Conceivably the jury had worded their verdict in this way in the hope that it might secure pardon.

[2] It used to be believed that the inquisition *de odio et atia* was the appropriate method of establishing grounds for pardon. This view was incorrect so far as appeals of homicide were concerned, but not entirely mistaken so far as indictments went. Its use for this purpose was sufficiently frequent to explain this belief, but it was a great exaggeration to regard it as the proper method.

ready to authorize the combination of the two types of inquiry in one inquisition. In 1236 he ordered the sheriff of Stafford-shire to postpone the outlawry of Ralph le Foun for the death of Robert son of Matilda, and in the meantime to inquire by the oath of lawful men of the county 'utrum idem Radulfus rettatus sit de morte illa odio et athia et quo odio et qua athia; an, si eum occiderit, ipsum occidit in felonia vel in se defendendo'.[1] This particular way of amalgamating the two types of inquisition did not continue, but the wording of the writ *de odio et atia* did influence that of the inquisitions con-cerned with mischance and self-defence. An example of jurors' finding that a killing had not been 'aliquo odio vel atya sed per infortunium' has already been mentioned.[2] If juries could use the terms as interchangeable with felony and malice afore-thought and their verdicts pass muster, Chancery clerks might also adopt part of the formula appropriate to one writ when drawing up another. Apparently, in one case in or before 1246 the writ for inquisition instructed the commissioners to inquire whether a father, who had killed his son with a knife-wound in the throat, had thrown the knife 'odio vel casu'; the verdict was that it was not done 'sponte nec odio sed per infortunium'.[3] The order for bail represented this by the orthodox phrase 'per infortunium et non per feloniam aut maliciam excogitatam'.[4] The clerks themselves sometimes used inappropriate terms, then, or substituted appropriate ones for the wording of the documents before them.

The terms of the writ *de odio et atia* had a lasting effect on the writs for inquisitions into the circumstances of a homicide. In 1243 the sheriff of Norfolk was ordered to inquire whether a child run over by a cart was killed 'casu inopinato et infortunio an per feloniam et [ex] malicia excogitata Reginaldi de Aylmereton qui duxit karettam illam . . . et si per feloniam et malicia predicti Reginaldi excogitata, per quam feloniam et qua malicia . . . '.[5] This final point is curious. There seems

---

[1] *Close Rolls, 1234–7*, 383; the verdict was that Robert had assaulted Ralph, who had killed him in self-defence 'quia non potuit aliter euadere manus ejus'. See *Bracton's Note Book*, ed. F. W. Maitland, iii, no. 1216. The decision to grant pardon was taken in the *Curia Regis* in 1237, though it was 'de gracia sua et non per iudicium'.

[2] Above, p. 76; cf. p. 81, n. 1. The clerks who translated and recorded the ver-dicts may sometimes have been responsible for the use of the phrase.

[3] See J.I. 1/318, m. 22, where the earlier inquisition was reported.

[4] *Close Rolls, 1242–7*, 491.

[5] Ibid., 50. The slayer was granted bail not pardon.

little need to ask what kind of felony was involved in a deliberate homicide, and the grounds for malice. Matters of this kind were certainly not taken into account when the homicide was being tried; either it must be shown that he had killed unintentionally or with justification, or he would be found guilty; his ultimate motives were of no interest if he had planned to kill or had killed knowingly and wickedly when he saw the opportunity. This formula seems inappropriate here. But a similar formula was included in the writs *de odio et atia*, which required the jury not only to say on oath whether a charge was brought of hatred and malice, but, if so, also to explain the cause of the hatred and malice—'quo odio et qua atia'. And this was an essential part of this type of inquisition. A return which failed to answer this question was inadequate and the king might demand a further verdict or more detailed reply before accepting the finding of *odium et atia*. It was too easy for neighbours friendly to the suspect to bring in a verdict that the charge was malicious; they must substantiate this assertion by showing that the appellor or members of a presenting jury had had reasons for malicious action, such as long-standing animosity or some specific recent quarrel. It seems evident that this formula was imitated in the writs, perhaps at first only in those used to obtain bail, which inquired whether a slaying had been by accident or in self-defence or by felony and malice, and if the latter, by what felony and what malice. But soon writs for inquisitions in which pardon was the object were also putting the question by what felony and what malice the killer had acted if the killing was found to have been felonious. This, if taken seriously, would lay the onus on the jury to establish a convincing proof of guilty intention unless they were prepared to swear that the slaying was excusable. It might seem to have given them encouragement to take the easier way out, and so given the whole investigation a certain bias in favour of the slayer. But in fact it was probably not taken seriously. It seems to have been a superfluous piece of verbiage, explicable only in terms of borrowing from the writ *de odio et atia*. Too much should not be read into these formulas, some of which were adopted, probably in Chancery rather than by the king in council, without due reflection on their implications.

It made more sense when the writ asked also what kind of

accident had occurred if the verdict should be accidental slaying. This question appears already in 1244, 1247, and 1248.[1] Both questions came to be included together. Thus in 1266 a jury was asked whether Walter Lemman killed Henry de Hales 'per infortunuim an per feloniam aut maliciam excogitatam, et si per infortunium qualiter et quomodo, et si per feloniam aut maliciam excogitatam per quam feloniam aut quam maliciam'. They replied that he had killed by accident, not felony or malice aforethought, and in reply to the inquiry 'quomodo et qualiter dicunt. . .'. Evidently this point was emphasized and they were careful to give a detailed —and very convincing—account of his accidentally killing Henry while they were both trying to beat out the flames when a dropped candle had started a fire.[2] But even without being asked this question it was usual for a jury to give a fairly detailed account.

In the 1250s another development appears in the writ ordering inquisition into alleged killing in self-defence. Not only the question, what kind of self-defence, was to be put, in imitation of the question about mischance, but also a much more specific one. A writ of 1255 ordered an inquisition to recognize 'si Robertus de Aula occidit Robertum le Aungevyn per feloniam et maliciam excogitatam aut se defendendo dum dictus Robertus le Aungevyn eum aggressus fuit, ita quod mortem evadere non potuit nisi eum occidisset'.[3] Thus the jury was to be asked whether the slayer had been in such straits that he could not have escaped death without killing his assailant. With this addition the formula ran: 'utrum interfecit . . . se defendendo, ita quod mortem propriam aliter evadere non potuit, an per feloniam vel maliciam excogitatam; et si per feloniam et maliciam excogitatam, per quam feloniam et

---

[1] C. 144/1, no. 1; J.I. 1/1185, m. 3: 'si per infortunium per quod infortunium et quomodo et qualiter'; C. 145/2, no. 26.

[2] C. 144/6, no. 6; *Cal. Inquisitions Misc.* i, no. 2127; cf. J.I. 1/1185, m. 3 (1257) and J.I. 1/1197, m. 6 (1264), where 'per quam feloniam aut quam maliciam' is omitted.

[3] *Close Rolls, 1254–6*, 199. The verdict was favourable and he was pardoned; see *Cal. Pat. Rolls, 1247–58*, 415. Similar writs appeared in 1260, *Close Rolls, 1259–61*, 247, and one is implied in 1256, ibid., *1254–56*, 313. Part of the phrase was used incidentally in 1258 in a verdict *de odio et atia* which stated that the prisoners were not guilty but that another man had killed in self-defence 'ita quod nullo modo potuit euadere nisi predictum Willelmum . . . euadendo percussisset' (C. 144/4, no. 46).

quam maliciam, et qualiter et quomodo'.[1] A question about escape was by no means a new idea. It seems to have been raised much earlier in the courts, at least in the *Curia Regis*;[2] and by the time it appears in the writs justices in eyre may have elicited replies to it also.[3] Probably, therefore, its inclusion was a matter of policy decided at governmental level, or perhaps suggested by some of the justices, rather than another —but far more business-like—example of the ingenuity or suggestibility of the Chancery officials. The question was a relevant one and points to a real effort to set a strict standard in these inquiries. To insist that self-defence against an attack which was not in itself of a lethal kind was no excuse for homicide was to assert a principle of some value. The force used in repelling attack must be commensurate with the force of the attack. Life might excusably be taken only to save life.

Now it has been seen that Bracton quoted from Raymond of Peñafort's account of killing *ex necessitate* in which he insisted that the slayer was guilty if he could have escaped without inflicting death. Thus the insistence on a verdict that the homicide had killed in self-defence, being unable otherwise to escape, may well have been due to canonist influence. However, it may well be that this particular doctrine was derived not from Raymond but from his predecessor, Bernard of Pavia, from whom he could have borrowed the fourfold division of homicide, committed *iustitia, necessitate, casu et voluntate*. For whereas Raymond did not define *necessitas* as being in mortal danger, Bernard had explained it thus: 'ut dum instante latrone vel hoste occidis eum, ne occidaris ab eo'.[4] At any rate, Bernard seems to have represented a stricter school of thought on this point, and it was this attitude which was adopted by the king. Unfortunately, he went even further. For to require that the slayer's own life should actually have been saved by his killing his assailant was to demand rather too much. There was no crime in forcibly repelling an attack which might reasonably be regarded as a threat to life or limb, even though this was to

---

[1] It is given, e.g., in J.I. 1/1197, m. 4 (1264).
[2] See above, p. 82, n. 1.   [3] Cf. J.I. 1/300ᶜ, m. 26.
[4] Quoted by Maitland, *Bracton and Azo*, Selden Soc. viii. 229, from Bernard's *Summa Decretalium*, Lib. v, tit. 10, *De homicidio voluntario vel casuali*. Maitland recognized the relationship between Bernard's treatment of the types of homicide and Bracton's, which seemed 'to have derived either directly or at second hand' from it.

exaggerate the assailant's aim. In practice, the commonest way for a jury to deal with this point was to seize on the word 'escape', rather than the whole phrase 'to escape death', and emphasize that the slayer had not defended himself until he had tried to run away but had been overtaken or cornered. But concern to establish the impossibility of his escaping without real risk to his own life led some juries to swear to rather implausible stories of flight and pursuit, whilst if the victim of an assault had had no opportunity whatever for flight the jurors might be perplexed as to the manner in which they could convey his unwillingness to fight back until he realized that he would be killed if he did not. None the less, the introduction of this question was valuable in so far as it avoided too great reliance on the jurors' subjective view of the relations between slayer and slain and the former's possible motives. It tried to supplement this by an objective test, based on his actual situation and the way he acted in response. But it still left too much to another subjective estimate of the jurors', their estimate of the victim's intention to kill.

In general, it may be concluded that the writs ordering inquisitions did not go very far towards establishing the criteria for determining that a homicide was justifiable or that there was good excuse for it. The only really helpful feature was the requirement that slaying in self-defence should be shown to have been necessary to save one's own life, but even this was a clumsy way of discriminating between reasonable and excessive use of force, and demanded an impossible assessment by the jury of the degree of danger which had threatened the slayer. It becomes necessary, therefore, to turn to the records of individual cases to discover the criteria which were commonly used, but generalization is peculiarly dangerous, since the prerogative was the final arbiter. Moreover, while the itinerant justices may have been considerably influenced by the wording of the special commissions, and it is evident that they generally tried to elicit answers to the same points from the jurors, there was nothing to prevent them from asking further questions, or airing theories of their own. If they were faced with difficulties or felt doubt as to the wisdom or equity of accepted practice they could raise these matters with the king. Some were prone to consult him, others to pursue their own, sometimes very individual course.

Precedents could provide some guide as to the boundary between justifiable and excusable homicide. In acquitting the justifiable slayer the justices were administering the law and so could formulate rules which should govern or at least guide, future decisions. Yet the binding force of precedent was still feeble, if it was recognized at all, and practice varied even here. If they were in doubt, the justices tended to consult the king, and since this might result either in instructions to acquit or in pardon this tendency itself opened the way for further encroachment by the prerogative. On the other hand, one or two types of homicide other than justifiable were often thought not even to require pardon and here the decisions of the justices kept the prerogative in check, though without establishing a recognized legal right to acquittal. The boundary between excusable and felonious homicide also depended to some extent on judicial decisions and thus precedents of a sort could be established. The justices, faced with the choice between referring a case to the king or condemning the slayer might choose the latter course in spite of some alleged excuse. If they were too severe the king could do nothing about it and was, indeed, unlikely to be aware of such decisions. It would have required legislation to check any tendency of this kind. But in practice, again, the justices were much more inclined to leave difficult decisions to him. Yet, in referring a case to him, and especially in remanding *ad gratiam*, they were always at least indicating their belief that pardon might perhaps properly be granted and generally were really recommending the homicide to mercy. The king might dissent from their view of an individual case or pursue a rather stricter policy in relation to certain types of killing if he chose to do so, but this was not altogether easy and required more determination and consistency than he was likely to show in matters which only occasionally engaged his full attention. On the whole he may be supposed to have recognized a moral obligation to accept judicial recommendations to mercy, only rarely asserting his discretion in an attempt to define culpability more strictly. The justices may be said, then, to have influenced his decisions to a considerable degree, and not to have been greatly affected by any guiding royal policy. In practice the emergence of some general rules can be discerned, but there was variation in their attitude towards them. Both accepted practice and the king's directives were flagrantly violated on occasion. More understandably, juries gave discordant verdicts in cases which would appear to have merited equal treatment. Legislation dealt with one minor point. But only at one moment did the king, Edward I, attempt a radical reform; for the rest his justices and commissioners had to struggle on without being given a more precise and official definition of excusable homicide. The boundaries which have to be traced were, then, wavering and discontinuous ones.

The problem of tracing these boundaries, particularly that between justifiable and excusable homicide, is aggravated by the fact that a good many justifiable slayers and *meticulosi* sought pardon before being brought to trial as a precaution, or as the quickest way of extricating themselves from an anxious and uncertain predicament. The fact that the king granted it did not imply that he thought it necessary, or that the justices would have hesitated to acquit if these cases had come before them. Thus the special inquisitions cannot be used in seeking to discover more precisely what types of homicide needed pardon. They can be used, though here some caution is necessary, to help establish what types were thought to merit it. They reveal the views of the jurors and perhaps the commissioners, though these might not have been acceptable to some of the royal justices. The king's acceptance or rejection of their views may be significant for his attitude at a particular moment, but his decision cannot always be ascertained, and he, of course, was not bound to act consistently when exercising his prerogative.

Justifiable homicide may be considered first, together with the killing of malefactors in conditions which rendered it unjustifiable, though excusable, or even inexcusable and felonious. The execution of a man sentenced to death by a properly constituted court was, of course, fully justified. The authority of the court might, however, be challenged.[1] The traditional powers of the local officials in the counties of the marches to execute captured outlaws and robbers, even though the latter had not resisted arrest, gave rise to some problems of this type.[2] But generally when the king's officials killed someone with insufficient justification it was in the course of making

---

[1] e.g. J.I. 1/1051, m. 5.

[2] See *Northumberland Assize Rolls*, Surtees Soc. lxxxviii. 70, 73; J.I. 1/657, m. 12, quoted below, p. 127.

arrests, or in their treatment of prisoners, especially if the latter had tried to escape. It was the duty of a gaoler to recapture escaped prisoners at all costs, but he was expected to take them alive if possible and might be in trouble if he killed them. The death of a prisoner was a matter for careful investigation. There was the possibility that he had been tortured to try to extort a confession and an appeal against accomplices. A coroner's inquest was held and the jury might include other prisoners, since they were in the best position to know the facts. A Newgate gaoler was condemned to death for killing a prisoner on the verdict of a jury which included other prisoners.[1] At one time no fewer than thirty-four prisoners died in Colchester Castle; at the eyre when this was presented the jury denied that they had died through the harshness of the prison or any restraint put on them; but later it was testified that one of them had died as the result of his treatment by the under-gaoler, who was found guilty of killing him and several others maliciously and feloniously and was himself condemned to death.[2] However, cases of this type did not come before the itinerant justices often enough for any particular policy to emerge in relation to them.

There were, on the other hand, enough cases of the slaying of returned outlaws and felons discovered in the act and resisting arrest for some general rule to have been established. Such homicide was in itself lawful, but problems might arise even in such cases, so that persons arrested for killing felons had to be brought before the itinerant justices and were not supposed to be released on bail in the meantime without the king's warrant.[3] There could be doubt as to the need to use force in making the arrest, or the degree of force used could seem excessive. It was very important that the attempt at arrest should have been made openly, so far as the circumstances allowed, and that the criminal discovered in the act should have been pursued with hue and cry raised. There could, of course, be doubt as to the truth of the allegation that the victim was a

---

[1] J.I. 3/36, ii, m. 10. An inquisition *de odio et atia* had earlier found that he was guilty of killing him maliciously by putting him in chains and irons which were excessively heavy and tight, so that his neck was broken, and to hasten his death he had sat on his neck (C. 144/30, no. 16).

[2] J.I. 1/249, m. 48^d. Cf. J.I. 1/954, m. 59, where a bailiff of Coventry was put in exigent for keeping a prisoner in the stocks until his feet got gangrene, as a result of which he later died.   [3] See J.I. 1/40, m. 29.

felon whose criminal attempt had just been foiled, or who had been detected at the moment of his getaway. Similarly, the man accosted and slain as a returned outlaw might not in fact have been outlawed, or he might himself subsequently have obtained the king's pardon. Accordingly, the justices had to probe carefully even in cases of ostensibly justifiable homicide, and they might think it incumbent on them to refer the matter to the king, for him to decide whether pardon was needed, and even if it was merited.

The logic of the justices' decision is not always apparent. For example, a verdict was given that a member of the watch and ward had accosted a suspicious character whom he found hanging about at night and had been attacked by him, eventually killing him in self-defence, and the justices ordered that he be kept in custody 'ad voluntatem domini regis, etc.', which indicates that they thought pardon necessary.[1] Yet several members of another watch, who had been attacked by a swordsman and had killed him believing him to be a thief resisting arrest, were acquitted at the eyre.[2] There is little to choose between these two cases, but if anything the second seems less justifiable, since the watch outnumbered the victim by four to one; perhaps his use of a sword against them turned the scales. On other occasions the justices seem to have taken the numbers on either side into account as well as the nature of the weapons employed. For example, they remitted Geoffrey le Skippere to gaol for having killed a thief who resisted arrest; they probably felt that he had used excessive force, since, although a number of other men were helping to make the arrest, he had killed him with a hatchet.[3]

Now and then the justices acquitted in cases which might well have been regarded as killing in self-defence rather than with justification.[4] Generally the tendency was in the other direction: homicides which might seem justifiable were treated as excusable because they were said to have been committed in self-defence. It has been seen that Bracton was inclined to require some element of self-defence if the killing of a thief was to be considered blameless.[5] This should have meant that

---

[1] C. 47/64/8, no. 221; cf. J.I. 1/371, m. 38^d, where the decision is given only as 'quousque, etc.' [2] J.I. 1/376, m. 76.
[3] J.I. 1/249, m. 27. The other men were acquitted.
[4] e.g. J.I. 1/65, m. 47. [5] Above, p. 73.

homicides of this kind were acquitted all the more readily, and occasionally they were indeed acquitted. But more often the justices seem to have seized on the notion of self-defence and interpreted it not as reinforcing the justification for the slaying, but as a factor detracting from it, since self-defence to them spelt the need for pardon.[1] It may have been for this reason that a distinction was made between killing a felon who resisted arrest and killing in resisting attempted robbery. While the former did not normally call for pardon the latter, despite Bracton's views, was often thought to require it.[2] When a robber was resisted and slain it would generally be the victim of his attack who killed him, so that it was all too easy for the courts to assimilate such cases to slaying in self-defence. This was done even when the robber was killed by a third party coming to the rescue of his intended victim.[3] One result of the confusion between the justifiable slaying of felons and slaying in self-defence was that justices of gaol delivery often burked the issue: when they were hesitant to acquit they tended to recommend release on bail pending trial at the eyre rather than pardon.[4] This way out of the dilemma was not open to the justices at the eyre where a final decision was expected.[5]

To kill a poacher in the forest was at first usually regarded as a more serious matter than to kill a thief caught in the act, even though he too resisted arrest. One forester who had done this when trying to arrest on the orders of the Justices of the Forest was remanded *ad gratiam* at the eyre.[6] As Maitland remarked, 'There was need in 1293 for a statute to say that in certain circumstances a forester or parker was to be acquitted of the death of a trespasser whom he was endeavouring to arrest and slew in the endeavour'.[7] Yet in 1262 the justices had taken

---

[1] e.g. J.I. 1/302, m. 53ᵈ.

[2] e.g. J.I. 1/46, m. 2, *Cal. Pat. Rolls, 1281–92*, 164, 167; J.I. 1/575, m. 82ᵈ, where a man who was attacked and chased by a professional highwayman turned when checked by a dyke and shot him.

[3] e.g. J.I. 1/915, m. 36, C. 144/17, no. 16.

[4] Cf. J.I. 1/1013, m. 4. A felon had been indicted before the coroner and the chief tithingman was ordered to arrest him. He went with others to do so and as the felon resisted arrest, one of them, William Blaunchard, gave him a fatal blow with a knife. William was bailed in 1288 after a verdict of self-defence had been given at the gaol delivery (*Cal. Close Rolls, 1279–88*, 502), and was acquitted at the eyre at 1289.

[5] Though very occasionally they released a slayer on pledges being found to guarantee that he would stand to right if prosecuted later on.

[6] J.I. 1/1098, m. 63. [7] *Hist. Eng. Law*, ii. 478.

a different view: three foresters had found poachers in a wood and tried to arrest them with hue raised; the poachers had shot at them and inflicted some wounds; the foresters, in self-defence, had returned their fire and killed one of them. At the eyre they were acquitted as they had acted in self-defence.[1] Here, then, is another example of the inconsistency in apprais-ing the effect of killing an offender in self-defence. This time a homicide which would not in itself have been lawful, since the victim's offence was insufficient, was rendered lawful by this additional excuse.

This boundary line between justifiable and excusable homicide remained uncertain till the Tudor period. The statute of Henry VIII[2] which dealt with this question decreed that the killing of evil-doers by those whom they 'attempt to rob or murder, or by any such Person or Persons being in their Dwelling-house, which the same Evil-doers should so attempt burglarily to break by Night', should not entail loss of lands or goods, but the slayers should be fully acquitted and dis-charged: they should not be treated in the same way as those who killed in chance medley. The statute was promulgated in order to put an end to the ambiguity surrounding this matter, so that it appears that doubt had continued as to the treatment of these cases.

The boundary between self-defence and felonious slaying also raised problems. The great majority of verdicts of self-defence related to killing in brawls, especially drunken brawls, and such episodes might be expected to present special difficulty to the justices since the survivor could always claim to have been defending himself. In practice they did not normally make difficulties over accepting a verdict of slaying in self-defence and remanding *ad gratiam*, but they did make some effort to see that the verdict met the main points which were raised in the writs ordering special inquisitions. Thus in the second half of the century they generally required a cate-gorical statement from the jurors that the killing had not been of felony and malice aforethought and that the killer could not otherwise have escaped with his life. It was desirable, therefore, for the jury to establish absence of intent by showing that the slayer had not started the fight, or that, if he had done so, he had not intended a mild scrap to get out of hand, and

<hr>

[1] J.I. 1/58, m. 25[d].   [2] 24 Henry VIII, cap. 5.

had not forearmed himself with any lethal weapon. Favourable juries often went into great detail to show that it was the ultimate victim who had been the original aggressor. The verdict was especially convincing if it could state that he had lain in wait for the prisoner; another good point to make was that he had pursued relentlessly when the latter had tried to break off the engagement; it was all to the good if the weapon or instrument used had been picked up by the unarmed victim of attack as he fled. These last points were useful not only in establishing absence of felonious intent, but also in showing that the defendant had been in a dire plight and had tried to get away. To comply fully with the requirement that he must have been unable otherwise to escape death it was, however, necessary to show also that he had taken every possible evasive action, turning at bay only when no further avenue of escape lay open to him. The back-to-the-wall position which was to become common form already featured in a great many verdicts, and, if they are to be believed, many a fugitive inadvertently bolted into a cul-de-sac. In dealing with the point that the force used in self-defence must have been no more than commensurate with the violence of the attack, a convenient rule of thumb was to judge it excessive if an edged weapon had been used against an assailant who was unarmed or armed only with a blunt instrument—a refinement of the Civil Law criterion. This rule was enforced with great strictness on occasion. For example, Adam Overstrod was brought before the itinerant justices in 1255 and charged with the death of Walter de Lacy; he imprudently admitted having killed Walter, but said that he had done so in self-defence; the jurors were questioned as to this and said that Walter had struck Adam with a staff and beaten him, and Adam had fought back, drawing his knife and giving Walter a fatal stab in the stomach.[1] On this verdict, Adam was sentenced to be hanged. A smaller discrepancy between the weapons was less serious but might still give rise to doubts.[2]

In theory the criteria of killing in self-defence were strict: an assault which was not murderous was no excuse for killing;[3]

[1] J.I. 1/361, m. 40ᵈ.

[2] e.g. J.I. 3/36, i, m. 10ᵈ; *Cal. Pat. Rolls, 1281-92*, 394.

[3] There does not seem to have been any clear rule as to the treatment of women who killed in defence against attempted rape. Few cases of this kind came before the justices, but one was reported at the Northumberland eyre of 1256, after the

in practice no doubt the gravity of the assault was often exaggerated and pardon was obtained. But other forms of provocation were not taken into account by the justices and there was little point in the jurors mentioning them, except when insult was followed by assault. Killing in a free-for-all might be represented as self-defence, but if this could not be done convincingly the justices would not recommend pardon. Some degree of culpability, such as voluntarily engaging in a brawl, or attacking under severe but not violent provocation, was enough to take a killing out of the category of excusable. Without the connivance of the jurors, those who had slain in extenuating circumstances of this kind would be held guilty. Their only hope was to try to get pardon by other means than inquisition or remand by the justices. They or their friends would have to approach the king and rely on money or influence to persuade him to grant it. Thus at the very level where the system of pardoning could have been valuable and appropriate, everything was left to the culprit's initiative and the king's discretion.

The emphasis laid on premeditation could, however, suggest one way of establishing excuse. If it was impossible to declare that a killing in a free-for-all had been in self-defence, whether because of the disparity in weapons or because the victim had not been the original aggressor, then there was a tendency for a well-disposed jury to fall back on the notion of a fortuitous cause—a chance rather than an accident in the modern sense. The inquiry whether the killing had been by malice aforethought could truthfully be answered in the negative if the parties involved had been strangers to each other and had quarrelled over some trifling matter, so that there could be no question of ancient enmity or even sudden provocation sufficient to create the intent to kill. A medley of this kind could be said to have occurred by chance, and its fatal outcome could thus itself be described as slaying by mischance.[1] But something

---

woman had fled to the sanctuary of Hexham. Her father offered 40 shillings that she might return to the peace; the justices accepted this and decided to consult the king; this probably implies that they considered she needed pardon (*Northumberland Assize Rolls*, Surtees Soc. lxxxviii. 85). Justices in eyre ordered that a woman who had killed a man who tried to rape her should be waived (J.I. 1/956, m. 41). She had earlier been released on bail after an inquisition *de odio et atia* had found the death accidental (C. 144/14, no. 16).

[1] The jurors took this line in *Cal. Inquisitions Misc.* i, no. 2087.

more than a verdict of this kind was generally needed to secure
pardon. Although verdicts of self-defence or mischance might
be based chiefly on the fact that slayer and slain were strangers
to each other,[1] the courts generally required much more than
the mere absence of malice aforethought to establish self-
defence. Neither of the verdicts mentioned in the last two foot-
notes seems to have succeeded in convincing the king, for no
pardons have been found in these cases. The man who killed
mota contentione needed to be able to show that he had not been
the aggressor but a reluctant participant.

The idea of a chance medley or chance encounter between
strangers was not the only form in which the element of fortuity
could be introduced into cases of what was primarily self-
defence. They could be emphasized with the object of ruling
out premeditation and pre-existing hatred, but some untoward
and unintended happening in the course of a fight, or, better
still, in the course of flight and pursuit could also be asserted in
the hope of convincing the king or his justices that the slayer
had had no immediate intention of killing even when under
sustained attack, that only the intervention of chance had foiled
his attempt to persuade his assailant to desist or to elude him
altogether. A good many men who were attacked drew sword or
knife, not with the intention of wielding them, but to scare the
attackers off, holding them out horizontally so that if the latter
persisted they were likely to run on these weapons—or so the
jurors were apt to declare when the headlong rush had ended
fatally. Such deaths could be ascribed to self-defence, but they
were also often put down to mischance.[2] The justices were
rightly sceptical of some verdicts of this kind. Even though he
had not struck out with his weapon the survivor of such an
affair had taken up a posture which inevitably suggested his
readiness to fight back and might in itself further have provoked
the aggressor. They might take the view that the attack had
not really been a lethal one, and that to unsheathe a sword
or knife when there was no threat to one's life involved some
responsibility.[3] An assailant might, however, be killed by his

---

[1] e.g. *Cal. Inquisitions Misc.* i, no. 2308; C. 145/48, no. 47, where it was stated
that the slayer had no 'noticiam' of the victim 'per quam maliciam excogitatam
nec feloniam ipsum interfecit'.

[2] e.g. *Cal. Inquisitions Misc.* i, nos. 2055, 2277; J.I. 3/90, m. 1; *Cal. Pat. Rolls,
1292–1301*, 40 (William le Carpenter).

[3] For an example of this attitude see below, p. 271.

own weapon. This could happen most easily if he was knocked down and fell with it beneath him, the point piercing him as it took his weight, but it could happen in other ways. The justices might consider his opponent partly to blame, but in practice they were quite often ready to acquit him, especially if he had been subjected to aggravated assault. If a pursuer came to grief by falling over a weapon in his haste, his quarry was likely to need pardon. Nor was the ownership of the weapon always decisive in such an event. Thus, according to the verdict at a gaol delivery, two men were ferociously set upon one evening by two others armed with swords and arrows; one fled; the other, James de Bolyngton, tried to defend himself with part of a bow which he was holding, but then he, too, fled; Richard Brontespage chased him with a sword and James, perceiving that he was catching him up, turned and warded off a threatened blow from the sword with the fragment of bow; the sword fell from Richard's hand and James scooped it up and fled; Richard drew a long knife and followed him; James stumbled over some rubbish and fell backwards into a thornbush with the sword in his hand pointing upwards; Richard was pursuing him at such a pace that he fell on the sword and fatally wounded himself, seeing which James raised the hue and ran to the village and gave himself up. The justices evidently felt it necessary to press for further information as to James's use of the sword. Had he, they asked, as he lay on his back voluntarily pointed the sword upwards and with it killed Richard of felony aforethought as he fell over him? The jurors said no, it was pointed upwards fortuitously, and Richard in falling over James killed himself by accident; if this mischance had not occurred Richard would have killed James. The justices then remanded him *ad gratiam* and he was pardoned on the grounds that the slaying had been accidental.[1]

Their question as to felony aforethought, absurd as it is on the face of it, illustrates the difficulty of establishing that the slayer had not finally under the stress of the moment wilfully killed his assailant, or at least wilfully resorted to unecessary violence, intending to injure if not actually kill him, and motivated perhaps by the desire to retaliate as well as by the instinct of self-preservation. For the jury to represent the case as one of mischance and to lay the blame for the accident, as well as the

---

[1] J.I. 3/24, m. 1ᵈ; *Cal. Pat. Rolls, 1292–1301*, 497.

attack in which it occurred, at the door of the assailant was a good way to distract attention from the state of mind of the man charged with his death; this might be dismissed as irrelevant if indeed the victim had brought it on himself both by his deliberate aggression and by his own clumsiness or precipitance. Mostly the justices accepted such accounts as evidence that there had been no deliberate killing, failing, perhaps, to give sufficient weight to the possibility of immediate intent and excessive violence when premeditation was ruled out. It is apparent that mischance was put forward very often and was preferred to self-defence as an excuse in these cases: slayers obtained inquisitions as to whether they had slain by mischance and juries sometimes affirmed that they had done so, although the details of their verdict would suggest that self-defence was more appropriate.[1] Sometimes they swore that a slaying had been both by mischance and in self-defence,[2] for jurors were often anxious to give all the help they possibly could. Verdicts of this kind were accepted so that the merging of the two was given a certain amount of official recognition. The authorities may have acquiesced in this way because of their own failure to analyse these concepts more thoroughly, but it is conceivable that they felt a certain relief, in such circumstances, at being presented with grounds for approving pardon without too obviously relaxing the criteria for an acceptable verdict of self-defence.

This preference for the excuse of mischance suggests that the assessment of responsibility for killing in a fight was generally somewhat severe or at least incalculable. In some respects actual practice did tend to severity, but in others it was surprisingly lenient. The emphasis placed on the absence of malice aforethought might have suggested that drunkenness would be a sufficient excuse. One jury, anxious to omit nothing that could be of help to the subject of the inquisition, asserted that he had not struck his brother, who had attacked him when drunk, 'per aliquam feloniam vel maliciam excogitatam; immo per infortunium et se defendendo et per ebrietatem', and added that there had never previously been any *odium vel atia* between

---

[1] e.g. *Cal. Inquisitions Misc.* i, no. 386; C. 145/9, no. 38; C. 145/34, no. 61. The *Calendar* is not always accurate and where necessary the reference is to the Chancery file.

[2] e.g. *Cal. Inquisitions Misc.* i, nos. 2097, 2168, 2286, 2295.

H

them.[1] But this piling up of excuses may have done more harm than good, for no pardon has been found in this case. Although a great many fatal brawls occurred in taverns, or when their patrons had just left to go home, and a great many of the eventual victims were said to have been uncontrollably drunk, the men who killed them in self-defence were generally represented as cold sober and as showing the greatest self-control. Probably it was felt that to admit that they too were drunk would cancel out the claim that they had been attacked without provocation and had fought back only when in mortal danger. It may also be that the authorities were not receptive to this particular excuse and that this became so widely known that jurors fought shy of it.

However, if the justices were strict on this particular point, their concern with intention and malice aforethought had one unfortunate effect for the maintenance of order. Because of it the category of mischance was allowed to include a type of killing which merited some punishment, killing with 'transferred intent', namely, the unintentional killing of one person by a blow deliberately aimed at another. This tended to run counter to Bracton's view that a slayer was guilty if 'unum percusserit et occiderit cum alium percutere vellet in felonia'.[2] There are hints that other people shared this view, or expected royal commissioners to share it. The jurors at one inquisition at any rate appreciated the advantage to the slayer of their being able to declare that he had not been attempting felony; he had, they said, shot not to hit but to frighten a hayward; the arrow had passed by him and gone over a wall and hedge, where it had come down on someone who had been hidden by them and had inflicted a fatal wound; they emphasized that the archer could not have intended to hit the hayward 'since they were standing so near together that he could easily have done so had he wished'.[3] But their care to establish this point was probably needless. The justices were generally ready enough to accept a verdict of accidental slaying without inquiring whether the intercepted or misdirected shot or blow had been felonious, intended to kill or wound someone else. It is true that in most cases of this kind there had been, as far as can be judged, no felonious intent. The typical case is that

[1] J.I. 1/1185, m. 3.　　　　　　　　　　[2] *De Legibus*, f. 155.
[3] *Cal. Inquisitions Misc.* i, no. 2103.

of the master of a household interrupted when chastising wife, child, or servant, a lawful occupation provided he did not pursue it with excessive violence. He can seldom have intended to inflict lasting, let alone fatal injury, yet in anger he might go too far. There are several instances involving the use or threatened use of an edged weapon, even a sword, by an enraged husband or master. For example, a husband and wife quarrelled and their lodger intervened, trying to pacify them; the husband threw a knife at his wife, but 'per infortunium' it pierced the lodger fatally in the stomach.[1] The king granted pardon on the record of the justices,[2] and in this and similar cases his pardon seems, if anything, overlenient. In some, at least, the action was illegal and had it achieved its true objective could have amounted to felony. In another respect, too, English justice was more lenient than Bracton, following Civil and Canon Law, would have approved. If a man was killed in a brawl only those who had actually struck him mortal blows were adjudged guilty of homicide; other participants were guilty only of breach of the peace, for which they could be amerced by the justices, always providing they had not held the victim whilst another killed him; had they done so they shared the latter's responsibility, unless it could be shown that their intention had been to restrain the victim from killing someone else. On these final points Bracton's statements[3] did accord with contemporary practice.

The official attitude to accidental killing was in general just as severe as it was to killing in self-defence; both were excusable, deserving but requiring pardon. On the whole, the justices showed little inclination to minimize responsibility for fatal accidents, yet there were certain exceptions, some types of accident being regarded with much greater leniency than others and acquittal for these being within their power. They seem, however, to have had, or at any rate to have ventured to use, very little discretion to acquit on the merits of individual

[1] J.I. 1/181, m. 31.
[2] *Cal. Pat. Rolls, 1281–92*, 23. Bail had been granted earlier; see *Cal. Close Rolls, 1279–88*, 153. Cf. J.I. 1/952, m. 43 (cf. above, p. 44, n. 2) and J.I. 1/676, m. 2, *Cal. Pat. Rolls, 1301–7*, 421. In the last of these cases a master attempted to strike a servant with drawn sword; a member of the family tried to prevent this and there was a scuffle in which the candle went out; in the dark his mother ran on the sword. This circumstance in itself was enough to warrant treating her death as accidental.
[3] *De Legibus*, ff. 121, 138ᵇ.

cases. It was not for them to make very searching inquiry into the question of negligence and base their decision on its presence or absence in each case. Fatal accidents fell into certain groups, in some of which negligence was apparently discounted, whilst in others it may have been taken for granted, despite all the efforts of well-disposed juries to absolve the slayer of even this negative kind of responsibility. This was a very rough-and-ready way of discriminating between accidental slayers who needed pardon and those who did not, and it resulted in the acquittal of some who had and the remand *ad gratiam* of some who had not been negligent.

The fatal accidents for which human responsibility was regarded as so minimal that acquittal was in order were those for which the uncontrollable movements of beasts or natural forces could be blamed. One sort of uncontrollable movement was that of the sea. No one could be held responsible in any way for the capsizing of boats on the sea, or for passengers or crew falling out and being drowned. The boats were not even deodand. A fatal accident on a river was regarded with more reserve: a boat which overturned here was liable to be deodand, but it was unlikely that any person would be held to have been negligent in such circumstances: poor boatmanship was not counted as negligence. Indeed, unless someone had fled, and so given evidence of a sense of guilt, there was little likelihood of any proceedings being taken at all. However, the victim's relatives might bring an appeal for his death at sea or on a river against the master of the boat, for example, and the latter might think it prudent to obtain pardon.[1] It was very rare for such cases to come before the justices except by appeal, but it may safely be assumed that they would not hesitate to acquit if the drowning had occurred at sea, and would be very likely to do so if it had occurred in a river.

A second group of fatalities in which it could be taken pretty much for granted that there had been no negligence was that in which tree-climbers were involved. Their own insecure position and the uncontrollable swaying of the branches could

---

[1] e.g. in 1269 the king pardoned one man and ordered the release on bail of five others to stand to right if anyone wished to speak against them for the death of a man who accidentally fell from a ship at sea. The ship and its cargo had been seized, but restored provisionally, pending the decision at the eyre as to whether they should be deodand. See *Close Rolls, 1268–72*, 52–3.

reasonably be held to absolve them from any responsibility if they caused the fall of some object, still more if they themselves fell on to someone else.[1] But while there was a strong feeling in favour of the climbers, they were not altogether sure of acquittal.[2] Fatal accidents when felling trees presented a rather more difficult problem. Those caused by persons who were lopping off branches could be treated leniently if this involved climbing,[3] but it was important to insist that every care should be taken to keep people out of the way when the whole tree was about to fall. Bracton, following the canonists and ultimately Civil Law, provided a norm by which to assess negligence in such cases.[4] Yet the justices might ignore this and hold that felling a tree so that it came down on someone required pardon, even though there was no real negligence.[5]

The third and largest group in which negligence was ruled out almost automatically consisted of riding, driving, and ploughing accidents. Some of these were attributable to the teams which drew various vehicles and which were difficult to guide or stop in an emergency.[6] The teams of oxen which might blunder into persons or obstacles in their path were usually slow-moving and evidently were sometimes left to their own devices. Horses too might be allowed to proceed without a driver, as when a cart drawn by horses, crossing the bridge at Leicester, went over a two-year-old child, the driver having remained behind; the jurors found that he was not to blame for the accident; the horses and cart were valued at 15s., since they were held responsible and so would be deodand.[7] Failure incessantly to keep an eye on the team was evidently not regarded

---

[1] e.g. J.I. 1/175, m. 38; J.I. 1/210, m. 31; J.I. 1/131, m. 3.

[2] One who was remanded *ad gratiam* would seem particularly deserving of lenient treatment: he had climbed a tree in a cemetery in order to take young crows; the branch on which he stood broke, but he clung to another and hung by his arms for a long time; meanwhile the broken branch came down on to someone's head and inflicted a fatal wound; see J.I. 1/1286, m. 29ᵈ. Cf. J.I. 1/739, m. 92ᵈ.

[3] e.g. William de Preston was acquitted of the death of a man hit by a branch which fell while he was doing this. Probably he himself was up the tree. See J.I. 1/982, m. 31.   [4] Cf. above, p. 71; *De Legibus*, f. 121; *Institutes*, Lib. iv, tit. 3.

[5] e.g. J.I. 1/422, m. 3ᵈ.

[6] e.g. J.I. 1/280, m. 18ᵈ. Ralph Pike was driving a cart drawn by six oxen and the cart went over a girl who was sitting in its path. This was adjudged an accident and the deodands were valued at 5 marks; cf. ibid., m. 29ᵈ: a man was up a ladder set against a hay rick; two oxen drawing a cart struck the ladder so that he fell and died at once. The oxen, the cart, and the ladder were all valued as deodands, at 16s. 2d.   [7] J.I. 1/455, m. 4ᵈ.

as negligence, and probably in general the animals concerned could be trusted to proceed at a staid pace; the person in charge of them could not be blamed for failing to foresee the unlikely people or obstacles which chanced to get in the way. However, what might be considered dangerous driving was also treated with considerable leniency. There was a tendency to blame the pedestrian who lacked the agility to get out of the way rather than the driver who could not control his vehicle. This is demonstrated in the acquittal at a gaol delivery in 1292–3 of Richard le Holdere who had been arrested for the death of John le Sprottere at Stratford Atte Bowe. John had been standing in the highway and Richard driving his wagon gave a great cry 'Fuge, fuge', as he could not hold his horses on a downhill slope since part of the harness had broken. One of the wheels struck and broke John's leg and he died three weeks later. The jury found that this was not due to Richard's malice or felony, but to misadventure with the horses and cart, and this on account of the feebleness and 'non posse' of John, who was unable to flee from the wagon.[1] This tolerance towards incompetent drivers goes back to an early time, for in the Yorkshire eyre of 1218–19, when it was presented that 'a boy was crushed through the stupidity of those who led the cart', the death was treated as entirely accidental and the cart and oxen were adjudged deodand.[2] The king accepted this view of death on the roads, if the justices thought it necessary to consult him. Thus in 1236 itinerant justices informed Henry III that two men brought before them for the death of another were not guilty, though the wheel of the cart they were driving had gone over him and killed him; the king instructed them to acquit.[3] Similarly, Edward I ordered the release of a carter, who had been driving a cart loaded with fish, the wheel of which had given a fatal blow to a girl 'whilst she was running impetuously across its course' against his will, as he was 'in no way guilty of her death'. The cart and horses were not even to be kept as possible deodands.[4]

There were, of course, cases of riding or driving casualties in which there was little if any negligence, but leniency might be carried too far. It is hard to see that the complete acquittal

---

[1] J.I. 3/36, ii, mm. 8; 2.
[2] *Rolls of the Justices in Eyre in Yorks.*, *1218–19*, Selden Soc. lvi, no. 657.
[3] *Close Rolls, 1234–7*, 340.   [4] *Cal. Close Rolls, 1279–88*, 257.

of William de Wilton was justified. He had driven a cart past Matilda le Pottere's stall and in doing so had knocked over her wares. Matilda tried to halt the cart, but William whipped up the horses and they drew it forward so that it went over her and broke her right arm. Of this injury she died a week later. William at first withdrew *pre timore*, but he appeared before the justices and was acquitted.[1] This was a case in which some punishment, if only a fine, would seem to have been appropriate. However, the horses and cart, valued at 17s. were deodand, so if they were his own he was at least penalized indirectly to this amount.

The reasons for this attitude to road accidents were manifold. The animals could be made the scapegoats and in this way the rider's or driver's innocence of intent could be emphasized, whilst the king's financial interest was safeguarded by his getting the value of the deodands. Too little attention was paid to the question of negligence. But both Civil and Canon Law showed some indulgence to riders who could not control their mounts,[2] so that the English courts cannot be blamed in this case for ignoring their guidance, though they might have learnt much from their analysis of negligence in other types of accident. Nor was the possibility that the victim had been deliberately run down entirely overlooked. In one case, at least, the justices rejected a verdict of accidental slaying and condemned the slayer to death. He had earlier fled and then been arrested and bailed after an inquisition *de odio et atia* had found him not guilty, asserting that the victim had died of illness.[3] His condemnation after two favourable verdicts is remarkable, but perhaps the discordant efforts to exonerate him gave rise to suspicion which was strengthened by his having fled.

It is noteworthy that Fleta repudiated the general leniency to dangerous driving. He quoted the familiar examples of slaying by chance 'as if a man should fell a tree which, in falling, crushed a passer-by or if a hunter should strike a man with a missile instead of the quarry', but he went on 'Nevertheless, if a man sets about his business improperly, as, for example, if he should drive oxen fast and one of them, meeting a man, should slay him with its horns, the deed will be imputed to the driver because he did not exercise the diligence he should

---

[1] J.I. 1/619, m. 74^d.   [2] See above, p. 75.
[3] J.I. 1/111, m. 27; C. 144/18, no. 36; *Cal. Close Rolls, 1272–9*, 522.

have done.'[1] In Fleta's view, then, this sort of fatality should be regarded as more serious, not less, than the ordinary types of accidental slaying. This was a tortuous inference from the authorities who had dealt with the subject in quite a different connection. Fleta took his examples from Bracton and from the canonists. But whereas Raymond of Peñafort had taken the cases of killing by ox or horse to be imputable to someone chasing them with intent to steal and Bracton had borrowed this, though he weakened the force of the insistence on an unlawful action by substituting 'insequitur' for 'furabatur', Fleta abandoned any idea of stealing and substituted exceeding a reasonable speed limit as the unlawful action. This was to attempt a complete reversal of a long-established trend.

Occasionally, the justices showed mercy in other types of accident. For example, they ordered that Katherine, wife of Alan le Netesherde, who had accidentally scalded her son so that he died, should be bailed to stand to right at the king's will.[2] A man was similarly bailed to stand to right if anyone wanted to prosecute for the death of a woman whom he was trying to persuade to take a drink she did not want, and who was accidentally but fatally wounded by his knife as he held her in his arms.[3] These decisions meant that there was no immediate need to seek pardon and it is most improbable that any further action was ever taken against these two. But in general other types of fatal accident were assumed to be imputable to any person who had been concerned in them, however innocently. The question of his having acted negligently was ignored, and he was deemed to need pardon.[4] In this respect the treatment of accidental slaying was even stricter than Canon Law, which recognized that if there was no negligence whatever such slaying should involve neither penance nor irregularity.

The main types of accidental killing for which pardon was

---

[1] *Fleta*, ed. H. G. Richardson and G. O. Sayles, Selden Soc. lxxii. 60. In one passage Bracton had expressed doubt as to how far the blame should rest on the inanimate object or animal which occasioned a death and how far on the man who acted foolishly, mentioning horses in a way which might suggest that he thought they were too often held to blame. See *De Legibus*, f. 136[b].

[2] J.I. 1/575, m. 66.   [3] J.I. 1/998[A], m. 40.

[4] An extreme example is that of William of Gerdeston who, rolling a cartwheel towards his home, lost his footing and fell so that the wheel rolled on by itself and fell on a young boy, injuring him fatally. He was remanded *ad gratiam* and promptly secured it. See J.I. 1/1098, m. 73; *Cal. Pat. Rolls, 1292–1301*, 40.

regularly thought requisite occurred in shooting at random or at a target, throwing some missile at an animal, playing games, working on the farm, in the kitchen. The rule was applied strictly in cases of shooting, no doubt because of the danger of a deliberate attack in the course of apparently innocent target practice. But in many of these cases there was no possibility of this, and in some the negligence if any was the victim's not the archer's. For example, Adam Glover and John Tailor had been playing and shooting at targets in Portmanmarsh; they each stood by one target and as Adam fired John tried to intercept his arrow in flight with his hood, so that it should miss the target, thinking the hood would act as a shield, but it did not and he was fatally struck in the throat. This would appear to have been entirely his own fault. Yet Adam was remanded *ad gratiam*.[1] Nor were other types of contributory negligence on the part of the victim considered to absolve the survivor from responsibility.[2]

There were a good many cases in which the injury inflicted had contributed to the death although it would not in itself have proved fatal. Juries were inclined to take a charitable view of injuries caused to persons who were already suffering from or later contracted some disease. Although a blow might aggravate an existing condition, and possibly prevent recovery, it was rare for jurors to take the line that but for it the patient would have recovered.[3] Equally, the possibility that ill usage had caused the disease from which the victim later died was seldom considered, except in the obvious case of septicaemia.

---

[1] J.I. 3/18, iv, m. 5ᵈ.

[2] e.g. a man was remanded *ad gratiam* after killing in the following circumstances: he was working in a wood; another came and asked him to lend him his hatchet to fell an ash tree in his garden, and suggested that he throw it over the hedge of the wood which was so thick and high that they could not see each other; the owner asked if it was safe to do this and before he threw it warned the borrower to look out, but it struck the latter fatally on the forehead (J.I. 1/1098, m. 76; cf. C. 47/86/31, no. 832; *Cal. Pat. Rolls, 1292–1301*, 77; C. 144/34, no. 5).

[3] They did so, e.g., in the case of the death of William de Neuton, who had attacked Hubert son of Hugh, threatening to kill him; as he reached for his knife, Hubert hit him on the head with a small hatchet, drawing blood. A fortnight later William became ill with ague and died after three weeks' illness. The jurors were asked if he died of the blow or of the illness; they said that the pain of the wound aggravated the illness, so that he died of both. The justices decided to consult the king as to what to do in this case (J.I. 1/1057, m. 61ᵃ). Hubert was pardoned on grounds of self-defence, though he would scarcely have qualified for pardon on these grounds alone, since William had not actually drawn his knife before he struck him. See *Cal. Pat. Rolls, 1272–81*, 430.

A coroner's jury refused to lay the blame for the death of an infant haemophiliac on his brother, who threw a stone which struck him on the head and drew blood; the victim died a natural death, said the jurors, 'quia omnes de illa progenie, si lesi fuerint ita quod sanguis exiuit, mortuus erit'.[1] This attempt to distinguish between a wound and the disease which rendered it fatal was not, perhaps, very convincingly expressed. Yet the notion of attempting some measurement of the gravity of the injury was sound, especially in this case, for the elder brother was himself only five years old. Juries, particularly at special inquisitions, sometimes stressed the point that the victim would not have died of his injury had he not neglected it, or aggravated its effects by immoderate eating and drinking.[2] It is not clear how far the justices were influenced by these particular statements if the verdicts which included them found slaying in self-defence or by mischance anyway, but they did accept verdicts of death from natural causes, even when these had been aggravated by some injury.[3]

A minor injury could have quite disproportionate effects in circumstances of which the culprit might or might not be aware. Generally the courts would not take this factor into account so far as homicide was concerned, but occasionally they would do so. Considerations of this kind were especially important when a pregnant woman suffered some injury which caused her to lose her child, and the law itself recognized this. Deliberate abortion and a deliberate and severe assault which brought it about could both be treated as capital crimes and according to some ranked as homicide. But when a miscarriage resulted from some minor scuffle or maltreatment it could be treated as trespass, and this was very generally done once the action of trespass was established. Accordingly, there was little need for the king's pardon for the death of the unborn child, and if one was granted it might be for trespass, not homicide.[4] In 1281, for example, Edward I pardoned three

[1] J.I. 2/266, m. 5ᵈ.   [2] e.g. *Cal. Inquisitions Misc.* i, nos. 2059, 2100.

[3] The Chancellor might consider an accumulation of such factors good ground for pardon (see below, p. 232) and the king would pardon on verdicts of this kind at special inquisitions. For example, *Cal. Inquisitions Misc.* i, no. 2073.

[4] There is an instance of pardon both for death and trespasses, for which Jordan Cloyet had abjured the Channel Islands. There was a plea of matrimony in the ecclesiastical court between him and Matilda Bonamy, whereby she 'obtained letters of excommunication against the said Jordan, and he, meeting her as she was carrying them, snatched them from her and threw her to the ground, and

men for their trespass against a pregnant woman, which caused the death of the child.[1]

Although the question of negligence was not entirely overlooked the justices very seldom raised questions about it.[2] They made little attempt to differentiate between its varying kinds and degrees, or if they did pursue the matter the eyre rolls failed to record their interrogation of the jurors, and the latters' response. However, cases which did not fall into one or other of the familiar categories sometimes created problems for the justices and they might take a special line of their own. In 1281, for example, a difficult case came before the justices in eyre in Wiltshire. A woman had brought her year-old son to the father, who refused to accept and care for him; she thereupon dumped the infant in the village street and during the following night he died from exposure. The jurors did not suspect either parent of causing the death, presumably intentionally, but the justices held both of them and the whole village responsible for it by their negligence; the matter was not treated as homicide, but all were amerced for their offence.[3] The treatment of the vill suggests that omission to take some action to save life might perhaps be considered culpable and in extreme cases punishable. But while the canonists might discuss the problem of omission, the secular courts were not likely to proceed far in this direction, and it does not appear that it was regarded as a matter for pardon.

It was, naturally, much easier to convince the justices that a slaying had been accidental than that it had been in self-defence. Accidental and intentional homicide were entirely opposed; they could scarcely shade off one into the other as self-defence and culpable homicide might do. Usually the circumstances were such that there could have been no question of the premeditated contrivance of an apparent accident. The jury's view of the matter could generally be accepted without further probing, provided they used the formula 'not

took away her purse containing the said letters and 16 pence . . ., by reason of which throwing, the child whereof she was pregnant died and was born abortive' (*Cal. Pat. Rolls, 1301–7*, 303).

[1] Ibid. *1272–81*, 444. The roll has the marginal note: 'de perdon. mortis hominis.'

[2] Though they might take it into account in what was regarded as accidental death, not homicide. Thus a man who had frightened a horse so that it threw its rider with fatal results had to fine for his foolish action, while the horse was deodand. See *Liber Albus*, ed. H. T. Riley, 97.   [3] J.I. 1/1004, m. 91.

by felony or malice aforethought'; certainly there could be no general rules as to the sort of alleged accident which ought to be regarded with suspicion, and it was only in a few atypical cases that suspicion was in fact aroused. The justices sometimes put one or two questions to the jury in order, apparently, to satisfy themselves that there could have been no felony, but in cases where this seems so obvious from the verdict that it is difficult to see why they bothered to do so.

In sum, the evidence shows that the attitude to justifiable and excusable homicide was, if not entirely incalculable, unpredictable at many points. Any guiding rules that commanded general respect were pragmatic. There were no definite, logical principles and no accepted authorities from without. At some points English practice conformed with Civil and Canon Law definitions of responsibility, but whether this was always due to deliberate or unconscious borrowing is very doubtful; common sense could have dictated the same attitudes. On other points a markedly divergent line was taken, and generally the criteria adopted by the English courts were the most stringent, as in their treatment of those who killed thieves and robbers in self-defence or poachers resisting arrest. In defining self-defence as the use of no more force than was in fact necessary to save one's life, the king was outdoing the most severe of the canonists. His justices paid far less attention when dealing with accidental slaying to the absence of negligence on the part of the slayer and to contributory negligence on that of the victim than did the latter. Pardons were necessary in cases in which only the smallest penance, penance *ad cautelam*, or even none at all was judged requisite and which did not debar clerks from promotion. In only one or two respects was English practice less severe: participants in fights were not held guilty unless they had themselves struck mortal blows; the justices were more lenient in their attitude to 'transferred intent', and they maintained the same or even greater leniency towards those involved in road accidents, ignoring the question of negligence almost entirely and here to the advantage of the slayer. Some justices were more tolerant or more inclined to follow Civil and Canon Law than were others and this inclination, while it benefited individuals, contributed to the general uncertainty as to the justifiable or excusable slayer's fate should he venture to appear in court.

IV

THE EXCUSABLE SLAYER IN COURT

THE boundary between homicides for which acquittal was in order and those which required pardon was not very well defined; that between excusable and felonious homicide was even less distinct, and this was natural since it depended to a greater degree on the king's use of his prerogative. Neither his actions nor the justices' were always consistent. Moreover, final decisions are not always on record. Thus great caution is needed in dealing with the treatment accorded to excusable slayers in court, but it is worth while to attempt some estimate of the prospects for those who appeared to stand their trial on indictment. The position of those who were appealed was radically different and will be considered in a later chapter.

The prisoner's fate depended on three sets of people, jurors, justices, and the king. The attitude of the juries, both presenting and trial juries, was of great importance. The justices might be unaware of a possible excuse if the jurors suppressed this factor, since the prisoner himself might fail to mention it when pleading not guilty. In the nature of the case, the eyre and gaol delivering rolls are not likely now to reveal what was hidden from the justices, and thus they give the impression that the risk of condemnation was all but negligible if the circumstances warranted pardon. This optimistic view is seen to be illusory as soon as other types of evidence become available, especially verdicts given elsewhere in the same cases. Such controls are provided by inquisitions obtained by prisoners in the hope of being released on bail pending trial at the eyre. In fifty-odd cases the account given at the eyre has been checked against that given at an earlier inquisition. In thirty of these cases slaying in self-defence was the finding on both occasions, and in ten slaying by mischance, though there were some discrepancies on points of detail. But eight men for whom a plausible excuse had been made out, on the strength of which they had been granted bail and would almost certainly have been granted pardon had they then applied for it, were found guilty at the eyre and hanged. Equally discrepant verdicts were brought in four other cases but the capital sentence could not follow because the prisoners had claimed benefit of clergy. Thus while the majority of these verdicts at inquisition and eyre were in general agreement, a disturbingly large minority, just on a quarter, were diametrically opposed. In some of these cases the eyre roll gives no hint that an excuse could have been put forward, the jury not apparently having given any details about the circumstances of the homicide. In others, details were reported at the eyre, but with factual differences or a shift of emphasis which proved fatal to the slayer. Generally, if not always, the jurors at the eyre must have been aware of the earlier, favourable verdict. They themselves might have to report that the accused had earlier been released on bail, and this in itself would suggest a favourable inquisition, even if this had not been well advertised locally, as one would expect it to have been. Thus they must have rejected the earlier finding deliberately, even if they did not expressly repudiate it, as they did on occasion.

It certainly cannot be assumed that the verdict of a special inquisition should generally be preferred to that of the trial jury. On the contrary, since it was not final and since it was obtained at the request of the accused or his friends who probably had some reason for confidence in its outcome, it must be treated with reserve. Yet some of these earlier verdicts cannot easily be dismissed. In one case a trial jury which found two men guilty differed not only from that at a special inquisition but also from the presenting jurors at the eyre itself;[1] the earlier accounts tally well enough and show convincing excuse if not indeed justification. In another the inquisition *de odio et atia* gave what seems a convincing account of the killing of Robert le Potter by Richard son of Richard Fitz-Ughtred. The bailiff of Preston, they said, came to attach a merchant who had committed an offence there. Robert, who was drunk, heard of this and struck the bailiff on the shoulder and elsewhere with a burning faggot; he then took a great stake in both hands and pursued Richard, who had accompanied the bailiff, meaning to strike him on the head. Richard for fear of death hit Robert on the head with an oak staff and

[1] C. 144/34, no. 11; J.I. 1/877, m. 53.

he died within a week of this blow.[1] This account rings true: it is not so favourable as to suggest that the jury had been influenced on Richard's behalf; a responsible person, the bailiff, was involved and the affair would seem to have been sufficiently public for misrepresentation to be risky. Yet at the eyre, although it was reported that he had earlier been bailed, the jury found him guilty and he was hanged.[2] There was some miscarriage of justice in the case of John de Okelesthorp and Hugh Nutel who killed Robert Turpin, though its exact nature is uncertain. In 1290 John was bailed on the strength of a verdict at a gaol delivery of killing in self-defence.[3] At the eyre in 1293 the following account was given.[4] John had been bailiff of Barkeston and Hugh sub-bailiff and they had distrained Robert by seizing a horse, which they led away and tied to a cart. Robert, armed with a pick-axe, followed them, released the horse and took it away. They chased him and he defended himself with the pick-axe, whereupon John shot him in the chest at a range of forty feet. Hugh then went up to him and laid hands on him, and John came up with drawn sword and as they belaboured him the arrow which was sticking into his chest was driven through his body so that he died. John shot at Robert in self-defence, to escape death himself. The justices, rather surprisingly, accepted this verdict and remanded him *ad gratiam*; the record was sent to the Parliament at London, and he was pardoned, though after some delay.[5] Yet Hugh, who would seem to have been far less responsible, had already been hanged for the death. If his condemnation was not unjust, it must be concluded that John's pardon was a misplaced act of clemency.

Very occasionally, the jury at the eyre was more charitable than that at the inquisition, acquitting altogether when the earlier verdict had amounted to killing in self-defence.[6] This suggests that some inquisitions at least resulted in verdicts which were not unduly favourable. The conclusion must be that neither the one type of verdict nor the other must always be preferred when they are at variance. Some of the men who were condemned despite an earlier finding of self-defence were

---

[1] C. 144/24, no. 9.
[2] J.I. 1/409, m. 16. He had a free tenement bringing in 29s. 6d. and chattels worth 27s. [3] *Cal. Close Rolls, 1288–96*, 103.
[4] J.I. 1/1098, m. 47d. [5] *Cal. Pat. Rolls, 1292–1301*, 141 (August 1295).
[6] e.g. C. 144/17, no. 14; J.I. 1/705, m. 21d. See below, p. 261.

guilty, but unhappily it cannot be doubted that some would have qualified for pardon had the true circumstances been revealed at the eyre.

In a few of these cases the disagreement was not as to the facts of the case, but as to the law applicable to those facts. Did they or did they not substantiate a charge of felonious slaying? The jurors generally supplied not only the facts as they saw them or chose to represent them, but also their own estimate of the nature of the homicide. They would state categorically that it had been in self-defence or by misfortune or both. But the justices were expected to scrutinize the verdict with care and form their own judgement on the facts. Normally, where self-defence was asserted, they were content to ask the jurors whether the defendant had really been in such straits that he would have lost his life had he not defended himself. The jurors regularly repeated on oath that this was the case. Very rarely, to judge by the entries on the eyre rolls, did the justices challenge the facts, but now and then they did press for more detail. For example, when a man who had been remorselessly attacked with a knife had eventually turned at bay and defended himself with a hatchet, the disparity of the weapons, though both were edged, may have given the justices pause, for they inquired whether he had given his assailant several blows; the jurors said no, and he was remanded to gaol, promptly to obtain pardon.[1] The justices did not always accept the jurors' assurances so tamely, but when they challenged the findings they were unlikely to break down the jury's determination to get the prisoner pardoned. Even if they were still unconvinced and consulted the king the chances were that he would take a favourable view. The difficulty and frustration which beset such efforts are well illustrated in the case of Robert de Caterale, who had killed Gilbert, son of William de Cherneleye, in the following circumstances: as they were riding home at dusk from a party with Gilbert's father and brother, Robert whipped William's mount so that it threw him. Seeing this, Gilbert struck Robert with his bow, breaking it, but continuing to strike him with a fragment. Robert fled till he came to a ditch over which stood a hedge, and as he jumped

---

[1] J.I. 1/739; m. 56; *Cal. Pat. Rolls, 1292–1301*, 5. The jury *de odio et atia* in this case had been careful to mention that it was a *little* hatchet; see C.144/30, no. 32.

this obstacle he clutched at a pale in the hedge, which broke away so that he fell into the water. At this moment Gilbert caught him up and assaulted him again with a piece of the bow, and Robert struck him on the head with the pale; as a result he died three days later. The justices did not find this story entirely convincing evidence of self-defence against a lethal attack and asked the jurors if Gilbert had had a sword or knife on him and had drawn either of them. The jurors said that he had been so armed but had drawn neither weapon. They were then asked whether Robert could have escaped death otherwise and said no. But since it seemed to the justices that this could not well follow from the first verdict, nine knights and three other men were added to the jury, which then swore that Robert could not otherwise have escaped death. So he was committed to gaol until the king's will should be known.[1] Later, he came with the king's pardon and was given firm peace. This pardon does not appear on the patent rolls. It would be understandable if the king had hesitated to grant pardon in view of the doubts which the justices themselves had entertained, yet it cannot be supposed that the latter would have been careless in scrutinizing the document put forward and it must be assumed that it was genuine.

The justices did not, then, always concur with the jury's estimate of the nature of the slaying, but they were unlikely to repudiate it altogether unless they had some other verdict on which to rely, such as that at the coroner's inquest. Many cases raised problems for them. With no hard-and-fast classification of justifiable and excusable homicide to help them they were often at a loss how to proceed. Sometimes they solved their problem in an unconventional way or sought some compromise. More often they tried to shift responsibility to other shoulders, deciding to consult with other justices or with the king.

One unusual and perhaps rather dubious solution was to release the killer on his finding pledges to appear in court in the event of his being prosecuted later. Examples of this have already been quoted.[2] It came very near to acquittal since there could hardly be subsequent prosecution at the king's

<hr/>

[1] J.I. 1/409, m. 31ᵈ. Cf. C. 144/29, no. 42, and *Cal. Close Rolls, 1288–96*, 11, 14, which show that he had been bailed three years earlier when an inquisition had found self-defence.   [2] Above, p. 104.

suit and there was very little chance of an appeal being successfully prosecuted at so late a stage. The prisoner could be
required to fine to be released in this way, but if this procedure
had become normal and no fine had been required it might
have provided the most satisfactory method of treating excusable homicide. It would have permitted the person who was
involuntarily involved in the death of another to be set free
provisionally without incurring the expense of securing the
king's pardon, but still with the undertaking, indeed a much
more compelling undertaking, to stand to right. Thus the
interests of the victim's family would have been no more ad-
versely affected than they were when the slayer was pardoned,
and the latter would have been saved expense and some of
the stigma which the need for pardon might perhaps impart.
But this course was seldom adopted and may have met with
some disapproval.

   It was also possible for the justices to allow a prisoner
charged with homicide to go free without any undertaking to
stand to right but on payment of a fine, which was a punishment for contributing to the death in some minor degree. The
prisoners themselves may have proffered fines which the justices
agreed to accept, even though this way of dealing with the
case had not been their original intention. In theory, no doubt,
recommendation to pardon was preferable to any form of
punishment, for it implied that the justices saw no need for
further prosecution, whereas fining implied some measure of
guilt, though not, of course, felony. But pardon involved delay
and expenditure, which could easily exceed a moderate pecuniary
penalty. Thus the prisoner might think it worth while to fine in
order to secure freedom at once. The justices themselves might
welcome this solution of their dilemma in cases in which they
hesitated to acquit but realized that pardon would be a matter
of rather unnecessary routine. If the prisoner could afford to
pay up at once, or could find pledges for future payment,
fining was probably the simpler and kinder way of disposing
of the case, however illogical it might be to punish those who
were innocent of any felony rather than advise the king to
remit his suit. The justices themselves are likely to have decided
on this course or to have indicated their willingness to consider
it in certain cases where it seemed appropriate, but the records
do not make it clear how often they did so. Their decision is often

recorded simply as remand in custody or to gaol, or, in the clerks' tantalizingly abbreviated phrase, 'ad gaolam quousque'. The order 'to gaol' certainly did not mean that the prisoner was to be punished by detention for an unspecified period. Apart from imprisonment for a stated term which had been decreed as the penalty for a few special offences, imprisonment was not a regular punishment at this period. For offences other than these and homicide, imprisonment after trial was indeed normally merely the prelude to a fine. Instead of sentencing the convicted defendant to pay an amercement fixed by themselves, the justices would send him to gaol until he proffered such sum as he could afford and they judged adequate. Even in cases of homicide they might be understood to intend the same result if they remanded the prisoner to gaol after self-defence or mischance had been established. On the other hand, such remand could well be taken to mean that the slayer was to be kept in prison until he obtained pardon: it could be the equivalent of remand *ad gratiam*, and indeed the entries on the roll may have been abbreviations of precisely that judicial order, for whereas sometimes the eyre roll records only that the prisoner was to be returned to prison the patent roll shows that he was pardoned at once on the record of the justices in eyre themselves,[1] and where another version of the entry survives it may reveal that the case was referred to the king.[2]

The intentions of the justices are, then, frequently inscrutable, but the remand to gaol at least afforded an opportunity for the prisoners to try to negotiate a fine, and this is likely to have been given to some of them deliberately. Fines were, so far as can be discovered, made only when participation in a killing had been very small, or when there had been a considerable element of justification,[3] or when the killing had resulted from a mischance of a type which tended to be treated with indulgence. These were precisely the cases in which the justices were reluctant to insist on the need for pardon but uncertain of their authority to acquit. Men who had taken part in a fatal brawl but had not themselves struck a mortal blow might also hope to fine with the justices, and it was possible to adjust their fines according to the degree to which they were held to have

[1] e.g. J.I. 1/181, mm. 31, 33, 13ᵈ, 37, 6; *Cal. Pat. Rolls, 1281–92*, 9, 20, 23.
[2] See above, p. 90, n. 1.
[3] e.g. J.I. 1/302, mm. 53ᵈ, 99 (Henry son of Reginald de la Forde).

contributed to the death. Thus while two men, who had come to help another in a fight in which he eventually killed his adversary, fined for one mark each, a third, who had held the victim's arm to restrain him from hitting back, fined for £10; no doubt he was thought to have contributed substantially to the slaying, whereas the victim had not been nearer to death or further from life from the blows given by the other two.[1] Although the justices generally thought themselves competent to acquit men involved in fatal road accidents they showed themselves slightly more severe in a case of speeding, which caused the death of Hamo le Blawer in a pile-up. He was going to market with two carts and Simon de Ikenouth came along in his so fast that in a narrow way he drove into one of Hamo's and the latter was crushed between them. The justices did not deem Simon entirely blameless but nor did they decide that the king's pardon was requisite. They ordered that he should be detained but eventually let him off with a fairly small fine, 2 marks; at the same time they treated the whole thing as an accident giving rise to deodand, so that he suffered the loss of his cart and two oxen, the total value being 16s. 6d. Hamo's cart was also valued, at 10s.[2] Deodands were not normally forfeit in cases which called for pardon; a hybrid of this kind, yielding both deodands and fine, might bring in a nice profit. But this case is most exceptional. Fines were occasionally accepted for other types of accidental death when there had been no negligence. For instance in 1268 John the Miller, who was suspected of killing his son, said that he had not killed him, but that his knife had got wrapped up in the tablecloth after dinner and when the tablecloth was shaken out the knife had fallen out and wounded his son in the head so that he died. The justices first ordered that he should be kept in custody until they had consulted the king, but later John was allowed to fine for half a mark, and this appears to have been the end of the matter.[3] It was, indeed, over-scrupulous to think the

---

[1] J.I. 1/653, m. 26. One of them, a clerk, claimed to have been acquitted earlier at a gaol delivery. Both had earlier been released on bail; see *Cal. Close Rolls, 1288–96*, 242 (Wallefeud and Coleville). The actual slayer had fled and was placed in exigent at the eyre.

[2] J.I. 1/359, m. 29d.

[3] J.I. 1/569A, m. 29. Cf. J.I. 1/1109, m. 2, where the man who tried to take a knife from another accidentally cut his own wrist on it and bled to death. The justices decided to have consultation, but then the suspect's son came and arranged a fine of 5 marks, as it had been found not to be a case of felony but misfortune.

king's pardon might be necessary in these circumstances, and even the small fine seems uncalled for.

These examples are enough to show that men charged with homicide were sometimes remitted to prison pending a fine rather than the king's grant of pardon. Unfortunately, so many of the extent eyre rolls lack the list of estreats that it is impossible to say how often the justices' discretion to act in this way provided some mitigation of the general harshness of the treatment of excusable slaying. The king was not opposed to the justices allowing a prisoner to fine with them if his responsibility was minimal, and when, on his accession, Edward I conceded that those who had slain before it should not be executed the justices allowed many of them to go free on payment of a fine or ransom, or finding pledges for future good behaviour.[1] But when in doubt as to the need for pardon they were far more likely to dodge responsibility and decide to consult other justices or refer the matter to the king himself. However, it sometimes dawned on them that they were being over-meticulous and the decision to have consultation was revoked. Nor must their inclination to leave the decision to others be exaggerated. Consultation with the king, especially with Henry III, did not necessarily mean that they were doubtful of the need for pardon. It was for a long time the normal course when they thought it was both needed and deserved and so was often no more than their manner of recommending to mercy.

It is difficult in many cases to know if an intended consultation ever took place. It has just been noted that the justices sometimes decided to fine the prisoner instead of carrying out their original decision to consult the king but it is also quite possible that they sometimes failed either to refer the case to the king as intended or to give any instructions as to the prisoner's fate, neither fining him nor letting him go scot free. Thus he would be left in the lurch, perhaps waiting hopefully for a pardon that never came, perhaps with no notion of what was likely to be done with him. On the other hand, consultation might actually take place but leave no trace on the rolls. The king might decide that no formal pardon was necessary and tell the justices to acquit. He might issue a formal pardon. He might decide that the prisoner did not deserve pardon. Only in the second event is evidence very likely to be available, and

---

[1] Cf. *Cal. Close Rolls, 1272–9*, 285; J.I. 1/1025, mm. 6[d], 8, 13, 15, 20[d].

even then there is an element of doubt, since even a formal charter of pardon, like Robert de Caterale's, might fail to be enrolled.

There is even greater uncertainty as to the results of some of the decisions entered on the roll simply as 'ad gaolam quousque', since this is in itself ambiguous. Such an entry may of course be an abbreviation of a clear-cut decision either to fine or to recommend to mercy. But it may also reflect the justices' own uncertainty as to the next move, or their failure to announce it in court. Their scruples and perplexities led to procrastination and vacillation which might easily turn to the prisoner's disadvantage, rather than alleviate his position. An equivocal decision meant that he did not know whether he was expected to take any action himself, or what action was appropriate. Perhaps he was being given the opportunity to proffer a fine, but he might not realize this or be able to raise an acceptable amount or find pledges for it. Perhaps he was expected to apply to the king for pardon, but failed to grasp that it was for him to take some initiative. Sometimes the justices certainly intended to reach a more definite decision, but there was a risk that they would fail to do so. The case might be shelved and forgotten. The prisoner was liable then to be detained indefinitely, or until his friends took action on his behalf, obtaining bail or pardon. The man whose fate was thus left in suspense at one eyre could be presented again at the next, whether he had remained in prison, obtained bail, or secured release in some more informal way.

As time went on the justices fell more and more into the habit of remanding to prison explicitly *ad gratiam regis*; this was normal under Edward I, though consultation did not cease and ambiguous remands continued—or at least ambiguous entries on the rolls. Remission *ad gratiam* was a clear indication that the justices intended the prisoner to apply for pardon and supposed that their record would ensure that he got it. But there is plenty of evidence that some prisoners expressly remanded *ad gratiam* were indifferent to the need to apply for pardon. Those particularly who were thus remanded at a gaol delivery might well not bother to do so.[1] The fact that the prisoner who qualified for pardon had himself to take certain steps, including, as a rule, paying the Chancery fees, must often

[1] See above, p. 50, for their tendency to apply only for bail.

have been a considerable disincentive. No doubt this would
not have been decisive for those who could manage to raise the
money had the alternative been a prolonged spell in gaol,
but bail was frequently obtained and, moreover, the order to
keep them there was not taken very seriously. One gaoler
allowed a prisoner to wander out of gaol after he had been
remanded in this way by justices of oyer and terminer and
was fined 10 marks for this dereliction of duty, but he was
unlucky.[1] Provided they put in an appearance at the next eyre,
the justices were unlikely to inquire how those remanded in
custody *ad gratiam* had spent the interval since their remand.[2]
A casual attitude to men who, after all, had been declared
on oath not to be felons, was probably very common,[3] and once
they were at large there was no urgent need for them to spend
money and perhaps find someone to act for them in obtaining
pardon. They would, of course, have to calculate with renewed
indictment at the next eyre, but probably felt that little was to
be feared from the itinerant justices; unless they now decamped
and so invited outlawry,[4] the earlier verdicts would be accepted
and the worst that could happen would be a second remand
ad gratiam, which might inconvenience them as little as the
first had done, so that some of these imperturbable slayers
still did not trouble to sue out their pardons. But the justices
did not, on their side, always consider it necessary to remand
again *ad gratiam*. For example, William Hogh appeared at
the eyre and was reported to have been so remanded at a
gaol delivery, and on hearing this they concluded, 'ideo nichil
hic de eo'.[5]

Not only could the justices be expected to be tolerant in
these circumstances; it might even be hoped that they could be

[1] J.I. 1/1339, m. 6.
[2] The constable to whom one defaulter was said to have been committed
entirely denied ever having had charge of him (J.I. 1/877, m. 63ᵈ). In the time of
Edward II a man who had been remanded earlier *ad gratiam*—though whether at
a gaol delivery or elsewhere is not stated—was reported to be no longer in prison;
the jurors did not know why, but alleged that he was at large in the country.
The ex-sheriff who was responsible laid the blame on two deputies who had been
bound to keep him in safe custody (*Eyre of Kent*, Selden Soc., xxiv. 87).
[3] But not all those remanded in custody contrived to get free; cf. J.I. 1/376,
mm. 23, 55ᵈ.
[4] As Samuel de Feringes did after being remitted to prison at a gaol delivery
till he should obtain grace. As he had failed to get pardon and did not put in an
appearance at the next eyre, he was then placed in exigent. See J.I. 1/238, m. 51.
Cf. above, p. 46, n. 5. [5] J.I. 1/1098, m. 24ᵈ.

hoodwinked into believing the prisoner had earlier actually
been acquitted. The conduct of Stephen Grazelyn throws much
light on this matter.¹ At a gaol delivery he had been found
to have killed in self-defence, so he had been remanded to
prison *ad gratiam domini Regis*. But he, too, had not obtained
pardon, and when he appeared before the itinerant justices he
claimed to have been acquitted by other justices and vouched
the record of their rolls. These being examined, it was found
that he had in fact been remanded as above, so he was sent
back to prison once again 'sicut prius, etc'. This time he did
take action, apparently applying to the king, who sent to the
justices in eyre for the earlier record; this was sent to him under
seal, and on the strength of it pardon was at last granted.²
But to attempt to mislead the itinerant justices by claiming to
have been acquitted when the prisoner had in fact only been
granted bail was a risky course. One prisoner at least was
hanged at the eyre after his claim to have been acquitted at a
gaol delivery had been falsified by the record, which showed
only that he had been granted bail and the trial jury had now
found him guilty.³ As this instance shows, the justices would not
normally accept claims of this kind without checking the records.

Explicit decisions to refer cases to the king for pardon did
not, then, always achieve the intended result. Quite often the
prisoner was content with bail; occasionally he did not get
either because the justices' intention was obscure. Moreover,
even if an application for pardon was sent off it might fail to
be delivered to the king or his council. Examples of this are
harder to pin down. Unless a second petition followed there is
little chance of evidence for the first having survived. The
patent rolls show that pardons usually came fairly promptly,
and it has been suggested that the applications were to some
degree organized, and that the organization was generally
reasonably efficient and expeditious, but sometimes it seems to

---

¹ J.I. 1/117, m. 74ᵈ; cf. C. 47/52/3, no. 108.
² *Cal. Pat. Rolls, 1301–7*, 145. Cf. the case of Henry Brun, J.I. 1/804, m. 73ᵈ,
Cal. Close Rolls, 1279–88, 445; and that of John Luytefot who also claimed at the
eyre to have been acquitted earlier, whereas in fact the record of the justices of
gaol delivery showed only his remand *ad gratiam*. He was now remitted 'quousque,
etc.', and was pardoned on grounds of self-defence; see J.I. 1/739, m. 75ᵈ; *Cal.
Pat. Rolls, 1292–1301*, 6. But the claim to have been acquitted may sometimes
have meant only that the earlier verdict had shown innocence of felony, not that
the justices had allowed the prisoner to go quit.
³ J.I. 1/302, m. 54.

have broken down. Thus failure or long delay in securing pardon may sometimes have been due to the hazards of medieval communications.

All these factors, ambiguous remands, the not-infrequent preference for bail, the risk of applications for pardon being lost in transit, constitute a zone of uncertainty surrounding the king's response to the calls on his clemency approved by the justices. For, in the absence of recorded refusals, the only way to estimate how often he withheld it is to compare the number of such applications with the number which succeeded, but neither figure can be accurately known. Failure to find a pardon for an individual on the patent rolls does not entirely exclude the possibility that he obtained one. The patent rolls are not quite complete;[1] complementary enrolments, such as the Gascon rolls, do not fill all the gaps. Identification often presents a problem; personal names were unstable; the clerks were sometimes careless in recording them, their spelling was not standardized and sometimes degenerated into a phonetic free-for-all. There is a margin of error on this side which is increased by the fact that enrolment was not absolutely necessary.[2] It cannot, therefore, be stated categorically that pardon was explicitly refused in any cases, though in some there is evidence to show that no charter of pardon had reached the prisoner after a very long period. But in spite of these uncertainties, it is possible to form some opinion as to the likelihood of a virtual recommendation to pardon by the justices being turned down.

It has been seen that such recommendation might take the form of consultation, remanding the prisoner 'quousque . . .' or explicitly *ad gratiam*. Consultation with the king generally resulted either in pardon or instructions to acquit. He was not, apparently, very often consulted because the justices doubted whether pardon was deserved. This doubt seems to have been in their mind in the case of Robert de Caterale, but the king pardoned him none the less.[3] Only one case of consultation has been found in which the absence of pardon seems at all likely to be due to the fact that the king definitely

---

[1] Some supplementary patent rolls recording only pardons were kept at times when these were being granted in great numbers. Only a few of these have survived from the time of Edward I.

[2] See above, p. 53.

[3] See above, p. 113.

decided against granting it. The circumstances were described
as follows: David Devaunt and Robert le Escot were at the
fair at Guisborough and Robert asked David to repay a debt,
but David denied that it was as yet due for repayment. Annoyed
by this Robert put an arrow in his bow to shoot him, and David
drew his sword and cut the bowstring, whereupon Robert
drew a knife and threatened him with it, and David in self-
defence, since he could not otherwise escape death, struck
Robert in the belly with his sword so that he died at once.
The justices remanded him to prison, 'et loquendum est inde
cum domino Rege'.[1] The absence of a pardon in this case could
reasonably be due to the king's taking the view that excessive
force had been used by the swordsman against one armed at
the end of the fray only with a knife and he may not have been
convinced that the sword had been drawn with the sole intent
of cutting the bowstring.

In spite of the ambiguity in the decision to remand to gaol,
or to gaol until . . ., it can be ascertained that very few of the
killers known to have been remanded in this way at the eyre can
have applied for but been denied pardon. Nearly all of them
can be shown either to have fined with the justices and thereupon been released or to have obtained it. In a handful of
cases neither outcome can be proved, but the absence of pardon
is explicable in other ways. In one case, for instance, the
prisoner, Andrew Webster, had been released on bail shortly
before and so it is not unlikely that he was one of those who
did not bother about obtaining pardon; he had strong claims
to have killed in self-defence after having been practically
besieged in his house and then ambushed in the orchard.[2]
Amfrisius de Normannia was presented and remanded at the
eyre in 1274;[3] the killing with which he was charged may have
occurred in the time of Henry III in which event he is likely
to have been allowed to fine for it. A strong case was made out
for him also, as he had been attacked and hemmed in between
the river Thames and a mill. However, it is just possible that
the king rejected a recommendation to pardon him, for although
his assailant, William, had felled him with a hatchet, as he
attempted a second blow the hatchet flew out of his hand, giving
Amfrisius the opportunity to get up and hit him in the back

[1] J.I. 1/1051, m. 27 (1268).
[2] Cal. Close Rolls, 1279–88, 317; J.I. 1/705, m. 11.   [3] J.I. 1/538, m. 16ᵈ.

with his knife. The jurors swore that William was still more infuriated by this and seized and beat him so that he scarcely escaped alive, but the king may have held that he had knifed an unarmed man, and so withheld pardon. In a third case there seems to have been confusion over the prisoner's name, and this may have held up application for pardon until finally it was abandoned in favour of bail.[1]

Remand explicitly *ad gratiam* provides more hope of establishing the king's response, but still similar difficulties arise, especially in considering such remands at gaol deliveries where, as already mentioned, prisoners were very apt not to sue out their pardons. The same inertia seems to have affected prisoners remanded in this way by justices of oyer and terminer. As general eyres were coming to be held at longer and longer intervals there was even less need to worry about being able to produce a pardon there later on. Thus it would be unprofitable to examine in detail the remands by commissioners of either sort which did not result in pardon. Most of them can be attributed to the prisoners' own failure to take any action or to their preference for bail. However, in some of these cases the king is known to have sent for the record and on receiving it to have ordered bail instead of granting pardon,[2] and in some it is clear that he was dissatisfied with the record, since he asked for further details. If on receiving them he was still unconvinced that pardon was in order the course of least resistance was to leave it to some future, increasingly hypothetical eyre to determine the merits of the case, and in the meantime release the prisoner on bail. The king's motive can only be surmised, but the evidence shows that the grant of bail, though rather imprudent, was not unlikely in these circumstances. Thus the first of the verdicts on John Tubbe, remanded *ad gratiam*

---

[1] At the Wiltshire eyre in 1289, John Rochel was found to have killed John Snel that same year in self-defence, and was remitted to prison (J.I. 1/1013, m. 18). No pardon has been found for him, but in 1292 Reginald de Burne was granted bail after justices of gaol delivery at Winchester had reported that he slew John Snel in self-defence (*Cal. Close Rolls, 1288–96*, 222). According to the account given at the eyre in 1289, which shows that the killer had fled and been cornered by Snel, two different men cannot both have killed him in self-defence, and it seems possible that a mistake was made over the slayer's name. This confusion may account for the absence of a pardon. On the other hand, of course, two men called John Snel may conceivably have been killed in counties of the same circuit within two or three years of each other.

[2] See above, p. 51.

at a gaol delivery, was deemed insufficient and not in due form. The king demanded another and proper one. John had been involved in a brawl in which Mariota Uppehille had intervened, trying to settle the quarrel, and he had struck her on the head accidentally 'per quandam retractionem cuiusdam baculi'.[1] The king may well have been perplexed by this account; at any rate he only ordered John's release on bail.[2] This was a case of the type the justices were apt to treat with a leniency which seems excessive in contrast to their severity to accidental killing when the slayer was not engaged in any unlawful activity.[3] The king was perhaps partly aware of the unwisdom of this, but failed to insist on a sterner policy. Allowing only bail might demonstrate his disquiet, while throwing the responsibility for further consideration of the case back on to his justices.

Again, a case might be of an unprecedented type, presenting the sort of problem which really did call for his discretionary powers. It was precisely because these cases must crop up from time to time that the prerogative of mercy was essential. They challenged the king to show wisdom and equity when the ordinary rules were inapplicable. Such a problem arose over killing in resisting arrest. The man, especially the official, who killed someone who resisted when he tried to attach him, or who became violent when asked for a pledge, thoroughly deserved pardon. But what if the matter went the other way, and the culprit in trying to escape was threatened with such violence that he killed his would-be captor in order to save his own life? The answer was far from obvious. Much would depend on the gravity or triviality of the original offence, and the degree of force used. Robert de la Nasshe, for example, tried to attach William le Monek to appear in his lord's court to answer for some trespass. William fled to the sea-shore and into his boat which was moored there; Robert pursued him into the boat with drawn sword, intending to kill him, and William hit him on the head with an oar. The jury at the gaol delivery said this had been in self-defence and he was remanded 'donec, etc.'[4] The discrepancy of the weapons should have told strongly in his favour. Yet as he was to blame for running

---

[1] C. 47/55/6, nos. 34–6.
[2] Cal. Close Rolls, 1296–1302, 25.　　　　　　　　　[3] See above, p. 98.
[4] C. 47/55/6, nos. 39, 40. This abbreviation here almost certainly means 'till he gets pardon'.

away in the first place it is easy to see why he was not granted pardon. The king's order to release him on bail until the first assize looks like a convenient way of avoiding the issue.[1] He had been given an opportunity to show the value of his prerogative but shirked exercising it when it involved a difficult question of principle and policy-making.

It remains to consider the fate of those remanded *ad gratiam* at the general eyre. In these cases a prompt and final decision might be expected from the king. While he might play for time when a prisoner had been remanded at a gaol delivery, releasing him on bail until the next eyre, since it could be argued that the greater authority of the justices in eyre fitted them to give a second opinion, to release on bail a prisoner who had been remanded at the eyre itself was nonsensical, especially when eyres were becoming infrequent and, as it turned out, on the point of disappearing. Yet this is what Edward I did in 1290 to John the tailor of Burbach, who had been so remanded the year before.[2] The case presented difficulties.[3] According to the verdict John had found two girls playing foolishly and attempted to punish them. John Giffard was indignant at this and went for him with his staff, chasing him from place to place and finally into the girls' house, where he saw a sword in a corner and picked it up, to hold it out between himself and Giffard, who ran on it without his striking out at him; whatever he did, said the jury, he did in self-defence and to escape death. The use of a sword against an assailant armed only with a staff was of course inexcusable, but then John of Burbach was said not to have wielded it actively; some juries would have described Giffard's death as accidental. Edward may have been in a quandary and taken refuge in the entirely inappropriate grant of bail. On the other hand, this seems so preposterous that it may be that John himself had asked only for bail. Fifteen years later he applied for pardon and Edward granted it on the record of the same eyre.[4]

[1] *Cal. Close Rolls, 1296–1302*, 523.

[2] See J.I. 1/1013, m. 16ᵈ; *Cal. Close Rolls, 1288–96*, 82.

[3] According to the presentment, hue had been raised against John de Burbach, and the victim had responded to it and was trying to attach him. The verdict as recorded did not mention this. The record including the presentment was sent to the king at this time (C. 47/84/10, no. 262). If he studied it, he may have realized that this constituted a special problem. His failure to solve it now left him unprepared to deal with Monek 12 years later.

[4] *Cal. Pat. Rolls, 1301–7*, 317.

Whatever the explanation, this case was exceptional. Nearly all those remanded *ad gratiam* at the eyre got pardon. Some ninety cases of this sort have been found; in all but nine[1] it was duly granted; in others it may have been so, for the general considerations apply here too, such as the possible non-enrolment of the pardons, or failure to identify the enrolments; allowance must also be made for the possibility of a prisoner's dying before he could secure pardon.[2] The small group of those not known to have secured pardon falls into two sub-groups. Five of the prisoners who have not been identified on the patent rolls as being granted pardon may be recognized elsewhere on the close rolls or returns to inquisitions, seeking or obtaining bail because they had killed in self-defence, while a sixth had been remanded, probably at a gaol delivery, for the same reason.[3] Whilst it would be rash to assume that none of them attempted to sue out pardon, it is very probable that most of them did not bother to do so, having already discovered from experience that they could get along well enough without it. This is a far more likely explanation than the king's refusal to grant it after two independent verdicts had found the killings excusable. It certainly can hardly be a coincidence that so many of those not known to have got pardon had already been in a position which is known in other cases to have induced a feeling of indifference to the need for it. The three other cases represent a very small proportion of those remanded *ad gratiam*, but it will be necessary to scrutinize them in detail before concluding that the king turned down three or four per cent of the known recommendations to his grace from justices in eyre.

---

[1] Or ten if one includes a case of slaying during the civil war (J.I. 1/538, m. 18) where the slayer was needlessly remanded; but it may be assumed that this was realized and the order revoked.

[2] This is known to have happened in some cases, e.g. J.I. 1/376, m. 55^d, J.I. 1/543, m. 60, but these have been omitted from the count.

[3] The cases are those of Thomas de Fauldon, bailed after an inquisition held by the sheriff had found self-defence (*Cal. Close Rolls, 1288–96*, 241; cf. J.I. 1/653, m. 12); John de Salenho and Thomas le Fraunceys, both bailed after the same verdicts at inquisitions *de odio et atia* (*Cal. Close Rolls, 1279–88*, 403; ibid., *1272–9*, 214; cf. C. 144/26, no. 9 and C. 144/13, no. 2; J.I. 1/11, m. 27, J.I. 1/497, m. 53^d which shows clearly that le Fraunceys had not obtained pardon); Ralph Smith, Simon le Pestur, both bailed after verdicts of self-defence at gaol deliveries (*Cal. Close Rolls 1279–88*, 167; ibid. *1288–96*, 60; J.I. 1/457 m. 36; J.I. 1/1098, m. 38) and Geoffrey de Assfeud who had been found on another occasion to have killed in self-defence; probably this had also been at a gaol delivery (J.I. 1/829, m. 51).

One case was described as slaying in self-defence, but the victim was a felon, found by night within a close stealing corn. The owner raised the hue on him and was attacked by him with a knife; he defended himself with his staff, breaking the thief's leg, so that he died next day.[1] This clearly was on the borderline with justifiable homicide. The discrepancy of weapons should have provided an argument in favour of the slayer: he certainly had not used excessive force. There was good reason to doubt whether pardon was necessary and here again it is likely that the justices revoked the remand *ad gratiam* and let him fine or go quit. It is inconceivable that the king would have refused pardon if he had been approached.

The last two cases raise more interesting possibilities. Neither was a homicide in self-defence or by accident. In one, a coroner's inquest had found a man guilty of killing a woman. A relative of the victim and two or three others, perhaps including the coroner, then compelled a certain Maurice the Scot to behead the slayer. Maurice was tried for his death and admitted that he had beheaded him, but said that he had been forced to do so by beating and ill treatment and threats that he himself would otherwise be killed. The jury stated that he had not slain him feloniously, but had been made to kill him by others as a felon against the king.[2] This occurred in Tyndale and the custom of the border helps to explain how such a thing could happen. The justices in eyre were far from recognizing its legality, but they remanded Maurice to prison to await the king's grace. No pardon has been found for him. In the Cambridgeshire eyre of 1285 a remarkable story was related: William de la Lutte was killed by unknown malefactors. He was working in the field with two labourers, spreading manure, when strangers approached him and asked the way to Swaffham. His reply, 'vos estis in regia via versus ibi et quia non potestis deviare', evidently did not satisfy them for they asked if one of the labourers might go with them until they could be sure of finding it. William refused and they went on, but presently came back and went for him with a hatchet, hitting him on the head and felling him to the ground. And afterwards they compelled one of the labourers, Walter son of Elyonore, 'per vim et compulsionem' to cut off William's head with the hatchet.

---

[1] J.I. 1/117, m. 74 (J. Jory taken for death of H. Dounman).
[2] J.I. 1/657, m. 12 (1293).

They then made off, leaving both the labourers bound.[1] The justices ordered that Walter be detained 'ad expectandam gratiam domini Regis', but again no pardon had been found. It is not clear whether William was already dead when he decapitated him; if they understood that he was the justices may have changed their minds and let Walter go quit.[2] But the similarity between these two cases may be significant. Both Maurice and Walter had been, or claimed to have been, coerced into beheading their victims. Maurice had the additional point in his favour that he had beheaded a felon against whom a verdict had been given at least at the coroner's inquest, but this was not enough to justify the execution. Both cases, then, raised the very important question whether compulsion could be accepted, if not as a defence, at least as a mitigating factor. Now, apart from the case of a wife acting under the authority of her husband, compulsion was not to be admitted later on as a defence for a criminal action in time of peace. It would have endangered a principle of great importance if the king had shown himself too ready to grant pardon to those who killed under threats or even actual violence to themselves. The justices may have failed to appreciate this when they remanded *ad gratiam*, but it is possible that the king, or members of his council, had grasped the principle and that pardon was deliberately withheld for fear of weakening its force.

There are, then, remarkably few cases in which the king seems likely to have decided against pardon when his justices thought it appropriate, but since there are some the question arises, what action did he then take, if any? The answer appears to be, none. No evidence has been found of his ordering the execution of a prisoner whom he declined to pardon.[3] Apparently, he did not desire to order immediate execution even if he could not bring himself to pardon. The slayer may simply have been left in prison, his petition unanswered, to await the

---

[1] J.I. 1/86, m. 44.

[2] The list of estreats is included in this roll. It contains no mention of any fine payable by Walter, so that the justices cannot have accepted one instead of insisting on his need of pardon.

[3] This lack of evidence may conceivably be due to a peculiar difficulty in conveying such an order in writing. Canon Law forbade clerks to pronounce the death sentence, or take any share in deciding upon it; they were even prohibited from transmitting it in writing. See *Decretals*, Lib. iii, tit. 50, c. 9. But it was assumed here that princes would have secular scribes available to write the letters ordering execution.

next eyre, when in theory he would be liable to be found guilty and hanged. But if any prisoner actually suffered this fate after an abortive remand *ad gratiam* the later eyre rolls seem to be silent on the earlier episode. When a previous remand was mentioned and no pardon produced the justices, so far as the surviving rolls show, remanded again. Nor do they seem to have inquired whether an unsuccessful application had been made to the king for pardon. There is no reason to suppose that such persons were eventually executed; if they were the whole business of the earlier remand would seem to have been suppressed. Together with prisoners who failed to apply for pardon or whose application went astray, they are likely to have remained in prison until they died or escaped, or were allowed to go after the next eyre. It is not unlikely, indeed, that the king was content to punish them by leaving them in prison for an indefinite period.

That he refrained from giving any instructions about them as a matter of policy is suggested by one or two cases in which a second petition for pardon succeeded long after the first had failed to produce any result. It may be that the petitioner had purged his guilt by a long spell in gaol and the king was satisfied with this punishment since the slaying, if not in his view a routine case of excusable homicide, had been in extenuating circumstances. There were, after all, degrees of culpability lying beween the most heinous and clearly excusable killing, however unwilling common law was to admit them. There was a delay of twelve years before Elias, son of Abel ad aquam was pardoned. He and his comrade, John de Acle, had deliberately gone to the house of an old enemy of his, Benedict le Clerk, intending to remove the inn sign; Benedict had come out and in trying to hit him with a hatchet, Elias had accidentally struck John, who died of the wound four days later. Elias was found to have killed him by mischance and was committed to prison to await the king's grace.[1] And there he seems to have remained from 1287 to 1299, when he was at last pardoned on the grounds that the justices last in eyre had found that he had killed by accident.[2] Now it has been seen that this type of slaying was regularly regarded as accidental when the intended

---

[1] J.I. 1/11, m. 27ᵈ.
[2] *Cal. Pat. Rolls, 1292–1301*, 403. The pardon stated that Elias was in Bedford gaol.

K

action was not felonious, sometimes even when it might have been considered so, but that Bracton would have objected to such a view of transferred intent. Thus it is tempting to see in this delay evidence of an attempt by the king or his counsellors to treat this offence with the severity it deserved, and perhaps to put a stop to the lax classification of similar cases as misadventures. But all this is the merest conjecture. Elias may not have tried to sue out his pardon earlier, or his application may have gone astray. It is uncertain, therefore, if the king definitely decided in any of these cases to inflict some form of punishment. If he hesitated to pardon he may also have deferred decision on an alternative course of action, and in the event allowed the whole matter to go by default. The king, in short, may have found it just as hard to reach a decision in a difficult and unusual case as the justices did.[1] This would have the result that the slayer would probably remain for a time, possibly a long time, in prison, with the added anguish of uncertainty as to his fate at the hands of the king. Thus the very desire to give an equitable decision—or, more precisely, not to give an inequitable one—combined with failure to review cases left over in this way aggravated the lot of some who merited, at most, some moderate punishment.

The treatment of non-felonious homicide in general was rendered far harsher than it need have been, granted even the over-harsh requirement of pardon for excusable slaying, by similar uncertainty, ambiguity, and vacillation at all levels. Some people at least had qualms about it which resulted in more positive action. The uneasiness of many of the justices at the inequitable and ill-ordered system they were required to administer is reflected in their attitude to those who had fled from justice, in relation to whom they were ready to assume greater discretionary powers.

---

[1] Grants of bail instead of pardon may sometimes have been due to his reluctance to reach a final decision. See above, p. 123.

V

METICULOSI AND FUGITIVES FOR
EXCUSABLE HOMICIDE

MOST of the people who killed in self-defence or accidentally, fled. Some thought better of it and came back
to stand their trial. Some went to the king to seek pardon.
Others took sanctuary and most of these abjured the realm,
though some came out of sanctuary and appeared in court.
Some of the fugitives were outlawed at once in the county
court on the appeal of the victim's next of kin. The rest could
expect to be put in exigent at the eyre and subsequently exacted and outlawed in the county court unless they surrendered
there. Others fled *pre timore* although they were in no way
responsible for a death, or had killed with justification, and
they might also apply for pardon, even though they were in no
real need of it.

There can be no doubt that many people—Bracton's *meticulosi*—fled in panic when they were in no way implicated in
a crime. That entirely innocent persons should take to their
heels just because they had been present at a sudden death
shows a disquieting lack of confidence in the course of justice,
although some allowance should be made here for superstitious
horror and an unfounded sense of involvement. Yet, when it
is observed that some men, including officials, who had killed
justifiably also fled, it becomes evident that there was great
doubt and confusion in people's minds as to the limits of criminal
liability for homicide, the need for and the prospect of obtaining pardon. Considering the uncertainties surrounding the
treatment of justifiable and even excusable homicide by the
king's justices at the eyre it is not surprising that the public
at large was ignorant just where the boundaries lay. It required
not only a cool nerve but an optimistic temperament as well to
stand one's ground and face trial. For those who could afford
it an immediate approach to the king was the surest and
quickest way to end an anxious situation. Thus many played

for safety and withdrew while they procured an inquisition. Their pardons were obtained as a precaution, often quite unnecessarily. Similarly, fugitives who had already been outlawed might obtain pardon, which in their case was necessary so far as outlawry itself was concerned, but for homicides which in themselves would not have necessitated it. The system of pardoning would appear even sterner and more irrational than it was if these cases were taken to illustrate the official view of liability for homicide. But they are worth noting as illustrations of the social effects of the system and the hardship and anxiety caused to innocent persons.

A fair number of men who had killed felons who resisted arrest secured pardons as a precaution, but most of them are not known to have fled.[1] Among them was a deputy-keeper of the peace.[2] The constable of Bristol Castle obtained pardon for beheading a prisoner who had broken gaol and been retaken,[3] as did a gaoler for the death of a prisoner suspected of larceny, 'through the severity and grievousness' of his prison, the victim having been placed in the stocks with a thick iron collar round his neck and left until the following day when he was found to be dead.[4] In these two cases there was some possibility that the court would have found that the officers had exceeded their powers, and the fact that they were sensible to this points to one merit in the system. Again, whilst men who had taken part in a fatal brawl, but who had not themselves struck the victim any mortal blow, were not deemed guilty of homicide[5] they might have reasonable doubts as to a verdict at the eyre finding that they had not struck him in this way. In these circumstances it was only prudent to withdraw and see what sort of verdict could be obtained by a special inquisition, or to seek pardon without an inquisition. But some of the cases of fleeing *pre timore* show astonishing sensitivity. A genuine sense of moral guilt must surely account for the flight of two clerks who had forcibly ejected a poor woman, a stranger, from a hospital, with the result that she died during the next night from debility and the cold.[6] Other cases show

---

[1] e.g. *Cal. Pat. Rolls, 1232–47*, 379 (the grantee was an outlaw); ibid., *1266–72*, 7, 14, 540; ibid., *1272–81*, 154; *Cal. Inquisitions Misc.* i, no. 1050.

[2] *Cal. Pat. Rolls, 1266–72*, 265.

[3] Ibid., *1281–92*, 152; cf. *Close Rolls, 1227–31*, 4.

[4] *Cal. Pat. Rolls, 1247–58*, 451; *Cal. Inquisitions Misc.* i, no. 2089.

[5] See above, p. 99. [6] J.I. 1/568, m. 37ᵈ.

sheer panic or stupidity. Thus in 1269 Richard de Baylloill took sanctuary for the death of John le Enveyse of Huntingdon; an inquisition found that as he was crossing a bridge he met John, who was carrying a truss of straw; Richard knocked against the truss so that it fell into the water; John went down into the river to try to save it, and was accidentally drowned.[1] Richard obtained pardon for his panic flight to the church; he had no need of it for the death. There was slightly more reason for the alarm felt by Richard de Troente, for although innocent, he was accused of the death of Hugh de la Forreste and so 'he ran away in his simplicity' and was outlawed;[2] but as he was a chaplain and so qualified for benefit of clergy he had little to fear, even if brought to trial. Some people fled as a precaution in case they were named as suspects at the coroner's inquest or presented in the hundred court or at the sheriff's tourn, or appealed, but, when it was apparent that no charge was being preferred against them, sought the king's permission to return to the peace.[3]

Whilst many fugitives for homicide secured pardon before the next session of the eyre, some quickly, some not until after they had been outlawed, a great many are not known to have sought it; probably they were too ignorant or too poor or both. Their flight and its presumed cause would be presented to the

---

[1] *Cal. Pat. Rolls, 1266–72*, 333. [2] Ibid. 348.
[3] e.g. *Close Rolls, 1261–4*, 179–80, where an inquisition was ordered to discover whether the fugitives were as innocent as they claimed. It was hardly safe to rely on the verdict at the coroner's inquest alone, for to judge by the few cases from this period where comparison with the eyre roll is possible such verdicts tended to find a death natural or purely accidental which later, as rumours spread about someone who had been present, were presented as homicide. In one such case feeling against a fugitive had clearly hardened by the time of the eyre. At the coroner's inquest the verdict had been that although Walter de Hardwyk had knocked down Gilbert Berenger the latter had died of ague not as a result of the blow. But at the eyre it was said that the two had struggled together and Walter felled him so that he was wounded in the head and died of the wound a week later. Walter was accordingly placed in exigent. See J.I. 1/10, m. 36; R. F. Hunnisett, *Beds. Coroner's Rolls*, no. 115. Similarly opinion might harden against those who had killed in self-defence; cf. ibid., no. 75: Gerleys, the groom of Nicholas Peyvere, was presented at the eyre for the slaying of William of Kendal; he was put in exigent, and there is no hint on the eyre roll that there might have been mitigating circumstances. But the verdict at the coroner's inquest had been very emphatic that the slaying had been in self-defence. According to this, the groom had found William threatening the rector of the church and also his own master; William at once assaulted him and struck him on the left arm with a drawn sword and then pursued him intending to kill him; it was only when he found that he could not escape that he turned and struck him with a barbed arrow through the heart.

justices and they were then likely to be placed in exigent. The circumstances of a death might or might not be described, but if the jurors believed the fugitive was in no way responsible they seem generally to have said so, and in this event the justices would not order outlawry but announce that the fugitive might return. It was unusual for anyone who was presented as having killed entirely justifiably to remain a fugitive up to the time of the eyre, but one example of this may be quoted: a man had shot a murderer as he fled refusing to surrender; the justices said the fugitive might return, but as he later fined with them for half a mark to return to the peace he was evidently already in the offing.[1] Some *meticulosi* were still afraid to come before the justices; for instance, people who were present when someone was drowned, in one case falling from a bridge, fled though they had not apparently pushed or even jostled the victims in any way; when the presenting jurors assured the justices of this they would declare that they might come back.[2] There were others whose flight was perhaps prudent, though as it turned out the juries put a favourable interpretation on circumstances which could easily have aroused their suspicion. The fugitive and the deceased might have been struggling together and the survivor might not care to bank on the jurors' regarding the other's death as entirely accidental. Some such mischances were improbable, as when a man tried to hit another but struck himself in the leg instead and died a week later.[3] A wrestling match might or might not be recognized to have been a purely friendly one despite its fatal outcome. Two men wrestled, somewhat imprudently, on the brink of a dyke and both fell in, one being drowned; the fact that the survivor had shared the risk of drowning no doubt helps to explain the jurors' failure to suspect him.[4] When someone died from natural causes not long after having been struck or injured by the fugitive the jurors might assert that the injury had not contributed to the death,[5] though again they could very easily have taken a different view of its effect. So long as they exonerated the fugitive entirely the justices would invite him to return, though his chattels, if he had any, would be

---

[1] J.I. 1/736, m. 37.

[2] e.g. J.I. 1/786, m. 4^d. In one case it was the fugitive who had been assaulted on a bridge and as he escaped from his clutches the assailant fell off it (J.I. 1/409, m. 6).   [3] J.I. 1/775, m. 18.   [4] J.I. 1/87, m. 37.

[5] e.g. J.I. 1/619, m. 65; J.I. 1/872, m. 36^d.

confiscated on account of his flight. In other cases it might still be up to him to seek pardon though the jurors indicated that he had acted excusably.

The jurors must often have found it hard to estimate how far the fugitive had been involved. When a man had been killed in a brawl they would have to try to discover who of those present had been active participants and who innocent bystanders. The latter might not unreasonably fear to be charged with complicity and were apt to flee.[1] But flight and failure to come back before the eyre naturally tended to raise a presumption of guilt, and many innocent men who might have been acquitted or not even indicted if they had stood their ground must have been outlawed because they fled. Similarly, when a slaying would have ranked as justifiable had the slayer appeared in court his flight might raise suspicions of this view of the matter and the justices place him in exigent,[2] for while genuinely justifiable slaying did not entail outlawry, a fugitive who had killed on unfounded suspicion that his victim was a felon, or who had used excessive force when he could have taken him alive would be outlawed.[3]

The justices did not, then, generally order the outlawry of those who had slain entirely justifiably and fled or others who had fled quite unnecessarily *pre timore*, if they were aware of all the circumstances and the jury was not prompted to set them in the worst light just because of the flight from justice. In intention, at least, the treatment of the *meticulosi* was not altogether unreasonable, and it does not seem to have involved any notion of their being blameworthy except on account of their flight. The punishment for this was no doubt harsh, though not grotesquely so. But there were some grievous disadvantages in the system so far as they were concerned. Firstly, even if the justices declared that they might return, the fugitives

---

[1] e.g. J.I. 1/56, m. 45.

[2] e.g. J.I. 1/829, m. 33, where a thief had been killed as he tried to break into a house.

[3] Fugitives were placed in exigent in the following cases: J.I. 1/85, m. 10, where the fugitive had killed a man he thought was a thief;

J.I. 1/65, m. 45, where a bystander who did not answer when challenged had been killed by a man pursuing thieves;

J.I. 1/376, m. 29^d, where a thief had been killed although he could have been taken alive;

J.I. 1/1043, m. 12^d, where two murderers had been killed by the victim's brother without his raising hue and cry.

might never get to hear of this and so never come home even though it was perfectly safe for them to do so. Secondly, in the absence of the person involved, the jurors might fail to give a full and true account of the circumstances which had led to his or her panic flight, and thus there was no guarantee that innocent persons would not be placed in exigent and eventually outlawed. Thirdly, in cases which raised some doubt, the flight itself might be taken as evidence of a guilty conscience and so just tip the scales.

Accidental slayers tended to flee even though they were not to blame through any special negligence. Most of them needed pardon and some may have preferred to withdraw while application was made for it, rather than face imprisonment and trial, after which, even if things went well, they would still need it. There was more point in withdrawing and obtaining a special inquisition instead of awaiting trial if one had killed in self-defence. This excuse was harder to establish, particularly in the absence of eyewitnesses. There was much to be said for having an inquisition held, especially if the fugitive was still at a safe distance, for if by ill luck it resulted in an adverse verdict he could at least save his skin by withdrawing still further. It came to be appreciated that this gave the fugitives an undue advantage, and for a moment an attempt was made to put an end to the holding of inquisitions while they were still at large.[1] This attempt was abortive. Inquisitions into their homicides continued to be held and pardons for outlaws and fugitives continued to be obtainable by their friends prior to their surrender. The wording of the writs ordering inquisitions has already been discussed, and the general criteria for pardon were the same as when prisoners were brought before the justices. If anything, the verdicts were more likely to be favourable than those given at the eyre, and although the king's attitude to them was a little more sceptical, they afforded a fairly reliable way of obtaining pardon although many excusable slayers did not obtain it in this way before the next eyre.

In theory, absentees who had fled after killing in self-defence or by accident should have been put in exigent on the order of the itinerant justices if they had not already been outlawed through an appeal. In this respect, however, the harshness of the system was considerably mitigated, especially for those

[1] See below, p. 281.

who had slain by misadventure, and for some time there was a tendency for the justices to show increasing discretion in refraining from putting the fugitives in exigent. It occasions no surprise to find that the early examples of this occurred chiefly in the treatment of road accidents. At the eyre in 1228 it was reported that the driver of a cart which had run over a girl had fled; the victim's mother did not wish to prosecute and said he was not guilty; the jury agreed with this, so the justices said that he might return if he so desired, but must find pledges to stand to right if anyone should wish to speak against him; the value of the cart was given as deodand to a neighbouring monastery.[1] In 1227, the justices ordered, not that two fugitives should be exacted, but that they should be attached, if they were found or came home, to stand to right. This would seem to be an indirect way of suggesting that it would be safe enough for them to return. One was concerned in a wrestling, the other in a riding accident.[2] But these were special cases and these fugitives could perhaps have been acquitted had they stood their trial. It was doubtful whether the justices could properly act in this way if the fugitive had killed by a mischance of another type,[3] but consultation as to the need to outlaw was sometimes held. It was very rare with colleagues but there is an apparent example of this from 1232.[4] Rather more often, the justices decided to consult the king. In the same year, in reply to their inquiry, he ordered justices in eyre not to promulgate outlawry against a man who had killed by mischance, but to let him be quit so far as the king was concerned.[5] It is noticeable that the eyre rolls generally show that they first ordered that the fugitive be placed in exigent and then decided to consult the king to see if he thought it necessary for the process of outlawry to be completed.[6] However,

[1] J.I. 1/54, m. 15.

[2] J.I. 1/358, m. 19^d; ibid. m. 16^d. The death as a result of wrestling was described as misadventure, not felony, and may not have been attributed to the survivor in any way.

[3] They continued to invite fugitives on account of fatal road accidents to return. See J.I. 1/37, m. 34^d; J.I. 1/455, m. 13^d; J.I. 1/954, m. 56^d; J.I. 1/1109, m. 21 (driving accidents); J.I. 1/1043, m. 1^d (riding).

[4] J.I. 1/62, m. 7.

[5] *Close Rolls, 1231–4*, 83. For other consultations see *Northumberland Assize Rolls*, Surtees Soc. lxxxviii. 111; J.I. 1/703, mm. 3, 7; J.I. 1/1109, mm. 25^d and 19^d, where a barber had dropped a razor on a customer's foot causing his death a month later.

[6] e.g. J.I. 1/734, m. 26^d; J.I. 1/300^c, m. 24.

they might decide to consult him and order that 'utlagaria interim ponatur in respectum',[1] or that the fugitive should be placed in exigent 'nisi dominus rex, etc.'[2] which implies they meant to consult him. Sometimes there is no indication of this intention except a marginal 'loquendum' against the order to exact,[3] and this suggests that there may have been a few other cases in which the king was consulted on the need for outlawry, though the surviving eyre rolls failed to note this.

Under Henry III the justices seldom extended the invitation to return without consulting him save to *meticulosi* and those who had fled after fatal road accidents. It was not until the time of Edward I that acting on their own authority they invited the return of fugitives who had fled on account of all sorts of fatal accidents. The first two decades of his reign saw a dwindling of the number of consultations with him and a corresponding expansion of independent action, especially when the fatalities had occurred in the more obvious types of misadventure, as in shooting,[4] at play,[5] in wrestling,[6] felling trees,[7] slaughtering animals,[8] hurling objects at birds or beasts.[9] At this time Edward does not seem to have objected to their using their own discretion in this matter, but there was a change in policy. In 1292 the justices were less confident in their power, or were actually forbidden to act in this way. Twice on the Lancashire eyre roll of this year the decision to allow return was noted and then deleted and the order to exact and outlaw or waive substituted;[10] both cases were the most obvious accidents. This unfortunate reversal of a sensible and humane trend was no doubt connected with the efforts to tighten up the business of pardoning at this juncture.[11]

The cases just listed were all ones which could properly be treated with some leniency, yet which were normally held to require pardon if the person involved appeared to stand his trial. The justices' declaration 'let him return if he will' gives no

---

[1] J.I. 1/1043, m. 16d.   [2] J.I. 1/872, m. 35.

[3] e.g. J.I. 1/56, m. 39. But it is not expressly stated here that the consultation was to be with the king himself.

[4] e.g. J.I. 1/981, m. 20d; J.I. 1/11, mm. 24d, 27d; J.I. 1/457, mm. 42d, 48d.

[5] e.g. J.I. 1/280, m. 1d; J.I. 1/457, m. 47d; J.I. 1/486, m. 37; *Northumberland Assize Rolls*, 362.

[6] e.g. ibid. 323, 348; J.I. 1/280, m. 6; J.I. 1/457, m. 38d; J.I. 1/1004, m. 79d.

[7] e.g. J.I. 1/131, m. 3; J.I 1/210, m. 31.   [8] J.I. 1/486, m. 11.

[9] *Northumberland Assize Rolls*, 343.   [10] J.I. 1/409, mm. 20d, 21.

[11] See below, p. 289.

indication of what was to happen if he did so, whether he had now to sue out pardon, or find pledges to stand to right at the next eyre, or needed to do nothing at all. When justices consulted the king it seems obvious that if he agreed that the fugitive might come back this would obviate any need for formal pardon. It would appear doubtful whether pardon was necessary either when the justices themselves declared simply that the fugitive could return. Maitland, however, considered that it was. He remarked that 'when a presentment of homicide by misadventure is made against a man who has fled, the roll sometimes says that he may come back if he will, though his chattels are forfeited; we do not think that this dispenses him from the necessity of procuring a pardon. He has not been tried and therefore has not been acquitted.'[1] This is a most reasonable inference, but there are grounds for doubting whether consistency and logic governed practice here. No case has been discovered of a fugitive obtaining a pardon after returning home as a result of the itinerant justices' saying he might do so.[2] This would imply either that the invitation to return was an empty gesture as fugitives never got to hear of it, or that those who responded to it did not obtain the king's pardon. The first explanation is not at all plausible. No doubt many fugitives lost touch with their friends and families and some of those who were not outlawed because they were deemed to have killed unintentionally never got to know of the justices' decision. But it is all too evident that a great many fugitives did not lose touch, and those with a clear conscience might be expected to make special efforts to find out what treatment was being accorded them *in absentia*. It is true that the accidental slayers who fled were likely to be particularly panicky persons. But for some flight was a calculated policy and among the fugitives, it may be suspected, there were many who withdrew only when the eyre was imminent, and then not without making arrangements for news of the decision to reach them. It would be astonishing if none of those invited to return did so, and thus the absence of pardons for men known to have been treated in this way is very significant, if negative evidence.

[1] *Hist. Eng. Law*, ii. 479, n. 4.
[2] There is an example of a pardon being granted (*Cal. Pat. Rolls, 1292–1301*, 4) to a man the justices said might return after a fatal accident, but the pardon was not obtained as a result of this statement. See J.I. 1/739, mm. 72, 92^d.

In one or two instances there is more positive evidence that the fugitive who was invited to return needed no pardon if he did so. Friends might take action on his behalf at the eyre and in one case the sheriff himself intervened. The justices had ordered that the fugitive be placed in exigent, but the sheriff of Yorkshire came and offered the king 2 marks to allow him to return to the peace. This sum was accepted, since it was found that the killing had been by misadventure not by malice, and the entry concludes: 'Ideo nihil de utlagaria. Ideo eat quietus.'[1] This seem to exclude any idea of his still needing a pardon. Justifiable slayers and *meticulosi* who were still fugitives were assured they might return, but only rarely were they said to be quit.[2] Usually, there was nothing to distinguish the invitation to them from that to accidental homicides. The former certainly did not require pardon; if the latter did require it, it is incredible that the justices should have given no indication of this, all the more incredible, indeed, because it was often difficult to draw a dividing line between the three categories. Occasionally under Edward I, the justices ordered the sheriff to arrest a fugitive who was said to have killed by accident and to keep him in prison to await the king's grace.[3] This singling out of some cases and specifying the need for pardon suggests again that normally fugitives who were allowed to return did not need this. The order to arrest them probably indicates that they were known to be at large in the neighbourhood, or at least believed to be so. The cases in question were not particularly serious ones and it is, in fact, rather an anomaly that these persons should require pardon if fugitives who were not yet within reach of the law did not. Only three or four rolls record such treatment, so it may have been due to some judicial idiosyncrasy. Possibly, the order was given through confusion

---

[1] J.I. 1/1109, 15ᵈ.   [2] There is one example of this, J.I. 1/996, m. 28.
[3] e.g. J.I. 1/486, m. 2: shooting through a window at a sparrow a servant hit a passer-by in the face; as this was by accident not felony the sheriff was ordered to arrest him and keep him safely to await the king's pardon; ibid., m. 15ᵈ: shooting at a target, the reeve's son hit a man who got in the way; the same order was given; his chattels were confiscated and the king was to have year and waste in his land; J.I. 1/664, m. 37: a man was fatally crushed while wrestling; the jurors said this had been in play; ibid., m. 45: a man shot at a wild bull; another man crossed between them as the arrow was in flight and received its blow. There is a similar case on J.I. 1/210, m. 32ᵈ; cf. J.I. 1/1004, m. 88ᵈ, where playing with his bow a man had hit a woman; it was testified that he was in the district and so he was ordered to be arrested, but there is no reference here to his awaiting pardon.

with the treatment of men who had killed in self-defence.[1] In
one case, at least, an order to arrest was rescinded because
it was realized that it was inappropriate.[2]

On the whole it appears most improbable that fugitive
accidental slayers required pardon if the justices simply declared
that they might return. It has already been remarked that in
no such instance is a pardon known to have been granted after
the eyre. Such a requirement could no doubt have been safely
disregarded until the next eyre approached. Since they had
not been outlawed and had been invited to come home they
were in no danger till then. If they appeared before the justices
they would doubtless now be remanded *ad gratiam*, but again
no case of this has been discovered. Indeed, no evidence has
emerged to suggest that the justices at subsequent eyres made
any inquiry about them. This is all the more significant since
they did check the cases of fugitives who were ordered to be
put under pledge if they came back.[3]

It was, then, within the discretion of the justices not to order
the outlawry of fugitives who had slain by misadventure, and
they used this discretion fairly often as the thirteenth century
advanced until they were checked in 1292. But it would give an
utterly false picture of the treatment of such killers if the cases
in which they failed to use it were not also surveyed. Whereas
they would not knowingly place undoubtedly justifiable slayers
and *meticulosi* in exigent, they often did not hesitate to do this
to those who were reported by the presenting jurors to have
killed accidentally. Moreover, with the usual exception of
road accidents, the main types of misadventure which led to
this treatment were the familiar ones: injuring or wounding
with a knife or other implement in the course of play,[4] or in
wrestling,[5] even in one case when the victim fell on his own
knife,[6] striking with a scythe while mowing,[7] striking with
missiles hurled at animals,[8] with knives or stones tossed about

[1] See below, p. 144.

[2] J.I. 1/65, m. 36^{d}.

[3] e.g. J.I. 1/1043, m. 20^{d}.

[4] e.g. J.I. 1/38, m. 33^{d}; J.I. 1/60, m. 22; J.I. 1/131, m. 7; J.I. 1/497, m. 31^{d};
J.I. 1/568, m. 26; J.I. 1/780, m. 23; J.I. 1/1060, m. 5.

[5] e.g. J.I. 1/111, m. 32^{d}.

[6] J.I. 1/176, m. 30.

[7] e.g. J.I. 1/40, m. 19; cf. J.I. 1/60, m. 22; J.I. 1/776, m. 27^{d}.

[8] e.g. J.I. 1/181, m. 18^{d}; J.I. 1/210, m. 28^{d}; J.I. 1/455, m. 11^{d}; J.I. 1/736, m. 43;
J.I. 1/775, m. 18; J.I. 1/954, m. 53; J.I. 1/1109, m. 2^{d}.

with no particular objective,[1] shooting,[2] scalding by overturning pots of boiling water.[3] The circumstances described by the jury might indicate that there had been no negligence and indeed no responsibility whatever; for example, two men wrestled; one was overcome with heat and sickness and died; the other fled and the justices ordered that he be exacted and outlawed.[4] They did so again when a sudden gust of wind had carried an arrow beyond the target and it had struck a man sitting nearby.[5]

It does not follow that the county courts outlawed all the fugitives whom the justices ordered them to exact. It has already been suggested that a decision to consult the king after all may sometimes have failed to be noted on the extant eyre rolls. But it is unlikely that this happened in a great many cases. On the other hand the fugitive might now surrender, or his friends might approach the king before the process of outlawry was completed, if they learnt that his case had been presented as an accidental slaying, and it is even possible that the justices themselves sometimes recommended mercy after ordering outlawry. In some cases, at least, pardon was promptly granted to fugitives on their testimony that the killing had been accidental, though there is no evidence to suggest that they had taken the initiative in drawing the king's attention to the matter.[6] But even allowing for some concealed cases of leniency on the part of the justices towards fugitives, it is clear that many who were stated to have slain by accident were outlawed and never obtained pardon. None has been found in the cases quoted in the last paragraph.

Some *meticulosi* and accidental slayers took sanctuary and

---

[1] e.g. J.I. 1/802, m. 47; J.I. 1/1060, m. 5.

[2] e.g. J.I. 1/238, m. 57[d]; J.I. 1/359, m. 33[d]; J.I. 1/457, m. 35[d]; J.I. 1/543, m. 58[d]; J.I. 1/575, m. 14; J.I. 1/653, m. 11; J.I. 1/705, mm. 18, 25; J.I. 1/804, m. 65; J.I. 1/829, m. 11[d]; J.I. 1/1108, m. 2; *Northumberland Assize Rolls*, 312–13.

[3] e.g. J.I. 1/174, m. 33[d].   [4] J.I. 1/569[A], m. 16.   [5] J.I. 1/575, m. 84[d].

[6] e.g. J.I. 1/371, m. 14, *Cal. Pat. Rolls, 1272–81*, 337; J.I. 1/778, m. 61, where two carpenters were moving planks to pick out ones suitable for a ship they were building and one fell on a boy sitting unseen on the far side of the pile crushing him fatally; as it was proved that the boy was nearer to death and further from life by their action the justices ordered their outlawry; but they were pardoned at once on the justices' record (*Cal. Pat. Rolls, 1247–58*, 485); J.I. 1/912[A], m. 35, *Cal. Pat. Rolls, 1258–66*, 263; J.I. 1/1109, m. 14, *Cal. Pat. Rolls, 1247–58*, 603. In the first and last of these cases the eyre roll contains no reference to accident, but the justices must have been informed of the circumstances since the pardon was granted on their record that the slaying had been accidental.

abjured the realm. Their number does not appear to have been very large, though no doubt the records are sometimes silent about the circumstances of a death when they mention abjuration on its account. It was within the competence of the itinerant justices to annul an abjuration, either on the grounds of some error in the actual proceedings, or because the sanctuary-seeker was innocent and should not have been made to abjure, or because he was under age. Alternatively, they might refer the matter to the king.[1] The killing might have been justifiable and the justices accordingly annul the killer's abjuration, as they did when a man who had killed a fleeing homicide to prevent his reaching sanctuary himself took sanctuary and abjured; he had acted, they pronounced, 'pro pace conservanda' and so should not have been made to do so.[2] Their assessment of culpability was as usual lenient when the abjuration had arisen from a road accident.[3] Although leniency was not entirely confined to this type of accident,[4] there is usually no suggestion of the justices' annulling or getting the king to annul an abjuration however strong the case for pardon would have been.[5] Nearly all the abjurations for accidental slaying which have been noticed were the result of fatalities in games, wrestling, or target practice.

Fugitives who had killed in self-defence were in a very different situation from those who had killed accidentally. It was unlikely that the jurors presenting the fatal outcome of a struggle and the flight of the survivor would declare that he had acted entirely in self-defence. There are many cases in which it may well be conjectured that he had done so, and a great many in which this circumstance could plausibly be alleged if pardon was sought from the king. In many of these the fugitives did in fact later obtain pardon on the grounds of self-defence; others obtained pardons which were probably

[1] e.g. J.I. 1/174, m. 43.   [2] J.I. 1/703, m. 3.   [3] e.g. J.I. 1/915, m. 12.
[4] e.g. J.I. 1/722, m. 10^d; J.I. 1/619, m. 68^d.
[5] They did not do so in the following cases:
J.I. 1/210, m. 28^d: where the victim was brought down in play on a knife;
J.I. 1/232, m. 11^d: a clerk threw a stone in play and it hit a boy in the head;
J.I. 1/562, m. 20^d: the victim was crushed while playing;
J.I. 1/568, m. 26: the victim was wounded by a knife in a scrum in a ball game;
J.I. 1/575, m. 84^d: here for once a wrestler discarded his knife first, but as he threw it away it bounced off a wall and struck a boy;
J.I. 1/619, m. 52^d: an accident while shooting at a target;
J.I. 1/653, m. 19^d: killing in play.

based on the same consideration, though they did not expressly say so. But it is impossible to hazard any guess as to the number who qualified for but failed to obtain pardon. Occasionally, the presenting jurors did mention self-defence, and while no case has been found of the justices simply inviting the fugitive to return, they did sometimes order that he should be taken and should await the king's grace.[1] Generally the man in question appeared before them shortly afterwards armed with the king's pardon, so that there can be no doubt that he had been somewhere within reach.[2] Indeed, in 1281 the justices decided to consult the king about a fugitive who had killed in self-defence, but at the same time, since it was testified that he was lurking in the district, they ordered the sheriff to take him.[3] On only two occasions, both in 1268, has evidence been found of the justices themselves pressing for further information and eliciting the verdict of self-defence from the jurors.[4] In another case, one bordering on justifiable homicide, the jurors themselves appear to have related the events in detail without prompting.[5]

When the jurors were well disposed towards a prisoner they sometimes, as has been seen, declared that he had slain by mischance when self-defence might have been a more appropriate description. This way of representing the slaying may have made little difference to the prisoner who would be remanded if either verdict was accepted, but it could be of real advantage to a fugitive, for it might well dissuade the justices from ordering his exaction and outlawry. In one such case at least they decided to consult the king, who may well have agreed that there was no need to proceed with it.[6]

The attitude to fugitive slayers was, then, in some respects more lenient than that to slayers who were arrested. If they had slain accidentally they were often allowed to return home without having to obtain pardon and a few who had killed in

---

[1] e.g. J.I. 1/664, m. 45[d], where a man who was attacked by a lunatic struck him on the head with a staff in self-defence; cf. J.I. 1/497, m. 26[d].

[2] e.g. J.I. 1/486, mm. 2, 9.

[3] J.I. 1/486, m. 31. C. 47/67/8, no. 316 shows that he later appeared before the justices and was remanded *ad gratiam*. His pardon is recorded, *Cal. Pat. Rolls, 1281–92*, 122.   [4] J.I. 1/1051, m. 10; J.I. 1/998[A], m. 27.

[5] J.I. 1/736, m. 29 (1272).

[6] J.I. 1/703, m. 3. The victim had followed Maurice le Marshal from an inn and given him several blows with a hatchet, then seizing a lance which Maurice was holding he had tried to pull it away and had struck himself on it in the body.

self-defence were not placed in exigent. It may have been felt that they had already suffered by their flight and so might be spared the further burden and expense of applying to the king for mercy. Yet it must be noted that the fugitive was liable to some punishment since his chattels were forfeit to the king, who would also enjoy year, day, and waste in any free tenements he might hold. This penalty was inflicted not only on fugitives who failed to appear in court but also on all those who had fled at any time for the slaying, even though they had thought better of it and returned, whether just in time for the eyre or earlier on. The king, it is true, not infrequently ordered the restitution of the chattels which should have been taken into his hand when the flight from justice first became known. But this additional grace would generally have to be bought and sometimes at something approaching the market value of the chattels. Moreover, he could order their restitution only when their confiscation would have been to his own benefit; if the fugitive's lord enjoyed the franchise of appropriating the chattels of condemned felons and fugitives, then the lord was entitled to them whether the king pardoned him or not, and this right could not be overridden. If the pardoned fugitive had actually been outlawed then he suffered not only forfeiture of chattels but total loss of his free tenements as well. These, after the king had enjoyed his year, day, and waste in them, escheated to the lord and the king could order their restitution only if they were held of him in chief.[1]

---

[1] Bracton, *De Legibus*, f. 132ᵇ. It has been seen (above, p. 33) that many pardons referred vaguely to outlawry if any. This may have been to the advantage of fugitive freeholders who did not know if they had been outlawed or not, for the positive inclusion of outlawry in the pardon for a homicide who had not in fact been outlawed might have disastrous effects, entailing escheat of his land. For example Michael del Fell held land and tenements in chief in Soureby by the courtesy of England of the inheritance of his deceased wife. On his death the bailiff of Soureby, understanding that Nicholas, his son, was a felon and that the property should escheat, held an inquisition in the court of Soureby with 24 jurors; the verdict was that Nicholas had slain William de Pulhou, but had been pardoned by Edward I and had fought for him in Gascony, and been killed there six years before his mother's death. Asked if Nicholas had been outlawed for the homicide, the jurors said no. Then, unfortunately, his daughter and heiress Margaret, thinking it would help her case, produced the charter of pardon which stated that he had been outlawed and that the king pardoned the outlawry. The bailiff thereupon decided that Nicholas could not have inherited and his daughter was equally incapable of inheriting through him. Margaret petitioned the council and the sheriff of Cumberland was asked to inform Edward II if Nicholas had in fact been outlawed. He, too, said that he had not been. See C. 47/94/1.

Forfeiture of chattels was a harsh punishment in many cases, hitting the less wealthy more often than those who could afford to buy them back. The poorest of all were not affected by it, since they had no chattels to be seized. Others may have succeeded in concealing what they had, or carrying everything away with them. The chattels once seized were entrusted to officials or others pending the final decision as to confiscation, and these people might resent any order to restore them to the pardoned fugitives, and accordingly be hostile to the notion of pardon or the invitation to return. The liability to forfeiture of land was particularly prejudicial to the comparatively small number of outlawed freeholders who sought pardon; if the lands were not restored they stood to lose heavily, while the possibility of restitution carried with it the danger that those to whom the king entrusted the lands during his year and day or after escheat to him would have a much stronger vested interest in seeing that he did not grant the pardon, which he might well follow up by restoring the estates.[1] There were, then, some secondary dangers in the liability to forfeiture of land and chattels, although by no means all fugitive slayers were exposed to them. In most cases the actual loss, if any, amounted to no more than a few shillings' worth of goods. The practice of forfeiture, however, was to spread and lead to an altogether unjustifiable change in the view taken of the nature of excusable slaying. It is worth while, therefore, to consider its implications rather more closely.

Forfeiture was a penalty and implied some guilt, but it was imposed for various reasons. It automatically followed conviction for felony, both free land and chattels being confiscated in addition to capital punishment being inflicted, so that the felon's heirs were disinherited. But forfeiture of chattels was also the regular penalty for fleeing from justice. It was incurred by all who withdrew on account of any type of felony, whether they were indeed guilty or not, and whether they had eventually returned to face trial or not. Only fugitives on account of mere trespass escaped liability to it. The chattels of *meticulosi* were confiscated. Flight by anyone suspected of crime or who thought he might be suspected was, then, an offence and this was the punishment for it. There was no need to assume that there must be some additional guilt, some crime, or some culpability

[1] For example of disputes over them see K.B. 27/102, m. 4; K.B. 27/173, m. 43ᵈ.

in regard to the event which had occasioned the flight. The justices were careful, when remanding a prisoner *ad gratiam*, to inquire whether he had withdrawn at any stage; if he had done so they ordered the forfeiture of his chattels *pro fuga*. Similarly, when they proclaimed a pardon and granted firm peace they asked if the grantee had absconded, unless he had been outlawed, in which case it was obvious that he had done so, and ordered forfeiture *pro fuga*, but only on that account. So long as only those who had fled were punished in this way the punishment did not hold any implication whatever of felony and if they had withdrawn on account of a death it did not imply even the smallest responsibility for it. Forfeiture of chattels by fugitive excusable slayers did not point to there being some element of guilt in excusable homicide.

A most deplorable change began in the 1330s. Until then, the justices in eyre continued to make the inquiry concerning flight when remanding *ad gratiam* or whenever a pardon for homicide was produced, unless the grantee had served in the king's wars, in which case they sometimes tended to be indifferent to the question of confiscation. However, the eyre was now on the point of disappearing and it was left to the justices to deal with the matter elsewhere, mainly in King's Bench and at gaol deliveries. The rolls of the latter sometimes record the inquiry as to flight, sometimes they do not. At first its omission may have been due to the clerk who wrote the rolls rather than the justices' disregard of the proper grounds for confiscation. Some gaol delivery rolls do not record confiscations at all; some continue to record the inquiry into flight for excusable homicide after the time when such inquiries seem to have lapsed altogether in the King's Bench. They were apparently being omitted there in the late 1330s in some cases, and fairly soon after this it became the normal procedure to declare the chattels of excusable homicides forfeit without reference to flight, though there were still exceptions. Gradually it became the established rule, and the compilers of Year Books were soon referring to forfeiture with no hint that it depended on flight.[1] The fact that this was an innovation does not seem to have attracted attention, and it may have been due to oversight rather than conscious policy. Some pardoned homicides still escaped this penalty for the simple reason that they had no

[1] e.g. *Liber Assisarum*, 287, Mich., 44 Edward III.

chattels to forfeit, but no one considered it necessary to think up some other punishment for them. Thus the infliction of the penalty on excusable slayers who had never fled does not necessarily indicate that they were already regarded as deserving punishment. Inevitably, however, it ensured that they would come to be regarded as culpable. The fact that a penalty was imposed on them would come to presuppose their guilt, though the question what sort or degree of guilt there was to call for punishment went unanswered.[1]

The extension of the practice of forfeiture of chattels had, then, a most unfortunate result for excusable homicides, helping to establish the belief that they were all guilty of some offence, whether or no they had fled. It must not, however, be taken for granted that it was the only reason for this attitude being adopted towards them. If an attempt is made to sum up the evidence of the last chapters in its bearing on this point it will be found inconclusive. No proof has been found that excusable slaying was widely regarded as an offence deserving some punishment, but it seems that the attitude of the king's justices varied. Some were ready to invite fugitives to return whereas others showed the greatest severity in ordering their exaction and outlawry. It is likely that there were differing schools of thought as to the nature of excusable homicide, as well as its scope. Such homicide, by definition, needed pardon. The original reasons for this, that all slaying must be screened if all culpable slaying was to be prosecuted and punished and that just claims to compensation ought to be given some recognition, had, no doubt, long been forgotten. Writers such as Bracton had no theory with which to replace these formerly utilitarian and now irrelevant considerations. The thirteenth-century justices had no logical guiding principle to indicate when pardon was needed, let alone why. The system, if such it can be called, had now no rationale, and the justices' perplexity is not surprising. Some seem to have thought the need for pardon harsh and to have seen no culpability in this type of killing, whilst others may have been tempted to construct a new justification for it, assuming some culpability and being determined to make the slayers suffer in some measure.

---

[1] Later it was even asserted that 'where one killeth another se defendendo ... or by misadventure ... this offence is felony, and he that committes it shal forfait his goods' (W. Staunford, *An exposicion of the Kinges Prerogative*, cap. xvi).

It is, however, only at the end of the thirteenth century that any explicit statements appear on this issue and then they are based on or provoked by a misunderstanding of the nature of the king's pardon. There was an ambiguity in the term pardon which tended to create a popular misunderstanding—the Queen's Pardon is still apt to be misunderstood in the same way. The term in ordinary parlance means forgiveness, and forgiveness implies that there is an offence or injury to forgive. But when the king pardoned a suspected homicide this could be assumed only by those who were ignorant of the way in which he used his prerogative and the motives for invoking it, or were over-influenced by Civil Law.[1] Pardon certainly was not tantamount to acquittal, but it did not necessarily imply any guilt whatever. In itself it was neutral. It was remission of the king's suit, a decision not to prosecute further, but neither implying nor excluding belief that the applicant was in some way to blame. There is plenty of evidence for this. Some pardons were granted just because inquisitions had found that the suspects were not guilty,[2] others because the alleged victims turned up alive and uninjured.[3] Accessaries could not be tried until the principal had confessed, been outlawed, or convicted. If the king pardoned the principal before conviction or after outlawry, then the accessaries would go quit.[4] This, too, indicates that the pardon was not regarded as proof of guilt; if it had been so regarded they could properly have been tried and convicted. The pardoning of excusable homicide cannot, therefore, in itself have implied that some guilt attached to it, and knowledgeable lawyers must have been well aware of this. Yet some people assumed that it did so, or at any rate thought this theory worth propounding. There are hints of this in the late thirteenth century. In 1286 it was suggested that the act of obtaining pardon was an admission of guilt. Men appealed of abetting a murder were arraigned at the king's suit after the actual slayer had obtained pardon, so,

---

[1] In a Civil Law passage it had been taken to imply some guilt; pardon 'does not remove the disgrace of the crime, but merely dispenses with the punishment' (*Codex*, Lib. ix, tit. xliii, 3; trans. S. P. Scott).

[2] e.g. *Cal. Pat. Rolls, 1266–72*, 465, where two men were pardoned because an inquisition had found that another had killed the victim by accident and that they were innocent. Cf. ibid., *1258–66*, 197, 249, 254, 501; ibid., *1281–92*, 412.

[3] e.g. ibid., *1258–66*, 247; ibid., *1281–92*, 190. Cf. Bracton, *De Legibus*, f. 127.

[4] For examples see K.B. 26/160, m. 7; K.B. 26/162, m. 36; below, p. 309, n. 3.

it was asserted, admitting the deed.[1] They put themselves on the country and were acquitted. The old attitude was maintained in 1305 when justices of gaol delivery decided that a large number of persons indicted for aiding, consenting to, and abetting a killing should not be impleaded, but be set free, because three of the alleged principals had just produced the king's pardon and so had gone quit, whilst a fourth had earlier been acquitted;[2] similarly, a woman was not to be impleaded for abetting unless her husband, who had been pardoned the king's suit for homicide, should be convicted at the suit of someone else.[3] But in 1313, the new argument was put forward again, in a case of receiving. The alleged thief had secured pardon, and the receiver claimed that he ought not to answer the charge when no one had been convicted of the actual felony. Spigurnel retorted that 'the words of this charter which he (the thief) himself purchased assume that he committed the felony'. To this it was replied that 'he had not in his charter . . . *unde convictus est*, but only *unde arretatus est*, words which suppose only that he was indicted, and not that he confessed himself guilty'.[4] This reply was not considered altogether convincing and the justices held that as the accused had not denied that he had received the stolen goods he must fine for the offence—which he did for half a mark. The Year Book bears the disapproving comment, 'But note that the Justices so did rather for the King's profit than to vindicate the law, etc., and they did it under fear.' The argument was thus still regarded as a sophism by some, but it was gaining ground, even on the Bench. Its continuing influence may have contributed to the practice of punishing excusable slayers by forfeiture of chattels, even though they had not fled, though it is unlikely that it alone was responsible for this. The practice no doubt reinforced the notion that pardon inferred some guilt, and the notion may have lent respectability to the practice.

While the indiscriminate confiscation of chattels had grievous results for excusable slayers as a whole, it has been thought to have had a decisive and beneficial influence on the treatment of

---

[1] J.I. 1/827, m. 50^d; cf. m. 49^d.   [2] J.I. 3/26, iii, m. 27.
[3] Ibid., m. 5^d.

[4] *Eyre of Kent*, Selden Soc. xxiv. 103. The argument had been put forward by an appellor in 1307 to show that her appeal against an outlaw had not been a false one. The court neither rejected nor expressly accepted it. See *Select Cases in the Court of King's Bench*, Selden Soc. lviii, no. 88.

one section of them. Infants seldom had any chattels to be confiscated, and since, on this view, by the fifteenth century it was only when chattels were to be obtained that the pardoning of excusable homicide had any point, they were no longer required to get pardon, but could be acquitted in court.[1] But this view is too cynical. Acquittal of the very young was common well before the practice had begun of confiscating the chattels of pardoned homicides who had not fled. It can have had nothing to do with such mercenary considerations; indeed, the king lost the payments for pardon. The reason for the tendency to acquit was the recognition that very young infants were incapable of deliberation and thus the problem of establishing the absence of felony and malice aforethought did not arise in their case. The justices could safely be allowed to presume it.

[1] See A. W. G. Kean, 'The History of the Criminal Liability of Children', *L.Q.R.* liii. 366.

VI

INFANTS AND THE INSANE

FOR a considerable period, infants were included in the system of pardoning. In many cases pardon was obtained for them before trial and it might be supposed that this was a precautionary move on the part of their parents and forestalled the acquittal which could have been expected there. But apparently this was not the position, at least before the time of Edward I. Their pardons were not superfluous. If the infant slayer appeared in court without one the justices were likely to remand him *ad gratiam*, so that sooner or later he had to seek the king's grace. This applied whether or no the slaying had been wilful, though in the great majority of cases it had been accidental. Children, then, really did stand in need of pardon for causing death, and this is all the more remarkable because it was already recognized that the very young were not fully responsible for criminal actions, though there was much uncertainty as to the age at which they could be held answerable for them. Later it was established that 'a child below the age of seven cannot be guilty of felony, that between seven and fourteen there is a rebuttable presumption to the same effect, and that over fourteen he is fully *doli capax*'.[1] In the first half of the thirteenth century there was already some accepted rule as to what constituted the age of full criminal responsibility and it looks as though it was either 13 or 14. Pardons for children of 12 seem often to have been granted on grounds of their being under age. None has been found for a child of 13, but it may be that it would have been thought risky to admit to this age, even though it was only at 14 that pardon was unobtainable on these grounds, so that 13-year-olds were represented as being only 12. The age of 7 does not appear to have had any special significance until the end of the century.

Although very young children admittedly should not receive punishment they were all supposed to be treated as liable to it

---

[1] W. S. Holdsworth, *Hist. Eng. Law*, iii. 372.

until the king or his justices decided otherwise. Local officials were not considered competent to decide on this point, though probably they often took it upon themselves to do so, especially with the very young. It was remarked at the outset that such children were arrested for homicide and kept in prison.[1] The case of Katherine Passeavant was by no means unique nor does it appear that the abbot or his officials were exceeding their duty in detaining her. A boy of 8 was detained in Canterbury gaol until itinerant justices had seen him in court and heard a verdict of accidental slaying; he was then remanded to gaol and pardoned on their record.[2] One of 10 was imprisoned until bail was secured for him on the strength of an inquisition by the sheriff which found accidental slaying; he was subsequently pardoned on the justices in eyre's record.[3] A seven-year-old, Robert Parleben, was imprisoned but released on bail as an inquisition *de odio et atia* found that he had killed a girl by accident while they were guarding cows and she got in the way as he threw a stick at one which was straying into the corn.[4] Another boy, aged 9, was delivered at a goal delivery because it was found that he had shot and killed accidentally.[5] At least two infants who were arrested and kept in prison died there; one was only 6.[6] In one case the justices were told that a boy of 10, another shooter by mischance, had been brought before the county court but allowed to go; they now remanded him to gaol 'quousque...', and amerced the district which had harboured him for six years,[7] but it is good to know that a county court could show some independence and humanity in this matter.

The parents of imprisoned infants were naturally anxious to secure their immediate release and for this purpose they might well obtain pardon rather than bail, as did Katherine Passeavant's father. The king obviously would not hesitate to grant it in such cases and it might be hoped that the matter would now be over and done with. Similarly, if the infant

---

[1] Above, p. viii.

[2] J.I. 1/371, m. 23; *Cal. Pat. Rolls, 1272–81*, 315.

[3] *Cal. Close Rolls, 1279–88*, 343; *Cal. Pat. Rolls, 1292–1301*, 35; cf. J.I. 1/1098, m. 70, which gives his age.

[4] *Cal. Close Rolls, 1272–9*, 475; C. 144/18, no. 16. He was pardoned 3 years later (*Cal. Pat. Rolls, 1271–82*, 457), but appealed at the eyre (J.I. 1/486, m 26ᵈ).

[5] J.I. 1/280, m. 3ᵈ.

[6] J.I. 1/739, m. 66ᵈ; *Rolls of the Justices in Eyre for Yorks*, Selden Soc. lvi, no. 919.

[7] J.I. 1/371, m. 21.

slayer was at large it was desirable to secure pardon quickly so that he or she should not have to grow up under the shadow of a future trial. Yet pardons for children even below the age of 7 were sometimes expressly conditional on their standing to right. In 1244 this proviso was included in one for a boy aged 3½ who had accidentally killed a contemporary,[1] and it was also included in one for a boy of 6, who duly produced it at the eyre in 1256 while he was still under age.[2] Generally, however, the proviso did not have to be implemented until the infant slayer had come of age.[3]

The conditional nature of pardons is not always as explicit in children's as in those for adults,[4] but it seems to have been taken for granted that it applied however young the slayers. Nor was the proviso an empty one, even in their case. Astonishing as it may be, a relative might rely on it and appeal the pardoned child. In the case of the seven-year-old cowherd, Robert Parleben, a jury *de odio et atia* gave a most circumstantial account of the accidental death, and Robert was released on bail and later pardoned.[5] Yet at the eyre he was appealed by a cousin of the little girl. Robert excepted to the appeal on various grounds: failure to specify the year, the hour, the place, the weapons used; failure to mention that he killed her *nequiter et in felonia*, etc. He did not mention his pardon until the appeal had been quashed. When he did produce it, as it required him to stand to right, it was solemnly proclaimed and he was given firm peace.[6]

Pardon was not always obtained before the eyre and some infants appeared to stand their trial. Most of them had killed by mischance and so qualified for pardon on this ground as well as that of their youth. The emphasis was often put on the element of mischance and this would be investigated as carefully as if the slayer had been an adult. For instance, in 1284 when

---

[1] *Cal. Pat. Rolls, 1232–47*, 433.

[2] J.I. 1/778, m. 47ᵈ; cf. *Cal. Pat. Rolls, 1247–58*, 143. Cf. J.I. 1/86, m. 47ᵈ where the pardon for a boy of 10 was proclaimed and he was given firm peace.

[3] e.g. Thomas Coleman was found by an inquisition to have shot someone fatally at the age of 12 and was pardoned 'on condition that when he is of full age he shall stand his trial if any one will proceed against him' (*Cal. Pat. Rolls, 1232–47*, 425).

[4] Cf. *Close Rolls, 1234–7*, 237. For a clear statement of this proviso see ibid., *1237–42*, 246.

[5] See above, p. 153; cf. below, p. 208.

[6] J.I. 1/486, m. 26ᵈ.

Alice le Ster was presented at the eyre in Cornwall because at
the age of 6, while playing with stones on the edge of a cliff, she
had accidentally knocked one over and it had struck and killed
a girl on the beach below, the justices took the trouble to ask
the jury if she had sent the stone over deliberately; they were
assured that she had not and remanded her *ad gratiam*.[1] At
first, it seems, the result of a verdict of mischance was likely to
be the same as in the case of adults: recommendation in some
form to the king's mercy.[2] Under Edward I, however, some
justices were taking a different line. In 1279 those in Northumberland asserted that a child of 4½ who had accidentally killed
one of 2 should have 'vitam et membra quoad praedictum factum
pro tenera aetate ejusdem',[3] and this was probably tantamount
to acquittal. By 1287 a boy of 9 years could actually be acquitted as under age,[4] and in 1292 one of 7 was also acquitted.[5]
Remands *ad gratiam* had not ceased—there was one in 1293[6]—
but the practice of acquitting was evidently gaining ground.

Not all the infants who killed did so entirely by mischance.
Their acts of violence might be wilful although they did not
foresee or could not appreciate their outcome. They might
even appear malicious. There was better reason to hold that
such infant killers needed the king's pardon. A boy of 6 hit
one of 8 on the head with a stone; his parents obtained pardon
for him in 1252 on the grounds that he was under age, and he
produced his charter in court.[7] There seems to have been no
suggestion that he had not meant to hit the victim. In 1249
itinerant justices decided to refer to the king a case of killing in childish anger. One boy, Robert, had climbed on to a
cock of hay and fallen off on to another boy, William, aged 12,
who was annoyed at this and hit him twice on the head with
a stick; this proved fatal. The jury at the eyre considered
William guilty, though rather through simplicity than felony.[8]
Earlier his family had made an attempt to hush the matter up,
giving the coroner 1 mark to conceal it, and the death had
been presented as entirely accidental, Robert's neck being said
to have been broken by his fall.

[1] J.I. 1/111, m. 27. Cf. above, p. 50.   [2] e.g. *Cal. Close Rolls, 1227-31,* 206.
[3] *Northumberland Assize Rolls,* Surtees Soc. lxxxviii. 323.
[4] J.I. 1/11, m. 29. Cf. J.I. 1/280, m. 3ᵈ.   [5] J.I. 1/739, m. 70.
[6] J.I. 1/1098, m. 70. Cf. above, p. 153, n. 3.
[7] See p. 154, n. 2.
[8] J.I. 1/996, m. 23ᵈ.

Acquittal in these cases seems to have begun at the same time as acquittal for infants who had killed by mischance. By 1272 it could be asserted that at 11 a fugitive was of an age when he could not undergo judgement.[1] In the 1290s a child of 5 was said to be too young to commit felony,[2] and a boy who had actually killed in a fit of temper was acquitted.[3] He had thrown a knife at another who would not give him part of his apple; he was said to be under age and so quit; unfortunately his age is not given, but the nature of the squabble suggests that he cannot have been much older. By the end of the reign the age of 7 seems to have been established as a dividing line. It was asserted in 1302 that 'a child indicted for homicide ought not to suffer judgement if he did the deed before he was 7 years old', and again in 1313–14 that those under 7 should go free of judgement.[4]

Some infant slayers could claim benefit of clergy. The same sort of development appears in their treatment. Under Henry III they were either handed over to the bishop to purge themselves in the church court,[5] or recommended to the king's grace. Adult clerks who had killed excusably were treated in the same way, so that no special concession seems to have been made as yet on grounds of youth.[6] But a change appears in 1287: Thomas de la Penne, at the time 9 years old, had been playing with Reginald, aged 10; the latter had seized him in his arms and brought him to the ground; Thomas, moved to wrath, had got up, drawn his knife, and struck him in the stomach so that he died next day.[7] By the time of the eyre Thomas's people seem to have taken steps to avert his punishment by making a clerk of him, for he now claimed benefit of clergy, but the justices apparently thought that because of his youth there might be no need for canonical purgation, and ordered his release on bail until the king gave orders about him. This probably meant that nothing more was heard of his homicide, and thus here again an infant killer was treated more leniently by this date.

As some of these examples show, it was realized quite early that a child might attack another voluntarily yet without felony.

---

[1] J.I. 1/802, m. 54ᵈ.   [2] J.I. 1/804, m. 70ᵈ.   [3] J.I. 3/91, m. 11.
[4] A. W. G. Kean, loc. cit. 364, 366, quoting *Year Books, 30–31 Edward I*, 511–13, and *Eyre of Kent*, i. 109.   [5] e.g. J.I. 1/736, m. 45.
[6] See Appendix II.   [7] J.I. 1/11, m. 30.

Bracton had quoted the Civil Law phrase 'innocentia concilii' and under Edward I these notions were at last allowed to influence practice to the extent of acquittal becoming permissible. But there was another side to the coin. If some children were too young to be capable of felonious intent others below the age of 14 might act in a way which could be taken to reveal it. In 1302 a boy was found guilty of felonious killing; he had been going through a village and had found a house with the door open and a girl of 5 alone in it; he tried to steal the bread he found there and the little girl protested; alarmed at her cry, he picked up a hatchet and struck her on the head, killing her; and when he had thus killed her he dragged her out of the house and threw her feloniously into a well in the adjoining garden. The jurors were asked how old he had been at the time and replied 10 or more. So he was sentenced to be hanged. He had no chattels.[1] His actions, both in silencing the girl because she objected to his stealing and in trying to conceal the killing, showed all too clearly that he was aware that he was acting wrongly, and this was taken to imply felony. Thus children between 7 and 14 could commit felony, although their misdeeds would not all be construed in this way; indeed, the presumption was probably already in their favour.

Over half the child homicides noticed on the eyre rolls had fled from justice, the age of the fugitives ranging from 5½ to 12.[2] They were liable to be outlawed, at least when they came of age. Although Bracton asserted that no one should be outlawed until he reached the age of 12,[3] it is difficult to tell how far this rule was respected. There is an instance of the outlawry of a boy of 11 in the county court, apparently on appeal, but he later surrendered and claimed that the outlawry had been irregular since he had been only 12 or under. A jury confirmed this and the outlawry was annulled in 1280.[4] This shows that the rule existed but was not always regarded locally. At about this period some justices in eyre when placing in exigent fugitives who had killed when they were under age were careful to establish that they had now reached age;[5] but it is not clear

---

[1] J.I. 3/26, ii, m. 4ᵈ.   [2] For the 5½-year-old see J.I. 1/85, m. 12ᵈ.

[3] *De Legibus*, f. 125ᵇ.

[4] J.I. 1/784, m. 14; *Cal. Inquisitions Misc.* i, nos. 2191, 2195. He was also found not to have been guilty, though present when several men committed the crime.

[5] Cf. J.I. 1/46, m. 7 where the fugitive was now 22 (1284); J.I. 1/827, m. 54ᵈ (1286—the killing had occurred in 1269).

whether others troubled to ascertain this.[1] Sometimes they had consultation with the king as to whether infant killers should be put in exigent,[2] and some of these may still have been under 12. Some of those whose outlawry was ordered had been only 8 or 9 when they had killed by accident; some presenting jurors, to their credit, concealed one of these cases.[3] Outlawry was ordered in about a dozen of those found, but in much the same number the justices decided that the fugitive might return if he wished, though in one they ordered that his chattels should be confiscated;[4] and one boy fined for 10 shillings when he appeared before them after their decision not to outlaw him.[5] The coroners were not authorized to accept abjurations of the realm by minors,[6] and this confirms the view that outlawry of those under age was regarded as inequitable. Probably it was felt that when they reached the age of 12 they should be held responsible for contumacy in refusing to stand their trial, even though they had not been responsible for their actions at the time they committed them and had, indeed, killed quite unintentionally. But outlawry for failure to appear in court was harsh treatment for young persons who had fled as infants and could have little knowledge of the law. As already noted, adult fugitives were often told they might return and it is evident that in this respect again infant slayers were treated in very much the same way as grown-up slayers by accident, some being outlawed eventually, some not.

It must be assumed that flight of this kind by very young children was generally not spontaneous. Whatever their immediate reactions had been they were not likely to have stayed away from home indefinitely. Their parents would later have sent them away to avoid arrest and trial, perhaps to friends in another county. Thus the harshness of the treatment

---

[1] But when the exact age of the slayer at the time of the slaying was stated together with the date of the slaying his present age was easily calculated. For example, one boy was stated at the eyre in 1286 to have been 11 when he killed in 1279 (J.I. 1/575, m. 5^d); another in 1278/9 to have been 10 when he killed temp. Henry III (J.I. 1/131, m. 9^d). Both could, therefore, be outlawed as having now reached full age.

[2] J.I. 1/979, m. 12^d (1256); J.I. 1/1025, m. 16^d (1275).

[3] J.I. 1/734, m. 22; J.I. 1/829, m. 37.

[4] J.I. 1/65, m. 41. It turned out, however, that he had none.

[5] J.I. 1/569^A, m. 6.

[6] See J.I. 1/700, m. 6^d. Cf. *Pleas of the Crown for the County of Gloucester*, ed. F. W. Maitland, no. 150.

of infant slayers was probably aggravated by the ignorance and folly of grown-ups. Yet mistrust of the system was not always due to ignorance. Too many points were undecided and the justices were too inconsistent in their practice for it to be prudent always to produce the infant in court.

Infant homicides were, then, liable to be treated with almost incredible severity despite the recognition that they were not fully criminally responsible. Their fate was sometimes abhorrent, though often justices and jurors were as sympathetic towards them as the law allowed. There was imperative need to define their situation more clearly, but for a time the availability of pardon afforded a way of avoiding facing up to these problems and anomalies. Thus while it was of use to many individual children it may have tended to hinder reform and even definition of the standing of infant slayers as a whole. However, under Edward I the practice of acquittal was superseding that of remanding them *ad gratiam* and in some other respects also the treatment of children was becoming less stringent.

Infants were not the only slayers who might be held incapable of felonious intent. Excusable homicide included slaying by the insane and those who suffered from diminished responsibility. There was much to be said in favour of some system of pardoning in these cases, especially where homicidal maniacs were concerned. There was good reason why each such case should be regarded as a special problem, one calling for executive rather than judicial decision. Even today the limitations on the courts' ability to determine their fate is recognized and flexibility in their treatment has to be allowed. Already, in the thirteenth century their actions were seen not to call for retribution and the problem of prevention was sometimes recognized.

Those who slew when suffering some mental derangement were in very little danger of being held criminally responsible. There was a very strong feeling indeed against executing people who were temporarily or perhaps permanently out of their minds, a feeling which may have been tinged with superstition as well as Christian charity and concern for the soul of the slayer. One clerk was said to have killed at the instigation of the devil, but he was also said to have been rendered mad and frantic by illness, so that he was not supposed to be suffering from demoniac possession.[1] No case has been found in which this was asserted. Nevertheless, some notion of this kind may have underlain the horror of destroying the unfortunate who might otherwise eventually have come to himself. But, as this case shows, medical grounds for mental disturbance were recognized. People who killed when they became violent from ague or in a state of delirium were not held responsible. There was no question of the king's suit resulting in their being sentenced to death, and the idea of executing such people was so detestable that prosecution of an appeal by the victim's relatives was almost inconceivable.[2] Nevertheless, pardons to these killers included the usual proviso of standing to right.

While there was no danger of an admitted madman being executed, the problem of what to do with him could not be solved merely by granting pardon; nor were his relatives always very eager to seek it for him. Even release on bail was often undesirable and it was at least prudent to investigate the slayer's present condition before agreeing to it. Homicidal maniacs would have to be kept in some sort of custody and their relatives might be glad enough to leave them in the sheriff's rather than making their own arrangements to guard them. Their victims included some men described as keepers who had been slain by their own charges.[3] In such a case the relatives were unlikely to be in a hurry to secure either bail or pardon and so have to find a new man for the post. Even when they were in prison homicidal maniacs could be dangerous, as Richard Pinnok proved to be; captured for killing one man and imprisoned at Bristol, he slew another in gaol; he claimed to have killed whilst suffering from frenzy and madness, and was remanded *ad gratiam*.[4] It may have been a relief to both his family and his gaoler when a madman died in prison.

It was obviously inexpedient that such slayers should be released, and so far as release pending trial went there might seem to be very little point in the relatives obtaining it.

[1] *Cal. Inquisitions Misc.* i, no. 2279.

[2] In 1285 an inquisition found that James de Ardena had killed during a fit of madness (ibid., no. 2275); the king ordered his release on bail and his writ as calendared stated that James had been appealed (*Cal. Close Rolls, 1279–88,* 334). But the actual enrolment used the term *rettatus*, not *appellatus*, so that this case was no exception. One lunatic was appealed in the county court, but the appeal was not later prosecuted; see below, p. 168, n. 4.

[3] e.g. J.I. 1/65, m. 39; J.I. 1/300ᶜ, m. 23; J.I. 3/96, m. 38.

[4] J.I. 1/286, m. 10.

Yet it was obtained in many cases, especially from Edward I.
Henry III seems to have granted it much less often; whether
because he judged it imprudent or because few attempted to
secure it does not emerge. In 1226 he ordered the sheriff to
hold an inquisition to discover if Alice de la Lade had killed
her baby from madness or maliciously and intentionally, and
to let her out on bail if the verdict found she had done this
through madness.[1] But after this he seems to have been more
inclined to allow abjuration of the realm,[2] or to pardon at once.
Thus in 1251, after an inquisition had found that a woman had
killed a small girl when demented, he told the sheriff to release
her and let her go where she willed; her pardon contained the
proviso of making peace with the relatives or standing to right.[3]
Five years later he showed a little more appreciation of the
risk of releasing madmen, for though he pardoned a man who
had slain two boys, the justices of gaol delivery having found
that he did this through madness and not through felony,
Henry optimistically instructed the sheriff to deliver him from
prison, but to take 'security that he will do no such damage
any more'.[4]

Early in his reign Edward I showed caution in dealing with
mentally disturbed prisoners. On one occasion at least he
ordered an inquisition to inquire not only if a prisoner had been
in a frenzy at the time of the killing six years before but also
whether he had now recovered or could not be released from
prison on the grounds of the aforesaid illness without danger.
It is not clear if he had been asked for pardon or only bail.
The verdict, probably given in response to this order, was that
the prisoner was not 'so far restored to sanity as to be set free
without danger, especially in the heat of summer', and neither
seems to have been granted.[5] But soon Edward was allowing

[1] *Rot. Litt. Claus.* ii. 158.
[2] e.g. *Close Rolls, 1234–7*, 461.
[3] Ibid., *1247–51*, 468–9; *Cal. Pat. Rolls, 1247–58*, 100.
[4] Ibid. 471.
[5] See *Cal. Inquisitions Misc.* i, no. 2202; C. 145/34, no. 59. These documents are
reproduced by N. Walker, *Crime and Insanity in England*, i. 20–3. The reference is
here given incorrectly as C. 154/34. The second document is wrongly dated and
its relation to the first is not made clear. Richard Cheddestan had been on trial at
a gaol delivery in April 1276 and had pleaded not guilty. The verdict was that
he had killed in a frenzy and was a chronic case. Subsequently the king was
approached and in July issued an *ex parte* writ for the inquisition to one of the gaol
delivery justices. It looks as though the verdict now taken was appended to the

bail almost as a matter of course if inquisitions found that the prisoners had killed when deranged by madness or frenzy.[1] The mainpernors had, however, special responsibilities for their charges, at least in some cases. When an inquisition had found that Hugh de Mysin had hanged his daughter and tried to hang himself while in a frenzy and not feloniously,[2] Edward ordered that he should be delivered in bail to twelve men of the county, 'who shall mainpern to have him before the king to stand to right if any one wish to speak against him, and who shall mainpern that he shall not hereafter injure anyone';[3] and a little later, the sheriff having informed him that mainpernors had been found, the king ordered him to deliver Hugh's goods and chattels to them to keep until otherwise ordered, 'provided that Hugh shall have his maintenance from the goods and chattels according to the judgment of the mainpernors, without making waste of the goods and chattels'.[4] When Matilda, wife of Walter Levyng, suffering from ague and frenzy, killed her two-year-old son and her daughter with an axe, her husband and the tithingmen led her to Oxford where she was imprisoned. The king agreed to her release on bail to twelve of her kindred or others, who perhaps were to share the responsibility of guarding against a further attack, which her husband alone did not feel up to doing.[5] Certainly in some cases continued restraint proved essential after the slayer had been released on bail.

earlier one, for they appear on one return, but the reference to the heat of summer and the apparent reply to the king's question indicate that the addition was of later date. Mr. Walker's comments on this case are misleading. It certainly does not show that the sheriff 'simply confined this homicidal man in prison' without trial (p. 19).

[1] There may have been even more cases than appear since writs authorizing release on bail might omit any reference to the prisoner's proved insanity. For example, *Cal. Close Rolls,1272–9,*449 records the order to release William Huelinesneveu, imprisoned for the death of his son Robert; C. 144/17, no. 53 shows that an inquisition *de odio et atia* had found that he had killed him with a little hatchet whilst raving mad and deprived of all sense, Robert having been only 6 months old. Nor were the enrolments inclusive: J.I. 1/181, m. 40[d] and J.I. 1/575, m. 20[d] mention orders for bail which do not seem to have been enrolled; the latter shows that the killer was still mad at the time of the eyre, yet he was again handed over to mainpernors who were to produce him *coram rege*.

[2] *Cal. Inquisitions Misc.* i, no. 2220.

[3] *Cal. Close Rolls, 1272–9,* 518.

[4] Ibid. 525. The case was reported at the eyre where he was called Hugh de Grene (J.I. 1/664, m. 37).

[5] J.I. 1/46, m. 3[d]; *Cal. Close Rolls, 1272–9,* 206. She was pardoned after the eyre (*Cal. Pat. Rolls, 1281–92,* 146).

James de Ardena who had been granted bail in 1285, after an inquisition had found that he killed Eva de Carleton in his madness, and was mad both before and long after,[1] failed to appear at the eyre in 1286, and it was then reported that he was still mad and was in a church, bound hand and foot.[2]

While the king might entrust them to mainpernors, the sheriff was not supposed to release on bail people who had slain while mad, however strong the case for leniency. The sheriff of Shropshire was amerced in 1272 for having allowed a woman to go after she had been imprisoned in the castle at Shrewsbury for killing her baby through insanity in childbirth.[3] On the other hand those who had taken sanctuary were allowed to abjure the realm in the ordinary way.[4] Presumably it was felt unnecessary to guard them specially so long as they did not relapse into homicidal tendencies before they had reached another country.

In the hope of securing either bail or, more often, pardon various types of inquisition were obtained by their friends to establish that the killers were insane: a special commission might be appointed to hold an inquisition as to their mental state, or justices of gaol delivery might hold one. The writs were drawn up on similar lines to those for inquiries into other allegedly excusable homicide. Thus the commissioners were to inquire whether James de Ardena had killed 'per infortunium aut furia inuectus vel alio modo, et si per infortunium, per quod infortunium, qualiter et quo modo. Et si alio modo, tunc qualiter et quomodo'; the jurors replied that he had killed 'furia inuentus et non alio modo' and was still suffering from the same infirmity.[5] It is perhaps not really surprising in view of the protean nature of the writ *de odio et atia* that this also was employed by the friends of homicidal maniacs, though it was peculiarly inappropriate to their case. There was certainly nothing improper in charging Joanna le Vagh

[1] See above, p. 160. n. 2.

[2] J.I. 1/829, m. 4. The justices decided to speak about him, probably to the king.

[3] J.I. 1/736, m. 40ᵈ.

[4] e.g. J.I. 1/538, m. 18, where a demented vagabond was said to have recovered his senses in Newgate; he was allowed to abjure at a gaol delivery there. It is interesting to note that he was stated not to belong to a tithing because he was a lunatic as well as being a vagabond.

[5] C. 145/44, no. 36.

with the death of her daughter. The jury *de odio et atia* in
1284 found that she had killed her in a frenzy while raving mad,
and that she was still in the same condition in Aylesbury gaol.[1]
Despite this final cautionary statement Edward I pardoned her
at once on the strength of the verdict.[2] Two years later she was
sufficiently recovered to appear before the itinerant justices with
her pardon; as this required her to stand to right it was now
solemnly proclaimed and she was given firm peace.[3] In the case
of William Huelinesneveu the jury roundly asserted that he
was not charged *odio et atia* but because he was indeed guilty,
though insane.[4] Another jury gave one of the twisted verdicts
with a new twist: Alexander de Tadeworthy, they said, did not
kill Alicia de Gydecote out of hatred and malice but was mad at
the time.[5]

A good many insane killers were brought before the justices
without pardon having been sought, or at least without its
having been granted, since many relatives shirked taking the
responsibility or the king recognized that it would be rash to
put it upon them. The justices had therefore to cope with these
difficult cases. There was no questioning the madmen's having
committed the slayings with which they were charged. If one
was ever falsely saddled with a sane man's crime no indication
of this has been discovered, and it never seems to have occurred
to the justices to consider this possibility. They accepted the
verdict easily enough so far as the identity of the slayer went.
The only points they were at all likely to raise concerned his
mental state. This was a particularly difficult matter to establish if he had now fully recovered. A prisoner's claim to have
been mad when he killed his victim might be a desperate
attempt to save his life. A man, who had abjured the realm but
had not left it and had been arrested, informed the justices of
gaol delivery at Newgate that he had been demented and in a
frenzy at the time of the slaying and was unaware of what he
did then or was supposed to have done.[6] This tale sounds
convincing enough until it emerges that another prisoner
from the same county was also said at the same delivery, but

---

[1] C. 144/24, no. 1.   [2] *Cal. Pat. Rolls, 1281–92*, 125.
[3] J.I. 1/65, m. 40ᵈ.
[4] See above, p. 162, n. 1.
[5] C. 144/18, no. 8. But on the strength of this verdict the king only ordered his
release on bail; see *Cal. Close Rolls, 1272–9*, 450.
[6] J.I. 3/35ᴮ, m. 16.

this time by the jury, to have killed while unaware of what he was doing.[1] The justices were not prepared to accept the first prisoner's own statement, which could have been suggested to him by the case of his fellow prisoner, but ordered the coroner to bring his record. One prisoner charged with killing his daughter said that he could not deny this, but that he had been out of his mind, and put himself on the jury as to this. The jury agreed, adding that he had been trying to commit suicide. The king's failure to pardon him is unlikely, therefore, to have been due to doubt as to his insanity.[2]

Often the homicidal maniac was said not to have recovered by the time of the eyre, and in this event the justices readily accepted the jury's opinion that he was mad—his appearance and demeanour may have confirmed it if he was brought into court. His condition might be so bad that this in itself was hardly feasible, but this would be equally convincing and could lead to his case being referred to the king. Yet the possibility that he was feigning madness was not always overlooked. Some justices raised the question, asking, for example, whether the slayer had acted from hatred or malevolence already existing between him and his victim and from felony, pretending to be insane. At the end of the thirteenth century it was usual for justices of gaol delivery or oyer and terminer to press for details as to the duration of an attack of insanity, or the frequency of periodic attacks. For example, John de Merihill, who had been bound because he was demented and *non compos mentis* and had bitten through his cords and cut the throat of a six-year-old boy, appeared before justices of oyer and terminer and pleaded not guilty; the fact that he was now apparently fit to plead may have made the justices sceptical of this presentment, but the jurors hastened to assure them, on oath, that he was insane but enjoyed lucid intervals. They confirmed the account, adding no doubt as proof of his mania, that after killing the boy he got back into bed and pulled the bed-clothes over his head. Asked how long he had been out of his mind before the slaying, they replied for fifteen days and at intervals during the last four years; asked how many times a year he suffered this illness, they replied three or four times. This seems to have satisfied the justices, who remanded him

[1] Ibid. m. 43[d].
[2] C. 47/79/10, no. 312; *Cal. Close Rolls, 1279–88*, 151. Cf. above, p. 51, n. 5.

ad gratiam.[1] Justices of gaol delivery, suspicious of one slayer's alleged insanity, inquired whether there was any prior enmity or ill feeling between him and his victim and whether he had killed in felony, pretending to be insane. But the jury insisted that he was mad at the time and for long afterwards, so he too was remanded *ad gratiam*.[2]

Once they were convinced that the slayer had been mad the justices nearly always remanded in this way or consulted the king. There is one statement, made by a party in an action for land, that the justices had ordered the perpetual imprisonment of a man who had confessed to slaying when he was out of his senses.[3] But it is doubtful if this is correct; they may only have remanded him to gaol pending a decision by the king, if he was approached by the prisoner's friends. No similar order has been found. On the other hand, although it was very rare for them to acquit, they sometimes did so when there was especially clear proof of insanity. For example, one women was acquitted for the death of her daughter, aged $1\frac{1}{2}$; she had thrown the child into a well and tried to drown herself also, but was pulled out by some men who chanced to come along; the jury found that she had been in a raving frenzy;[4] the attempt at suicide no doubt confirmed this. It is harder to understand the independent line taken by the justices in the case of Geoffrey de Riche. He, because mad, wanted to sleep with Agnes Fuller and as she would not let him have his will took a sword and cut off her head. After the deed he ran to the neighbouring houses and announced that he was a pig and got under a trough; later he went home and took needle and thread and sewed the head to the body. The jury swore that he was demented before and after this deed and still was, so that he ought not to undergo judgement. Two men then fined with the justices for his judgement for 20 marks and he was allowed to go quit.[5] While Geoffrey's insanity was beyond question, the justices might still have been expected to consult the king before agreeing to accept the fine, and guarantees of his future surveillance were certainly highly desirable, yet they are not

---

[1] J.I. 1/847, m. 2; the record of this case was twice sent to the king and eventually Edward II granted pardon; see *Cal. Pat. Rolls., 1307–13, 152.*

[2] J.I. 3/96, m. 10^d.

[3] Bracton's *Note Book*, iii. no. 1878, Cf. N. Walker, op. cit. 19.

[4] J.I. 1/376, mm. 50, 80.

[5] J.I. 1/1109, m. 18.

recorded to have laid down any conditions about his custody by his friends or made them responsible for any future acts of violence by him. In other cases they did this. On one occasion justices of gaol delivery decided to hand over to mainpernors a man who had killed his wife in a frenzy; the mainpernors had to undertake to guard him in future so that he did no harm; if he did any harm they were to be held responsible for him.[1] However, to act in this way without the king's authorization might get the justices into trouble. They ran the risk of being fined if they delivered a madman without consulting the king,[2] but sometimes thought it enough to consult with their fellows or take time to deliberate among themselves.[3]

Unfortunately, despite recognition of the importance of preventing further maniacal acts of violence, when precautions were laid down they were quite inadequate. There was really no way of ensuring the safety of others if lunatics were handed over to their relatives; and if the latter did take their responsibilities seriously they might have no means of restraining them except by keeping them tied or chained up. Many seem to have been left in prison, where their treatment is likely to have been even worse, though the danger to society was less. The chances of their recovery there and ultimate pardon and release were small.

Insane clerks were sometimes handed over to the bishop to be kept in prison by him; some, no doubt, were able to purge themselves in court Christian, but one at least failed to make purgation there and was degraded.[4] The secular authorities might be only too glad to let the church take over responsibility for these particular members. But most clerks who had slain through madness were remanded to await the king's grace. Some got pardon, but none has been found for others. Most of the laymen, too, who had killed when insane, according to the surviving plea rolls, did not secure it after remand *ad gratiam*, or if they did their charters were not enrolled. However, the patent rolls of Edward I include a certain number of pardons on grounds of insanity, granted on the record of justices in eyre, of gaol delivery, and oyer and terminer, in cases not

---

[1] J.I. 3/35ᴮ; m. 54ᵈ.
[2] Cf. J.I. 1/135, m. 13ᵈ. The madman here was guilty of arson, not homicide.
[3] e.g. J.I. 3/26, ii, m. 3; J.I. 1/818, m. 48ᵈ.
[4] See *Reg. Greenfield*, Surtees Soc. cxlv, no. 571; cf. no. 946 (1312).

found on the plea rolls, and there may have been some in additional cases disguised as killing by mischance.[1] It does not appear, then, that it was in any way contrary to the king's policy to pardon those recommended to his mercy if the necessary steps were taken. The ordinary fees of the seal had to be paid,[2] but no special proffer or inducement seems to have been necessary.

There are very few instances of the justices ordering that a madman should be outlawed.[3] It may be that such slayers were generally too crazy to think of escape. One of the handful who were put in exigent was described as becoming 'demens vagabundus per patriam' and as having then withdrawn; probably he had wandered off with little if any idea of fleeing from justice.[4] No case has been noticed of the justices announcing that one who had fled might return.

Although drunkenness was not in itself an excuse for slaying it might be of significance if the slayer was of unstable mind even when sober. For instance, Thomas le Potter, who was subject to fits of lunacy, went out to supper and got drunk; when he left, his host followed him to see him safely home; infuriated by this solicitude, Thomas killed him. He was led to do this said the jurors, by lunatic illness, raving fury, and drunkenness, and the justices remanded him *ad gratiam*.[5] Feeble-minded persons also qualified for pardon though fewer cases have

---

[1] As in the case of Richard Russel, who was presented as having killed his wife through insanity; he appeared and put himself on a jury, which said that he had been entirely out of his mind when he found her asleep in the house and, wanting to wake her, called her without immediate response, so that he took an axe and struck her on the head. He was remanded to gaol and pardoned on the grounds that the slaying had been by mischance (J.I. 1/181, m. 31[d]; *Cal. Pat. Rolls, 1281–92*, 20).

[2] One madman, Nigel Coppeden, is known to have paid the full sum of 16*s.* 4*d.*; E. 101/211/4, m. 4; cf. C. 47/81/6, no 196; *Cal. Pat. Rolls, 1301–1307*, 416.

[3] For exceptional cases see: *Rolls of the Justices in Eyre in Yorks, 1218–19*, Selden Soc. lvi, no. 526; J.I. 1/376, m. 24, where a woman who had fled after throwing her daughter into a well when mad was ordered to be waived. In each case the fugitive was stated to have had no chattels. This implies that the insanity of the fugitive made no difference so far as forfeiture of chattels was concerned. N. Walker thinks that a distinction was made between anyone who 'had killed by accident or self-defence, or if he was an infant' and the insane man, their chattels being forfeit but not his (op. cit. 24). Their chattels were not confiscated at this period unless they had fled, any more than were the madman's. The question of forfeiture arose only after flight, but it then arose in his case as well.

[4] J.I. 1/780, m. 17[d]. He had earlier been appealed, but the appellor did not now come before the justices to prosecute the appeal.

[5] J.I. 1/422, m. 4.

been found of their needing it, probably because they seldom attacked others. One idiot, William Pilche, was pardoned for killing Augustine le Fevere as it appeared by testimony of the coroner and other trustworthy persons 'that the said William was passing along the high road by night when he was met by the said Augustine, in the disguise of a terrible monster uttering groans and refusing to speak though adjured in God's name, on account of which the said William rushed upon him as a monster and killed him'.[1] People suffering from ague, *febris acuta*, sometimes killed while delirious, and were treated in the same way as the temporarily insane, though there was less need for concern about their future conduct and pardon could be granted promptly.[2] A rather different problem was presented by the deaf and dumb. Such people might be fully responsible, though in the absence of methods for teaching them they must often have had little understanding of law and morality. Since the dumb could not plead or put themselves on the country, they were treated as being incapable of defending themselves and so of being judged. One mute, who knew enough to take sanctuary after killing a man, remained in the church for eight and a half years; Henry III then allowed the abbot of Shireburn to take him to his abbey and keep him there, provided he never went beyond its walls.[3] But pardon might be obtained for a deaf-mute.[4]

Women who killed in childbirth were sometimes regarded as responsible, sometimes not. One who killed her child when it was a few hours old claimed that it had been stillborn, but also declared that she had been demented at the time and put herself on the country as to this. The jury found that the child had been born alive and that she had been in her right mind. Perhaps her defence showed too much presence of mind to be convincing. She was sentenced to death by burning.[5] This is the most shocking case found. Provided mental derangement was mentioned at all, punishment was extremely unlikely. How many deranged persons were executed because their condition was not recognized it is impossible to guess.

[1] *Cal. Pat. Rolls, 1258–66*, 407.

[2] e.g. one was remanded *ad gratiam*, received his pardon at the same eyre and was given firm peace by the justices (J.I. 1/1098, m. 74. Cf. *Cal. Pat. Rolls, 1292–1301*, 40).

[3] *Close Rolls, 1231–34*, 38.   [4] e.g. *Cal. Pat. Rolls, 1292–1301*, 250.

[5] J.I. 1/818, m. 47.

Although insanity was not always accepted as an excuse, most of the slayers suffering from it or from diminished responsibility were treated as incapable of felony and as deserving both pardon and care. The worst feature of their treatment was the general one affecting all the insane, lack of provision for them in conditions which would prevent their being a danger to others and might promote their recovery. That many of those who stood in need of pardon did not secure it was probably as much the fault of their families' reluctance to receive them, as of official reluctance to hand them over. If there was an element of uncertainty as to their fate this was due, in the main, to the special problem of prevention, not to doubts about their deserts. The risks involved in their release did not, however, deter some justices from acquitting them, particularly those whose insanity was most unmistakable, and the king pardoned others who were equally deranged.

VII

THE RIGHT OF APPEAL

THREE sets of people were concerned in the system of pardoning homicide, the king, the killer, and the victim's kin. The king, representative of public order, decided that in certain cases punishment might be remitted, but his decision was permissive only and did not, in theory, affect the kinsman's right to prosecute a capital appeal. Indeed, even where excusable slaying was concerned, the question of pardon might never arise, since the appeal normally took priority over the king's suit and the slayer was liable to be tried and convicted on appeal without the king's intervening in any way. Thus a slayer who deserved pardon might have no chance to secure it if his victim's relatives were set on seeing him punished, while one who had obtained pardon, whether or not deservedly, might still be tried and convicted if they remained irreconcilable. The victim's feudal lord or man shared the right to appeal, though the latter would have little chance of succeeding unless he could claim to have been an eyewitness of the slaying and, indeed, to have been injured at the same time. Appeals of this sort were uncommon; it was very rare for the victim's lord to bring one, though it was not unknown. The king's pardon did not affect this right of feudal associates; the proviso of standing to right if appealed meant that the grantee must answer to an appeal brought either by a kinsman or by his lord or man. But appeals by the last two were such a remote contingency that it will be unnecessary to deal with them separately. What is said of appeals by the victim's relatives may be taken to apply to them also.

In theory the relatives of a slain man retained the right to appeal the homicide whatever the circumstances and in spite of the king's pardon of his own suit. The appellor could not take excuse or mitigating circumstances into account when he formulated his appeal since this had to allege felony, though he might show readiness to compromise it later. If he believed

the slaying to have been felonious, or if he was so vindictive
that he aimed at the capital sentence even when it had not been,
then his course was apparently straightforward: he would
appeal of homicide in felony and breach of the king's peace
and offer to prove his charge by battle or such other proof as
the court might award. In practice the matter was less simple,
and it will be necessary to attempt some estimate of the practical
value of the right of appeal against alleged homicides who had
been pardoned, and also against those who had slain excusably
but had not yet been pardoned. The right of appeal against
people who had slain unintentionally may appear to have been
a regrettable survival and not in itself of much interest; yet
its converse, the liability of the excusable killer to capital
punishment on conviction at the relatives' suit, is an issue
of considerable social and legal concern. The fact that he
needed the king's pardon is shocking enough; if the law actually
allowed him to be executed at the will of a vindictive and
unreasonable kinsman of his victim then his situation was far
worse. On the other hand, if the king was too generous with
pardons to intentional slayers, the right of appeal might
conceivably serve as a useful corrective, and it is worth asking
whether there is any evidence of its so doing. From the point of
view of the bereaved family, their right to compensation may
have been more highly valued than that of appeal, whereas
the king was unlikely to take much interest in this aspect of the
system. Its ultimate failure to conserve even a moral claim to
reparation was one of its most serious defects. The status of
such claims in the thirteenth century must be considered.
Rights acknowledged in theory were in practice to some extent
at the mercy of both the king and his justices; nor were the
relatives necessarily always eager to exploit them. Public
opinion itself could affect their attitude, or their own consciences
inhibit them. It is necessary, then, in trying to discover how
the theoretical claims of the victim's family were affected by the
system of pardoning, to ask how far they were respected by
the authorities and then what use was made by potential appellors of such powers as remained to them. Again, the conduct
of the slayer himself must be taken into account. If he stood his
ground he faced trial on appeal, but might hope for a settlement.
If he took to his heels he was likely enough to be outlawed on
appeal in the county court. The manner in which the authorities

might aid him depended on which course he adopted. Their attitude to the homicide who was available for trial will be considered first.

If the king was aware that an appeal was going to be prosecuted against a slayer who had been arrested it was not his policy to grant pardon. Indeed there would be little advantage to the appellee in securing a pardon which contained the proviso of standing to right, for this would leave him very much where he was, still bound to defend the charge before the king's justices. Prisoners arrested on appeal seldom appear to have attempted to get pardon, either because they recognized that it would be of little avail to them, or because they knew it would be refused. Most arrested appellees were content to obtain release on bail, but those of optimistic temperament might obtain a special commission of oyer and terminer or gaol delivery to try them at once. Occasionally a prisoner was pardoned the king's suit although it was uncertain whether an appeal was pending, but if there was doubt about this special care would be taken to ensure that the pardon should not obstruct the effective prosecution of the appeal. Thus Henry III, in pardoning a man who had slain by accident and had voluntarily surrendered to prison, ordered that he should be released only if he could find twelve free and lawful men to go bail for him.[1] Or the king might give instructions that the pardoned prisoner should be released only if no appeal was pending,[2] and even without such instructions it appears that the sheriff might detain him if he was aware of an appeal against him.[3] Edward I ordered that a prisoner should be allowed to fine for release if not appealed 'as has been wont to be done in the like case at other times'[4] and some of his orders for bail included this condition.[5] Occasionally, the king did not pardon outright but reduced punishment to abjuration of the realm, going on crusade or entering a monastery, but in so doing he might

---

[1] *Close Rolls, 1227–31*, 148. Cf. *Cal. Pat. Rolls, 1247–58*, 130, where John le Gerdlere was pardoned but released only on finding pledges to stand to right. British Museum Charter 5153, m. 1 shows that an appeal was begun against him but not prosecuted. J.I. 1/318, m. 24, has a case of a prisoner who had been appealed being pardoned, but it sounds as though the appellors were ready to make peace.

[2] e.g. *Close Rolls, 1251–3*, 356.

[3] Ibid., *1256–9*, 90, *Cal. Pat. Rolls, 1247–58*, 576, 601; cf. *Close Rolls, 1261–4*, 317.

[4] *Cal. Close Rolls, 1272–9*, 285.

[5] Ibid. 109, 177; ibid., *1279–88*, 216. It would of course be unnecessary if release followed an inquisition *de odio et atia* which found the appeal malicious.

postpone the departure or entry until the relatives had had a chance to appeal. In one case pilgrimage to Jerusalem was suspended for five years, but it does not appear whether this slayer was in prison.[1] The slayer might be allowed to abjure at once provided he was not appealed, though one sheriff delayed for over four years before being reminded to let his prisoner abjure.[2] The king was careful, then, not to jeopardize the prosecution of an appeal by premature release of a prisoner. Moreover, once the prisoner had been released on bail he would not apparently pardon him if he knew the appellor still wanted to prosecute. Pardons were obtained by homicides who had been appealed and were out on bail, but in some of these cases the appellors may already have agreed to withdraw; at any rate the king would not seem to have been told that they were prosecuting. However, since bail was generally granted after an inquisition *de odio et atia* the appeal might have been found to be malicious and in that event there would be no reason to hesitate in pardoning the appellee.

If the slayer had remained at large it was anomalous for him to secure pardon if it was known that he was being appealed. The king might, of course, easily be deceived on this point, but it was a serious offence to conceal that an appeal was being actively prosecuted when applying for pardon. Robert de Welly was fined the very large sum of 200 marks for obtaining for himself and his men a charter of pardon for the death of John de Hellewe, of which the widow had appealed them. The charter stated that she had withdrawn her appeal, but at the eyre they were found to have deceived the king, since she was still prosecuting it.[3] A good many appellees may have secured pardon when appealed without subsequent detection; indeed, in a few cases the grant of pardon may in fact have persuaded the appellors to withdraw, but the king would not deliberately pardon in such a way as to hinder the continuation of an appeal. There is an early example of the king 'pardoning an appeal' in so far as pertained to him, but this pardon was clearly only permissive: it did not debar the appellor from

---

[1] *Cal. Pat. Rolls, 1258–66*, 426–7.

[2] e.g. *Close Rolls, 1231–4*, 194; ibid., *1242–7*, 70; ibid., *1247–51*, 29.

[3] See above, p. 33, n. 3. Subsequently she did in fact withdraw it, and the appellees were given firm peace in accordance with their pardon, despite its having been improperly obtained. The pardon is summarized, *Cal. Pat. Rolls, 1247–58*, 353.

prosecuting her appeal if she chose to do so, but made with-drawal easy by remitting any amercement for it.[1] As pardons normally contained the proviso of standing to right they would not, in any event, exclude the prosecution of the appeal; they could at most create a certain prejudice against it. Thus while it was not totally impracticable for an appellee to secure pardon before trial, special strings were likely to be attached, and the prospect of being required to face the appellor in court was not likely to be diminished by this means. Licence for a concord, on the other hand, might be but seldom was obtained at this stage. Generally, the appellee waited until his trial before adopting this method of averting proof and possible conviction.

At the time of the trial it was not the king's policy to prevent the hearing of an appeal or stay the proceedings. This is indicated in passing by Bracton, who raises the question what point is there in a widow's prosecuting an appeal for the slaying of her husband since there will have to be trial by jury, just as there would be at the king's suit. The widow's appeal has an advantage, he decides, in that the king's suit is sometimes remitted *de gratia* but this cannot happen if she prosecutes.[2] The king might, however, issue a general decree prohibiting prosecution for acts of violence during civil war and reinforce this by instructions to the justices in individual cases to quash private appeals.[3] Normally he observed a self-imposed limitation, but this was a matter of general policy which the demands of equity or expediency could be expected to transcend on occasion. Yet it is remarkable how difficult it is to discover such occasions. The outstanding exception to the rule of not pardoning prisoners known to have been appealed is the general amnesty granted as a pious gesture on the death of Queen Eleanor in 1204, but

---

[1] *Rot. Litt. Claus.* ii. 200.   [2] *De Legibus*, f. 148b.

[3] e.g. *Close Rolls, 1264–8*, 440. Another kind of intervention appears on *Rot. Litt. Pat.* i. 66, where men who had killed apparently on the king's order were to have peace if accused. This obviously was a very special case and does not in any way reflect normal policy. There is one most unusual writ ordering the itinerant justices to hear an appeal both of homicide and of ordering and abetting it, and then send the record to him, and not to give judgement or promulgate outlawry against the appellees, who included Miles Basset, until the king gave them further instructions (*Close Rolls, 1231–4*, 591–2). The sheriff was ordered not to proceed to outlawry in the county court, but postpone it till the eyre (ibid.; cf. ibid. 465 for an earlier postponement). The killing had occurred in 1233 or earlier and the widow had appealed other persons but had been found to have done so *de odio et atia* (ibid. 227). This circumstance and possibly some connection with the political crisis at this time will explain Henry's peculiar action in this case.

even in this case those accused of homicide were to find pledges
to stand to right if appealed; if they could not or would not
find pledges, they were to remain in prison or abjure the realm.[1]
This requirement sharply distinguished homicide from other
crimes, the pardons for which on this occasion had no such
proviso.[2] The one later example which may be quoted shows
that something quite abnormal, indeed miraculous, was
needed before the king would depart from his general rule and
grant a pardon that prevented appeal. It has been noticed
earlier that a few convicted criminals survived hanging, either
because the rope broke or because they were cut down before
becoming asphyxiated. Such survival was taken as a divine
manifestation of the wrongfulness of the sentence and pardon
was granted. One of these pardons went to a homicide who had
been appealed, convicted, and hanged, but survived because
the rope broke, 'ex quo per divinam clementiam ei est vita
reservata'.[3] Obviously no demand by an appellor for a second
execution could be entertained after this supernatural exculpation.[4]

While the king's policy was not entirely consistent in practice,
he did, then, show considerable care for the relatives' right of
appeal. His justices also were at some pains to ensure that there
was an opportunity for appeal even in cases in which pardon
seemed appropriate. Thus when the jury presented a homicide
as accidental, they might inquire whether anyone wished to
appeal. The justices in eyre in Northamptonshire in 1253 were
particularly punctilious about this. When a man had been
accidentally killed during a game, according to the jury, they
asked his father, who was present in court, if he wished to
prosecute and he said no, as it had been an accident.[5] And when
the jury reported that a woman had killed a man by mischance, a
staff slipping from her hand as she tried to hit a cock, the justices
inquired if any one wished to sue, though no one did so.[6] In
each case no decision was given as they wished to consult their
fellows. This suggests a particularly severe attitude to accidental

---

[1] *Rot. Litt. Pat.* i. 54.

[2] Although one of the prisoners charged with breach of the peace was in fact
appealed again after his release. See *Rot. de Oblatis*, 381.

[3] *Close Rolls, 1234–7*, 6.

[4] But in a similar case Edward I pardoned only what belonged to him (*Cal.
Close Rolls, 1279–88*, 34; cf. J.I. 1/653, m. 19ᵈ).

[5] J.I. 1/615, m. 7.   [6] Ibid., m. 8ᵈ.

slaying on this occasion, yet it might be helpful to the slayer if the king could be informed that the next of kin concurred with the jury's view. Whatever the justices' motives, it is clear that they were ready to entertain an appeal although they had reason to believe that the slaying had been by mischance. Invitations of this kind do not appear when homicide in self-defence was presented, but appeals were not discouraged.

This respect for the rights of the relatives is remarkable in view of the fact that appeals had only a small chance of success if they were prosecuted before the king's justices. By the thirteenth century they were obstructed by a farcical accumulation of procedural rules, so that most of them, if not already withdrawn, were quashed for some technical error. Sometimes, before this happened, the appellor asked that the prosecution should be taken over by the Crown, but this solution was, of course, of no use to an appellor who was trying to get a conviction when the killing qualified for pardon. The justices showed themselves reluctant to allow appeals to reach the stage of proof, whether by battle or jury; they quashed them almost automatically if exceptions were raised. One might expect to find they were particularly reluctant when they had reason to believe that a case was really one of homicide by misadventure. It is thus significant that they were so scrupulous about allowing or even inviting appellors to come forward in such cases.

Usually the justices would not know more of the circumstances than the appellor revealed,[1] and he could not, even if he so wished, state that the slaying had been accidental or in self-defence, since the correct formula for appeal included the allegation that the slaying had been in felony and breach of the king's peace. The appellee in his defence could not, at least during most of this period, draw attention to circumstances such as self-defence and accident either. As Maitland remarked, 'we see no trace of his being able to set up the misadventure by way of exception'.[2] He must be ready to prove

---

[1] They might have learnt more from the indictments and coroners' rolls, but they could not or would not use this knowledge to quash the appeal if it was made in due form.

[2] He was referring here to the late twelfth century. See *Hist. Eng. Law*, ii. 482. Britton and *The Mirror of Justices* said that this could be done but they may have been inaccurate, although there was an important modification in the treatment of appeals under Edward I. See below, p. 277.

that he was in no way responsible for the death, that the deceased had not been further from life or nearer to death through his action, or he would be convicted of felonious homicide. This rule did not apply if the victim had himself been a felon, found in the act and killed while resisting arrest. The appellee could defend himself on this ground and hope for acquittal.[1] Otherwise exceptions were confined to such matters as the status of the appellor and his or her deviation from the proper formula and omission or variation in the account of the slaying. Only when the appeal had been quashed on such grounds and the prisoner arraigned at the king's suit could the justices go into the circumstances and decide to recommend him to mercy.

Although the king would not normally and deliberately pardon while an appeal was being prosecuted he would sometimes give permission for a concord to be made, but in cases of homicide his justices had no power, as they had in cases of rape, wounding, and assault, to authorize the making of a concord between appellor and appellee. In theory this required the king's own consent. Thus his grace would have to be invoked by the prisoner or on his behalf, and licence for concord obtained, or the appellor might get leave to withdraw and accept compensation. Concords were more easily authorized in the course of proceedings in the court *Coram Rege*, and if the king himself was present there need be no delay.[2] But the king was by no means lavish with such licences. It seems that he would grant them only in exceptional circumstances or in return for a very considerable payment—as much as 100 marks might be paid even when the concord was made in the *Curia Regis*. Moreover, his granting licence did not mean that he or his justices generally put any pressure on the victim's kin to come to terms. This is brought out by a conditional clause in some licences to make peace with the relatives or widow, 'si pacem cum eis possit invenire',[3] or 'quod . . . pacem faciat cum predicta Felicia de predicto appello, si ipsa Felicia voluerit'.[4]

---

[1] e.g. J.I. 1/1043, m. 14; K.B. 26/143, m. 5.

[2] Adam de Port, impleaded by Philip de Lucy over a medley between their men in which one of Philip's was killed, was said by John to have made peace 'coram nobis cum eodem Philippo et cum parentibus mortui' (*Rot. Litt. Claus.* i. 52).   [3] *Close Rolls, 1231–4*, 23.

[4] Ibid., *1234–7*, 119; cf. 126. On 11 June 1207, Elyas de Beuney was granted the king's peace until Michaelmas 'et quod interim si possit pacem faciat cum parentibus'. See *Rot. Litt. Pat.* i. 73; *Rot. de Oblatis*, 372.

In one case the *Rotulus de Oblatis* notes that the concord has in fact been made.[1] Thus the licensing of concords in no way detracted from the right to prosecute a capital appeal. At the same time it did provide a means—the only official means—of giving substance to the alternative right of the kin to compensation.

So far only support for the prosecution of appeals in court against appellees who appeared there has been considered. But the question of appeals against fugitives could also confront the itinerant justices. In the thirteenth century eyres were coming to be held at increasingly long intervals and generally there was ample time for the process of outlawry in the county court to be concluded before the next one. But in a few cases it intervened before the process had been completed. If the appellee did not now put in an appearance, the justices would probably instruct the appellor to carry on with the appeal in the county court.[2] Occasionally, they hesitated to do this if they knew the slaying had been accidental, as is shown by the case of Richard Benne, who had fled after the death of Geoffrey de Kamele. The latter's father, Roger, appeared before the itinerant justices in 1249 ready to prosecute his appeal, but the jurors said that Geoffrey had been run over by a wagon, drawn by four oxen and driven by Richard, accidentally and not by felony. The justices did not instruct Roger to continue his appeal until Richard was outlawed in the county court, but decided to have consultation on the matter.[3] This was a most noteworthy interference with the right of appeal, and is doubtless to be explained by the usual tenderness shown by the courts towards those responsible for road accidents. Normally they gave every support to the appellor when outlawry was involved.

While the king himself took some care not to pardon appellees who were in prison, and his justices encouraged appeals against fugitives, the right of appeal was bound to be affected when the king pardoned fugitives from justice. He could not always know whether an appeal was being actively prosecuted

---

[1] Ibid. 127.

[2] As they did in the case of John de Saham, appealed by Amphelisa Harding; see J.I. 1/87, 42ᵈ. He had in fact already been pardoned on grounds of self-defence (*Cal. Pat. Rolls, 1281–92*, 23). Cf. C. 47/67/8, no. 317, where a jury had already sworn that the fugitive had killed in self-defence.

[3] J.I. 1/996, m. 23.

in the county court and might grant pardon before the process of exigent could be completed. Occasionally, he even held it up while the circumstances were investigated.[1] He pardoned men outlawed on appeal just as readily as those whose outlawry had been ordered by the justices.[2] Indeed, he came to grant pardon to persons who apparently did not know if they had been outlawed or not, as the common formula 'outlawry if any' in the pardons shows. On one occasion at least, the justices queried a charter of pardon which was so worded since the grantee had been outlawed on appeal.[3] But generally no objection was taken, and in any case the king's charter could not be overruled. Thus very often the patient work of an appellor was undone. But since the pardon would nearly always contain the proviso of standing to right he could start it all over again if he chose. There was in fact a chance that a new appeal would be prosecuted, either by the original appellor or by someone else entitled to appeal, and steps might be taken officially to ensure that the appellee was available. The king would order the arrest of a man whom he had pardoned if an appeal was subsequently brought and the appellor asked him to do so.[4]

Not only fugitives and outlaws but also those pardoned after the justices had referred their cases to the king were required to stand to right. The king, then, went through the motions of providing safeguards for the rights of the family, even though his pardons, especially those to fugitives from justice, inevitably had the effect of postponing if not destroying any hopes of making them effective. The pardons, with very few exceptions,

---

[1] e.g. *Close Rolls, 1231–4*, 342; ibid., *1234–7*, 2, where the appellee claimed that the victim had been outlawed for killing his uncle; ibid. 244 and *Cal. Pat. Rolls, 1232–47*, 155.

[2] For an exception to this see below, p. 313. In special circumstances, the king might pardon outlawry provided it had been at his suit. See J.I. 1/827, mm. 49^d, 50^d. A commission of oyer and terminer had recently been appointed for the appeal against the grantee and others in this complicated case (*Cal. Pat. Rolls, 1266–72*, 476; cf. ibid. 420).

[3] J.I. 1/736, m. 29^d. The pardon was based on an inquisition finding that Hugh Carbonel had killed in self-defence. Cf. *Cal. Pat. Rolls, 1266–72*, 104, 134.

[4] e.g. in April 1246 Henry III pardoned John le Vadlet his suit for the death of Martin Malherbe, for which John had abjured the realm (ibid., *1232–47*, 477), but in November he issued general instructions for John's arrest wherever he was found, as he was appealed of the death. A marginal note shows that this order was made at the request of Martin's widow, who was no doubt now bringing the appeal (ibid. 493).

were conditional on these rights being respected. Indeed, there is some reason to believe that the family's right to appeal remained unaffected whether it was expressly safeguarded or not.[1] However, the wording of the letters patent is of some interest for significant modifications came to be made in it.

Especially in the early part of the thirteenth century the formulae employed were not entirely stabilized. Many pardons specifically remitted the king's suit, but it was not invariably mentioned and when it was omitted the proviso of 'standing to right if any will speak against him' might quite sensibly be taken to mean that the grantee could still be presented by the jurors and tried at the king's suit. But this was not the intention and the king would sometimes send an order to the justices in eyre not to allow this.[2] It was only if appealed that the grantee must stand to right. In some pardons the relatives' continuing right to take action is indicated only by implication: it may be stated that the king has pardoned the homicide 'quantum ad ipsum pertinet', or 'quantum in ipso est', implying that the pardon does not prejudice the rights of others to prosecute. Or it may be said only that the king has pardoned his suit, or *sectam pacis sue*, implying that he has not forbidden trial at the suit of the relatives.

Most often the pardons rested on explicit conditions. 'Provided he make peace with the family and stand to right if any one will speak against him' seems to have been the full and correct formula early in the thirteenth century. Very often this comprehensive formula was used in individual pardons, but it appears that either section of it could stand for the whole in the enrolments. Most pardons as enrolled on the early patent rolls of John included only the proviso that peace must be made with the relatives, but this did not mean that the latter's right to appeal was excluded. Every now and then they also mentioned 'standing to right'. For example, in 1202 Henry de Cunde was pardoned his flight and outlawry 'ita quod faciat pacem etc. et standi recto etc.', and Godfrey le Berruer was pardoned his flight 'ita tamen quod faciat pacem etc. Et pleg. inveniat standi etc.'[3] On the same membrane and between these

---

[1] This is suggested by *Select Pleas of the Crown*, Selden Soc. i, no. 47 (*Northants. Record Soc.* v, no. 66), and seems to have been assumed in the 1290s; see below, p. 186.

[2] e.g. *Close Rolls, 1231–4*, 493; *Cal. Pat. Rolls, 1232–47*, 100 (cf. 102), 104, 109, 155.

[3] *Rot. Litt. Pat.* i. 13.

two entries is one recording that Adam de Worminton has letters patent of pardon for his flight and outlawry for the slaying of his nephew 'ita tamen quod faciat pacem etc.', and it is hard to believe that the 'etc.' here stood for less than the whole formula so briefly indicated in the other two entries. Moreover, these early pardons sometimes appear to omit any reference to making peace but do mention standing to right,[1] and from 1208 to 1214 all the pardons recorded on the surviving patent rolls refer to this and not to peace with the kin. Yet it it is clear that this does not indicate any substantial change but merely a different fashion in the wording of the entries, for a later reference to one of them shows that the actual letters patent issued to the grantee contained the whole formula.[2] In 1214 there is a reversion to the earlier style of entry, but evidently no importance can be attached to these variations; they may well have been due to nothing more than the labour-saving devices of the clerks who enrolled the pardons. During Henry's minority the whole formula was practically always entered,[3] but then the entries began to be abbreviated again; one on the patent roll of 1233 runs 'on condition that he stand his trial if anyone etc. under the usual words'.[4] The two parts of the formula are sometimes run together, as in the proviso 'that he make peace with the relatives if any will proceed against him'.[5] It is still difficult to be sure of the actual wording of the letters patent of pardon since one summary may give both parts of the formula while another gives only one.[6] One must be very cautious, therefore, in seeing significance in the apparent omission of part of the normal formula.[7] However, at this period the condition of making peace with the family is often omitted in the enrolment and sometimes at least this seems to mean that it was absent from the charter of pardon

[1] Rot. Litt. Pat. i. 15, 53; cf. Pipe Roll, 3 John, 274.

[2] Rot. Lit. Pat. i. 114 'ita tamen quod stet recto'; Rot. Litt. Claus. i. 597: 'ita tamen quod pacem faceret cum parentibus . . . et staret recto si quis inde versus eum loqui voluisset'.

[3] There are only two or three exceptions before 1225: Pat. Rolls, 1216–25, 19, 288, 294 (abjuration).

[4] Cal. Pat. Rolls, 1232–47, 35.

[5] Close Rolls, 1227–31, 552; cf. Cal. Pat. Rolls, 1232–47, 255.

[6] Ibid., 1232–47, 102, 100.

[7] One entry does suggest that the omission of part of it might be deliberate, for standing to right was entered and then cancelled and making peace substituted. This pardon was for a clerk, and it is possible that the proviso of standing to right was omitted because benefit of clergy would make it futile. See ibid. 357.

itself. In one entry, for example, this proviso was crossed out though 'stet recto' was left.[1] It appears more regularly in the 1240s than in the 1230s, to judge by the enrolments.[2] This proviso certainly seems to have been regarded as less significant. When a pardon was produced at the eyre the clerk might record some details of it on the roll, and it is noticeable that the proviso of standing to right may be included but that of making peace dropped even though the enrolment indicates that the actual letters patent included it.[3] This is understandable, since the one proviso called for action in court and the other did not. It was the duty of the itinerant justices to make sure that the grantee appeared in court, ready to implement the undertaking to stand to right, unless he had already done so. The clause was a reminder to them to proclaim the pardon and invite any would-be appellor to come forward. But the justices were not concerned with the making of peace in accordance with the alternative proviso. The grantee was under some moral obligation to negotiate peace with the victim's kin, but this was no longer a legal obligation. Occasionally, the court was informed that peace had been made, but this was to show that the relatives were not now prosecuting their appeal, rather than that the pardoned appellee had fulfilled his undertaking.[4] The courts could ignore this proviso and the eyre rolls omit it when summarizing the pardon; it must gradually have dawned on those concerned that there was little point in including it in the actual letters patent. If the slayer would not make some payment voluntarily the only way in which pressure could be brought to bear on him was to threaten to appeal him on the strength of his obligation to stand to right. None the less, the ultimate dropping of any reference to making peace could have a detrimental effect on the relatives' claim to compensation. So long as it was mentioned

---

[1] C. 66/44, m. 7.

[2] The printed calendars generally do not reveal these details and it is necessary to refer in most cases to the rolls.

[3] e.g. the pardons for Adam le Reve of Nesse, J.I. 1/734, m. 29^d, C. 66/64, m. 8; William son of John le Webster, J.I. 1/1109, m. 4^d, C. 66/63, m. 2; Philip Caillewey, J.I. 1/174, m. 36^d, *Cal. Pat. Rolls, 1232–47*, 104; Walter son of Benedict, J.I. 1/300^c, m. 24, C. 66/62, m. 10.

[4] e.g. justices in 1262 decided that Hugh de Bley should go quit, since it was testified by the jury that he had made peace with the relatives and no one else was present who wished to prosecute. See J.I. 1/954, m. 63^d; cf. C. 66/64, m. 8 (1253). His was one of the last pardons to include both provisos.

in the pardons it at least countenanced their attempts to obtain it; their moral right to it could hardly be doubted. Its total omission might lead to the eclipse even of this moral right, so that those who sought to obtain some payment would now be regarded as mercenary, if not vindictive.

It was apparently in a very casual way that this proviso was allowed to drop out. It was normally included in the early 1250s, down to Henry III's visit to Gascony from August 1253 to December 1254. The first pardon for homicide which he granted there also included it, but for the remainder of his stay it was omitted from the pardons, or at least from the enrolments. It is very probable that it was omitted in the letters patent themselves, for some of these were produced at subsequent eyres the rolls of which have survived, and whenever the roll quotes the pardon in any detail the proviso of standing to right appears, but not that of making peace,[1] though as has just been seen this is not conclusive proof of its absence from the actual charter. The enrolment of the first pardon granted after Henry's return included it again,[2] but after that it only appeared in the enrolments spasmodically during 1255,[3] and then disappeared there altogether. Evidently Henry's stay in Gascony was responsible for the elimination of this proviso. He is most unlikely to have given the matter special thought while there, or to have been able to discuss it with counsellors who might be specially interested in it. The decision to omit the proviso is much more likely to have been taken by the clerk who drew up the warrants, or the omission may even have been inadvertent because the clerk now doing this work was not sufficiently familiar with the pardons to know that it was generally included. Thus the displacement of royal administrative departments and consequent makeshifts or changes of personnel are the likely reasons for this change in the formula. Once the proviso had been dropped, however casually, it would become apparent that there was little point in restoring it, and it was soon allowed to lapse entirely.

---

[1] See the pardons for Fuleham and Short, J.I. 1/233, m. 52ᵈ, C. 66/66, m. 5; Thomas de Bregges, Matthew Ferthing, J.I. 1/361, mm. 57, 40 (where Ferthing is stated to have crossed to Gascony to get the pardon), C. 66/66, mm. 11, 6; Walter de Gissing, J.I. 1/568, m. 12, C. 66/66, m. 11.

[2] William Doget de Bosco's, C. 66/69, m. 17, J.I. 1/778, m. 43. An inquisition, ordered by the regents in March 1254 had found him not guilty; see *Cal. Inquisitions Misc.* i, no. 2085.   [3] C. 66/69, mm. 5, 7, 13, 14, 16.

The stipulation of standing to right was nearly always included, even in the enrolments, although this fact is concealed by the *Calendar of Letters Patent*, where after 1252 it is generally omitted, presumably as common form. Sometimes it was abbreviated in the enrolment to a mere 'ita tamen etc', but even in this diminished form the clerks thought proper to include it, and rightly so, since this proviso really mattered. The grantee was expected to have his charter proclaimed in court and would be in trouble if he failed to appear and give a would-be appellor the opportunity to prosecute. For some years under Edward I, however, it was omitted when pardon was granted in certain circumstances. If the grantee had just been remanded at the eyre then the proviso might be dropped. This seems to have happened in a few such cases in 1279–80,[1] but it was generally included until 1282, so that the first experiment in omitting it seems to have been short-lived. In 1282 it was revived and became the normal practice when pardon followed remand at the eyre.[2] It is particularly noticeable during that of 1292–3. Since the enrolments of practically all the pardons granted immediately after remand *ad gratiam* by itinerant justices omitted the proviso and nearly all other pardons as enrolled included it, there can be no doubt that this was a matter of policy and that the engrossed letters patent themselves corresponded with the enrolments in this respect.[3] Indeed, one such letter patent has survived, that for Thomas son of Robert de Nateby, and it does in fact omit any reference to standing to right.[4] Those remanded at the Cornish eyre of 1302 were not required to stand to right, but pardons after remand by justices of oyer and terminer regularly included the proviso, as did those after remand at gaol deliveries. The

---

[1] e.g. the pardons for John de Fonte and Walter le Whyte, C. 66/98, m. 6; John le Carpenter, ibid., m. 5; their remands are recorded on J.I. 1/371, m. 7; J.I. 1/915, m. 10ᵈ; J.I. 1/323, m. 57ᵈ. In 1280 Robert de Skercroft seems to have received a similar pardon, see C. 66/99, m. 5, but evidence of his remand has not been found.

[2] Only one exception has been noticed in 1282, the pardon to Richard Russel, C. 66/101, m. 13. His case was exceptional in that he was a lunatic; see above, p. 168, n. 1. It may have been thought desirable to require him to stand to right when he recovered.

[3] Exceptionally, it was included in the pardon for Roger Garlaund who was remanded *ad gratiam* and then produced his pardon before the justices. The account of it on the eyre roll confirms the enrolment on this point. See J.I. 1/409, m. 3; C. 66/111, m. 7.

[4] C. 202/H/3, no. 58. His remand to prison is recorded on J.I. 1/986, m. 1.

omission was, then, deliberate but by the end of the reign very infrequent as the eyre was being superseded by other types of commission.

The dropping of the proviso in special cases does not mean that Edward I was lax in requiring that pardoned slayers should appear in court and answer any appeal that might be brought against them. After all, the recipients of these pardons were already prisoners who had just been in court ready to stand trial. Appellors had at this very moment the opportunity to appeal them. If they failed to avail themselves of it now they would have virtually no chance to command a hearing at a future eyre, since failure to prosecute it there at the earliest opportunity was fatal to any appeal. Moreover, the omission of the proviso did not obviate the need to produce the pardon before the justices; on the contrary, pardons of this type seem to have been devised to meet the case of those who could get them through before the end of the session and have them proclaimed there in the ordinary way.[1] The remanded prisoners would not be released, or at least not officially released, until the pardons came. Thus they should automatically be available for trial if an appeal was now made. The justices evidently did not consider that the solemn invitation to appellors to come forward was superfluous if a pardon failed to mention standing to right, but included it as usual in the proclamation, before granting firm peace.[2] In short, it was just because the grantees were in no situation to avoid standing to right that there was no need to stipulate that they should do so. Edward was certainly not intending to let them off this liability. Indeed, just at this period he was making very special efforts to ensure that fugitives surrendered to prison and a number of pardons were conditional upon their doing so by a given date.[3] These generally also stated specifically that they must stand to right. Thus the king, or one of his ministers, was showing some interest in this matter and may well have recognized the futility of inserting this requirement in pardons for those who were not only in prison at the moment, but had just been answering to the charges against them in court and

---

[1] Those pardoned in this way in 1279–80 are not known to have produced their pardons at this eyre, and it may have been their failure to get them in time that led to the suspension of this type of pardon for a couple of years.

[2] See J.I. 1/374, m. 79ᵈ and J.I. 1/409, m. 28 for clear statements that this was done.   [3] See below, p. 287.

would have to produce their charters there as soon as they received them.[1]

The situation was quite different if a prisoner was remanded *ad gratiam* at a gaol delivery. Even though proclamation of a pardon was possible there it did not command the same publicity as at the eyre, and the original proceedings might not be notified to potential appellors. Thus pardons on the record of justices of gaol delivery needed to include the proviso. So, of course, did those granted after special inquisitions. When Edward, in the following years, began to grant pardon in return for service in his wars, the proviso of standing to right was, however optimistically, regularly included and the recruits had to find mainpernors not only for their military service but also for standing trial.[2] Moreover, at first, he made some gesture of excluding men who had been outlawed in the county court through appeal from recruitment in this way.[3] Thus Edward still followed a deliberate policy of respecting the right of appeal ostensibly at least.

Much earlier, and then very occasionally, the proviso of standing to right was qualified by a particular method of proof being required if an appeal was made. A couple of John's pardons provided that proof must be by judicial combat. Henry de Stratton was pardoned the death of a man in 1202 on condition of finding pledges 'standi recto si quis erga ipsum loqui voluerit et se defendendi per corpus suum ad corpus, sine alia lege'.[4] In 1205 Alured Morwy was pardoned the death of Tokina, wife of Osbert Wringe, 'nisi aliquis per duellum eum appellare voluerit inde qui duellum facere velit et possit'.[5] These pardons certainly limited the possibility of appeal; the first would exclude any appeal by the widow, if there were one. But no later instances of such limitation have been found, and Bracton mentions a modification of procedure in just the opposite direction. According to him the method of proof was restricted when a pardoned outlaw was appealed anew by the original appellor, but the restriction was in favour of the latter. He would have the trouble of renewing his appeal

---

[1] Only one or two pardons of this kind seem to have been granted when the eyre was over, e.g. that for Alice le Ster, but as she had been only 6 when she accidentally caused a death the omission is explicable on that ground alone. See above, p. 50.
[2] *Cal. Pat. Rolls, 1292–1301*, 107.
[3] See below, p. 313.
[4] *Rot. Litt. Pat.* i. 15.
[5] Ibid. i. 53; cf. *Pipe Roll, 7 John*, 172.

but at any rate this should be made easy for him. The fact that the appellee had once fled did not establish his guilt; this had still to be proved, but by his flight he had forfeited his right of choice between defending himself by combat or putting himself on the country, and must now submit to trial by jury whether he wanted to or not. Thus the appellor would not be required to fight to prove his charge.[1]

It appears, then, that the king took some care not to prejudice the right of the relatives to secure the trial and conviction of pardoned homicides. In view of this it is surprising to find Maitland asserting that the king's pardon protected the appellee from capital punishment.[2] Maitland did not, of course, overlook the proviso of standing to right. He recognized that 'the king could not protect the man-slayer from the suit of the dead man's kin',[3] but he thought that the pardon averted punishment in life or limb on the appellee's conviction. The pardon which purported to safeguard the appeal would, then, drastically affect its outcome; not only would it allow the culprit to make peace with the relatives, at a price, if they were agreeable, but it ensured that even if they were inexorable their appeal would result in nothing more serious for him than pecuniary punishment. There seems to be nothing whatever in the wording of the pardons to justify this interpretation. It becomes necessary, therefore, to look very closely at the evidence upon which Maitland relied for this paradoxical view. He quoted only one piece of evidence in support, but this, as he presents it, seems irrefutable. After noting that 'the king could not protect the man-slayer from the suit of the dead man's kin', he continues:

What could the kin do in such a case? They could make themselves extremely disagreeable; they could extort money. In Henry III's day Mr. Justice Thurkelby was consulted by a friend who had obtained a pardon, but was being appealed. The advice that the

---

[1] *De Legibus*, f. 133ᵇ.

[2] Holdsworth apparently agreed with him: 'In the old days of *wer* and *bot* the person who slew another, even though it was by misadventure or in self-defence, had been liable to pay the statutory sums to the deceased's kin. . . . The fact that the result of conviction upon an appeal or an indictment was no longer a money payment, but death or mutilation, made no difference to the liability; and the mercy of the king would suffice where it was clearly wrong that such liability should be enforced' (*Hist. Eng. Law*, iii. 312–13).

[3] *Hist. Eng. Law.* ii. 482.

expert lawyer gave was this:—You had better go to battle, but
directly a blow is struck cry "Craven" and produce your charter;
you will not be punished, for the king has given you your life and
members.[1]

But this advice of Thurkelby's must be placed in its proper
context. It is known from a book of legal precedents, *La Corone
pledee devant justices*, where it is quoted in reply to a question
arising out of a particular and very unusual case. A man has
been appealed by his victim's widow, tried and acquitted as
his exception is upheld. He has obtained the king's pardon of
his suit of the peace, on condition of standing to right. Now he
is appealed by a relative of the slain man. The problem is what
does the condition of standing to right entail in these circumstances? Some people say that he fulfils the condition of standing
to right if he is ready to find pledges 'de fere gre' to the relatives;
but if he cannot do this because the appellor is 'de si gros grein'
that his wrath cannot be assuaged, then it may be said that he
must fight, and Thurkelby's advice follows (though it does
not refer to life and members being spared). But Maitland
did not include all of it, for while Thurkelby advised the appellee to surrender at once if he did not feel sure he could defeat
the appellor at the first stroke, he advised him to fight on if
he was confident he could do so and thus obtain judgement in
his favour. The defeated appellor would then be imprisoned not
only until he fined for his recreancy but also until he obtained
the king's grace for contravening his charter and grant of peace.
As this shows, an appeal in such circumstances was unlawful in
itself: the appellor was liable to punishment for bringing it.
Since there had already been acquittal on the first appeal,
that of the widow, and the king's suit was pardoned the appellee
had no further need to stand to right, and Thurkelby's scheme
seems to have been quite uncalled for except as a trap to involve
the appellor in double punishment. The marginal comment
'nota doctrinam' points to its novelty, and it must be doubted
whether he ever gave this advice to anyone actually appealed
after acquittal and pardon. It seems probable that he was
giving an ingenious but far-fetched answer to a colleague or
pupil who had raised a quibble about the effect of the proviso
in a hypothetical case, one in which it would actually no longer

---

[1] Ibid. ii. 483, quoting Cambr. Univ. Library, MS. Mm. i, 27, f. 124.

apply. One of the shorter and much more popular versions of the same set of precedents dismissed the matter thus:

pur ceo ke le roi lui ad pardone sa suite de la mort, issi qil estoise adreit si nul homme veut rien de ceo parler envers li, et quant il vient et respent a lapeel la Femme et il abate lapeel, *si esta il adreit* et si nad il a nul homme a respoundre si al roy noun. Cum de ceo fet et quant il ad pardone ceo que a lui apent et par iugement est il qites de lapel la Femme, et si est il de tot quites.[1]

This concludes the discussion in this version. The man acquitted on the widow's appeal and pardoned the king's suit is totally quit. Nothing more need be done to fulfil the condition of standing to right; and so Thurkelby's subtleties are besides the point. His 'doctrine' was probably only a piece of legal theorizing or even of legal humour. Even if his 'advice' could safely be followed when the appeal was unlawful, there is no reason to think that it would apply when there was a lawful appeal after pardon.[2] There is no evidence here for the view

---

[1] British Museum MS. Harl. 6669, f. 2; seventeen similar shorter versions are known. Only two other longer versions, including the Thurkelby story, have been found: Cambr. Univ. Library, Dd. vii, 14; Christ Church, Oxford, C. 111.

[2] Another view of the relationship between pardon and appeal based on this work has recently been put forward by J. M. Kaye in his edition of it in *Selden Soc. Supplementary Series*, iv. The fullest version gives two answers to the question what is the meaning of the proviso in the given circumstances. The first runs: 'akune gens dyent ke yl esta en dreyt quant il vint en la court le Roy et mostre sa chartre de pees, ke nostre seignur le Roy li ad grante, par la resone ke par tant est le apel la femme abatu: et kaunt le apel la femme est abatu sy nest il tenu a respoundre, si au Roy non; et quant le Roy li ad pardone ce ke a li apent donk est il quites par jugement' (p. 6). He translates the first part of this as follows: 'Some people say that he "stood to law" when he came into the king's court and showed his charter of peace, which our lord the king had granted to him: because by this means the woman's appeal is abated . . .' He concludes that 'the charter remitted the king's suit and also abated the appeal of the present appellor, but without prejudice to the rights of any other person who might have brought an appeal against the appellee on the same facts' (p. xxxii). He comments that 'this is an arbitrary limitation since the private suit concept would logically prevent the king from interfering at all: the most he might do would be to prevent the justices from holding an inquest *pro pace observanda* on the original appeal being abated'. Variants on this perplexing passage appear in some of the shorter versions, though the one quoted above and some others discard it. Possibly it derived from a misunderstanding of the lost original; 'par tant' may have referred in a wider sense to the situation as it now existed. But whatever the author meant to say, it is quite clear that the king's pardon did not abate a present appeal any more than it prevented a future one. The system of pardoning was not as illogical as all that. There is one case from 1235 in which the problem was rather similar to that supposed here and the Latin of the eyre roll shows very clearly that the king's pardon and the abating of the appeal were quite distinct matters. A widow, Alice, had appealed Roger

that pardon protected the duly convicted appellee against execution.[1]

Other evidence does not point to this view. Bracton, in his discussion of the renewal of the appeal when outlawry has been pardoned, says that the king remits his suit, 'quod quidem facere poterit sine praeiudicio aliorum', and that the appellee 'iudicuim sustinebit',[2] which does not suggest anything less than the usual capital sentence Actual examples of the trial of homicides appealed after being pardoned are hard to come by. One letter close—of particular interest because it rules that the lord of a slain man shares with the relatives the right of appeal after pardon—orders that the appeal shall proceed according to the law and custom of the realm, but it is likely

---

of killing her husband, but admitted that she had not been present. The appellee put himself on the country, but she later came and withdrew her charge. The king had remitted his suit for the death, 'et quia dominus Rex remisit ei hoc quod ad eum inde pertinebat et appellum Alicie nullum est eo quod ipsa non locuta est de visu et auditu et preterea ipsa retraxit se, consideratum est quod Rogerus eat quietus de morte illa imperpetuum' (J.I. 1/864, m. 15^d). The decision is given in detail here because it was not obvious whether her appeal had been abated in such a way that any future appeal was blocked, or whether it had merely been withdrawn. Evidently it was considered that it had gone far enough to have been quashed and so Roger was finally acquitted for ever. Normally, there was no need to go into such detail. But it is perfectly clear that so long as the appellor was in court and was prosecuting his appeal the king's pardon could have no effect on it. This is shown by a number of actual cases. It was only when the appeal had been quashed and he was arraigned at the suit of the king that the prisoner mentioned that he was pardoned and produced his charter. Had it had the effect of abating the appeal he would obviously have produced it at once, without raising exceptions and relying on them to secure his acquittal so far as the appeal was concerned. Thus in the case quoted on p. 192 Robert Fuleham first excepted to Eleanor's appeal and it was quashed; only then did he produce the pardon. Robert Parleben acted similarly (above p. 154). For other examples see J.I. 1/538, m. 18^d; J.I. 1/568, m. 7^d; J.I. 1/804, m. 76; J.I. 1/1051, m. 10^d; J.I. 1/1057, m. 53^d; K.B. 26/161, m. 16^d; Select Cases in Court of King's Bench, Selden Soc. lviii, no. 88. In one or two cases a pardon was produced in abating an appeal, but only because the appellor had failed to come to an earlier eyre and firm peace had then been proclaimed. See above, p. 62, n. 4 and J.I. 1/486, m. 40^d.

[1] In his Constitutional History (p. 480) Maitland says nothing of such protection: 'The king by pardon might free a man from indictment, but not from appeal.'

[2] De Legibus, f. 133^b. He adds that if the appellee refuses trial by jury 'quasi pro convicto habetur, ita quod in patria non poterit remanere: et si rex eum in patria sustinerit, hoc esset ad iniuriam appellantis', which suggests that he would predict further and undue leniency on the part of the king. But the point was probably an academic one, since the king could have extremely few opportunities to commute the penalty in this way. Nor, of course, does it prove that the king could interfere also with the punishment which would follow on conviction. Fleta insists, 'ne fiat injuria appellanti', on perpetual imprisonment for the pardoned appellee who 'patriam recusaverit' (Lib. i, cap. 28).

that in this case the appellee had now fled and that the appeal resulted in his outlawry.[1] This, in fact, was the most probable outcome if anyone persisted with an appeal after pardon. The fact that pardoned homicides who knew that their victim's relatives were irreconcilable preferred flight and outlawry to running the risk of trial and conviction in itself suggests that the punishment would be severe. A few appellees saw fit to stand to right, but their optimism was justified by the appeal being quashed. Just one case has been found in which the appellee was arrested, tried, and executed despite pardon. His fate would prove conclusively that the pardoning of the king's suit was no protection against capital punishment on appeal if it were certain that the pardon—a joint one for him and another man—had reached him before his trial. But this is not certain. Eleanor, widow of Ellis le Waleys, had appealed Robert of Fuleham of her husband's death in 1252 and Robert Short and Robert Dote as accomplices. Dote was outlawed at her suit and does not seem to have secured pardon. Fuleham was imprisoned but was released on bail.[2] The king, in Gascony, granted pardon to him and Short on 4 September 1254 but in the enrolment the letters patent were dated 17 September and they cannot have been handed over earlier than this.[3] The appeal against Fuleham was being heard in the King's Bench in mid October but was adjourned to the eyre in Essex.[4] Dote and Short had not appeared in the King's Bench and the sheriff was ordered to summon them to appear at the eyre. Itinerant justices were appointed for Essex and Hertfordshire on 12 October and were at work there very soon after.[5] Eleanor came and prosecuted her appeal against Fuleham,

---

[1] Cal. Close Rolls, 1251–53, 263: 'Quia rex non perdonavit Radulfo Champeneys nisi sectam pacis que ad ipsum pertinet de morte Johannis de Coueleg', unde rettatus fuit, ita quod staret inde recto in curia regis, si quis versus eum inde loqui vellet, mandatum est vicecomiti et coronatoribus Linc' quod appellum Johannis Carbunel, domini predicti Johannis interfecti, quod facit versus eundem Radulfum et alios pro morte predicta, admittat, et in eodem apello procedat secundum legem et consuetudinem regni, non obstante perdonacione antedicta.' (The pardon is entered in Cal. Pat. Rolls, 1247–58, 137.) Since these instructions were sent to the sheriff and coroners it is likely that Ralf Champeneys had fled and was in process of being outlawed.

[2] Close Rolls, 1251–3, 94.

[3] Cal. Pat. Rolls, 1247–58, 332.

[4] K.B. 26/147ᴮ, m. 3ᵈ.

[5] Cal. Pat. Rolls, 1247–58, 373. Some essoins were taken on 19 October (J.I. 1/233, m. 1).

but it was quashed and he then produced his pardon. It was reported, however, that Short had been arrested for the death and had been hanged at Newgate.[1] If this occurred as is likely, after the hearing in the King's Bench there should have been time for the pardon to reach him, but Fuleham may not have made it available.[2] His case, therefore, does not afford proof, but there is later evidence that the king's pardon would not in itself save a criminal convicted on appeal from execution. In the time of Henry IV a man was appealed of robbery, found guilty and condemned to be hanged; he thereupon alleged that he had the king's charter of pardon and asked for a writ of *scire facias* against his opponent. It was maintained that when the plaintiff had judgement in his favour the king could not pardon, and since the plaintiff could not be deprived of execution the defendant could not have *scire facias*, but should be executed. Then the party at whose suit he was appealed came into court and declared that he did not wish to press his suit further, wherefore the king's charter was allowed.[3] This appears to be the usual reaction, at this period, to a pardon. It may be surmised that it was not the done thing to take advantage of the proviso of standing to right, but that is the furthest one can go. In law, the pardon left the appellee at risk of his life.

Thus in theory the rights of the victim's kin were safeguarded. As a rule the king would not pardon if he knew that an appeal was pending or already in progress, while a pardoned killer was required either to make peace with them or answer to a capital charge. In practice it was not always easy to assert these rights; the next of kin might shrink from doing so; local opinion might be hostile to them. It is necessary, therefore, to inquire what they amounted to in practice and how far they were exploited.

---

[1] Ibid., m. 52^d.

[2] There is another element of doubt in this case, since according to the presenting jurors it was Dote who was hanged at Newgate and Short who had been outlawed (ibid., cf. J.I. 1/235, m. 23^d).

[3] *Year Books of Henry IV*, Mich. 11 Henry IV, no. 36. Staunford remarked in this connection: 'Car al appeal del partie, le pardon le Roy nest plee, eins que le felon serra mise a mort, ceo nient obstant' (*Les Plees del Corone*, Lib. ii, cap. 35).

VIII

THE VICTIM'S KIN

OF the alternative rights ostensibly assured to the relatives of slain men, even when the king was ready to remit his own suit, that to compensation would seem likely to have been the more highly valued. It would also seem likely that the relatives would be most inclined to come to terms if the slaying had been excusable, yet the evidence suggests that concords were not very common and were even less frequent in such circumstances than for other types of homicide.

The licensed concord was the appropriate way of securing compensation in court, but appellors seldom seem to have begun their appeals with this end in view. The licences were nearly always obtained by the appellees rather than the appellors, and were only permissive.[1] It was for the appellees to persuade the appellors to come to terms. Occasionally the licence is said to have been bought by both the slayer and his appellor so that they must already have got together and it may be that sometimes when the appellee alone appears to be responsible for getting it, he had in fact already made contact with the appellor, perhaps even already negotiated acceptable terms with him. But it was not, apparently, at all usual for the appellor to take the initiative in seeking the licence or indicate his willingness to come to terms until approached by the appellee. Bereaved relatives who were ready all along to accept compensation would generally let this be known before making any appeal, or would withdraw their appeal without licence.

The decision to allow a concord had to be certified to those concerned and it was obviously desirable that it, like a pardon, should be on permanent record in Chancery, but still there was less need for it to be in documentary form and enrolled. The king's 'licence' must not be thought of as necessarily a formal document handed to the appellee. Occasionally letters patent were issued which did constitute a sort of official

---

[1] See above, p. 178.

licence, but more often the king's consent was notified less formally. There was in fact no great need for documentary confirmation other than the rolls of the court: their record would be decisive if any dispute arose later as to the genuineness of the authorization claimed for a concord. But appellees might seek permission for a settlement before proceedings in court had begun. Their proffers, if they could not pay cash down, were recorded on the *rotuli de oblatis* and the pipe rolls. Permission obtained in this way could be notified direct to the justices who would otherwise have dealt with the appeal. A few letters close concerning licences were enrolled,[1] but so few that this was probably not thought necessary, being done only if the parties concerned elected to pay extra for the enrolment. There might, then, be no permanent record of the king's permission at all, or only the entries dealing with the financial negotiations, if the appeal was compromised before the trial started.

If the concord was made in court the rolls would record it, and possibly itemize its conditions. It does not appear that the parties generally had their own written copies of it, corresponding to the chirographs in land actions. In one case the appellor on withdrawing her appeal gave the appellee a charter 'quitclaiming' it; although nothing is said of compensation being paid, probably she got some *quid pro quo*. She renewed the appeal and he successfully produced her charter and was acquitted.[2] Once agreement had been reached the appellor could not repudiate it. If the appellee failed to carry out his part of the bargain it was unlikely that the appeal could lawfully be renewed, but the agreement itself might include a clause stating that failure to carry it out rendered the appellee liable to execution. Thus in 1208 it was agreed that one appellee was to go to the Holy Land 'and remain there in the service of God for the soul of the slain for seven years, . . . and if within that term he shall return, let justice be done on him as though he was convicted of the said death . . .'.[3] But this drastic threat

---

[1] e.g. *Rot. Litt. Claus.* i. 362. Cf. ibid. 213 where, however, the chief function of the writ was to authorize release on bail.

[2] This case is dealt with below, p. 211.

[3] *Select Pleas of the Crown*, Selden Soc. i, no. 102; *Curia Regis Rolls*, v. 245. In 1262 John Galun, who had obtained pardon on condition of becoming a monk, but had left religion, secured a grant that the pardon should stand despite his defection. But his pardon was for trespasses, not homicide, and a stricter line might have been taken if he had made concord for the latter. See *Cal. Pat. Rolls, 1258–66*, 197.

was most unusual. Indeed, another man implicated in the same death had to agree only that the court might distrain him to fulfil his share of the bargain, namely, to make one of the victim's relatives either a monk or a canon and to pay 40 marks to the kinsfolk in four instalments. Most concords apparently left the question of enforcement open, but it was possible to bring an action for failure to carry out the agreement similar to the action *quod teneat ei finem factum*. This was done against Eustace de Bekering, who had made concord with those who were appealing him in 1220 of the death of William de Tillbrook; later in the year he was summoned 'ad audiendum judicium suum de hoc quod non tenuit concordiam factam . . . de morte predicti Willelmi'.[1]

Concord after proceedings had begun in court was by no means infrequent in appeals of assault and could be regarded as a quite probable outcome—in the form of marriage—of an appeal of rape, but is comparatively seldom recorded in cases of homicide. This is natural so far as the eyre rolls are concerned, since the itinerant justices themselves could authorize the settlement in the first cases but not in the latter. Although the king's permission to compromise an appeal of homicide could be sought much more easily if it was being heard in the *Curia Regis*, the number of appeals dealt with there was small, and those in which concord was made were dwindling away by the middle of the thirteenth century. Appeals were likely to be brought there by or against wealthy and influential people, people who could afford to pay large sums for permission to come to terms in addition to whatever they undertook to pay as compensation to the victim's family. One licence cost 400 marks;[2] another cost £100, but this covered bail and the appeal included robbery as well as homicide.[3] In a case involving several men 100 marks were proffered for the licence.[4] Rather less would suffice for one man appealed of one crime only, but the figures suggest that concord was the rich man's resort.

It does not follow, however, that the king was bribed into permitting concords regardless of the merits of the case.

---

[1] *Curia Regis Rolls*, ix. 329.

[2] *Excerpta è Rot. Finium*, i. 264. Fourteen years earlier the appellee, John of Bayeux, had been appealed with Eustace de Bekering and others for the Tillbrook killing and had made a concord. See *Select Pleas of the Crown*, Seld. Soc. i, no. 197, *Curia Regis Rolls*, viii. 381, ibid. ix. 27 (cf. 167–8).

[3] *Excerpta è Rot. Finium*, i. 293.   [4] *Rot. de Oblatis*, 126–7; *Pipe Roll, 3 John*, 31–2.

Moreover, the attitude of the appellors was just as important as his, and in several cases it is likely that the appellee who secured a settlement had not in fact been personally involved in the slaying. Thus a lord might have been appealed of instigating or even participating in a fatal struggle in which his followers had engaged, but the appellor might be persuaded to come to terms with him, although the actual slayers were excluded from the concord. Similarly, an appeal against members of one family might be continued against one while another was able to reach a settlement.[1] This would seem to indicate that the appellor had been convinced that the latter had not been an accomplice after all and permission for concord was only proper in such a case, if the appellor would not otherwise withdraw. It is noticeable that appellees who were apparently entirely innocent quite often bought off the appeal in this way. In one case the licence was actually conditional on an inquisition *de odio et atia* finding the appellee not guilty,[2] and in some other early cases the concord was made apparently in despair of reaching a conclusion to the matter in any other way.[3] It seems, however, that the appellees sometimes felt morally responsible for slaying and were ready to make expiation by going on crusade or providing for a monk. There was a strong religious element in some of the concords; three were licensed at the instance of the bishop of Durham,[4] and this suggests that atonement was being made for slayings which incurred some degree of guilt, but not perhaps felony and malice aforethought. On the other hand, licensed concords explicitly for excusable homicide were conspicuous by their rarity.[5]

[1] e.g. while Elyas was given licence to make peace, Jordan de Beuney was eventually defeated in the judicial combat (in spite of having been allowed out of prison to practise duelling) and condemned. See *Rot. Litt. Claus.* i. 88, 90, 104; *Rot. Litt. Pat.* i. 73; *Curia Regis Rolls*, iv. 187, 225.

[2] *Rot. de Oblatis*, 405; *Pipe Roll, 10 John*, 68. Cf. *Close Rolls, 1227–31*, 544; *1231–4*, 9, 23.   [3] e.g. the case of Robert de Walterville, below, p. 340, n. 4.

[4] *Close Rolls, 1234–7*, 119, 126.

[5] One was authorized in an unusual case of misadventure. Six of the earl of Chester's serjeants, lying in wait by night for thieves, were attacked by worthy men of Preston by mistake and themselves in turn mistook the latter for thieves. The two groups exchanged fire—'ad invicem se intersaggitantibus'—and one of the men of Preston was fatally wounded. The king instructed the itinerant justices to make diligent inquest, and, if they found that the slaying had in fact occured through this mischance, allow peace to be made between the serjeants and the wife and relatives of the slain man (*Rot. Litt. Claus.* ii. 165).

Such concords did not, then, provide a regular method of negotiating peace between appellor and appellee in cases of homicide and so substitute agreed compensation for the old fixed wergild in appropriate cases. One obvious disadvantage lay in their tending to involve long delay, since the appeal would not normally be prosecuted in court until the next eyre. If the relatives of the slain were prepared to accept compensation they would naturally like to obtain it as soon as possible. A much speedier settlement might therefore be made out of court, perhaps at a loveday. If the relatives had this in mind from the beginning they would refrain from starting an appeal before the coroner and in the county court. If they began an appeal of felony but changed their minds about the circumstances of the death, or were successfully approached by the appellee with a proffer of compensation, they would soon drop it. A concord was quite legal provided no appeal had been begun; it was an offence, punishable by a small amercement at the eyre, to abandon an appeal once started, yet even a concord made after appeal seems to have been regarded as having some validity. It was doubtful, however, by what means the parties could be compelled to respect it, and its breach could have disastrous results for the appellee. The king himself might be petitioned in the last resort over breach of such a concord.[1] The appellee who was a party to an unlicensed concord ran a much more serious risk, however, than renewal of the appeal which he thought he had bought off. At the eyre the whole business would have to be presented and he would be tried at the king's suit. The fact that the victim's relatives had been ready to make peace might influence the jurors in his favour, but this was very far from being a foregone conclusion. He was liable to be found guilty and executed despite the concord.[2]

[1] e.g. in 1260 Henry of Bath was commissioned to inquire into 'a complaint made on behalf of Aylwina Grenegres and Richard her son that whereas Robert le Clerk . . . lately appealed them of the death of . . . his brother, and they, though innocent, as they assert, to avoid expense made peace with the said Robert in 5s. on condition that he should cease from the said appeal, . . . the said Robert without their knowledge again appealed them, whereby they were outlawed; and find whether Robert appealed them maliciously' (*Cal. Pat. Rolls, 1258–66*, 101). Cf. *Cal. Inquisitions Misc.* i, no. 2170 for a similar inquiry, though it does not appear whether the appeal here was for homicide; the appellor seems to have tricked the appellee into some breach of the agreement and then secured his outlawry, but at the suit of the king, not her own.

[2] As Robert Basset found to his cost in 1221. At the price of a marriage and a marriage settlement he had made peace with his victim's widow, with the consent of

From the guilty slayer's point of view, the extra-judicial concord was in the long run of little use unless he also obtained
the king's pardon. However, such concords appear more often
than licensed ones.

Appellors themselves may sometimes have come under some
pressure from public opinion or influential individuals to agree
to out-of-court negotiation. A lord might arrange a settlement,
going over his tenant's head. A monastic chronicler throws
some light on the way in which these affairs were handled.
A villein had been killed in the course of a forcible attempt to
get seisin of land given to the monastery of Meaux by Amandus,
son of Saier, and the widow and brother appealed some of the
monks, lay brethren, and their servants of the death, supported
by Saier, who held the land. 'Nos ergo', says the chronicler,
'pertimescentes damnum pergrande, per consilium amicorum,
eidem domino Saiero dedimus sexaginta marcas et medietatem
totius tenementi supradicti . . . appellumque mulieris . . . et
omnis parenteli dicti viri nativi sui retrahi faciebat.'[1] Such
intervention was not always welcome. On one occasion the
appellors complained to the king's justices that the abbot of
St. Albans had forced them to make peace for the death of their
child. The entry on the plea roll breaks off abruptly, but one
on the pipe roll of 1204 indicates that they had appealed
Baldwin the reeve and his son of the death.[2] Whether the abbot
was acting in his spiritual capacity or as lord of the borough to
avert the reeve's suspension from his functions does not appear.
Saier's motive in accepting the monks' overtures seems to
have been quite simply that the bulk of their payment was to
be his rake-off. Local feeling as expressed in the county court
probably helps to explain connivance in a concord by the
sheriff, but he, too, might be bribed or at least receive some
small gift in recognition of his compliance. Thus, Robert
Basset gave the sheriff of Gloucester half a mark,[3] and in a case
from about 1250 the sheriff of Suffolk got 40 shillings for

their son, after she had sued her appeal in two sessions of the county court. Half a
mark had gone to the sheriff for allowing this. At the eyre the son was one of the
presenting jurors and in this capacity tried to conceal his father's slaying, but in
spite of his efforts it came to light, and Robert was found guilty and hanged.
See *Pleas of the Crown for the County of Gloucester*, ed. F. W. Maitland, no. 101.
Cf. J.I. 1/174, m. 27, where a man was hanged for a death for which he had made
a concord with the victim's daughter.

[1] *Chronicon de Melsa*, ii. 6–8.
[2] *Curia Regis Rolls*, iii. 83; *Pipe Roll, 6 John*, 33.   [3] See p. 198, n. 2.

suffering peace to be made with the victim's mother and brother whereas the latter were paid 20 and 22 marks by the two appellees respectively.[1] Other people who assisted at an unlicensed concord between appellor and appellee were liable to amercement, as well as the actual parties to it.[2] The amercements were generally small—half a mark—but an appellor might risk considerable punishment. One offered as much as 20 marks as a fine for having made peace without the king's leave with those whom he had appealed of the death of his father, on which account his land had been taken into the king's hand.[3] Those who arranged or connived at the concord might fine for smaller amounts. In one case the chief peace-maker fined for 4 marks, and another for 1 mark. The appellee had paid £11 and more to buy off this appeal.[4]

Although unlicensed concords were probably more common than licensed ones unfortunately it is impossible to make any estimate of their number. Since, in the absence of an appeal, there was nothing improper in coming to terms concords did not all have to be reported at the eyre. It was only when an appeal had been launched and then withdrawn that a concord was irregular and called for amercement by the justices, and therefore ought to feature on the eyre roll. A fair number have been noted, including some in cases of justifiable slaying. The families of men allegedly killed as felons often resented the smear on the deceased's good name and appealed the slayers of felonious homicide. Although justifiable slayers stood in little danger of conviction and had little need to come to terms,[5] some must have thought it advisable to buy the appellors off,[6]

---

[1] This case is recorded in the Hundred Rolls of 1274–5 (*Rot. Hundredorum*, ii. 175). Reginald de Paveli was involved in a dispute over presentation to a church; he came with lord Roger de Bavent and Reginald le Deveneys to help his nominee to collect the tithes, and in the resultant fight Deveneys killed a parson from Norfolk, but the other two were appealed and it was they who made the concord. This was an old affair, for which de Paveli had obtained pardon (*Cal. Pat. Rolls, 1247–58*, 95) in 1251 and the sheriff in question, Hamo Passelewe, was in office in 1248 (ibid. 11).

[2] e.g. J.I. 1/95, m. 50ᵈ: 'Et juratores testantur quod concordati sunt. Et quod Egidius de Barenton interfuit concordie. Ideo in misericordia.' Cf. *Pipe Roll 1 Ric. I*, 135, 152; J.I. 1/569ᴬ, m. 30.   [3] *Rot. de Oblatis*, 379–80.

[4] J.I. 1/569ᴬ, m. 30. This was a case of self-defence and the killer, Nicholas son of Nicholas, was pardoned. See *Cal. Pat. Rolls, 1266–72*, 252.

[5] See above, p. 178, for their right to plead justification.

[6] e.g. J.I. 1/802, m. 47ᵈ, where a concord was made between the widow and the man who had beheaded her husband after he had stolen a horse and refused to stand to the king's peace.

and possibly the mere threat of appeal was sometimes enough to extract some payment. The records also reveal a small number of unlicensed concords made in cases of slaying in self-defence.[1] In most of these cases it looks as though there was genuine doubt about the circumstances, and the appellors were ready to come to terms once they were convinced that the slaying was excusable. Their change of mind may have been brought about by the holding of a special inquisition at the instance of the appellee or his friends, generally in order to secure bail, occasionally, though this was irregular, in order to obtain the king's pardon. In a few instances the sequence of events can be traced and the inference can fairly be made that the appellor was prepared to compromise because of a favourable verdict. Thus a widow prosecuted her appeal until the fourth session of the county court, at which the appellee was granted bail on the king's order, an inquisition *de odio et atia* having found that the killing had been in self-defence.[2] The widow thereupon made a concord, for which, in spite of the circumstances, she subsequently fined for half a mark. In other cases it does not appear whether concord was made before or after the holding of the inquisition. One concord, which was reported at the eyre when the appellee produced the king's pardon, may have been made as a result of it.[3] The appellor was amerced for not appearing rather than for making the concord, which may hint that it came after the pardon.

While positive evidence for unlicensed concords for slaying in self-defence does not suggest that they were at all frequent, some allowance must be made for the possibility that juries were inclined to conceal them if they could. When they reported that an appeal had been withdrawn, the justices might be careful to inquire whether there had been a concord, but statements on this issue occur much more often on some rolls than others; it may be that some justices pressed for information on this point, whereas others let the matter pass and the jurors were not expected to volunteer a statement. There are plenty

[1] e.g. p. 200, n. 4; J.I. 1/569ᴬ, m. 12ᵈ; *Cal. Pat. Rolls, 1266–72*, 80; cf. 135 and *Close Rolls, 1264–8*, 316, 410. Cf. J.I. 1/409, m. 32ᵈ; ibid., m. 33, C. 144/26, no. 26; J.I. 1/1051, m. 14ᵈ *Cal. Pat. Rolls, 1258–66*, 476; J.I. 1/1098, m. 44ᵈ.

[2] J.I. 1/409, m. 32ᵈ; C. 144/25, no. 4. This verdict was confirmed at the eyre, and the slayer was pardoned. Cf. J.I. 1/1098, m. 31, C. 144/27, no. 32, *Cal. Close Rolls, 1279–88*, 461.

[3] J.I. 1/1051, m. 28ᵈ; *Cal. Pat. Rolls, 1258–66*, 391, shows that the killing had been in self-defence.

of instances of appeals against slayers in self-defence being dropped before or at the eyre; in some the jurors actually stated that no concord had been made,[1] but in many nothing was said either way.

There were a good many blackmailing appeals, especially in cases of fatal accidents, whether it was plausible to connect the appellee with the accident in some way, although he had not caused it, or if he could not plausibly be connected with it at all and had not even been present. It might be expected, therefore, that many people who were genuinely involved in fatal accidents would buy off appeals brought against them really only in the hope of obtaining compensation. But no direct evidence for this has been found. In one case of killing by mischance an appeal was reported to have been made and withdrawn;[2] perhaps concord had been made, although the jurors failed to say so; their sympathies may well have lain with the parties whose coming to terms would morally have been the right course. Other juries may have concealed the fact that an appeal had ever been made when they approved its having been compromised in this way. Unless they tended to do so, very few appeals can have been made in cases of this kind, for very few were reported. If, then, compensation was secured at all often for accidental slaying it must have been possible to achieve this without launching an appeal. An appeal had to be begun promptly so that in order to anticipate it the killer would have to start negotiations at once. The mere threat of appeal might be enough to persuade him to do this within the time available, but it seems improbable that things were often arranged with such speed. The kin were not always in a strong position to bargain for compensation. The killer and his family must often have been too poor to be able to pay any substantial sum and it would be a waste of time to haggle with them over the amount. But the difficulty might be just the opposite. The killer might be too powerful, rich, and influential for a humble family to dare tackle him in this way. They would have to be content with whatever he deigned to offer, and if he offered nothing they would be well advised to put forward no demand. The slayer's own ignorance may sometimes have allowed him to be stampeded into paying all he could afford although the

---

[1] e.g. J.I. 1/1060, m. 41ᵈ; *Cal. Pat. Rolls, 1266–72,* 478, 504.
[2] J.I. 1/131, m. 11ᵈ; *Cal. Pat. Rolls, 1266–72,* 240.

relatives had already missed the chance of making a successful appeal, but the relatives themselves might be equally ill informed and find that their hesitation had stiffened the slayer's resistance to their demands. Agreed compensation after pardon is scarcely in evidence.

All in all, the business of reparation had fallen into utter confusion. Yet the term 'blackmail' is too strong for the efforts of relatives to secure it for excusable homicide even under threat of appeal. Their moral right to it was so to say officially recognized until the middle of the thirteenth century; their right to prosecute an appeal even if there were grounds for judging the homicide an excusable one was recognized throughout. This lever was deliberately put at their disposal when the king granted pardon; their hands were not forcibly removed from it when he gave permission for concord. He could hardly object to their using it at an earlier stage in cases in which compensation was admittedly appropriate unless he himself provided more effective means for securing it. It was not the relatives who acted reprehensibly in this regard, but the king who failed to supply an adequate substitute for wergild for excusable homicide. It was futile to suppose that anything short of a legal right, enforceable by an action in court for damages, could give the admitted moral claim of the relatives any practical validity. As it was, extra-judicial concords were dependent on many factors amongst which the equity of the claim was not conspicuous. They occurred in cases of intentional homicide as well as when there were excuses or extenuating circumstances or when the death had been justifiable or purely accidental, and the most deserving claimants were just those who were least likely to be able to apply any effective pressure. Moreover, the very fact that some entirely innocent people were appealed simply in order to extort money tended to discredit the whole notion of obtaining agreed compensation for a kinsman's death. The need to use the threat of appeal on a capital charge in order to secure it would also tend to antagonize fair-minded people even when it was being sought for excusable homicide. Thus public opinion gradually turned against it in such cases. Some jurors evidently did not sympathize with attempts to secure compensation for accidental slaying by launching an appeal,[1] and fear of incurring local

[1] e.g. C. 144/16, no. 42. Cf. J.I. 1/1060, m. 24.

disapproval might discourage some deserving relatives from seeking compensation under threat of appeal.

There is no reason to suppose that the king deliberately abandoned the policy of salvaging something of the ancient right to compensation. The inclusion in the pardons until the mid thirteenth century of the stipulation that peace be made and also his willingness to license concords for homicide indicate some continuing respect for it. Yet neither method afforded it effective protection. The reason for this may be partly that the relatives of slain persons failed to avail themselves of such chances of getting compensation in court as remained to them. The too costly licensing of concords was certainly a failure as a substitute for wergild payments. But the main fault lay in the fact that, when pardon had been granted, there was no sure way of securing the award of compensation by a court. The proviso of making peace was really no more than a pious exhortation to the pardoned slayer; its omission was no more than the tacit admission of its futility as far as legal action was concerned. Thus neither the proviso of making peace in the pardons nor licences for concord could prevent the catastrophe whereby the legal right to compensation for homicide became a total loss. Action out of court lingered on, but was becoming somewhat disreputable. It appealed more to the ruthless and greedy than to the decent and deserving. The threat of appeal was suspect as a way of blackmailing the innocent and was of little avail in securing a fair settlement of just claims to damages.

It follows that the alternative stipulation of standing to right cannot be defended as the only effective lever for prizing some sort of reparation out of those who had slain excusably or in extenuating circumstances. It was far too clumsy and unselective an instrument, and any small usefulness it may have had in this direction was insufficient to warrant its retention, especially if it was likely to be abused by vindictive relatives to frustrate the proper exercise of the prerogative of mercy. By now any continuing usefulness it had lay rather in the sphere of felonious homicide. Royal clemency was sometimes misplaced and when this occurred appeal was the only means of bringing about due punishment. The requirement of standing to right gave appellors an opportunity to redress matters to the benefit of law and order. By taking regular advantage of it they might have neutralized the encouragement given to criminals by the king's leniency and venality. The use and abuse by bereaved relatives of their opportunities to bring to trial both pardonable and pardoned slayers must now be examined.

Certainly some appeals were prosecuted against slayers who fully deserved pardon, either forestalling it or forcing the grantees to implement the proviso of standing to right. Others were even brought against justifiable slayers who had no need to secure remission of the king's suit. But it must not be taken for granted that all these appeals sprang from savage and relentless vengefulness. The aim of vindicating a slain relative's good name[1] was not altogether reprehensible and there might be neither malice nor vindictiveness when an appeal was brought against a man whom a jury held to have killed in self-defence. Honest disagreement could easily arise as to the division of responsibility between the parties to a fight. Nearly always, it is true, the account given by the jury attributed it entirely to the man who was ultimately killed, but there are some instances in which it was admitted that the man who killed in self-defence had been the original assailant. He might have started a minor brawl with no intention whatever of letting it develop into a serious fight, and without having armed himself with any lethal weapon. In such a case, though the king might be persuaded to grant pardon, it would be understandable if the victim's family wanted to see the slayer punished. Nor should it be taken for granted that the appellor was always guilty of exaggerating the charge if the accused managed to put the notion of self-defence across at some inquisition.[2] Juries at special inquisitions may have been too ready to take a lenient view. The general reliability of their verdicts will be examined more closely later on, but it can be said at once that it was not only the appellor who might show wrongheadedness in assessing the degree of responsibility and guilt for a homicide. The withdrawal of appeals was common and was not always

---

[1] e.g. K.B. 26/143, m. 5; K.B. 26/204, m. 26ᵈ.

[2] e.g. there is no need to doubt the good faith of William de Chanedun, who appealed Brother Walter le Juvene, Maurice, monk of Binedon, and others of killing his nephew, Henry le Scoyn, and prosecuted his appeal at the eyre, where they came and claimed benefit of clergy. The jury actually found Walter and Maurice guilty, yet Walter eventually secured the king's pardon on the grounds that the slaying had been in self-defence. See J.I. 1/202, m. 27; *Cal. Pat. Rolls, 1266–72*, 178.

due to concord having been made out of court. A number of appellors may have withdrawn unconditionally when they had had time to recover from the first shock of bereavement and review the circumstances more calmly, recognizing that there had been some excuse. Killings which juries were later to regard as having been committed in self-defence led to such abortive appeals in a fair number of instances. It looks as though a good many appellors were open to conviction when local opinion came down on the side of the slayer's innocence of felonious intent in killing in a brawl although the coroner's inquest alone might not convince them. Only a few persisted with their appeals.[1]

A certain number of appeals were made in cases which at the time might have ranked as accidental killings, cases of transferred intent, in which the killer was engaged in punishing or fighting with one person, but unintentionally hit another. It may be felt that the appellors had reason on their side rather than the king who granted pardon. The victims could not always be said to have been responsible for provoking or attacking the killers; they might have been law-abiding bystanders who intervened only to try to stop the fight. In such a case the killer was acting unlawfully, perhaps even of malice prepense though not towards the actual victim. In his case pardon may be judged over-lenient—Bracton would have judged it so— and the appellor to have been doing no more than his duty, contributing more to the suppression of crime than was the king.

Very few appeals have been found to have been prosecuted before the justices in cases which are known to have been regarded as accidental homicide. In two or three instances such appeals were started and then withdrawn, but they are very few compared even with cases involving self-defence. Accidental death was frequently caused by a member of the victim's own family, and it is natural that appeal was extremely rare in such cases, though it was not impossible; for example the widow might appeal her brother-in-law. But although this factor should be taken into account the rarity of appeals in cases of accidental killing is still striking. It appears that there was considerable reluctance to bring an appeal when the accidental nature of the killing was recognized. The relatives

[1] For examples see below, p. 276, n. 1.

would shrink from making a charge they knew to be exaggerated when there was no pre-existing enmity between them, or the victim, and the killer, or withdraw one made when distraught by grief.[1]

Except when the homicide had been justifiable, an appeal might be prosecuted without the circumstances being revealed, since neither appellor nor appellee could mention them.[2] It may be, therefore, that some appeals of felonious homicide conceal the prosecution and even conviction of excusable slayers. But certainly there can have been very few such cases. This can easily be established, for if the appeal was quashed the appellee would be arraigned at the king's suit, and now the excuse of accident or self-defence could be put forward. Only an appeal which was prosecuted until he was convicted could effectively conceal the circumstances altogether; only a handful of appeals of homicide resulted directly in conviction, and thus the number in which the appellee can possibly have killed excusably is very small indeed. The right of the next of kin to appeal did not, in practice, involve any considerable danger that excusable slayers would be convicted and executed.

The victim's relatives could reasonably interpret flight as tacit confession of guilt and it is probable that many more excusable slayers were outlawed on appeal than were prosecuted and actually tried on it before the king's justices. But it is not possible to make any sort of estimate of the proportion outlawed in this way. Although the fact of outlawry would have to be reported at the eyre there would be no need for the presenting jurors to detail the circumstances of the slaying. Vast numbers were outlawed and many excusable killers may have been among them, but as a rule only those who later obtained pardon can be recognized as such. Very few pardons for slaying by accident are known to have been granted to men outlawed on appeal, though the eyre rolls do reveal some. The patent rolls record only a few pardons on grounds of misadventure to outlaws, and it does not of course follow that they

---

[1] As did the appellor of Simon of Flanders in 1235, confessing that he had appealed him of the death of his son Gregory, accidentally drowned at Scarborough, 'cordis anxietate et dolore nimio quem concepit occasione mortis ipsius Gregorii et non eo quod idem Simon de predicta morte culpabilis fuit' (*Close Rolls, 1234–7*, 139).

[2] At any rate for most of the period under discussion. See above, p. 177.

had all been outlawed on appeal.[1] While the number of these
entries is very small, some allowance must be made for the
fact that the enrolments sometimes omitted any mention of
outlawry when as other evidence shows the grantee was an
outlaw, and also of accident when the slaying was elsewhere
held accidental. All that can be inferred from these rolls is that
some other accidental slayers may have been outlawed on appeal,
but that this is likely at most to have happened extremely
seldom. Pardons after outlawry on appeal appear to have been
slightly more frequent in cases considered by juries to be slaying in self-defence. Eight probable examples have been noticed
and two more doubtful ones. But again it is not safe to assume
that the finding was always correct and the appeal unreasonable.
Another jury might reject the charitable view of the killing
and endorse the appellor's.[2]

Appellors may be given the benefit of the doubt when the
slayers were as yet unpardoned fugitives, but their motives
are more suspect when they appealed those who had secured
pardon on grounds of excuse. Here at least they would seem to
have acted with deliberation, either dissenting from the verdict
or refusing to be appeased by it. The possibility must not be overlooked, however, that they might be unaware of the pardon,
which might only just have come to hand when the appeal was
made. In fact no clear example has been found of an appeal
being prosecuted at the eyre against an excusable slayer who
appeared there with his pardon apart from the case of Robert
Parleben which has already been mentioned.[3] Robert had been
only seven when he accidentally killed a contemporary; the
appeal was not made in due form and the appellor was a
cousin of the victim; such a relationship was unlikely to be
accepted as entitling him to appeal. In view of all these factors
it may be assumed that this appeal was brought to annoy
rather than with any expectation of securing conviction and
punishment. It was only when the pardoned slayer absented

[1] e.g. *Pat. Rolls, 1225–32,* 393; *Cal. Pat. Rolls, 1232–47,* 370, 376; ibid., *1247–58,*
26, 97, 127, 142. In the first of these cases it is unlikely that the grantee had been
outlawed on appeal, since the victim was probably a member of his own family.
There were also pardons which covered 'outlawry if any'; e.g. ibid. 422, ibid.,
1266–72, 535. These grantees may or may not have been outlawed.

[2] e.g. the case of William, son of Madoc de la Hethe, *Cal. Pat. Rolls, 1281–92,*
79; *Cal. Close Rolls, 1279–88,* 279; *Cal. Inquisitions Misc.* i, no. 2166; J.I. 1/739, m. 54.

[3] Above, pp. 153, 154.

himself yet again that appellors were at all likely to renew the charge.[1] It may be significant that the cases noted come from the eyre of 1247–8. In the second half of the century feeling against renewing appeals against excusable homicides may have been too strong to be easily flouted even when they had absconded after obtaining pardon.

It has been seen that few of those outlawed on appeal in the county court are known to have been excusable slayers. Many homicides were outlawed in this way and it may be concluded that the great majority of them were murderers, people who fully deserved punishment. As long as outlawry was tolerated as a form of punishment the appellors may be said to have been contributing usefully to the task of retribution. This function of the appeal was still valued at a time when it was seldom allowed to achieve conviction if the appellee appeared in court. It was not the fault of the appellors that outlawry was not best calculated to repress crime, its use as a deterrent being more than offset by its providing opportunity and incentive for a career of brigandage. In appealing murderers the victim's relatives were discharging a duty to society; occasionally their appeals led to capital punishment, far more often to outlawry. The same duty could usefully be performed when the prerogative of mercy was abused by the pardoning of felonious homicide. It remains to consider how far the continuing right of appeal was exploited after pardon had been granted to those who had slain without excuse.

An appeal could be brought on the strength of this right against someone who had secured pardon without having been outlawed, either because the process of exigent had not been completed or because no appeal had been made in the county court. In the first case there would be no special difficulty for the appellor at the eyre, but in the second he would almost certainly run into immediate trouble, since he had not gone through the essential preliminary stages. Mostly these appeals would be against pardoned outlaws, and there would be no such difficulties if a first appeal had been made punctually and carried on to its successful conclusion. But there might still be some legal obstacles—for example the appellor might

[1] Hugh Hoyde of Blaby was outlawed at the suit of Edith, widow of William Smith, but pardoned. At the eyre she was ready to appeal him again, but as he was not present she was told to continue the appeal in the county court until he

be a woman and the deceased her son or brother[1]—and there might also be psychological ones. The original appeal would have been a tiresome and prolonged business; the resolution of many appellors flagged and they did not stay the course until the fifth session of the county court. For those who had persisted doggedly and got the slayer outlawed the nullification of their efforts by the king's pardon must have been exasperating, and the right to renew their appeal have seemed something of a mockery. Most of those who had shown enough stamina to last out the first five laps lost heart at the prospect of starting off again.

It might even be dangerous to appeal a pardoned slayer. A powerful appellee could take measures both in and out of court to avoid having to implement the proviso in his pardon

was outlawed once more (J.I. 1/455, m. 10, Leics. 1247). If, as seems most probable, this Hugh is to be identified with the Hugh de Whetstan who was pardoned his outlawry for the death of William the Smith of Cosseby, this killing had been in self-defence according to an inquisition (*Cal. Pat. Rolls, 1232–47*, 468). The justices ordered that William King be placed in exigent for the death of Ralph de la Grave, but as it was then testified that he had already been outlawed and pardoned the order would have been revoked had not Ralph's son come forward and said that he wished to prosecute (J.I. 1/909[A], m. 20); according to an inquisition, Ralph had run upon William's lance so that the killing had been in self-defence and by mischance (*Cal. Inquisitions Misc.* i, no. 2055; cf. *Cal. Pat. Rolls, 1232–47*, 484).

[1] This need not have prevented outlawry on her appeal. In spite of Magna Carta, cl. 54, appeals of homicide brought by women other than the victims' widows were generally regarded as quite permissible so far as outlawry was concerned, though not quite always. For example, the justices in eyre in Yorkshire in 1231 amerced the county for having outlawed a man on the appeal of the victim's mother (J.I. 1/1043, m. 15) and those in Suffolk in 1296 did so when a man had been outlawed and a woman waived on a similar appeal (J.I. 1/829, m. 15). More often it was the county court which declined to allow this sort of appeal, and the justices were likely to amerce the suitors for failure to outlaw, not for doing so. In 1280 Nottinghamshire county court was in trouble for having failed on two occasions to outlaw on the appeal of a daughter of the victim, 'quia unusquisque appellatus de felonia tam de mulieribus quam de hominibus si non comparuerunt ad quartum comitatum debent utlagari' (J.I. 1/664, mm. 41, 42). This firm statement of the view that outlawry was lawful in all types of appeal by women was elaborated in 1284 by the justices in eyre in Leicestershire. A woman had appealed three men of the death of her sister. They had not appeared, but at the fifth county court they had not been outlawed as they should have been, because the court had held that she could appeal for the death only of her husband. The justices decided 'quia Comitatus allocabat Remedium statuti hiis qui nullum remedium petierunt eo quod absentes fuerunt, Ideo ad iudicium de toto Comitatu' (J.I. 1/457, m. 47[d]). If the appeal was made at the eyre itself and the appellee did not come, the justices would instruct a woman appellor to continue it in the county court until he was outlawed, regardless of the victim's not being her husband. For example, J.I. 1/569[A], m. 10.

of standing to right.[1] There might be local sympathy with the grantee and it would require considerable resolution to appeal him. If an appeal was begun the appellor might find himself under considerable pressure to withdraw or at least accept an offer of compensation. He, or more likely she, might yield to this, albeit reluctantly. For example, when Walter de Skandelby came to the county court of Leicester in 1245 and produced his pardon for the slaying of Michael de Retherby the widow, Alice, came forward and renewed her appeal, but 'since the lord king granted him peace on condition of standing to right if any one wished to speak against him concerning the said death, he prevailed upon Alice to withdraw her appeal and release him, in so far as pertained or could pertain to her, from the appeal made against him, . . . and that by her charter which she drew up for Walter'.[2] But she had been persuaded against her better judgement, and later renewed it. In 1247 the king ordered the itinerant justices 'to make inquisition whether Alice had withdrawn her appeal and released Walter from it; and when they were making this inquisition Alice came before them and yet again renewed her appeal; and since it is testified by the coroners and by the record of the county court, and also by her charter which Walter produced that she withdrew and quit-claimed as above, it is considered that he have firm peace for the future, and she is committed to gaol'.[3] Woman appellors were notoriously apt to change their minds, and others besides Alice did so more than once. Two, who had appealed a man in the county court for the death of their brother, said at the eyre when he had the king's pardon that they no longer wished to prosecute and had made peace with him. But afterwards one of the sisters appealed him again in the county court; at the following eyre she came before the justices,

[1] e.g. Geoffrey Payn of Weston came before the itinerant justices armed with the king's pardon for the death of William son of John de Lonwath; since he had earlier been appealed by John and another son and cousin, who did not now appear to prosecute him, Geoffrey offered 5 marks to have his pardon proclaimed; this, apparently, was done at once; it looks as though he was trying to accelerate the procedure to make sure of being given firm peace before they turned up. He was evidently known to have tried to intimidate them, for 12 men had to act as his pledges that no harm should come to them in future through him or his men or at his procurement; see J.I. 1/569^A, m. 14^d; cf. *Cal. Pat. Rolls, 1266–72*, 13, which shows that the pardon was granted at the instance of Edmund, the king's son.

[2] J.I. 1/455, m. 7^d.

[3] Ibid. His pardon shows that he had been outlawed; see *Cal. Pat. Rolls, 1232–47*, 449.

but again withdrew her appeal.[1] Thus even her persistence
failed in the end. Very few cases have been found in which
both appellor and pardoned appellee were present at the eyre.
Those which have been noted suggest that the risk of conviction
was virtually negligible. One appeal was quashed because it
omitted date and time;[2] another because it had never been
made in the county court;[3] a third because the appellor was
the victim's sister.[4] It has already been remarked that only one
case of conviction and execution after pardon has been found,
and in that one there are elements of doubt.[5]

Appeals after pardon were, then, very infrequent. There
are many factors which help to account for this. Many pardons
were not obtained for years. The person best entitled to appeal
might have died meanwhile, and it was difficult after such a
lapse of time for survivors to recall the details which were
essential to a successful appeal if the appellee appeared in court.
There would have been plenty of time for anger to cool.
Failure to take advantage of the invitation to appeal may often
have been due to weariness with the whole business and ultimate
apathy, or surrender to outside pressures. But probably the
main reason was that appeals were declining anyhow. It was
not unknown for an appeal to result in conviction and execution,
but this outcome was rare, and both the withdrawal and the
quashing of an appeal entailed the amercement of the appellor.
It was still worth while, so some people must have thought,
to bring one in order to ensure the appellee's arraignment at
the suit of the king when it failed, as it was almost sure to do.
But if an ordinary appeal, punctually prosecuted, had small
prospect of success, an appeal after pardon was a forlorn hope,
and now conviction at the suit of the king was ruled out.
There was, on the other hand, no legal obstacle to bringing
about the outlawry of a fugitive; all the appellor had to overcome was his own lethargy and irresolution, or, more serious,
his lack of time and money to cover his expenses in attending
the county court. Galling as it must have been for the individual
who had earlier sustained the tedious process there to see the
outlaw permitted to return, there would be some consolation
in the fact that he had already undergone a period of punish-

---

[1] J.I. 1/1109, m. 34 (1257).
[2] J.I. 1/573, m. 40 (1286).
[3] J.I. 1/569^A, m. 14^d (1268-9).
[4] J.I. 1/1060, m. 21 (1279).
[5] Above, p. 192.

ment as a fugitive, even though he escaped life-long exile. Thus the appellor who had succeeded once might not feel it incumbent on him to try to get him outlawed again. However, if he did still feel vindictive, and the slayer knew it, he might well be given a chance to bring about a second outlawry. Advantage was taken of this just often enough to show that the right of the victim's relatives to bring about punishment despite pardon was not a dead letter, but probably second outlawries were not secured often enough for criminals and fugitives from justice to take the possibility into their calculations. If the king's readiness to pardon weakened the deterrent effect of threatened capital punishment or permanent outlawry, the remnants of the right of appeal can have done nothing to counteract this.

The system of pardoning did, then, contribute to the decline in the position of the relatives and their share in determining the fate of the culprit, even though it was technically still possible for them to press a capital charge after pardon. So far as capital punishment was concerned the effect was slight because here the right of appeal for homicide was rendered all but nugatory by other means. So far as outlawry was concerned the effect was rather greater, if only because outlawry was brought about by appeal so much more frequently. The ostensible protection of the family's ancient right to prosecute was largely illusory. When the pardon was for excusable homicide the kin generally concurred in this view of the matter and had no wish to prosecute further. How often intentional slaying was pardoned will have to be considered later, but until 1294 this practice had not reached scandalous proportions and it is not surprising that before that date the number of appellors who felt strongly enough to struggle on after pardons had been produced is noticeably small. Conversely, the protection pardon gave to homicides was greater than appeared on the face of it. Although the proviso of standing to right must be taken to mean what it says and Maitland's gloss dismissed, yet in practice the danger of execution as the result of a successful appeal after pardon was negligible.

IX

THE KING

IT was the king's prerogative to grant pardon for felony and
his monopoly of this power was almost, but not quite, entire.
The lords of the Marches enjoyed it, but within England
only the very greatest franchises, the palatinates, did so. Lapsley
observed that in the palatinate of Durham, 'In respect to the
privilege of preventing the consequences of the law by means
of a pardon, the analogy between the Bishop and the king is
practically complete.'[1] He went on to show how the bishop's
pardons were granted both for excusable and felonious homicide within the liberty, and how the king's pardon to one of the
bishop's men might be confirmed by the bishop. On one occasion the validity of a royal pardon for men of the franchise was
challenged and one of them was arrested; he was not finally
released until the liberty was in the king's hands in 1302.[2] The
earl of Chester enjoyed the same authority within his palatinate,
but after 1237 this was secured by the Crown and was granted
only to the king's eldest son. A highly suspect charter of
William I authorized the abbot of Battle to save thieves from
execution.[3] The franchise was also claimed by the abbot and
monks of Glastonbury and supported by a spurious charter of
Edgar, purporting to grant 'eandem quoque libertatem et
potestatem quam ego in curia mea habeo, tam in dimittendo
quam in puniendo', and adding 'Si autem abbas uel quilibet
monachus loci illius latronem qui ad suspendium uel ad quod-
libet mortis periculum ducitur in itinere obuiam habuerit,
potestatem habeant eripiendi eum ab imminenti periculo in
toto regno meo.'[4] This alleged grant would have given them

---

[1] G. T. Lapsley, *The County Palatine of Durham*, 68.

[2] C. M. Fraser, *Antony Bek*, 97.

[3] *Cartae Antiquae*, Pipe Roll Soc., New Series, xvii, no. 208.

[4] J. M. Kemble, *Codex Diplomaticus Aevi Saxonici*, iii. 67–8. The claim to authority to pardon may account for a serious dispute between the king and the abbot in
1286–7. Robert de la Lauendrie had killed a clerk, Walter de Wrington, and the
king ordered the sheriff and coroners of Somerset to hold an inquisition as to
whether the slaying had been in self-defence; but as the abbot complained that

authority to pardon thieves not only within the twelve hides of
Glastonbury, where they had franchises of an exceptional kind,
but throughout the realm. It was of little, if any, use to them.
While the king alone could grant pardon for homicides committed in England outside the two palatinates, it does not follow
that he himself necessarily took the decision on each petition
or each recommendation to mercy. The evidence points to personal decisions by John, some of whose pardons were of an
unusual type; though it would be impossible to call them
irregular, they certainly seem to manifest the *voluntas regis* un-
trammelled by counsel or administrative formalism. But the
minority of his son afforded an opportunity for the king's advisers to influence the evolution of the system of pardoning.
The first pardons of Henry III were granted on the authority
of the regent, William the Marshal, and after his death in 1219
Hubert de Burgh generally dealt with the pardons, sometimes
in association with Peter des Roches, more often with the
council.[1] While William the Marshal was regent pardons were
sealed with his seal, as appears from a payment of 40 shillings
in 1222 by Richer de Shagbiry for new letters patent under the
king's seal to replace those granted to him in 1218 under
William's.[2] There seems to have been no hesitation about exercising the prerogative on the king's behalf but soon after the
Marshal's death there was a change in the nature of the pardons.
They were now to be effective only until the king came of age,

such an inquisition would prejudice his liberty the prisoner was handed over to
him, the king then appointing two commissioners to see that the abbot's bailiffs
did justice, as the case came under his jurisdiction (C. 66/105, m. 22^d. The summary
in *Cal. Pat. Rolls, 1281-92,* 255, is misleading). The abbot refused to allow this
joint commission to deliver his gaol but appointed two of them and two others
as his justices, not the king's to deliver it. They held the inquisition and found that
the killing had been in self-defence. Still the abbot refused to let Robert go, either
on bail, or by judgement or in any other way. The sheriff was therefore ordered by
a writ *non omittas propter libertatem* to bring Robert to the Tower of London to appear
coram rege. When he did so, the abbot's bailiff demanded his return: 'And because
some arguments of the aforesaid abbot remain still undetermined and the aforesaid
prisoner, so it seems to the court, cannot altogether be set free without the lord
king or restored to the aforesaid abbot, and also it does not seem to the court that
he ought to stop in prison since it is proved that he acted in self-defence, day is
given to the aforesaid abbot at the next parliament . . . and the aforesaid Robert
de la Lavandrye, saving the claim of the aforesaid abbot, is handed to . . . bail'
(*Select Cases in the Court of the King's Bench,* Selden Soc. lv, no. 111). No pardon has
been found for him.

[1] *Pat. Rolls, 1216-25,* 200, 206, 234, 238, 288, 336, 377.
[2] *Excerpta è Rot. Finium,* i. 90; cf. *Patent Rolls, 1216-25,* 159, 335-6. Henry's own
seal appeared at the end of October 1218; see ibid. 177.

'usque ad etatem nostram'.[1] Yet this alteration probably had no great significance and does not necessarily indicate a change of policy and greater respect for the prerogative on the part of Hubert de Burgh, for some months before the Marshal's death, when Henry had his own seal at the end of October 1218, it was laid down that no letters patent of confirmation, sale or gift or anything which might become a perpetuity should be sealed with the great seal until he came of age.[2] It may have been felt that some similar though lesser restriction would be appropriate in grants of pardon, and thus though the seal was used for them, the same time limit was imposed. In the event, only a few of the grantees are known to have obtained new pardons after Henry's majority. It must have been difficult to know when the original ones would be deemed to have run out, since Henry came of age by stages. Although for some purposes he was considered of age by the end of 1223, pardons granted in 1224 were still limited 'usque ad etatem', even though one bore the 'Teste ipso rege'.[3] A letter close ordering the release of a pardoned prisoner in 1225 does not refer to this limitation, but the actual pardon may have done so.[4] However, in the summer of 1226 Henry III himself seems clearly to have taken part in the pardoning of an irregular outlawry for theft and there was no hint of any time-limit,[5] so that it would appear that he was exercising the prerogative at least some months before he declared himself of full age in January 1227.

The Marshal and Hubert de Burgh do not seem to have made any other particular innovations in relation to pardons. They granted them in return for money for the king's use,[6] and also at the request of important persons, such as the king of Scotland and the earl of Chester.[7] They do not appear to have required inquisitions into the alleged circumstances when pardons were sought for fugitives. The proportion of pardons for felonies other than homicide was high, but this may point to willingness to pardon any kind of felony rather than reluctance to pardon

---

[1] *Patent Rolls, 1216–25*, 200. All the enrolled pardons now included this phrase.
[2] Ibid. 177.   [3] Ibid. 425; cf. 450.
[4] Ibid. 549. But the released prisoner, who had earlier abjured, was now to leave the realm, so the limitation would have little point.
[5] Ibid., *1225–32*, 36–7. Cf. above, p. 43, n. 1.
[6] e.g. Richer de Shagbiry's first pardon in 1218 cost him 5 marks; *Excerpta è Rot. Finium*, i. 14; cf. ibid. 16, for a proffer of 4 marks.
[7] *Patent Rolls, 1216–25*, 237, 450.

felonious homicide. On the other hand, there is evidence to suggest that some other people were concerned to modify the system at this time. Justices in eyre referred a case of accidental killing by a child to the *Magna Curia*, not to the regent, thinking, perhaps, that such a case required judicial decision at a high level rather than the vicarious exercise of the royal preroga-tive; but later he was pardoned 'pro Rege'.[1]

During the period of baronial ascendency the council played a greater part than usual in the decision to pardon. A pardon for ordering a felony was granted explicitly 'by the counsel of the magnates of the council';[2] but it seems that the Justiciar, Hugh Bigod, was particularly concerned in the decisions, and that not only when Henry was in France.[3] During the king's absences in Gascony, the regents in England seem to have had no authority to grant pardon. Petitioners would be well advised to seek the king on the Continent. For some of them who had already abjured or been outlawed and gone abroad this may have been no hardship; the king would be more accessible.[4] During his stay in 1242–3, Henry granted over two dozen par-dons for English homicides, with a handful for other offences, and even more during the slightly longer spell there in 1253–4.[5] But on this occasion, a good many of those in need of pardon seem to have waited until he was nearer to England on the return journey. One was granted at St. Maur,[6] and eleven at Boulogne, of which nine were for homicide.[7] When Henry visited France in the winter of 1259–60, he granted a few par-dons; none are dated there during his next two visits, but in 1264 he again granted several whilst he was on French soil. In the early part of the reign of Edward I no pardons appear on the surviving patent rolls of the periods when he was abroad, but the close roll for 1273 includes an order to the sheriff of Suffolk to allow William de Benges, who had slain in the last

---

[1] *Rolls of the Justices in Eyre in Yorks.*, *1218–19*, Selden Soc. lvi, nos. 448, 1134.
[2] *Cal. Pat. Rolls, 1258–66*, 1.   [3] Cf. ibid., *1247–58*, 652.
[4] e.g. *Pat. Rolls, 1225–32*, 391, where Halengrat the Balister was pardoned his abjuration of the realm of England for a killing. Bordeaux, where the pardon was granted, was his home town; he obtained pardon for abjuration again in 1243, on Henry's next visit (*Cal. Pat. Rolls, 1232–47*, 396).
[5] Once at least during this visit, however, he instructed the Chancellor to hold an inquisition whether a slaying had been accidental or of malice aforethought, and if it found it accidental to make a pardon of the king's suit 'per sigillum regis Anglie', thus leaving the final decision to him (*Close Rolls, 1253–4*, 318).
[6] *Cal. Pat. Rolls, 1247–58*, 385.   [7] Ibid. 387–9.

reign, to have peace until ordered to appear before the king or his justices, twelve mainpernors having been found for him;[1] this suggests that the regents had authority to concede something very much like pardon for homicide committed under Henry III. During Edward's absence, probably in May–June, 1279, a petition was made to 'the prince' by an elderly chaplain, who claimed to have been falsely indicted of homicide and outlawed without his knowledge of the charge, to be admitted to the prince's peace.[2] But it is doubtful if anything was done until the king's return, when one of his first acts appears to have been to grant pardon for this death and any consequent outlawry.[3] There is evidence elsewhere that he granted pardons whilst he was in France and Gascony from mid 1286 to mid 1289.[4] The whole business of obtaining an inquisition and then pardon on its findings might be put through while the king was in Gascony. Communications could be surprisingly punctual. On 1 May 1289 Edward, from Condom in the Agenais, wrote ordering an inquisition whether Stephen son of Richard de Honesworth killed his brother Richard in self-defence.[5] The inquisition was held on 9 June and brought in a favourable verdict. Pardon was granted at Bonnegarde on 1 August, though this is known only from the transcript of the charter on an eyre roll of 1293.[6] There are several other instances of pardons produced at the eyres but not discovered on the patent or Gascon rolls at this time, which were most probably granted while the king was in Gascony, but as their dates are not mentioned on the eyre rolls this cannot be proved with certainty.

At first sight the patent rolls suggest a change of policy during the king's absence in Flanders in 1297–8. One pardon for homicide granted at Ghent in October 1297 is enrolled,[7] but from 21 November till his return in March all the entries on the patent roll, including a considerable number of pardons for

---

[1] *Cal. Close Rolls, 1272–9*, 13.

[2] S.C. 8/335, no. 15816. The prince would be the regent, Edmund of Cornwall. The clerk had surrendered to Newgate and an inquisition had brought in a verdict of not guilty. He asserted that the actual murderers had caused him to be indicted 'saying that he could easily by means of his clerical privilege be acquitted and purged of the offence'. [3] *Cal. Pat. Rolls, 1272–81*, 317.

[4] J.I. 1/1267, m. 7. [5] *Cal. Inquisitions Misc.* i, no. 2305.

[6] J.I. 1/804, m. 61[A]. That his charter was genuine is shown by an entry on the close roll for 1290, ordering the sheriff to replevy his chattels for the time being as the king had pardoned him (*Cal. Close Rolls, 1288–96*, 76).

[7] *Cal. Pat. Rolls, 1292–1301*, 313.

homicide, were tested in England by Edward the king's son.[1] This would suggest that the council under the nominal presidency of the thirteen-year-old prince was exercising the royal prerogative of mercy. Yet this becomes doubtful when it is observed that nearly all those who received pardon for homicide were serving with the king in Flanders, and had taken an oath not to quit without leave. Other evidence proves that in fact it was the king, or those with him in Flanders, who had decided to grant these pardons. For each one a privy seal warrant has survived, dated there a couple of weeks or more before the date given on the patent roll.[2] Moreover, a great many other warrants were issued by the king at this time although the resulting pardons do not appear on the surviving patent rolls or were not entered there until after his return to England.[3] Thus Edward I was very active in granting pardon while he was abroad, and that for the simple reason that most of the recipients were much-needed recruits for his army. There was every reason why he should not relinquish his prerogative at this time, and it is clear that he did not share it with the council in England. Some of his warrants evidently went direct to Chancery; others were routed via the council which sent the instructions on to Chancery, where the resultant pardons were entered on the patent roll as tested by the prince.

While the king was on campaign, however, the normal applications for inquisitions into excusable slaying and for pardon based on their verdicts continued, and the difficulty of having all the documents sent for his inspection and attending to them did lead him, apparently, to delegate one or two final decisions to the Chancellor. But even so he did not relinquish his responsibility as much as appears at first sight. Late in 1297 he wrote from Ghent enclosing a petition from Master John Paternoster, who was staying with him in the army, which asserted that he had killed William of Gloucester for saying that he wished the king was dead; Edward instructed the Chancellor to inquire into the truth of this and make letters of pardon if the verdict was satisfactory.[4] But a second unconditional warrant for the pardon was issued on 3 January 1298,[5] so that there was now

---

[1] Ibid. 321–34.   [2] C. 81/13, 14, 15 *passim.*

[3] See *Cal. Chancery Warrants*, especially pp. 79–90, for many of these warrants, but others must still be sought in the C. 81 files.

[4] *Cal. Chancery Warrants*, 76; cf. C. 81/12, no. 1189.

[5] *Cal. Chancery Warrants*, 80.

no need for the Chancellor to take the final decision. Moreover, this was, of course, a highly unusual case and one in which Edward at least might think that the provocation fully justified the slaying. A more convincing example comes from 1301, when he wrote to the Chancellor saying that he had heard that the record of an inquest at a gaol delivery into the slaying of Rychier Berd by Thomas Margarete had been brought to Chancery, and instructing him to make letters patent of pardon if the inquisition was sufficiently in his favour and the case one of the kind in which 'we are accustomed to pardon the suit of our peace'.[1] The enrolment of the pardon mentions that Thomas had slain in self-defence;[2] the gaol delivery roll fully bears this out and shows that he was remanded *ad gratiam*.[3]

This case is particularly significant since Thomas had been remanded *ad gratiam*. The king's own decision was obviously desirable when a petition for pardon was based on the finding of a special inquisition, but it could be argued that pardon on the virtual recommendation of the king's justices trying the case was a formality which did not really demand it. Indeed, already in the early years of Edward III it could be assumed that when the accused was 'acquitted' on grounds of self-defence the justices would send their record to the Chancellor, apparently without waiting to be asked for it, and that he would then make out the charter of pardon 'par cours de ley', without speaking to the king;[4] by now, it seems, a pardon could issue from Chan-

---

[1] C. 81/27, no 2660. Cf. *Cal. Chancery Warrants*, 151. The Calendar suggests that Edward told the Chancellor in 1300 to inspect the inquisition which he enclosed concerning Robert de Foxholes and grant pardon or not according to his own judgement 'if he be not guilty' (ibid. 115). But the warrant actually stated that he was to make the pardon 'inspecta inquisitione . . . per quam perpendere poteritis quod inde culpabilis non est' (C. 81/22, no. 2166ᴬ). The warrants sometimes told him to use his discretion in formulating the charter, but this did not mean that he had any discretion as to whether or no pardon should be granted. See, e.g., C. 81/23, no 2256.

[2] *Cal. Pat. Rolls, 1301–7*, 8.

[3] J.I. 3/47, iii, m. 5; the record is C. 47/70/4, no. 107. On his return from Flanders in March 1298 Edward informed the Chancellor that he had heard that an inquisition at a gaol delivery had found slaying in self-defence; at the instance of John Carbonel he wished to show special grace to the slayer, John Bogeis, so the Chancellor was to issue pardon in due form if he found by the inquisition already held, or one to be held and returned to Chancery, that the killing had indeed been in self-defence (C. 81/16, no. 1517). The Chancellor sent for the record of the gaol delivery, which was as reported to the king, and pardon was granted a month later (C. 47/79/10, no. 315; *Cal. Pat. Rolls, 1292–1301*, 347).

[4] A. FitzHerbert, *La Graunde Abridgement*, Corone, pl. 361.

cery in the king's name but without having actually received his fiat, and this was certainly the regular procedure later on. But this case shows that even under abnormal conditions Edward I was at least informed of the record of a gaol delivery. Normally it would certainly have been delivered to him. Most of the surviving warrants under privy seal for the drawing up of pardons relate to those for men who earned them by enlistment or to those who obtained special inquisitions, but there are enough based on verdicts of excusable slaying given at the eyre or at gaol deliveries to prove that their records were produced before the king and that he then communicated his decision to Chancery by a privy seal.[1] There is evidence that remands *ad gratiam* in the King's Bench also were actually considered by him.[2]

Petitions for pardon might be presented in Parliament, and two are known to have been granted there as early as 1279.[3] The second of these decisions shows some awareness of the way the justices normally acted. The victim had been killed as a thief, and so justifiably, and an inquisition held by the king's justices or commissioners had established this. The king accordingly remitted his suit, but recognized that there was really no need for a formal pardon, and the entry concludes 'Habeat cartam si velit'. The killer does not, in fact, appear to have bothered to secure one. But the king was unlikely to respond more readily to petitions here than elsewhere. On the contrary, he may have been tempted to make a special show of reluctance to use his prerogative in any but the most obviously deserving cases on an occasion which was likely to give it more publicity than usual. In three early cases at least he did not grant the petition. In 1290 a clerk, Ralph son of Adam de Claghton, who was now in prison at Oxford, petitioned for pardon as an

---

[1] e.g. *Cal. Chancery Warrants*, 146, 174, 254; C. 81/5, nos. 416, 417, 418, 420, 426, 428, 429; C. 81/20, no. 1890.

[2] In 1302 a jury there found that Andrew Smith had killed in self-defence and he was accordingly handed back to the Marshal to be detained until the king showed him grace; meanwhile he was to sue to the king through his friends. The king granted his charter of pardon and Andrew was thereupon told to sue in Chancery, etc. This no doubt meant that he must now apply there for the engrossed pardon, which in fact he obtained and produced in court (K.B. 27/164, m. 58). It seems clear that when he was told to sue to the king this phrase was to be taken literally, that Chancery acted only when the king had signified his consent, and apparently he did this to the justices themselves, not directly to Chancery.

[3] *Rot. Parl. Anglie Hactenus Inediti*, Camden Third Series, li. 2, 3.

inquisition had found that he had killed in self-defence, but the king merely ordered that he should be released on bail.[1] At the eyre in 1293 he came and claimed benefit of clergy. The jury then gave a very convincing account of his slaying in self-defence, at the age of 16, a man who was strong and powerful and had thrown him into the fire, holding him there so that he would have died if he had not drawn his knife and stabbed him in the thigh.[2] He was now remanded *ad gratiam*; the record was sent to the king,[3] and he was pardoned in time to have his charter proclaimed at the eyre.[4] There seems to have been no reason at all for Edward's earlier refusal to pardon him in Parliament. His rejection of another petition in 1290, that of Roger de Haliwell, who had been bailed earlier on, is less puzzling, although he, too, got pardon after remand at the eyre.[5] The delay in the difficult case of John de Okelesthorp, which has already been mentioned, is easy to understand.[6] These cases suggest that it was a waste of time to go to Parliament in search of pardon.[7] A favourable result might be expected with more confidence if the supplicant found someone to hand his petition to the king on a less formal and busy occasion. In fact few homicides seem to have chosen to petition him there, and so it is improbable that Parliament at this time had a direct influence on the use of the prerogative of mercy.

It appears that governmental policy in relation to this prerogative was normally determined by the king, although he may often have been influenced by his council or a particular minister. If pardons were sometimes authorized by the council alone the evidence does not reveal the fact. It is particularly difficult to know how far the young Henry III was responsible for the decisions attributed to him in the late twenties and early thirties. There was something of a new approach to the granting of pardon in these years, signs of a more responsible attitude, but whether this was due to the king's own realization of his inexperience and the wish to act only on adequate information and with prudent advice, or to pressure from his ministers' efforts to inculcate a sense of responsibility is a matter for

---

[1] *Rot. Parl.* i. 62[b]. The inquisition held in the preceding year had found that he had killed in self-defence and not *odio et atia*. See C. 144/29, no. 47.

[2] J.I. 1/1098, m. 5. [3] C. 47/86/27, no. 698.

[4] *Cal. Pat. Rolls, 1292–1301*, 67; J.I. 1/1098, m. 5.

[5] See below, p. 263, n. 3. [6] Above, p. 111.

[7] But one successful petition was made in 1290. See above, p. 51.

speculation. In 1227 Henry sought advice from Martin de Patishull on a case which had come before the latter at the eyre asking 'quam gratiam . . . dominus Rex decenter facere possit'.[1] A little later he was at pains to show how carefully he weighed the information supplied to him, and perhaps also to stress that the decision on it was his own, writing in 1231, 'audito infortunio ex literis S. de Sedgrave et sociorum suorum de morte Ricardi filii Stephani, quem Adam filius Walteri per decensum cujusdam sagitte quam sursum traxerat occidit, visum est regi et verisimile est quod non ex malicia aliqua excogitata per feloniam set eodem Adam invito obiit, unde rex pietate tactus quantum in se est, eidem Ade mortem predicti Roberti perdonavit'.[2] If, then, excuses were put forward as grounds for pardon the king needed to be convinced of their cogency, and it was from this moment that special commissions to inquire into them began to be appointed if the case had not already come before the king's justices.[3]

As inquisitions became more and more frequent and similar cases were regularly reported from the eyre and gaol deliveries, pardons on grounds of accident or self-defence became frequent enough to constitute the norm; by contrast with them pardons for intentional homicide began to appear as abnormal and reprehensible. No doubt the general improvement in the enforcement of order and respect for law was enough to render excessive use of the prerogative unwelcome anyway, but the cases of excusable homicide provided scope for its acceptable use, and so may have facilitated attempts to confine it within reasonable bounds. There were still very exceptional, unforeseeable situations which called for the king's discretion; there would always be isolated occasions when only the true prerogative of mercy could avert gross inequity, and for these no rules could be laid down. But while there was a residue of indefinable causes calling for its intervention, there was a strong tendency to contract its ordinary scope. The king, at least, now needed to be more circumspect in exercising it, and his letters patent of pardon normally gave the grounds which justified it, or emphasized a religious and charitable motive, though sometimes they merely stated that he acted at the instance of a worthy advocate. The habit of giving good grounds for his pardons served to highlight the arbitrariness of his action when he pardoned a homicide,

[1] *Rot. Litt. Claus.* ii. 165.   [2] *Close Rolls, 1227–31*, 552.   [3] See above, p. 37.

inquisition into which could only have been an embarrassment to the petitioner. While the king naturally clung to his power to pardon at will and influential subjects sometimes had good reason to support this aspect of his prerogative, it did not escape criticism. Bracton would have liked to see felonious homicide excluded altogether. In treating of outlawry he remarks: 'ubi felonia denotari poterit, numquam deberet talis admitti ad gratiam vel non nisi cum magna difficultate.'[1] A little later, he says: 'si quis autem per feloniam et in assultu praemeditato alium interfecerit, talis numquam de iure restitui deberet nec de gratia.'[2] In both passages he adds the very sound reason for refusing pardon in such cases: 'quia . . . ex tali veniae facilitate non solum inlagatis verum etiam aliis in hoc confidentibus datur materia delinquendi'; 'ne talis gratia aliis praebeat audaciam consimilia perpetrandi . . .'. He recognized that the king did not in fact confine himself to pardoning homicide which was not felonious, but thought that this was contrary to justice, even in the case of a homicide outlawed at the king's own suit, and with the saving proviso of standing to right.[3]

Thus by the mid thirteenth century homicide in self-defence or by accident had come to predominate in the system of pardoning and if Bracton could have had his way felonious homicide would have been excluded from it altogether. Unfortunately, by the end of the thirteenth century the balance had been reversed; felonious homicide, even of the worst kind, was not to be excluded for a long time yet. But until 1294 excusable homicide remained at the core of the system. Many such homicides were investigated at the eyre or at gaol deliveries and the justices were prepared virtually to recommend pardon. The king seldom dissented from their view of the merits of the case. In so far as uncertain communications and administrative inefficiency permitted pardon for the prisoner was largely a matter of routine. In difficult cases the king, like his justices, was sometimes at a loss and played for time. Occasionally he took a more severe view, it seems. What he could not do, in these cases, was to show clemency at will and abuse the prerogative by remitting his suit against undoubted felons. Only cases in which there were pretty good grounds for clemency were referred to him. Indeed, these decisions had in practice almost a judicial character: there was comparatively little room for royal discretion.

---

[1] *De Legibus*, f. 132b.   [2] Ibid., f. 133.   [3] Ibid.

But the prerogative had free play when the king was approached before the trial or after the outlawry of the slayer. His response to such approaches should reveal his own conception of his power and responsibility, and also his susceptibility to various types of influence.

Henry III was piously disposed. He would pardon a homicide as a gesture of reverence for a saint or simply out of charity, perhaps at the prompting of some ecclesiastic.[1] It was not difficult, in this connection, to soften him up. His pliability in the hands of members of his family and his favourites was notorious. A man to whom he was specially indebted might exploit his position by acting almost as a pardon-monger. Roger de Leyburn had saved Henry's life at the battle of Evesham; in the succeeding years he or his wife secured pardons for seventeen slayers.[2] For political reasons, too, it was sometimes expedient to show clemency. Pardons at this particular moment may have been granted more easily as part of the effort to pacify the country. The most famous pardon, that to Earl Warenne in 1270, granted after his attack on the la Zuches in Westminster Hall but before Alan's death, may have been due in some degree to political calculation or to kinship or genuine friendship, but it came only after his trial and the imposition of the colossal fine of 10,000 marks and a public act of penance; as Sir Maurice Powicke remarked, 'the significance of this story lies here: one of the most powerful men in the kingdom, a close friend of the lord Edward, was instantly brought to justice'.[3] His pardon was, then, more of an act of reconciliation after punishment than remission of the latter. It cannot be taken as in any way typical. It certainly does not imply that pardon could regularly be obtained by undertaking to pay a very large fine, or that members of the aristocracy could always count on it.

The king may sometimes have been venal, but he was not in the habit of selling pardons simply to raise money. He did not usually require very much heavier payments for pardons for culpable than he did for excusable homicide: a mark or even half a mark of gold sufficed in some cases. Such sums, though they must have been a heavy burden to some of the suppliants,

[1] e.g. Cal. Pat. Rolls, 1247–58, 533. Cf. J.I. 1/58, m. 20.
[2] Cal. Pat. Rolls, 1258–66, 560, 579, 585, 614, 630, 644; ibid., 1266–72, 10, 35, 50, 95, 212 (two cases), 228, 240 (two cases), 304, 552.
[3] F. M. Powicke, Henry III and the Lord Edward, 585.

were not exorbitant, and cannot be regarded as sufficient in themselves to induce him to show clemency when he was not otherwise disposed to do so. Rather larger amounts were sometimes promised, from 2 to 6 marks of gold, and these may indicate that he or his officials made some show of reluctance, but they may reflect only the grantee's being able to afford more. When Robert Malenfant promised 100 marks for a pardon for his outlawed son he may well have bidden high for clemency in circumstances in which it would ordinarily have been refused.[1] Edward I seems seldom to have acceded to proffers of this kind, but when he did so he might stand out for a high figure. For example, in 1305, after the appeal *coram rege* against John son of Reginald for the death of William de Heyworth had been abandoned and the charge against him at the king's suit had been adjourned from term to term for the best part of two years, the bishop of Coventry arranged for his pardon at the cost of 60 marks, which the bishop guaranteed.[2] Since the appeal had not been prosecuted there was little risk of conviction and it was perhaps mainly to reach a conclusion of the affair that John, who had been mainperned, fined for pardon. Whether or no he was guilty his action was unusual, and evidence of this kind is far too scarce to give any help in estimating how often culpable homicides bought the king's pardon. In the first part of the thirteenth century, as has been seen, some slayers were able to buy licences for concord, though at considerable cost. Such licences were few in number by the middle of the century, though it is not clear whether this was due to the king's reluctance to grant them or the fact that they were no longer sought.

It is remarkable how few members of the nobility, knights, or squires obtained pardon for homicide. Except for political assassinations, such as that of Henry Clement in 1235,[3] murders were not often thought by juries to have been committed or instigated by them. It is true that their men, in carrying out their orders, might get embroiled in fatal affrays and it was not uncommon for an appellor to charge the lord with sending them forth to kill and receiving them back after the deed had

---

[1] *Excerpta è Rot. Finium*, ii. 68.
[2] K.B. 27/176, m. 72; *Cal. Pat. Rolls, 1301–7*, 383.
[3] For this see F. M. Powicke, op. cit., Appendix B. Some of those implicated were pardoned between 1248 and 1252; see *Cal. Pat. Rolls, 1247–58*, 24, 85, 150.

been accomplished. But appeals of ordering homicide were pretty sure to be quashed since the appellors could not claim to have witnessed the giving of the order. The lord could afford to wait for the eyre at which he could confidently expect the quashing of the appeal. Receiving the homicides after the deed was a rather more dangerous accusation and it might be worth while to secure pardon, but this was done comparatively seldom. It was certainly not the case that the king often pardoned the guilty simply because of their social status, or even personal friendship, if only because such people seldom stood in need of pardon, or disdained to seek it, preferring to be acquitted. When he was approached, he was not unaffected by the rank of the slayer or the instigator and harbourer of slayers, but he might try to take a strict line despite or just because of it.[1]

Churchmen were more likely to seek pardon for procuring homicide than laymen. Disputes over presentations to benefices sometimes resulted in the attempt to remove one presentee or provisor by force, and the death of one of the participants.

---

[1] This is shown by his treatment of William de Monte Caniso of Edwardeston, a tenant-in-chief and also a mesne tenant of lands in several counties. At the eyre in Essex in 1285 it was presented that five men of his mainpast had killed Hugh Bukkey by night and had then returned to his house. The jurors testified that they had acted on his orders, one of them being his steward, and that William had known of their presence in his house after the deed, to which he had consented (J.I. 1/249, m. 18; cf. mm. 14ᵈ, 22ᵈ). They were all placed in exigent. There can be little doubt of William's guilt. But next year he was pardoned 'for certain trespasses charged against him before the justices last in eyre in the county of Essex, for which he fled and was put in exigent... on condition that he go to the Holy Land before Midsummer twelvemonth, and remain there in God's service for ever. He is to receive 100 marks yearly out of the issues of his lands in England by the hands of the Master of the Knights Templars or of the prior of the Hospital of St. John of Jerusalem in England' (*Cal. Pat. Rolls, 1281–92*, 247). His lands had already been taken into the king's hands, but apparently his heir was to be allowed to succeed to them on his death (*Cal. Inquisitions Post Mortem*, ii, no. 610). There were complicated dealings with them for a long time and William was later permitted to answer any claims to them by a parliamentary decree (*Cal. Pat. Rolls, 1292–1301*, 72; ibid. *1281–92*, 394). He had apparently failed to depart for the Holy Land by the stipulated date, and was in prison in London in 1290 (ibid.; *Rot. Parl.* i. 50ᵃ), but in February 1291 he was said to be about to leave for Acre and the king ordered the restitution of some at least of his chattels—arms, silver, robes, jewels (*Cal. Pat. Rolls, 1281–92*, 422). Three months later Acre fell and there is some reason to think that William had not departed by 1292 (see *Select Cases in the Court of the King's Bench*, Selden Soc. lvii, no. 49), but he eventually left England. In 1297 he was pardoned for Hugh's death and all other trespasses and given licence to return (*Cal. Pat. Rolls, 1292–1301*, 235). A little later his lands were restored (ibid. 253, 256). He certainly cannot be said to have been punished lightly; eleven years was no short term to spend deprived of his estates and goods, partly in prison and partly in exile.

The king was generally ready to hand out pardons all round, especially if one of his own clerks was involved. The attempt to remove Henry de Wengham from the church of Tentwardenn to which he had been provided resulted in the death of one of the attackers. After many appeals in the county court the case was heard *coram rege* and Henry pardoned all those concerned.[1] Walter Chamberleng found it prudent to obtain pardon at the instance of the Papal Nuncio for the death of John de Elynton and receiving the slayers; no doubt he was guilty on the latter charge, for he continued to harbour them after getting it. When indicted for this he claimed benefit of clergy, but then fined for another pardon with 60 marks.[2]

A few laymen of substance stood in need of pardon for actually slaying someone themselves and obtained it, apparently, without any difficulty. Edward I, for example, granted pardon for homicide 'dilecto et fideli nostro, Johanni de Boclande', without specifying any grounds for it.[3] Secular lords were not likely to kill in self-defence, and their escorts were more likely to quarrel among themselves than have to act in their defence. If they caused fatal accidents these were seldom reported. Their favourite sport of jousting could, however, prove fatal, and pardon would then be needed. Lesser individuals who engaged in the same sport might flee and be outlawed for slaying in this way.[4] Forest offences, abduction of heiresses, neglect of feudal duties, and non-payment of dues and fines made tenants-in-chief familiar enough with the process of obtaining pardon, but so far as serious crime went they were much more likely to intercede with the king on behalf of others than to seek pardon for themselves. On the rather rare occasions when a lord charged with having ordered his men to kill, or having harboured slayers among them, or both, did seek pardon, he might be expected to do what he could for his men also. A few lords and ladies did in fact persuade the king to pardon both themselves and their men.[5] But as has already been seen when they sought licence

---

[1] J.I. 1/361, m. 46; *Cal. Pat. Rolls, 1247–58*, 169.

[2] J.I. 1/1188, m. 23ᵈ; *Cal. Pat. Rolls, 1247–58*, 626, 627; ibid., *1258–66*, 29; cf. *Excerpta è Rot. Finium*, ii. 305.

[3] See K.B. 27/162, m. 59ᵈ. Cf. J.I. 3/26, iii, m. 17.

[4] e.g. J.I. 1/998ᴬ, m. 28ᵈ.

[5] e.g. Mabel de Aumbley obtained pardon for harbouring her men after the slaying of John de Middelton, and Henry also pardoned them at her instance (*Close Rolls, 1254–6*, 237).

for concord, lords who got into this predicament might try to extricate themselves from it regardless of the fate of their dependants. The actual slayers might be servants and not tenants and their lord would not be under the same moral obligation to protect them if there was no feudal bond. But often he seems to have been anxious to dissociate himself entirely from his men's misdeeds.

When there was no suggestion of his complicity a lord might be readier to back an application for pardon, and there are examples of this both for servants such as warreners, foresters, and grooms as well as for feudal tenants. The feudal lord's duty of maintaining his vassals in court might be taken to extend to giving them assistance of this kind, and even villeins might have some claim to it. Yet the slayer was not particularly likely to turn to his lord for help; if he did so it was generally because his lord was in the king's service or high in his favour. Some lords, however, may have shown themselves particularly ready to help their tenants. Roger de Somery, for example, interceded for seven men in 1266 and 1267, all of whom may well have been his tenants, though scattered over five different counties.[1] He may have been influenced by his son-in-law, Ralph de Cromwell, who had spoken for an accidental slayer in 1263.[2] Few other lords shared this concern for their tenants. About 15 per cent of the pardons granted *ad instantiam* before 1294 were granted on the intercession of some eighty great lords and ladies and smaller landowners, but in only a few cases is it clear that the grantees were their tenants and in a good many the evidence does not suggest this. The grantees' surnames do not all reveal their place of origin and unless the victim's does so, or the locality of the homicide is known, there may be no clue whatever to a possible tenurial connection, but so far as can be judged comparatively few of the patrons approached the king simply because the slayers were their tenants and they expected him to acknowledge their right and duty as feudal lords to intervene on their behalf. However, when a lord was in a specially good position to influence the decision it was another matter. He, or his homicidal tenant, would note the opportunity and he might be ready enough to exploit it. This kind of opportunism was demonstrated during Simon de Montfort's short-lived

---

[1] See *Cal. Pat. Rolls, 1258–66*, 614, 650; ibid., *1266–72*, 67, 68, 104; *Cal. Inquisitions Post Mortem*, ii, no. 16; J.I. 1/802, m. 43. [2] *Cal. Pat. Rolls, 1258–66*, 302.

ascendancy in 1265, when one of his knights, Saer de Harecourt, lord of Kibworth, interceded for Wodard de Kibewrth. Pardon was granted late in April and the opportunity would soon have passed.[1]

A number of men who were serving or had served in local offices, sheriffs, constables of castles, justices of Chester also helped to obtain pardons. Some of them may have done so for their own tenants or servants;[2] but it is likely that in many cases they were asked to help because of their professional experience in such matters and also because of their standing with the king. Incidentally, helping others in this way increased their familiarity with a procedure which they might need one day to follow on their own behalf. William la Zuche, who had been sheriff of Surrey and Sussex and held other important offices, helped Henry Pelerin to secure pardon in 1265; three years later he stood in need of it himself, also for homicide, and it was granted to him and a number of others.[3] Royal justices themselves are sometimes named as persons at whose instance pardon was granted and again it is very hard to tell whether they were acting as personal patrons or in a more or less official capacity. In one case pardon was said to have been granted at the instance of Richard de Middelton, but two days later it was enrolled again and this time was said to be granted on the testimony of Middelton and another itinerant justice that the victim had been killed while fleeing from arrest, apparently as a poacher.[4] The use of *ad instantiam* in the first pardon may therefore have been a clerical error, and it certainly does not imply that pardons granted on the record of the justices could properly be said to have been granted at their instance. It is possible, however, that in some of the other cases the justice took pains to assist a homicide who had appeared before him or put in a special word on his behalf. Such men were not likely

---

[1] *Cal. Pat. Rolls, 1258–66*, 418; *Cal. Inquisitions Post Mortem*, ii, no. 247. But as an inquisition had found that he had killed in self-defence (see J.I. 1/1197, m. 19) this could hardly have mattered. He himself was later murdered. Cf. C. 144/13, no. 25.

[2] e.g. William de Lancaster, Keeper of the Honour of Lancaster, helped get one for his yeoman. See *Cal. Pat. Rolls, 1232–47*, 435; *Close Rolls, 1247–51*, 108; *Lancs. Assize Rolls*, Record Soc. for Lancs. and Cheshire, xlvii. 101.

[3] *Cal. Pat. Rolls, 1258–66*, 456; ibid., *1266–72*, 197. Hugh Saunzaver intervened on behalf of two men, one in 1264 the other in 1267; in 1272 he himself was pardoned for the death of Ralph le Keu. See ibid., *1258–66*, 307; ibid., *1266–72*, 177; *Close Rolls, 1268–72*, 491.

[4] *Cal. Pat. Rolls, 1266–72*, 203, 204.

to be asked to act in this way except by persons who deserved pardon, and the king was not yielding to pressure but accepting trustworthy advice when he showed clemency to their protégés. It is true that one justice at least, John de la Lynde, who was generous with aid in securing pardon, spoke to the king about one of his own tenants who had killed, but he was said to have done so in self-defence and it may be presumed that John had satisfied himself of this.[1]

People of many other classes appear as soliciting the pardons. Churchmen, of course, would intercede from motives of charity, perhaps also from concern for the reputation of members of their own order or to ensure respect for sanctuary. Sometimes they were protecting their own tenants or relatives. Many of those at whose instance pardons were granted were royal clerks. Occasionally the clerk was taking advantage of his position to assist a member of his family or a neighbour,[2] even perhaps a tenant, but usually there is no suggestion of any personal connection. It appears that many homicides got hold of any member of the household they could and sought his help in presenting their petitions. Often this help is likely to have consisted much more in advice and in drawing the king's attention to the matter than in persuading him to show clemency in a doubtful or improper case. An extreme example of such help being obtained when there could be no doubt whatever that pardon was appropriate is that of the chaplain, Richard de Troente, pardoned at the instance of Peter de Wintonia, Keeper of the Wardrobe.[3]

So many pardons for homicide and other crimes were granted between August 1269 and March 1271 at the instance of Henry III's household clerk, Thedisius de Camilla, that it looks as though he was the appropriate person to deal with petitions for pardon, and that it was more a matter of his putting them forward after some preliminary vetting than of his using his influence over the king to obtain them.[4] Other clerks who are named in a considerable number of pardons probably had the same function. The Chancellor himself might back a petition. That made on behalf of John Clerk gave a long account of the

---

[1] Ibid. 302. For other pardons granted at his instance see ibid., *1258–66*, 571, 630; ibid., *1266–72*, 209, 229.

[2] e.g. the pardon of Thomas de la Cornere granted at the instance of Magister William de la Cornere, king's clerk; *Cal. Pat. Rolls, 1266–72*, 629, 635.

[3] See above, p. 133.

[4] *Cal. Pat. Rolls, 1266–72*, 361, 371, 404, 448, 457, 458, 492, 493, 505, 506, 524.

death of Philip de Hednesberhe, which was due to three factors: a blow on the head by John with a small stick which neither drew blood nor broke a bone, a kick in the chest from the hind hooves of the victim's own horse, and the falling sickness; John, hearing of his death and destitute of counsel and the help of friends, took sanctuary and abjured the realm, although no one charged him with the death, apart from the bailiff of the late king who made him abjure. Since John was not entirely to blame for the death and so ought not to suffer perpetual punishment for it, the Chancellor together with John's friends asked Edward I, for the soul of his father and for Christ's pity, to deal mercifully with him.[1] It may fairly be assumed that he had checked this account of the death, and that his support of the petition was more or less official. The resulting pardon did not mention him or John's friends, but it referred to an attached schedule, now lost, which may have included the petition.[2]

Probably Henry III yielded most often to the pleading of members of his own family, his half-brothers, and in-laws to pardon the undeserving. A visit by his daughter Margaret and her husband, the king of Scots, was sure to be the occasion for a number of pardons granted at their instance, and there were some between visits. The recipients were likely to be fugitives from justice who had taken refuge across the border. Evidently the Scottish royal train could be expected to include a number of hopeful English outlaws, and Henry saw fit, when planning the visit in 1256, to provide that if Alexander was prevented from coming Margaret's safe-conduct should extend to 'those she brings with her, except outlaws'.[3] Whether the Scottish monarchs' solicitude for homicides was due to the belief that they had killed excusably or to a natural wish to secure the return of undesirable immigrants to England is hard to judge. Many of those pardoned at the instance of Alexander in 1251–2 were required to find 'security to attempt nothing against the peace',[4] which suggests that they were notorious criminals, but this inference is uncertain since the same condition might also be imposed in a pardon for homicide in self-defence.[5] One man,

---

[1] S.C. 8/335, no. 15817. John was given firm peace at the eyre in 1279 (J.I. 1/371, m. 21). The pardon as quoted there was one of those which used the phrase 'quia testatum est per fideles' when giving accident as the grounds, and it extended to 'abjuration if any', although the petition made it quite clear that he had abjured.

[2] *Cal. Pat. Rolls, 1272–81,* 145.   [3] Ibid. *1247–58,* 484.

[4] Ibid. 122–3.   [5] Ibid. 125.

pardoned at Margaret's instance later in 1252, had been outlawed for robbery as well as homicide,[1] but their influence was
certainly exerted sometimes on behalf of excusable slayers,[2] and
Alexander may have judged that after eighteen years in exile
Ralph Drenge had been sufficiently punished even for culpable
homicide.[3]

It certainly must not be assumed that help was sought only
because the applicant for pardon knew he had a weak case.
One pardon was granted at the instance not only of the king
of Scots, but also at that of the slayer's lord, Henry de Bohun,
yet even this joint effort was quite unnecessary since an inquisition actually held by justices in eyre had found that he had
killed in self-defence.[4] The formality of the backing of some
requests for pardon is revealed in the case of Richard de Beau-
compe, pardoned on 24 June 1270 at the instance of John, son
of Edward the king's son; the patron on this occasion had cele-
brated his fourth birthday a fortnight earlier! Nor can there
have been any need to get the infant to hand the petition to his
grandfather in order to soften his heart and incline him to
clemency, since the slaying had been found by inquisition to
have been due to mischance.[5] Statements suggesting that pardon
was granted merely because of someone's intercession must not,
then, be taken at their face value.[6] One reason why a slayer was
anxious for support emerges when it is stated that the king has

[1] Ibid. 145.

[2] e.g. ibid. 461, 531, 578 (cf. J.I. 1/1109, m. 32ᵈ). Alexander obtained pardon
for the keeper of one of his own prisons who had killed an escaped prisoner south of
the border; see *Cal. Pat. Rolls, 1247–58*, 497. He does not always seem to have been
efficient in getting the pardon delivered to the grantee: in 1255 he obtained a
second for a man for whom he had got one in 1253 (ibid. 256, 409; cf. *Close Rolls,
1254–56*, 233).

[3] *Cal. Pat. Rolls, 1247–58*, 122; *Close Rolls, 1231–34*, 424 shows that he had been
outlawed before mid 1233.   [4] *Cal. Pat. Rolls, 1247–58*, 531.

[5] Ibid., *1266–72*, 436; cf. ibid. 481 for the appointment of commissioners to hold
it.

[6] Individual documents can give a very misleading impression of the king's
yielding to improper influence. For example, in 1261 Henry III wrote to the sheriff
of Berkshire about the disposal of the property of Roger Gambun, whom he had
pardoned of his special grace at the instance of special friends of the king, although
an inquisition held by the itinerant justices had found that he had manifestly
killed John le Hopper, for which manifest felony the property had been taken
into the king's hands (*Close Rolls, 1259–61*, 479). This suggests that pardon had
been obtained for felonious homicide through the influence of some favourites of
Henry's. But the pardon was actually granted at the instance of Laurence del
Broke, who often served as a commissioner for inquisitions into the circumstances of
slayings, and was based on a verdict given at the eyre that Roger had slain John

not only pardoned him but has ordered the restoration of his
chattels and perhaps his land at the instance of someone else.[1]
Financial help was sometimes provided more directly to meet the
costs of the letters patent of pardon.[2] Help was also given in securing the holding of the inquisition which established some excuse.[3]

While they reveal that some homicides sought help even
though there were excellent grounds for clemency, the enrolled
pardons taken by themselves do give the impression that the
king was all too apt to succumb to pressures exerted on behalf
of felonious homicides. This impression is especially marked in
the calendars for the period 1247 to 1272, when well over half
the grants were said to have been made at the instance of a
third party.[4] In only about one-quarter of the pardons of this
type as enrolled is there any mention of justification or excuse.
Of some 600 grants made during these twenty-five years without
good reason shown in the enrolments, four-fifths are said to have
been made *ad instantiam*. There is thus a very strong primafacie
case for the charge that at this moment pressure was being frequently and successfully exerted; indeed it seems that at this
time not far short of half of all the pardons for homicide were ex-
tracted or wheedled out of Henry to the benefit of those who had
slain intentionally. But this evidence is misleading. For one thing,
the clerks who enrolled the pardons showed more concern to
mention the fact that they were granted *ad instantiam* than the
grounds for them. No case has been noted in which the pardon
as recorded on the eyre roll mentions that it was granted at
somebody's request whereas the patent roll entry omits this
factor.[5] It appears, therefore, that it was the normal practice to
include it. But perhaps the clerks did not wish to lengthen the

by mischance (*Cal. Pat. Rolls, 1258–66*, 109, 146). The eyre roll provides details,
which show that Roger had responded to the hue and cry when there was a medley
outside his house, had tried to break it up by brandishing a hatchet, but had
accidentally struck a great friend of his without seeing he was there (J.I. 1/701,
m. 30ᵈ; cf. m. 21ᵈ, where Roger was placed in exigent).

[1] e.g. *Cal. Pat. Rolls, 1266–72*, 48, *Close Rolls, 1264–8*, 306; *Cal. Pat. Rolls, 1247–58*,
387, *Close Rolls, 1254–6*, 25; ibid., *1264–8*, 341, *Cal. Pat. Rolls, 1266–72*, 88.
[2] Cf. above, p. 55, n. 1.   [3] e.g. *Cal. Pat. Rolls, 1272–81*, 268.
[4] Where two or more men were pardoned for the same death at the instance of
the same patron they have been counted only once for the purpose of estimating
how often the king yielded to pressure. Where one man was pardoned twice for
the same death but at the instance of different patrons the case has been counted
twice, since the king acceded to two requests.
[5] The printed Calendars nearly always include it, but one or two additional
cases emerge from a check with the rolls.

entries by doing so, and accordingly compensated for including this additional matter by omitting the circumstances which showed some excuse or extenuation. In many cases other evidence reveals that there were good grounds for clemency; in some it is clear, in others likely that the actual pardon had referred to them. However, even the letters patent of pardon might be silent on this point, to judge by some of those which appear to have been copied out *in extenso* on the eyre rolls. It is unlikely that an excuse would not be put forward when the patron or go-between asked the king to pardon the homicide if there was in fact a perfectly good one to hand. It is conceivable that the king very occasionally acceded to a request in ignorance of, or without paying particular attention to the arguments which could be used to support it, but generally it must be supposed that he took them into account, even if rather more perfunctorily than he would have done if there had been no influential backing. Failure to mention self-defence or accident in the enrolment, even perhaps in the pardon itself, did not, therefore, necessarily imply that it was not granted in part at least on these grounds. In individual cases they can be shown to have existed in the view of a jury, whilst in others they can be shown at least to have been alleged.

Evidence for inquisitions into the circumstances provides a useful check on the enrolled pardons. In a comparatively small number of cases the actual returns to inquisitions whether a slaying was felonious or by mischance or in self-defence have survived. In a larger number the appointment of commissioners to hold such inquisitions is enrolled, especially from 1255 on.[1] Even if the returns have not survived to prove that the king had a favourable verdict before him, it can be taken for granted that he was acting on the strength of such a verdict when he granted a pardon shortly after appointing commissioners, although its enrolment does not refer to it. Some thirty instances of this kind have been noticed, and they are enough to show the danger of relying on the enrolled pardons alone. The chief alternative source of information is, of course, the plea rolls, especially the eyre rolls, but also those of the *Curia Regis*.[2] Here one may hope to discover independent accounts of the homicides in question, though unfortunately many rolls are missing, and there are the

---

[1] But many inquisitions are known to have been held the orders for which have not been traced.   [2] The coroners' rolls are scarcely helpful at this point.

usual problems of identifying individual cases. Moreover, even
when a case can be confidently identified on a plea roll, the
entry may be too summary to be helpful. It is only in a limited
number of cases that it is possible to judge if pardon *ad instantiam*
was, or could have been, based on adequate grounds. Nevertheless, it will be worth while to attempt some estimate of the
proportion of such pardons which were granted for excusable
homicide, or at any rate for homicide with some degree of
extenuation, among the cases identified on the plea rolls. In
June 1294 Edward I began to recruit troops by pardoning
criminals, and after this his commanding officers might put in
recommendations for those who had enlisted and served under
them. It would distort the picture altogether if pardons granted
during the wars were included. Accordingly only the period
from 1226, when Henry III was beginning to take some part in
granting them, down to mid 1294 will be considered. The
sample consists of over 180 cases which have been identified from
these years. Evidence for there being reasonable grounds for
clemency has been used whether it is on the plea roll or elsewhere,
including the enrolled pardons themselves and the inquisitions.

A few of those pardoned *ad instantiam* did not really need
pardon at all. They could have afforded to await trial, but
preferred, no doubt, to get the matter cleared up at once. Some
had probably not slain anyone or participated in any way.[1] Some
could have pleaded justification. Robert le Wastur recognized
a man who had been outlawed for forest offences, tried to arrest
him and shot him as he fled.[2] Another killing which at one time
would have been accounted justifiable was that of a chaplain
found in bed with the slayer's wife,[3] but by now it was certainly
prudent to seek pardon in such circumstances. Until 1293 the
killing of offenders in forests and warrens who resisted arrest

---

[1] e.g. Master Geoffrey de Everleye, clerk of the king of Spain, obtained a pardon
for Alice of Everleye who had been charged, together with three men, with killing
her husband (*Cal. Pat. Rolls, 1272–81*, 147; J.I. 1/371, m. 17ᵈ). One of the men had
been hanged at a gaol delivery, but Alice had been acquitted there, although she
was later indicted at the eyre. Her pardon was, perhaps, a wise precaution, but
it seems likely that she was innocent.

[2] J.I. 1/1004, m. 97; *Cal. Pat. Rolls, 1272–81*, 296. For what may be a similar
case see above, p. 230, n. 2.

[3] J.I. 1/202, m. 27ᵈ; *Cal. Pat. Rolls, 1266–72*, 237. Cf. Pollock and Maitland,
Hist. Eng. Law, ii. 484. The husband with two companions beat, wounded, and
castrated the chaplain, as a result of which treatment he died three months later.
This suggests too deliberate an assault, but the plea of provocation should have
been enough to persuade the king to grant pardon.

was not normally considered justifiable, but it was generally treated as excusable. There are three cases of killing by foresters or warreners in which the victim is not actually stated to have been poaching but where this is not unlikely to have been the occasion for the affray.[1] Pardons *ad instantiam* were particularly likely in such an event, for the killer would have been defending his lord's property and acting in the line of duty. There is one other case in which the slaying is stated to have occurred in a forest or park and the circumstances may have been similar, but this is more conjectural.[2]

In eight of the cases identified on the plea rolls the slaying had been accidental, though it is noteworthy that in only three of them is this known from the pardons as enrolled.[3] Among the other five, Philip le Teler could certainly not be held to blame for the death, which occurred 'per maximum infortunium' as he was carrying the victim on his back and he slipped off, piercing himself on Philip's arrow. The other four accounts show that there was no doubt whatever about the accidental nature of the fatality. There is an additional case in which the enrolled pardon refers to an inquest having established that the slaying was by mischance, but the account at the eyre suggests only that it could possibly have been described as self-defence.[4] In sixteen cases the slaying was in self-defence according to the enrolled pardon or the eyre roll or both. In a seventeenth the victim had threatened to strike the slayer;[5] this was not in itself enough to warrant describing his action as self-defence, but it

---

[1] The duke of Brittany's forester was harboured by him for a time after slaying a man in the forest, was then outlawed, but finally pardoned at the duke's instance. See J.I. 1/1060, m. 1; J.I. 1/1098, m. 83; *Cal. Pat. Rolls, 1292–1301,* 67, 68. Randolf Russel was also a forester who may have killed a poacher, but as several others were also appealed this is uncertain (J.I. 1/736, m. 25; *Cal. Pat. Rolls, 1258–66,* 309). Another slayer, Nicholas de Hatfeud, was a warrener (J.I. 1/573, m. 44^d; *Cal. Pat. Rolls, 1266–72,* 462).

[2] That of Thomas Ladde Best, J.I. 1/131, m 6^d, *Cal. Pat. Rolls, 1266–72,* 371.

[3] These three were for Andrew Bukstan, *Cal. Pat. Rolls, 1258–66,* 11, J.I. 1/343, m. 15^d, cf. below, p. 256; Thomas de Carleton, *Cal. Pat. Rolls, 1266–72,* 79, J.I. 1/569^A, m. 23, cf. below, p. 303; Roger Payn, *Cal. Pat. Rolls, 1281–92,* 22, J.I. 1/1004, m. 86^d. The others were for Nicholas de Caldecote, *Cal. Pat. Rolls, 1266–72,* 577, J.I. 1/85, m. 9^d; Baldwin Wynepole, *Cal. Pat. Rolls, 1281–92,* 53, J.I. 1/86, m. 38^d; Thomas le Archer, *Cal. Pat. Rolls, 1266–72,* 444, J.I. 1/736, m. 27; Philip le Teler, *Cal. Pat. Rolls, 1247–58,* 456, J.I. 1/1022, m. 31; Roger son of Fulk, *Cal. Pat. Rolls, 1258–66,* 404, J.I. 1/1051, m. 8.

[4] John le Marescal, *Cal. Pat. Rolls, 1258–66,* 147; J.I. 1/998^A, m. 32.

[5] Richard Graffard, *Cal. Pat. Rolls, 1266–72,* 643; J.I. 1/1060, m. 21.

constituted some extenuation, and pardon was perhaps not altogether out of place. Richard Wyther's pardon has not been found on the patent rolls, but it is recorded on an eyre roll as granted at the instance of the bishop of Exeter and on a verdict of self-defence at an inquisition; he had, it emerges, killed a vagabond thief in self-defence as he was trying to attach him.[1] In seven other cases although the eyre roll does not mention self-defence, it can be assumed that the pardon was granted on these grounds because an inquisition had been ordered shortly before the grant to ascertain whether the slaying had been in felony or self-defence.[2] Doubt arises, however, in three others in which an inquisition had been ordered three or four years earlier.[3] The verdicts may have been favourable but for some reason or other were not followed up; possibly the inquisitions were not in fact held. In either event the accused might well find it necessary to get someone to draw the king's attention to the omission. But, of course, it may be that they were held and the verdicts were unfavourable, and that it was just for this reason that a friend at court had to be found to secure a pardon. Nevertheless, the fact that the slayers had thought it worth while to obtain the inquisitions in the first place suggests that a case could at least be made out for excusable homicide. Finally, the case of Robert le Palmer should probably be included. He was not said to have killed in self-defence, but had earlier been granted bail and this suggests that an inquisition de odio et atia had brought in a favourable verdict; moreover, the jurors at the eyre said that one of his two alleged victims had been killed by someone else in self-defence, and it looks as though there had been a fight between the four and that these grounds could plausibly be put forward on his behalf as well.[4] Thus in twenty-five cases self-defence seems clearly to

---

[1] J.I. 1/202, m. 24d. The pardon as quoted here referred to a verdict of self-defence at an inquisition held by William de Stanton and John de la Strode.

[2] Cal. Pat. Rolls, 1266–72, 262, 290, J.I. 1/1060, m. 10; Cal. Pat. Rolls, 1258–66, 489, 496, J.I. 1/1051, m. 24; Cal. Pat. Rolls, 1266–72, 44, ibid. 1258–66, 670, J.I. 1/1051, m. 37; Cal. Pat. Rolls, 1266–72, 454, 479, J.I. 1/736, m. 39d; Cal. Pat. Rolls, 1266–72, 504, 478, J.I. 1/1060, m. 41d; Cal. Pat. Rolls, 1266–72, 407, 471, J.I. 1/573, m. 2; Cal. Pat. Rolls, 1266–72, 424, 474, J.I. 1/736, m. 51d.

[3] Cal. Pat. Rolls, 1266–72, 405, 131, J.I. 1/1051, m. 38d, J.I. 1/1060, m. 47; Cal. Pat. Rolls, 1266–72, 228, ibid., 1258–66, 482, J.I. 1/1051, m. 37; Cal. Pat. Rolls, 1266–72, 669, 162, J.I. 1/60, m. 23d. (The identification here is not certain.)

[4] J.I. 1/619, m. 62; an appeal had been brought against him but was not now prosecuted; cf. Cal. Pat. Rolls, 1266–72, 519.

have provided grounds for the pardons, and in four others it may have done so.

Over forty of the 180-odd pardons granted *ad instantiam* in cases identified on the eyre rolls can, then, be accounted for in ways which suggest that no improper influence was being brought to bear on the king. In many of them there were excellent grounds for clemency. In the most dubious cases there were at least plausible grounds. There are several other pardons which, on a charitable view, could be attributed to adequate excuse being found or even to exoneration by a jury rather than to such pressure. It is noticeable how often—in thirty cases—the account on the eyre roll mentions that the slaying occurred *mota contentione* or *orta lite*, although the pardon does not refer to self-defence. Now, there are a great many instances of pardon being granted explicitly on grounds of self-defence when the eyre roll goes no further than to speak in these terms of a quarrel having broken out. It was precisely in these fatal free fights that it was most difficult to determine what degree of responsibility for starting the scrap or for turning it into something more serious rested on the survivors. Presenting jurors often would not commit themselves until asked to pronounce on this, whereas jurors at a special inquisition would generally be ready enough to lay the blame on the deceased. It is quite possible, therefore, that inquisitions had been held in many of these thirty cases and had given verdicts of slaying in self-defence, though no reference to them has been found. It is significant, however, to find that very few pardons for slaying *mota contentione* but with no reference to self-defence were granted without the assistance of some patron: only five have been noted. Thus help was secured in a very high proportion of them and this suggests that there was real need for it. The claim that such slaying was excusable could be asserted with some plausibility but it was unwise to rely on it alone. In such cases mercy might well be thought proper and influential people might feel constrained to support applications for it. This support may sometimes have proved decisive. Thus it would be rash to regard all thirty cases as routine pardons for homicide in self-defence which could easily have been secured without any influence having been brought to bear on the king. It may reasonably be inferred that some of them would have been granted simply on the merits of the case, but it looks as though men who killed in a free fight were in particular need of some backing when they sought pardon, since the element of self-defence was difficult to assess and jurors could not always be relied upon to recognize it. This points to some strictness in the normal treatment of these cases, and pardoning them *ad instantiam* may not indicate undue laxity resulting from improper pressures. The same considerations may apply, though more doubtfully, to killing in a tavern. This would almost always imply a drunken brawl, and it was not difficult for the survivor to blame the deceased for starting it. One such killing has been noticed, pardon for which was granted *ad instantiam* but made no reference to self-defence.[1]

It has been remarked that when a man was killed in a brawl only those who had given him mortal blows were held guilty. This probably means that some men who were pardoned *ad instantiam* would have qualified without such backing for several such pardons went to participants in large-scale brawls, and it may well be that these grantees were not directly responsible for the fatal outcome.[2] Men appealed as accomplices in smaller affrays got similar pardons.[3] More remote complicity was probably alleged in other cases.[4] There might be real doubt whether the victim had died as a result of the injury admittedly inflicted.[5] The pardons granted at the request of various people in some of these cases were not routine matters, but on the other hand it is likely that a case for leniency could be made out in most, if not, indeed, all but one of them, and they hardly look like a serious abuse of the prerogative of mercy.

In some of the cases already mentioned an appeal had been made but had failed or been withdrawn. In eight or nine other cases this had happened, and in two more concords had been made. Appeals were often withdrawn even though the presenting and trial jurors thought the appellee guilty. At the same time it is evident that many appellors came to recognize that

---

[1] That for William or Walter Elys, J.I. 1/238, m. 49ᵈ; *Cal. Pat. Rolls, 1258–66*, 523.

[2] e.g. J.I. 1/1109, m. 24; *Cal. Pat. Rolls, 1247–58*, 496, 497.

[3] e.g. J.I. 1/700, m. 11, *Cal. Pat. Rolls, 1258–66*, 309; J.I. 1/701, m. 29, *Cal. Pat. Rolls, 1247–58*, 332, 340, *Close Rolls 1259–61*, 367; J.I. 1/568, m. 7ᵈ, *Cal. Pat. Rolls, 1247–58*, 122; and perhaps J.I. 1/998ᴬ, m. 41, *Cal. Pat. Rolls, 1266–72*, 211. This prisoner was appealed of holding the victim while another slew him. If he had done so Bracton would have considered him guilty of homicide.

[4] J.I. 1/998ᴬ, m. 34, *Cal. Pat. Rolls, 1266–72*, 82; *Placitorum Abbreviatio*, 148–9; *Cal. Pat. Rolls, 1247–58*, 626, 627. Cf. above, p. 228.

[5] e.g. J.I. 1/1109, m. 18; *Cal. Pat. Rolls, 1247–58*, 536.

they had appealed someone who was altogether innocent, or had slain justifiably or excusably. This may well have been the explanation in some of these cases, especially in four of them, in which the appeal was summoned to Westminster and was there withdrawn or failed. Pardon was likely to be obtained forthwith, so that the appellee would not have to wait to be arraigned at the king's suit at the eyre.

Samson Foliot is entitled to the benefit of the doubt as to his intention in striking his son what proved to be a fatal blow. Himself a justice of gaol delivery, he knew the ropes and could doubtless have secured pardon easily enough without the intervention of the Queen Mother on his behalf.[1] In hitting a servant on the head with a tripod, Peter the Marshal inflicted an unduly forceful punishment, but his pardon was not unreasonable since the death was obviously not premeditated and presumably not intended even in the heat of the moment.[2] This type of killing was discussed by Bracton and his authorities; it was taken to involve some degree of culpability, but could hardly be regarded as intentional homicide when such an unlikely implement was used. Finally, two cases may be mentioned in which the culprit appears to have gone straight to the king to get pardon, one at the instance of Robert Burnel, in whose house the killing had occurred.[3] The confidence with which they went off to seek pardon suggests that both could put forward some excuse as well as having a friend at court.

If, in granting some of these pardons, the king showed more mercy than he might otherwise have done, at any rate they do not suggest that influential people were intervening on behalf of murderers whose crimes were of the most heinous and premeditated kind. There is thus some evidence in 100 of the 180-odd cases identified on the plea rolls to suggest that pardons granted *ad instantiam* may have been deserved or at any rate were not gravely misplaced. Some went to excusable slayers, others, perhaps, to those who could even have been acquitted. A large proportion went to men who had been involved in chance medleys or in more large-scale incidents in which they had taken only a minor part; had they stood trial

[1] Ibid., *1272–81, 441*; cf, 338; J.I. 1/1004, m. 85ᵈ.
[2] J.I. 1/361, m. 61ᵈ; *Cal. Pat. Rolls, 1247–58*, 402.
[3] J.I. 1/323, m. 43ᵈ; J.I. 1/361, m. 40; *Cal. Pat. Rolls, 1266–72*, 507; ibid., *1247–58*, 329.

some would have been found guilty of breach of the peace but
not of felony. In some cases excuse or extenuation is highly
conjectural, but it may fairly be regarded as probable in half
of the 180.

Conversely, they include cases in which there are definite
indications that influence was used to secure pardon for felonious homicide. But these are extremely few. The Lord Edward
persuaded his father to pardon a man who had killed 'per
vetus odium', according to the presentment at the eyre.[1] Three
men pardoned at the instance of Henry's half-brothers were
charged with both murder and robbery, but a great many
others had been appealed of the same robbery and affray
and it is doubtful if these three were the ring-leaders.[2] Robert
Russel was pardoned for a homicide of which his father had
been absolved by a jury de odio et atia, which stated that Robert
was guilty.[3] Both had abjured the realm. The pardon for the
death of Ellis le Waleys has already been discussed;[4] Short at
least was deemed guilty by two sets of jurors. In a couple of cases
the patron who secured the pardon undertook suretyship for the
grantee's future good behaviour, or someone else was found to
do so.[5] This requirement raises a presumption that the grantee
was guilty, or was at least a suspect and unruly character, but
it does not prove that he was believed guilty of felonious homicide, since, as already noted, the same requirement is sometimes
found in cases of excusable killing. William Clive was probably
guilty; he and his brother were stated to have killed a woman
and buried her in their father's grange; a year later they
quarrelled and one of them appears to have revealed the felony;
William fled and secured pardon; his brother was found guilty
but handed over to the bishop as a convicted clerk.[6] Only nine
cases of pardon for probable though by no means certain
felonious killing have been found, then, to set against 100 for
killing which probably was not premeditated although it was
pardoned ad instantiam.

---

[1] Robert Spurecat, Cal. Pat. Rolls, 1266–72, 111; J.I. 1/569ᴬ, m. 9ᵈ.

[2] Cal. Pat. Rolls, 1258–66, 180, 211, 544; J.I. 1/874, m. 31.

[3] Cal. Pat. Rolls, 1266–72, 248; J.I. 1/323, m. 54; J.I. 3/85, m. 16; C. 144/6, no. 3.

[4] Above, p. 192.

[5] Those of Robert Seys (Cal. Pat. Rolls, 1247–58, 532; cf. K.B. 26/161, m. 12ᵈ; J.I. 1/736, m. 30) and Walter le Noreys (Cal. Pat. Rolls, 1258–66, 378; J.I. 1/998ᴬ 24ᵈ).

[6] Cal. Pat. Rolls, 1258–66, 627; J.I. 1/954, m. 51.

There remain some seventy cases identified on the plea rolls in which no clue has been found as to the nature of the homicide pardoned in this way. Either the slayer came before the justices armed with his pardon or he was said to have fled and was put in exigent. In the event of his producing his pardon there was no need for any examination of the circumstances in which he had killed, and there would have been no particular reason for the presenting jurors to mention them if they knew that he was in court and had been pardoned, while if the slayer was a fugitive there was no need for them to say whether his slaying was excusable, though it has been seen that they sometimes did so. It was normal for homicides which later turned out to have been excusable to be presented as felonious. Such presentments on the eyre rolls are, therefore, neutral: they do not even raise the presumption that these pardons *ad instantiam* were misplaced. Moreover, three-quarters of them come from the last years of Henry III and the first of Edward, who granted that no one should lose life or limb for any homicide or other felony committed in his father's time.[1] There was less need for thorough investigation of such homicides at the eyres held in the new reign, and so all the more reason for the eyre roll to omit any reference to the circumstances. On the other hand, it is likely on general grounds that pardons were granted more readily to culpable slayers for much of this period. Slaying in the months of open civil war might not necessitate pardon, but in the troubled years as a whole there were many homicides which it would have been impolitic to regard too severely. Henry III could not easily refuse the requests of supporters like Roger de Leyburn, who, as has been seen, secured many of these pardons for his protégés.[2] On the other hand, when the baronial party was predominant, petitions seem to have been scrutinized more carefully than usual, and pardons granted at the instance of more responsible people. One, for example, was granted at the instance of the bishop of Lincoln, and with the approval of the Justiciar Bigod.[3] These are likely to have been based on some consideration of the circumstances. The Justiciar's brother, however, and other baronial leaders also

[1] See J.I. 1/323, mm. 42, 44.

[2] Above, p. 225.

[3] *Cal. Pat. Rolls, 1258–66*, 41. In 1265 the Justiciar, Hugh le Despenser, himself held a number of the inquisitions leading to pardon. See ibid. 424, 427, 430, 431, 433.

seized the occasion to put in their recommendations and it
may well be that the king pardoned without good reason shown
in an appreciable number of cases, but then the times were
abnormal.

The seventy neutral cases, then, no doubt contained some
pardons *ad instantiam* for felonious homicide, and it would be
unsafe to assume that the proportions of excusable or near-
excusable and felonious homicides among them were much the
same as in the cases where further information is available, i.e.
of the order of 100 to nine or under. But even if they are assigned in a purely arbitrary way half to the one group and half
to the other, the proportion of excusable homicides or homicides
in extenuating circumstances would be about 75 per cent of
the total pardoned *ad instantiam*, and it seems unlikely that the
true figure fell short of this. It may well have been considerably
higher. Thus although the king sometimes yielded to pressure
and pardoned felonious homicide he was not persuaded to do
so as often as might have been expected. Whether he often
refused requests from influential people cannot be ascertained,
but it may be that he showed some restraint in the exercise of his
prerogative even when it meant denying a favour to a courtier.
In so far as the king pardoned homicides without more or less
plausible grounds he did this, to judge by the cases identified
on the eyre rolls, most often, though not exclusively, at the
prompting of some influential person, or at least some one with
easy access to him. But while these disreputable pardons were
likely to be obtainable only with assistance it must not be
thought that assistance was given primarily in such cases.
Very seldom indeed is there positive evidence for such obvious
abuse of the system. What does emerge from this survey is
that help was given especially in cases of killing in the course of
brawls where self-defence might be asserted but not, perhaps,
with much confidence unless such backing was to be had. In
listening to recommendations to mercy in these cases the king
was not necessarily deliberately transgressing the limits on
his prerogative approved by Bracton, nor were patrons themselves necessarily consciously inflating the claims of their
clients to his clemency. Perhaps they were somewhat gullible
or biased and so too ready to believe the clients' stories without
further investigation. But the cynical abuse of the system of
pardoning was the exception rather than the rule. In a con-

siderable number of cases their intervention can have made no difference whatever to the success of the plea for pardon. Where it may most often have turned the scales was in cases of minor complicity or of unpremeditated killing in a fight in which greater force had been used than was really vital in self-defence.

Of the cases identified on the plea rolls between 1226 and 1294 only just over a third involved pardons *ad instantiam*. In many of the other cases, of course, pardon followed remand *ad gratiam* by the justices because an excuse had been established in court, or an inquisition obtained before trial. There is evidence for excuse, including mental derangement and infancy, in the vast majority. If the five cases in which the slaying was said to have occurred *mota contentione* are included, then there is clear evidence in just on 92 per cent of them that pardon was granted with good reason or at least when extenuating circumstances supplied some grounds for it. Half of the remaining pardons went to men who may have deserved them since appeals against them had been withdrawn or they had perhaps taken only a minor part in a fatal brawl. Most of the rest went to men who had been outlawed, some on appeal, and no details are available, but it is likely that in over 96 per cent of these cases pardon was not undeserved. There is only one in which the evidence positively suggests that the grantee had killed feloniously.[1] It must be emphasized again that both sets of figures, those for pardons obtained with and without the help of patrons, are very rough and there is liable to be some subjective bias in the interpretation of very sketchy information. For what they are worth, when added together, they suggest that in a sample of well over 500 cases identified on the plea rolls[2] pardon is very unlikely to have been granted to felonious killers in more than 20 per cent, and even 10 per cent may well be considerably above the mark.

The impression that the king showed a certain restraint in the use of his prerogative down to 1294 is confirmed if one glances

[1] That of Robert de Neuburgh, pardoned 'de gratia speciali' for two homicides, robberies, and other crimes (*Cal. Pat. Rolls, 1281–92*, 160; J.I. 1/210, m. 46). He was a free tenant with chattels valued at £6, so he may have paid a fairly large amount for his pardon.

[2] Cases in which justices of assize were instructed to hold special inquisitions when the applicant for pardon was not on trial have, of course, been omitted from the sample.

at pardons for crimes other than homicide. They were, of course, granted in a wide range of other matters from arson, mayhem, rape, robbery, harbouring felons, prison-breaking, rescuing prisoners, permitting them to escape, political offences, forest offences, counterfeiting and clipping coins, breaches of the peace, to breaches of trading regulations, a host of offences and defaults by those in his service, and breaches of feudal rules such as marriages of heiresses without his permission. People outlawed for failing to appear in court especially in actions of trespass were coming to obtain pardon increasingly from Edward I. Most of these offences were in no way comparable with homicide and readiness to pardon them is no indication of the king's excessive leniency towards serious crime. In order to obtain some idea of his treatment of the latter it is enough to consider pardons for arson, mayhem or mutilation, rape, robbery, burglary, and larceny. No detailed examination of pardons in these cases has been attempted. The recipients were expected to stand to right and produce their pardons before the itinerant justices, where they would be proclaimed and firm peace given, just as in cases of homicide. But comparatively few proclamations of pardon other than for homicide were recorded in the eyre rolls,[1] to judge by which this sort of pardoning did not reach significant proportions. The patent rolls by themselves will afford a better but still very rough comparison between the frequency of pardons for homicide and for the other crimes under consideration, in the period from 1226 to mid 1294.

The total number of pardons enrolled on the patent rolls of these years for homicide, arson, mayhem, rape, robbery, burglary, and larceny is well over 1,900. Of this total, all but some 140 were for homicide. Thus the proportion was around 93 per cent for homicides, to 7 per cent for the other felonies. This in itself suggests that Henry and, up to this point, Edward were restrained in their use of the prerogative of mercy so far as felony was concerned, granting on an average only two pardons a year for these felonies other than homicide. But even this figure is too high, for in some of these cases no felony had in fact been committed, or there had been mitigating circumstances or only outlawry was pardoned. Thus of the fifteen cases of alleged maiming (including three of castration), one

[1] For some examples see J.I. 1/486, m. 41^d; J.I. 1/829, m 5; J.I. 1/1060, m. 24.

had been found to have been an accident,[1] and in another the grantees had been outlawed through fraud.[2] Six outlaws were pardoned because they had been outlawed whilst abroad and unaware that charges had been made against them, one because his outlawry on appeal by an approver had been irregular in some way. Two were pardoned outlawry because they had surrendered at once and stood their trial. Six people were pardoned because it had been found that they were innocent or at least that they had been accused out of malice, and an appellee on the withdrawal of the appeal. Three robbers who had been found guilty and hanged but had survived, two because the rope broke, and one because he had been cut down when unconscious but still alive, were pardoned in accordance with custom as they were supposed to have been miraculously exonerated. Thus only some 118 persons were pardoned outright although they were, apparently, guilty of these felonies, an average of 1·7 a year.[3] These pardons were rather scarcer in the first decade after 1226 (in contrast with the preceding decade), rather concentrated in the last years of Henry III; otherwise they were fairly evenly distributed over the period.

It is evident that before 1294 the business of pardoning was not carried on altogether recklessly for the benefit of professional robbers and deliberate murderers. It generally needed the good offices of a friend at court, and probably a fairly influential one, such as a member of the royal family, for the culpable homicide to win the king's grace. Pardons for such men allowed a number of undesirable individuals to escape punishment by outlawry and return to their native districts, but they were not granted on such a scale as to jeopardize any deterrent effect the inadequate penal system may have had.

On his return to England as king, Edward I showed good intentions in this matter, He yielded to fewer requests from his family and courtiers to grant pardon than his father had done. Yet it was Edward who introduced the policy which made pardon available to every able-bodied male criminal who cared to earn it by military service. In 1293 he pardoned Thomas de

[1] *Cal. Pat. Rolls, 1247–58*, 569.
[2] Ibid., *1258–66*, 194.
[3] Some pardons may not have been enrolled, but their number could scarcely affect this average.

Luton a homicide 'for his services in Wales'.[1] This was an isolated grant; the plea that he deserved some reward may have been put forward by Thomas or his lord. But in the following year Edward, in urgent need of troops, grasped the possibilities of pardon as a means of large-scale recruitment which this case may have suggested. It was in June 1294 that he first resorted to this expedient, enlisting outlaws, fugitives, and prisoners for service in Gascony by the promise of pardon for their various crimes.[2] Roger Brabazon and William de Bereford were commissioned to receive the manucaptions of such recruits, who had to find mainpernors both for their service and for standing to right on their return to England. Proclamation was made in the counties that felons who wished to come to the peace in this way should come before the commissioner or before the king himself either in person or through their friends. The wording of the commission and the proclamation is hypocritical to the point of keeping total silence over the real reason for it: the desperate need for troops. Edward claims to be taking this course

because we are moved to pity for that so many and divers men of our kingdom so often incur the penalty of loss of life or limb, of whom some are suspected and indicted and others appealed by approvers of homicides, robberies and other crimes and various trespasses against our peace, and some for forest trespasses, who wander about the countryside, doing, committing and procuring many different evil deeds, whereby some of them are imprisoned, some outlawed and some fugitive, and with the aim of avoiding such ills and the hope of the betterment of such malefactors and for the quiet of the people of our realm, at the request, moreover, of the prelates, earls, barons and others of our council.

By 1303 this method of recruitment was so familiar and the reasons for it so patent that Edward stated them frankly when enlisting criminals for the Scottish campaign. At this time he had recourse to the sanctuary-men who were living in the large permanent sanctuaries or banleucas such as those of Beverley and Ripon, and the bailiff of Holderness was empowered, 'the king being in great want of men able to bear

---

[1] *Cal. Pat. Rolls, 1292–1301*, 16.

[2] Cf. F. M. Powicke, *The Thirteenth Century*, 648; *Rôles Gascons*, ed. C. Bémont, iii, cxxxvi–cxxxix, nos. 3032, 3033, 3038. *Cal. Close Rolls, 1288–96*, 349, where the promise seems implicit, is one of the earliest individual cases: 4 June.

arms, to receive the mainprises of persons indicted of homicides and other trespasses, who, in accordance with the liberty of the town of Beverley, have fled for safety to that town and are dwelling there, and who are willing to go to the king in Scotland before Trinity and remain there on the king's service during pleasure'.[1]

This policy of Edward's was undoubtedly dictated by expediency and he had no intention of allowing it to become permanent or even to modify the normal principles on which pardon could be recommended in any way. His own efforts, and still more those of Chancery, to maintain the proper standards when possible, are striking witness to this, though the actual methods and results were unimpressive. During the wars excusable slayers still had to obtain inquisitions to establish their excuses and some strictness was shown in scrutinizing the verdicts. Enlistment may have seemed to offer a way of avoiding this investigation. A considerable number did in fact enlist although they had slain with some excuse. The patent rolls reveal this in some cases, the plea rolls in some additional ones. One motive for enlistment may have been that the killer could not afford the expense of securing the appointment of commissioners to hold an inquisition and the Chancery fees for the pardon—the latter were sometimes remitted if the grantee had done service.[2] If this was a common motive it underlines the inequity of the normal treatment of excusable killers, and would imply that the system of recruitment had one good result in making pardon accessible to those who fully deserved but were too poor to obtain it otherwise. But enlistment did not necessarily obviate the need for an inquisition. For example, between August 1300 and April 1301 out of fifty pardons for killing in self-defence at least thirty-five went to serving soldiers or veterans, yet inquisitions were held to establish the circumstances. Why the king insisted on this does not emerge, but many of the inquisitions were ordered by him in person and the writs went out under his privy seal. They caused confusion in other respects and seem to have been something of an aberration on the part of the household secretariat.[3] Even later, however, inquisition was sometimes required, despite military service,[4] though by now it must have been evident that an

[1] *Cal. Pat. Rolls, 1301–7*, 138. [2] Cf. above, p. 57, n. 1.
[3] See below, p. 292. [4] e.g. *Cal. Chancery Warrants*, 169.

adverse verdict could not prevent his granting a service pardon. Excusable slayers who had not fought for him had still to have the circumstances investigated. It may have seemed hard that they were treated as harshly as before when so many felons were being pardoned, and this anomaly may have encouraged juries to give favourable verdicts almost as a matter of course when an excuse was put forward.

The policy of limiting pardons, in the main, to excusable homicides was throughout greatly dependent on the honesty of the jurors at special inquisitions and in court. The king was sometimes deflected from this policy by influence or bribery, but this did not occur often enough to wreck it. Chronic corruption or partisanship among the jurors could undermine it disastrously. In order to assess its worth when it was not under excessive strain from military necessity it will be necessary to consider the general reliability of their verdicts.

X

THE VERDICTS

UNDER Henry III and down to 1294, the great majority of pardons for homicide went to persons who were believed to have slain with excuse. After 1294 Edward I continued to pardon such homicides and to require equally stringent proof of their merits, even in the case of some of the excusable slayers who had fought in his wars. A great many homicides were now being remanded *ad gratiam*, especially at gaol deliveries. But to say that pardons were based on supposed excuse is not to affirm that they were fully deserved. The king acted on information about the circumstances of the slayings, but this information was not necessarily reliable. The enrolled pardons sometimes suggest that he had been persuaded to accept an affirmation that the slaying had been in self-defence or by mischance without having a special inquisition held and without the record of a court. He pardoned one man because the slaying had been accidental, 'as is said';[1] another because 'he is said to have killed in self-defence';[2] a third because 'it appears on sufficient testimony that he killed him in self-defence'.[3] But it is not certain that no formal inquisition had been held in these cases, since similar phrases occur in the enrolment of pardons which were in fact based on inquisitions or the justices' records. Thus in 1280, Edward pardoned a man for another's death, 'on sufficient testimony that the latter was killed by misfortune', but there is a rider to this on the patent roll, 'and the like was found by inquisition which the king ordered to be made by the sheriff of York'.[4]

---

[1] *Cal. Pat. Rolls, 1266–72*, 551. This was at the instance of Raymond de Beyvill.

[2] Ibid. 117, at the instance of Peter de Chaumpvent and Imbert de Muntferaunt.

[3] Ibid., *1272–81*, 362, at the instance of the bishop of Bath and Wells. These phrases occurred in letters patent of pardon as copied on eyre rolls; they were not simply abbreviations by the clerks enrolling them. See J.I. 1/705, m. 13 (cf. *Cal. Pat. Rolls, 1281–92*, 6); J.I. 1/739, m. 94.

[4] *Cal. Pat. Rolls, 1272–81*, 398. The inquisition is *Cal. Inquisitions Misc.* i, no. 2239. A presentment at the eyre seems to agree with its verdict of accidental homicide. See J.I. 1/1098, m. 11.

Pardons were regularly granted 'on the testimony' of justices and commissioners,[1] so that the phrase in itself certainly does not imply information given by the associates of the homicide. But occasionally it may have been used when no actual inquisition had been held,[2] and for lesser crimes it is clear that the king was prepared to grant pardon without the formality of an inquisition.[3]

Pardons for excusable homicide granted on unsworn information were at most exceedingly rare after the 1230s. From then on the king normally pardoned such homicide only on receiving a favourable verdict given before either justices in eyre, justices of gaol delivery, or, later, of oyer and terminer, or specially appointed commissioners. As a rule he accepted these verdicts without further investigation; no doubt he did so in good faith, yet the possibility remains that he was deceived. The reliability of the verdicts is problematical. Those from special commissions may well be suspect, since they were obtained on the initiative of the slayer or his friends. It is surprising, therefore, to find that a very considerable proportion, well over one-third, of the inquisitions shown by the patent rolls to have been ordered were not followed up by pardons enrolled there. At first sight this would suggest that the jurors were remarkably impartial, but these figures cannot be accepted as establishing the number of unfavourable verdicts. For one thing, an inquisition into an alleged excuse was not necessarily aimed at securing pardon. A prisoner might obtain one with bail as his objective. It is true that the writ *de odio et atia* was frequently brought by excusable slayers in order to get bail; but strictly speaking it was inappropriate, since it sought to prove that the charge was malicious and altogether unfounded, rather than that the prisoner, though indeed responsible for the killing, had committed no felony. The charge would have been brought duly and bona fide; it was of the essence of the system of reserving to the king the decision to remit his suit against excusable homicides that such present-

---

[1] e.g. *Cal. Pat. Rolls, 1272–81*, 393, 441, 464.

[2] An example is quoted above, p. 232, n. 1; cf. *Cal. Pat. Rolls, 1272–81*, 281; J.I. 1/827, m. 27.

[3] e.g. J.I. 1/739, m. 92, where a man charged with the arson of his father's house produced a pardon granted by the king on the father's repudiation of the charge: 'nos attendentes ex relatu eiusdem patris sui quod . . . maliciose rettatus fuit'. Cf. *Cal. Pat. Rolls, 1281–92*, 162.

ments should be made. Thus a literal-minded killer might reject the writ *de odio et atia* as a means to release on bail if he thought he was entitled to it because he had slain excusably. There are eleven cases among the calendared *Miscellaneous Inquisitions* where a verdict of excusable slaying was followed by bail, not pardon. In two or three other cases, the inquisitions into alleged excuse ordered according to the patent rolls were clearly followed by bail. Others may have been so too, since orders for release on bail were not invariably enrolled on the close rolls. Secondly, it is unsafe to assume that the commissioners always actually held the inquisitions. This is shown by the fact that it was sometimes necessary to appoint others later on. There may have been no second appointment in some cases; a judicial visitation might have intervened or the applicant might have died, or, if he was a fugitive, lost contact with his friends. Again, pardon might after all have followed a favourable verdict but not have been enrolled. For example three inquisitions were evidently held as the writs on the patent rolls instructed, although no consequent pardons appear there, and brought in favourable verdicts, for the killers in question had secured their pardons before the Yorkshire eyre of 1268.[1] Similarly, three of the verdicts among the *Miscellaneous Inquisitions* resulted in pardons which are mentioned on eyre rolls though absent from the patent rolls.[2] Finally, there are other instances where the verdict itself has survived and is unequivocally favourable despite its apparent failure to result in pardon.[3] Since these verdicts are still among the surviving Chancery documents, there can be no doubt that they reached their destination, though they may never have received the king's own attention. Thus the proportion of inquisitions which brought in favourable verdicts was certainly appreciably higher than two-thirds, and may have been a great deal higher.[4]

[1] J.I. 1/1051, mm. 14ᵈ, 24ᵈ, 40; *Cal. Pat. Rolls, 1258–66*, 476; ibid., *1266–72*, 125, 134.

[2] *Cal. Inquisitions Misc.* i, nos. 2204, 2278, 2305; J.I. 1/1004, m. 101; J.I. 1/573, mm. 3ᵈ, 4; J.I. 1/804, m. 61ᴬ; cf. *Cal. Close Rolls, 1288–96*, 77.

[3] e.g. *Cal. Inquisitions Misc.* i, nos. 2107, 2187, 2189, 2190, 2267, 2309. No. 2308 was also favourable but it rested partly on the assertion that slayer and slain were unknown to each other and this may have rendered it suspect. Cf. above, p. 95, n. 1.

[4] The danger of relying only on the patent rolls is well illustrated in the case of Nigel le Turner. In July and apparently again in September 1266 the king ordered

Taken by themselves, the surviving verdicts of special inquisitions go to the other extreme. Practically all the returns to this particular type of inquiry among the calendared inquisitions confirmed some sort of excuse, and a cynic might be tempted to conclude that verdicts were 100 per cent favourable and so utterly unreliable. But this conclusion, too, must be rejected. When a commission was appointed to inquire into an individual case its return had a far greater chance of surviving if it involved further administrative action. It might itself be endorsed with the royal assent and thus serve as the warrant to Chancery to draw up the pardon or grant of bail; generally it would be included in a covering writ ordering one or the other.[1] It would be useful for the clerks to have it to hand when drafting the letters patent. But there was less point in preserving adverse verdicts. Evidence for these must be sought elsewhere. Sometimes there was no need to appoint commissioners *ad hoc* when there was an application for an immediate inquisition; justices of assize might be in the county and could be instructed to hold it and the verdict would then be entered on their roll. Only a few entries of this kind have been found, but they include at least one that was altogether hostile.[2] Thus it would be quite unwarrantable to conclude that the inquisitions were

an inquisition to ascertain whether he had killed Richard le Cudier in self-defence (*Cal. Pat. Rolls, 1258–66*, 671, 678). This was apparently not held, for in October 1267 Robert de Messenden was ordered to take a similar inquisition (ibid., *1266– 72*, 161), but in the summer of 1268 the *Curia Regis* ordered the sheriff to send jurors to make the inquisition before it, since Robert de Messenden, who should have held it, had not been able to do so because he was busy on the king's affairs. The jurors duly came and found that Richard had assaulted Nigel with an axe and given him a great wound on the shoulder and another, almost mortal, in the back; Nigel had fled seeing he meant to kill him, but as he could not escape he had turned round and struck him on the head with a very small axe, one ell in length, which he had in his hand, and felled him, leaving him on the ground. Richard later got up and went home where he lay ill for three weeks or more; he summoned his neighbours and made his will and enjoined on all his friends that they should not lay the responsibility for his death on Nigel, who had struck him in self-defence and could not otherwise have escaped death (K.B. 26/185, m. 9). At about the same time justices in eyre were in the county and the presenting jurors there, too, mentioned self-defence, though they omitted the death-bed scene (J.I. 1/703, m. 3). The justices decided to speak with the king about outlawry, and possibly it was on this account that the matter was taken up in the *Curia Regis*. Although no pardon has been found for Nigel it can hardly be doubted that he now at last obtained remission of the king's suit. Yet going by the evidence of the patent rolls alone, one would conclude that an inquisition was probably held eventually but brought in an adverse verdict.

[1] e.g. *Cal. Inquisitions Misc.* i, no. 2232; C. 47/79/11, no. 356.
[2] J.I. 1/1197, m. 16.

entirely useless as a means of checking alleged excuse or justification, but it must be recognized that they were more likely to confirm the slayer's claims than the patent rolls suggest, and the suspicion that some of them were biased cannot be dispelled by the apparent disparity between the number of inquisitions ordered and the number of pardons resulting therefrom.

The result of the inquisition was sometimes at least a foregone conclusion. It has been seen that the homicide who obtained one for a consideration might even pay at the same time for the pardon which he confidently expected to follow. Robert de Aula did this, paying 3 marks of gold to the Wardrobe for an inquisition whether he had slain Robert Angevyn in self-defence or by felony and premeditated malice, and for having the king's peace in accordance with the finding of the inquisition. Henry of Bath was appointed by letters patent to hold it and to send the verdict to the king. Later the king pardoned Robert the suit of his peace for the death for 3 marks of gold and he went quit.[1] Since the inquisition was held by Henry of Bath and others of the king's council and the pardon was granted by their counsel its outcome was presumably fair and thus Robert was properly confident of the merits of his case. But in general there was a very good expectation that the verdict would be favourable, and probably few slayers and their friends got the king to order an inquisition until they had sounded local opinion and found it reassuring, or had taken more positive measures to ensure that it would bring in the desired verdict. Thus the results of these inquisitions cannot be taken at their face value. Some way of testing them is needed, but although further information has been found in many cases much of it is useless either to confirm or refute them.

That Henry III's clemency was sometimes misplaced, despite the holding of an inquisition, is suggested by the evidence of one of the few surviving coroner's rolls of his reign. An inquest was held in June 1269 into the death of Richard de Uphil, found dead on the king's highway beside the bridge of Gringelford. The coroner's jury found that Richard and William le Louerd had been driving together with two loaded carts and when they approached the bridge they quarrelled as to which of them should cross it first; William got down, drew his knife

[1] See above, p. 41.

and struck Richard in the back, piercing him to the heart; he then drove on to their destination.[1] There was an eyewitness to this slaying who raised the hue, and there seems no reason to doubt that his account of the matter was correct and was the basis of the verdict. Yet Henry ordered an inquisition to ascertain whether the slaying had been in self-defence,[2] and in February 1270 he pardoned William, at the instance of John de Burgo the elder.[3] Long after, at the eyre of 1286, the slaying was presented, without any suggestion of self-defence on the roll other than *mota contentione*, and William was placed in exigent, but he then appeared and produced Henry III's pardon.[4]

Not many coroner's rolls have survived even from the reign of Edward I, and those which are extant are not helpful on this particular point. The eyre rolls contribute further information in far more cases, but still it is not very easy to get corroboration of inquisitions into the circumstances if the verdict was favourable and led to immediate pardon. The entry on the eyre roll, if it can be found, is likely, as has already been remarked, to be very brief, for if the slayer did not appear there was no necessity for the indictment to go into any detail, nor was it necessary if he came already equipped with his pardon. It is, therefore, only by good chance that corroboration of the verdict of inquisitions of this type has been found in presentments on the eyre rolls in fifteen cases. In another eight the presentments mentioned that the parties had quarrelled or had been coming from an inn when the slaying occurred, statements which, had they been amplified, would very likely have accorded with the inquisitions' findings of self-defence. One inquisition which had found that the accused had shot a poacher is partially confirmed by the presentment, but this shows that the poacher had been tricked into going into the forest on that occasion by an *agent provocateur*.[5] In some cases the presentment is sufficiently detailed to provide circumstantial confirmation. For example, according to one inquisition, Andrew Bukstan killed Richard de Freskeneye, his man, by accident. Having come home from the fair at St. Ives where he had bought a new sword, he tested its flexibility on a trestle which collapsed so that the sword glanced off and struck

---

[1] J.I. 2/266, m. 4.   [2] *Cal. Pat. Rolls, 1266–72*, 471.   [3] Ibid. 407.
[4] J.I. 1/573, m. 2.   [5] *Cal. Inquisitions Misc.* i, no. 2290; J.I. 1/1098, m. 17[d].

Richard, who was sitting too close by.[1] According to the presentment at the eyre, Andrew held a sword in his hand and as he tried to bend it, it shot out of his hand and struck Richard in the leg.[2] The degree of agreement here carries conviction. It is not so close that one might suspect the presenting jurors of merely echoing the earlier verdict and having no independent knowledge of the accident, or deliberately suppressing knowledge which conflicted with it. On the other hand, the discrepancies are no more than could easily arise from the accounts of two independent eyewitnesses; indeed, they are little more than matters of selection and emphasis.

In a smaller number of cases the presentment at the eyre gives enough detail to cast doubt on the truth of the verdict on which pardon had been granted.[3] In one of these cases the pardoned slayer failed to appear at the eyre, so there is some reason to think that he had a guilty conscience and that the verdict had been false.[4] There were other cases of men pardoned because inquisitions had found their slayings excusable defaulting in this way, and being put in exigent.[5] One was definitely stated to have withdrawn from the county and to be suspected of guilt.[6] The others may have absconded because they had reason to fear that they would be appealed, but some may have died, or have failed to realize the need to put in an appearance. It cannot be assumed that they were all guilty of felonious slayings and that the inquisitions had all been perjured or not sufficiently informed of the facts, but it must be suspected that some of them were. Very occasionally, the veracity of a verdict at an inquisition leading to pardon was openly challenged. Thus in Yorkshire in 1257 Roger son of Adam Smith was presented for having killed his brother, but he came forward with the king's pardon, granted because the king had been given to understand that he had killed him by mischance. It was now testified by inquisition, however, that he had killed him by felony, not by mischance. This contradiction presented the justices with something of a dilemma. They could hardly

---

[1] *Cal. Inquisitions Misc.* i, no. 2101. [2] J.I. 1/343, m. 15[d].

[3] e.g. *Cal. Inquisitions Misc.* i, no. 367, *Cal. Pat. Rolls, 1266–72*, 353, J.I. 1/827, m. 12; *Cal. Inquisitions Misc.* i, no. 2208, *Cal. Pat. Rolls, 1272–81*, 223, J.I. 1/1004, m. 89. [4] See above, p. 209, n. 1.

[5] J.I. 1/739, m. 54; *Cal. Inquisitions Misc.* i, no. 2166. Cf. ibid., nos. 2135, 2243, 2307; J.I. 1/703, m. 8 (1268); J.I. 1/619, m. 57 (1285); J.I. 1/302, m. 66[d]; (1292).

[6] Ibid.

ignore or dispute the validity of the king's pardon, but they were unwilling to let the culprit go scot free. So they solved the problem by committing him to prison until he fined for 5 marks, and then, as no one now wished to prosecute, proclaimed firm peace, But they also amerced the jurors of the first inquisition.[1] A verdict at the eyre might implicitly reject one at an inquisition, as when two men obtained pardon for killing a felon as he fled from the peace but a third was hanged at the eyre, where the jurors asserted that they had killed him deliberately in a house.[2]

These cases suggest that the justices in eyre were likely to take more trouble to elicit an honest verdict than the individual justices, sheriffs, and coroners or others commissioned to hold special inquisitions. This would be understandable. Since special inquisitions were unlikely to be obtained unless there was a good prospect of a favourable verdict the commissioners were conditioned to expect one and tempted to regard the whole business as a routine matter with a foregone conclusion. They might themselves be subject to local influence or at least have some subconscious bias towards the slayer. The justices in eyre acting as a group might be more efficient, and as the verdict given before them would be a more solemn matter should themselves have felt the greater sense of responsibility. Yet they also needed to be on the alert, for jurors at the eyre were quite capable of trying to present a case in the most favourable light. For example, a presentment against a fugitive clerk, John le Felter, was found to have been gravely misleading, the court deciding 'quia xii juratores subvertere voluerunt feloniam istam in quoddam infortunium, ideo ad iudicium de eis'.[3] Thus while verdicts here should have been less open to influence than those given before special commissioners at the slayer's own request, their greater reliability cannot be taken for granted. If the slayer appeared in court it would generally be because he had reason to hope for a favourable verdict—it was not hard to evade arrest and all too easy to jump bail—and though his friends could have put out feelers and let him know the attitude of the neighbourhood towards him, they might again have judged it prudent to canvass his cause and even resort to bribery before advising him it was safe to appear.

[1] J.I. 1/1109, m. 5.   [2] J.I. 1/409, m. 12d.   [3] J.I. 1/46, m. 11.

Verdicts at the eyre or at sessions of oyer and terminer of
slaying in self-defence or by accident can seldom be checked
except by comparison with earlier inquisitions which had
resulted in release on bail.[1] It is not unlikely that jurors who
knew that only bail was being sought would take their duties
rather more lightly. Their verdicts cannot, then, provide full
corroboration of the verdicts later given at the eyre. It says
something for the reliability of the latter, however, that they
did not always endorse earlier findings of excusable slaying
even when the slayers appeared in court. In over fifty cases, as
already noted, the two types of verdict can be compared. In
nearly a quarter of them the slayer who had secured bail was
found guilty at the eyre. Yet it may be that it was sometimes
the second verdict which was at fault. It is difficult to reject
the first, more detailed verdict in at least one case, that of
Richard, son of Richard Fitz Ughtred.[2] In another case, the
contradiction was obviously due to the juries' differing estimates
of the slayer's motive. A man who had fled for murder returned
and was recognized by the villagers; he killed one of them and
would have killed his brother also if the latter had not killed
him in self-defence. So said the inquisition *de odio et atia*. But
according to the presentment at the eyre, it was not a question
of self-defence but of taking vengeance for the death of his
brother in a fight between the lot of them.[3] There were other
cases in which the difference in interpretation was less critical.
When the victim had run on the prisoner's sword or knife, for
example, one verdict might find him not guilty, while the
other found that he had killed in self-defence or by mischance.
Verdicts of this kind were obviously independent of each other,
and may be accepted as corroborative so far as the facts and
the absence of felony went. Or again, when two verdicts appear
to contradict each other there might have been a difference
only in interpretation or assessment of the effects of an injury.[4]

[1] The coroner's inquest might have taken a more severe view of the case than the
presenting jurors. See J.I. 1/111, m. 24[d], where a man was hanged although the
latter asserted that he had killed his son by mischance. But more often the inquest
was less hostile, to judge by the few surviving rolls. See above, p. 133, n. 3.
[2] See above, p. 110.   [3] C. 144/25, no. 13; J.I. 1/653, m. 10.
[4] The verdicts on the death of John de Wyndibank may be an example. In
1301 an inquisition found that John de Faldworthing had been accused *odio et
atia* of killing him and that he had died a natural death (C. 144/33, no. 6). On the
strength of this verdict Faldworthing got bail (*Cal. Close Rolls, 1296–1302*, 435).
In 1306 he appeared before the justices of oyer and terminer at Lancaster and the

Nevertheless, a verdict might by adroit selection and emphasis present a more impressive account of the slayer's predicament and his exemplary self-control than an unedited recital of the events would have given. It is just when two or more verdicts are in general agreement that this sort of touching up of the picture can be detected and, paradoxically, that suspicion of bias, if not corruption, most often arises. And in this respect the trial verdicts show up badly. Bail was granted more readily than pardon; to secure it the verdict *de odio et atia* had to affirm either innocence or excuse, but it was not necessary for it to meet all the requirements which the writs for inquisitions postulated when pardon was sought. The prisoner who had secured release on bail might realize that the verdict had included matter which would tell against him at his trial, or had omitted points which would be helpful. When his life was at stake, rather than his freedom, he would be determined to ensure that the second verdict was an improvement on the first. The trial jurors themselves, if well disposed towards him, might consider how they could outdo their predecessors' efforts on his behalf. The result might be serious distortion, even perjury, or it might be a more honest reshaping of the material.

There was very serious discrepancy in one of these cases. The inquisition *de odio et atia* found that there was a quarrel between John de Stone and William le Muner, who secretly lay in wait for him and struck him on the head with a 'baculum ad pilam' at the corner of a field; thus cornered and unable to flee in any direction, John in self-defence struck William with a small 'Handex' on the head, wounding him as he could not otherwise escape death.[1] At the eyre the verdict was as follows: William followed John and hit him three times on head and shoulders with a staff and meant to kill him; John fled and came to a certain ditch which he could by no means cross

verdict there was that he had killed Wyndibank, but 'totaliter se defendendo' (J.I. 1/422, m. 2). The jurors, however, gave a very long account of the matter, and it is easy from this to see that their predecessors might reasonably have considered him free from any responsibility. Indeed, immediately after the assault, it was Wyndibank and his accomplices who fled, because at that time it was thought that Faldworthing was dying, rather than Wyndibank, who survived for 9 months. Thus there may have been genuine disagreement as to the effects of the blow which he had received, and the earlier verdict, though disingenuous, may not have been perjured. The king sent for the record on 22 December, and his pardon was dated 18 March 1307. See C. 47/65/4, no. 93; *Cal. Pat. Rolls, 1301–7*, 503.

[1] C. 144/22, no. 11.

because of its depth and breadth, so he defended himself and hit William with a 'baculum' on the head, whence he died. He was now remanded *ad gratiam* and promptly pardoned.[1] The serious discrepancy here is over the weapons employed on either side. The trial jury found that John hit William with a staff or stick, whereas according to the inquisition it was an axe, an edged tool, even if only a small, hand one. As has been seen, to have used an edged weapon against a man armed only with a blunt instrument might prove fatal to a plea of self-defence. Thus the difference between the two accounts may have been literally vital to John de Stone.

There is one instance of acquittal at the eyre after a verdict of slaying in self-defence at an inquisition *de odio et atia*. According to its verdict, given in 1277, the charge against John Payn of Clanefeld for the death of William Sauvage of Benney was not made of any hatred or malice, but it happened that as the two were going together from Faringdon towards Rudcote they quarrelled and William struck John on the forehead with a hatchet and wounded him, causing him to fall to the bottom of a dyke. There he hit him again on the crown of the head, and planted his feet on him and kicked him severely and pummelled him all over. John managed to escape and took to flight, hotly pursued by William, and just reached a cart driven by a boy; he ran round and round the cart, still chased by William in a state of fury. Fearing for his life, John seized a pole hanging in the cart and hit William on the head so that he fell. John immediately ran away leaving William lying there; but the latter got up and some men who came along took him home and he lived from that Monday until the following Sunday; the jurors definitely believed that he died of that blow.[2] As a result of this verdict John Payn was allowed bail.[3] At the eyre in 1285 the following presentment was made: John Clerk of Claneford, William le Sauvage of Claneford, John Milot, and William's brother, Richard, were coming together from the fair at Faringdon and quarrelled. The other three assaulted John Clerk and William gave him two blows on the head and then the trio pursued him meaning to kill him, so he ran to his cart and seized its pole to defend himself. The

---

[1] J.I. 1/376, mm. 4, 71, 77 which shows that he now had his pardon proclaimed; cf. *Cal. Pat. Rolls, 1292–1301*, 14.   [2] C. 144/17, no. 14.
[3] *Cal. Close Rolls, 1272–9*, 397.

others hemmed him in so that he could not escape their hands
and in self-defence he struck William on the head with the
pole, so that he died a week later.[1] John, who had surrendered
to his bail, now came before the justices, pleaded not guilty
and put himself on the country. The trial jury, consisting of
the presenting jurors together with jurors from the neighbouring
vills, now swore that John was in no way guilty, but that
Richard Milot, who had since died, had killed William le
Sauvage. The jury did not in the least suspect John of the death,
but since he had been present and had not arrested Richard he
was amerced. The jurors also were amerced for having said at
first that he had killed William and then acquitted him. This
acquittal is highly suspect. It looks as though John's friends
feared that the first account of the matter might not be enough
to secure pardon—perhaps because it indicated that William
had abandoned his hatchet and was content to go for him with
feet and fists. The presentment, which may represent a second
story put about to improve on the first, made out that the odds
against John were three to one, but it was still unsatisfactory on
the matter of weapons. It may be that the hatchet had been an
invention and that the assailant or assailants had been unarmed.
At any rate neither story was altogether certain to secure
pardon, and it looks as though the death of Richard Milot
offered a better way of saving John by attributing William's
death to someone who was not there to give the lie to the
charge or suffer punishment for it.

It is possible to compare a few detailed verdicts given at
subsequent sessions of the eyre or of oyer and terminer, with
those at gaol deliveries. A verdict at a gaol delivery of killing
by mischance or in self-defence would result in the prisoner's
remand *ad gratiam*. Normally, he would indeed now obtain pardon. But it has already been noticed that a considerable number
of prisoners remanded in this way only obtained bail. In theory,
this meant standing trial again later on, and some of them
actually did so. Sometimes the justices in eyre would accept
the earlier verdict without requiring a new one and remand
ad gratiam again,[2] but sometimes a second verdict was required.
In a few cases both have survived and provide useful mutual
checks. On the whole they support each other well. The gaol

[1] J.I. 1/705, m. 21[d].
[2] e.g. J.I. 1/374, mm. 77[d], 12[d]; cf. C. 47/64/7, no. 201.

delivery verdicts seem to have been more reliable than those
of inquisitions *de odio et atia*, and to have carried greater weight
with the justices in eyre.[1] The chief difference lies in the greater
prolixity of the verdicts at the gaol delivery as compared with
those at the eyre or oyer and terminer, or at least in the greater
fullness of the entries on the rolls. But although the verdicts
at the eyre tally pretty well with those at gaol deliveries there
was the same tendency to enhance or invent discrepancy
between the weapons used on either side, or to select only the
most favourable features in the account.[2]

In a few cases three separate verdicts have survived in some
detail, no two of which fully agree.[3] The differences between
them cannot always be explained by the wish to give greater
assistance to the defendant. They might be equally helpful
but still discordant over details. This occurs particularly in
the three verdicts which have survived into the slaying of
William le Walker by Robert Clerk. A jury *de odio et atia* found
that Robert had come ashore at Liverpool and William had come
out of a house with a knife in his hand and had run after him,
meaning to kill him with it; Robert had fled as far as the wall
of the earl of Lancaster's stable, and had there drawn his
sword to defend himself; William pursuing him with his
knife had run on the sword and so had killed himself; he had
not been killed in any other way.[4] Robert, who was then in
Shrewsbury gaol, may have obtained bail as a result though
this is not recorded. On 3 October 1300 he was tried at the
delivery of Lancaster gaol, so that he seems either to have

---

[1] But the subsequent behaviour of a prisoner sometimes suggests that the
verdict had been lenient and he was afraid to face trial at the eyre. For example,
J.I. 1/374, m. 12[d], where a prisoner pardoned on the strength of the gaol delivery
verdict of killing in self-defence failed to appear at the eyre and was put in exigent.
Cf. *Cal. Pat. Rolls, 1281–92*, 196.

[2] This appears in two returns which have survived concerning the slaying of
Robert de Alreton by Gilbert de Speke. The first, the record of a gaol delivery in
1285, stated that Robert had leapt out at Gilbert from a field of rye and assaulted
him with knife and staff; Gilbert had fled to a thorn hedge but had not been
able to climb over it, and so had pulled a stick out of it and struck him once on the
head (C. 47/65/2, no. 58). This verdict was followed by bail (*Cal. Close Rolls,
1279–88*, 395). Later, at the eyre of 1292, it was found that Robert had lain in
wait for him in the field but that he had attacked and chased him with a sword
(C. 47/65/2, no. 58). Gilbert obtained pardon at once and was able to produce
it before the same justices (J.I. 1/409, m. 28).

[3] e.g. the case of Roger de Haliwell, C. 144/28, no. 20; *Cal. Close Rolls, 1279–
88*, 515; *Rot. Parl.* i, 65[b], no. 247; J.I. 1/409, m. 6; *Cal. Pat. Rolls, 1281–92*, 502.

[4] C. 144/32, no. 4 (b).

surrendered now for trial, or to have been moved from one
prison to the other. The verdict this time was far more detailed. Robert, said the jurors, went to the Isle of Man on a
trading trip; while he was there an unknown man told him
that his servant, William le Walker, had surreptitiously taken
his sword against his will, a sword which he dearly loved, and
prayed him to bring it back on his next visit to those parts.
Robert promised to do so if he found that William had indeed
gone off with the sword in this way. He then returned to
England, landing at Liverpool, and found William coming
to meet him. He at once taxed him with the matter and William
replied in anger, 'You accuse me of theft when I am not
guilty.' Drawing his knife he strode towards Robert, who took
to flight. Hastening after him, William caught him up and
gave him a great blow between the shoulder-blades. Robert
spurted and reached the stable of the earl of Leicester, where
he could flee no further, and so drew his sword. Trying to hit
him with his knife William ran upon the sword.[1] The very day
after the trial the king sent for the record and thereupon ordered
that Robert be released on bail.[2] In 1306 he appeared before
the justices of oyer and terminer and the jury now gave a
totally different account of the quarrel. Robert and another
man, William Brown, were coming together from Chester;
they were partners, and Robert had received the money,
goods, and chattels arising from their trading activities.
William Brown asked him to account for them, and when
Robert declined, he replied very roughly and they began to
quarrel. Still arguing, they came to Liverpool, where William
le Walker, a cousin of Brown's, heard them, advanced to his
help, and insulted Robert with abusive words, drawing a long
knife to strike him. Seeing this Robert fled for his life to a
corner, blocked in by two buildings; the other two pursued him
with intent to kill. Unable to get away Robert drew his sword
and held it in his hand to defend himself. William, bent on
killing him, ran upon him, trying to stab him through the
body, and struck him through his mantle, but in so doing
impaled himself on his sword.[3] On this verdict, Robert was remanded *ad gratiam* and was soon pardoned.[4] The differences

---

[1] C. 144/32, no. 4 (d). The earl of Lancaster was also earl of Leicester.
[2] *Cal. Close Rolls, 1296–1302*, 370.
[3] J.I. 1/422, m. 1.　　　　　　　　　　　[4] *Cal. Pat. Rolls, 1301–7*, 505.

between the second and third verdicts are very serious. The first does not explicitly support either account of the quarrel but its reference to Robert's coming by ship points to agreement with the second. Over the actual death there is substantial agreement in all three accounts, and Robert's pardon was surely merited, despite his delay in applying for it, and at first, perhaps, even in obtaining bail.

The variations in the verdicts are, then, sometimes unaccountable. They may suggest that the juries were ignorant of the facts or had forgotten them, or were simply guessing at motives. But, on the whole, discrepancies between two or more verdicts were over details of location and the sequence of events, the sort of thing on which independent witnesses could easily differ. Total agreement would in fact raise the suspicion that one verdict was directly derived from the other, or worse still, that both were dictated by the culprit's friends. Since there was often an interval of several years before the trial verdict, allowance must be made for the strain on the jurors' memory and the tendency for an epic to be built around a dramatic and fatal local engagement. The impression which these comparisons give is of pretty general agreement on the issue of self-defence or accident, with enough disagreement over details to exclude the notion of all the accounts being based only on the defendant's own statement. But it must be remembered that the defendant might himself try to amend his story, that his own memory might vary, and that some of the discrepancies might come from his or his friends' attempts to make doubly sure of pardon. Sometimes the modifications in the story were so obviously to his advantage that the jurors themselves can hardly have failed to be aware of them. Yet although they were inclined, even at the eyre, to be on the side of the slayer and make such adjustments as seemed best calculated to secure his remand *ad gratiam*, it may be that such action was generally not due to bribery or influence. The jurors may have sympathized with him just because they were convinced that he was no murderer, that his execution would outrage true justice. The whole muddled system of pardoning was an invitation to fair-minded men to supply the justices with the sort of verdict that would make pardon certain. Only seldom does it emerge from comparing verdicts given in court that one was a complete fabrication.

There are other verdicts which cannot be checked but which may be thought lacking in verisimilitude, or which include what now seems irrational matter. Very few are obviously perverse though some are rather implausible. Peculiar behaviour, especially under stress, should not be viewed with too much scepticism; jurors who wanted to help the suspect were unlikely to concoct an odd and elaborate story when there were many straightforward cases of self-defence to serve as a model. Throughout there is a noticeable commonsense attitude. Apart from one reference to a madman acting at the instigation of the devil,[1] in only one verdict is there any suggestion of supernatural forces to explain a death. This verdict is, indeed, highly remarkable and in utter contrast with all the others noted. In 1287 Richard Lucas and his brother William were found not guilty of killing Adam son of Lawrence. The jury was then asked who had killed him and stated that Richard and William went with nets to catch birds in the fields of Langeford and met Adam with others; Richard and Adam quarrelled and Richard struck him on the right shoulder with the handle of a hatchet. Adam, frightened, fled towards his home and when he came to a place called Castle-ditch he met the devil in the form of a house, and it took him and crushed him to death: Adam was killed by the devil, and not by the beating Richard gave him. The justices accepted this verdict and acquitted Richard,[2] perhaps concluding that Adam had indeed been killed by the collapse of a house— a not infrequent cause of accidental death—but with some reservation as to the agency which caused its collapse at the critical moment. There are other more credible cases in which the jurors found that the slayer had acted through fear of some supernatural being or force, and the justices themselves accepted this as sufficient defence.[3] In some a joking attempt to frighten someone by pretending to be a ghost or monster resulted in the joker's death. The jurors and the justices had no difficulty in believing that the victim of the hoax had been genuinely taken in and had slain in terror and self-defence.[4] It might be

---

[1] See above, p. 159.

[2] J.I. 1/11, m. 26[d].

[3] e.g. *Northumberland Assize Rolls*, Surtees Soc. lxxxviii. 343–4.

[4] e.g. two servants spent the evening in different taverns; one of them, being drunk, had the fatuous notion of wrapping himself up in a sheet like a corpse and waiting in the cemetery through which the other would have to pass on his way

that he was known to be rather simple and it was for this very reason that he had been subjected to it.[1] But whilst recognizing the superstitious fears of others, juries themselves, with the one exception, gave down-to-earth explanations of events.

What arouses greater doubt than the oddity of some individual accounts is the similarity between cases, especially that between cases in the same county within a short period. It may be judged that too many slayers in self-defence pulled stakes from fences and poles from carts, bolted into culs-de-sac or tried and failed to climb walls, were brought up against dykes or rivers, found swords unexpectedly but conveniently to hand or made random knife-thrusts that just happened to hit vital spots. The suspicion that some of these circumstances were borrowed from other cases is bound to arise. Eventually, the verdicts would tend to become divorced from the realities: even if a slaying was rightly deemed excusable its individual circumstances would be subsumed under some common form. This does not appear to have occurred by 1307, however. There was more variety in these accounts than appears at first sight, and for the most part they were widely spaced over a long period. Victims of assault naturally reacted in a similar manner when they found themselves in similar predicaments. In saying that the slayer had chanced upon a sword or axe in his random flight through his house, jurors may have misrepresented his natural and reasonable dash to the spot where he kept his weapons or his most serviceable tool, but there is no need to suppose that they were resorting to common form. This was an obvious way to emphasize the gravity of his plight, and his unpreparedness to fight back. Apparent similarity is often only superficial. It is largely due, perhaps, to the paucity of many of the clerks' Latin vocabulary. In struggling to translate stories which were various enough but inevitably tended to have some features in common, they fell back on the same terminology, anticipating the clichés of modern police-court proceedings. The impression of sameness would be relieved if, for example, they had known Latin terms to differentiate between stick, staff, stave, club, pole, cricket bat,

home. He alternately growled like a bear and barked like a dog. The other thought he was the devil or a spirit and fled, making the sign of the cross, but as he could not climb over the cemetery wall he drew his knife and his tormentor ran on it. He was remanded *ad gratiam*. See J.I. 3/92, m. 5.

[1] Cf. above, p. 169.

hockey stick, goad, instead of having to fall back on the ubiqui-
tous *baculum*. Moreover, even clerks with greater pretensions as
latinists had favourite expressions which they used in their
reports with little regard for the actual words of the jurors.
One who accompanied justices of gaol delivery travelling
about the country from Berkshire to Devon was much
attached to the phrase 'neque fugere [*or* evadere] potuit a
dextris neque a sinistris', using it in recording verdicts given at
Windsor, Wallingford, Oxford, and Exeter.[1] The oral verdicts
themselves were, no doubt, more varied than his Latin versions
suggest. When two more or less concordant verdicts survive
in one case the differences between them are nearly always
such as to suggest that they are based on evidence from eye-
witnesses and that, despite touching up, they refer to actual
not to fictional events. Moreover, many of the circumstances
described were unique. Thus the jurors were not yet falling
back on one or other of a set of prefabricated tales which could
be borrowed, disguised only with minor variants, to substantiate their declaration that slayings had been in self-
defence. They, or the slayer and his friends, in putting out his
account of the affair, may sometimes have borrowed or over-
emphasized some point which had been well received in another
case, but that is as far as the tendency towards reliance on
common form seems to have gone as yet.

Still, some verdicts were false in substance, those given
before special commissioners probably more often than those
at the eyre. It would have been unwise to accept all of them
implicitly. They provided the alleged facts and the interpretation put on them by the jurors, but it was for the king to decide
whether their sworn accounts were credible and, if so, whether
they warranted pardon. It has been seen that he monopolized
the right to grant pardon for homicide almost entirely, and he
seems to have gone through the motions of deciding on the
merits of each case, though very occasionally, when abroad or
on campaign, he left the final decision to the Chancellor. It
is hard to believe that he always paid close attention to the
verdicts submitted to him. Nevertheless, he scrutinized some
of them carefully, or possibly his councillors did so and drew
his attention to dubious points. At any rate they did not all
pass muster. Naturally, fault was more likely to be found with

[1] J.I. 3/103, mm. 4ᵈ, 6ᵈ; J.I. 3/104, mm. 21, 13ᵈ.

the verdict of a special inquisition but even the record of the justices in eyre or of gaol delivery might be queried.

When an inquisition *de odio et atia* was obtained with a view to pardon and the petition referred to this, the return was probably examined more closely than it would have been if only bail was requested. It may be guessed that this was the reason for the apparent fluctuations in the fortunes of Oliver de Manhisleg. In 1277 a jury *de odio et atia* found him guilty of the death of Thomas Winter, but in this manner: there was a brawl in an inn, in the course of which Thomas hit Oliver on the head with a stout wooden staff and chased him from the inn to his home; Oliver hit back at him with a hatchet, striking him on the head in self-defence.[1] The return bears a note of the decision: nothing is to be done in this case since the inquisition found him guilty. This decision may have been a refusal to grant bail, but it seems more likely that it was turning down an application for pardon, since a few months later Oliver did obtain bail on the grounds that he had killed in self-defence.[2] Whether a new inquisition had been held does not appear; the original one might possibly be considered good enough for bail. Oliver enjoyed two years' freedom and evidently hoped that pardon itself would be obtainable after the justices in eyre had heard the manner of the slaying. But he miscalculated. A shorter account of the fight was given at the eyre and the jurors found him guilty, no doubt because the disparity of weapons told against him, and he was hanged.[3]

Edward I was on his guard against granting pardon when an inquisition was obtained with intent to mislead him. In January 1284 he ordered one to ascertain whether William of Whittonstalle had killed John Turney in self-defence.[4] The verdict given in February was that he had done so, but it declared that he had shot him as he was following him about meaning to kill him with a big stick.[5] This verdict was not altogether convincing and Edward granted only bail.[6] William then made another attempt to get pardon, falling back on a writ *de odio et atia*, issued on 16 April. The return to this was extremely short: 'non aliter eum interfecit nisi se defendendo, ita quod mortem suam nullo alio modo evasisse potuit, et non

---

[1] C. 144/16, no. 36.   [2] *Cal. Close Rolls, 1272–9*, 383.
[3] J.I. 1/181, m. 1ᵈ.   [4] *Cal. Inquisitions Misc.* i, no. 2264.   [5] Ibid.
[6] *Cal. Close Rolls, 1279–88*, 255.

per feloniam nec per maliciam excogitatam'.[1] The king did not, however, forget the earlier verdict, and would again only grant bail. The warrant for this was attached to the return, and from the wording it is clear that he feared a second attempt to secure pardon rather than bail: 'Fiat breve juxta inquisicionem presentibus interclusam quod ponatur per ballium usque ad iter justiciarum et licet aliqui petant plus debito et extra forman juris sub colore mandati nostri non ideo magis facias eisdem.'[2] His caution was commendable in the light of the information so far provided, but at the eyre in 1293 a rather better case was made out for William; his assailant was now said at first to have brandished a burning faggot, and then to have chased him with a stake; he was raising this to bring it down on William's head when the latter at last shot his arrow. The jurors were further interrogated about the possibilities of escape and explained in detail how he had been hemmed in. The justices accepted the verdict, though shooting at such close quarters might have seemed rather implausible, and remanded *ad gratiam*.[3] Edward now pardoned him on their record.[4] One verdict of killing in self-defence which had been given at a gaol delivery did not satisfy the king and he instructed the justices at a later delivery to hold another inquisition and forward its verdict to him; probably the earlier findings had been impugned by someone, for the defendant was now charged with killing 'in premeditated assault and not in self-defence'; he declared that he was 'bonus' and not guilty of the death; the jury again found that he had killed in self-defence and described circumstances which seem to leave no doubt about this.[5] Satisfied, the king now pardoned him.[6] A check-up of this kind was valuable. But there are very few examples in which the substance of a verdict was suspect and checked in this way.

There is some reason to think that the king did not always receive a completely full and accurate record of proceedings, even at the eyre. Some rolls of a particular session might be fuller than others, especially on a case which was not completed in one day. Where the record has survived it may prove to give

---

[1] C. 144/24, no. 14; *Cal. Inquisitions Misc.* i, no. 2264.
[2] Cf. *Cal. Close Rolls, 1279–88*, 267.   [3] J.I. 1/653, m. 19.
[4] C. 47/72/4, no. 90; *Cal. Pat. Rolls, 1292–1301*, 30.
[5] J.I. 1/1286, m. 23.   [6] *Cal. Pat. Rolls, 1292–1301*, 5.

information that is not included in the surviving eyre roll. Evidently such a record was copied from a more detailed roll, probably that of the leading justice. But although his roll was the one which was likely to be consulted and regarded as definitive, it might not in fact have been kept up to date as well as one of the others, or it might not be available when the record was wanted. There was thus some slight possibility that the record sent to the king inadvertently omitted some information. There was also a possibility that there might be an omission which was not inadvertent. This may be observed in the case of Alexander de Pilkington. At the eyre in 1292 it was found that he had not struck Adam del Wode, but that the latter had run on his knife while attacking him; however it was considered that Alexander 'extraxit maliciose cutellum suum ad ipsum defendendum, cum non esset in aliquo periculo mortis'.[1] When the record was sent to the king most of this damaging information was suppressed, unless it is to be supposed that it had been omitted by chance from another roll.[2] He pardoned Alexander forthwith on this record:[3] it would be interesting to know how he would have reacted to a fuller one. This particular record did not arouse any suspicions; others may have done so, but the great majority of verdicts were accepted by the king. It was only in a few cases that he was incredulous of the facts as stated, or, more likely, unconvinced by the interpretation put on the facts by the jurors; he rarely asked for any confirmation. In some cases there had been earlier investigations and the returns to some of these would still be on file in Chancery; some are still in the Public Record Office. Comparison between them and the record, for example, of a verdict given in court might have proved disconcerting. But Chancery kept files which were not indexed in any way, and nobody bothered to research too deeply when application was made for pardon. It was bad luck if some official chanced to remember earlier, less favourable information on a particular case, or bad management if the applicant sought a second inquisition before there had been time for the first to be forgotten. More official attention was given to the formulas used

---

[1] J.I. 1/409, m. 28. The last clause is inserted on this roll.

[2] The record is C. 47/65/2, no. 56. Alexander had earlier been bailed after an inquisition *de odio et atia*. The return from this has survived, but is badly torn; it does not appear to mention this damaging point; see C. 144/27, no. 20.

[3] *Cal. Pat. Rolls, 1281–92*, 503.

in the verdicts than to the circumstances which were, sometimes, forced to fit them.

The king was not, then, as critical as he might have been, nor as consistent. Relevant information might not be brought to his notice. Pardons were granted for homicides which probably, on a strict view, did not meet the criteria for slaying excusably. But these criteria, as set out in the writs for inquisitions, were too exacting and too rigid; if juries supplied dubious details in order to satisfy them, or accepted the more favourable of alternative accounts, so far as can be established they were seldom guilty of substantial misrepresentation. Most of the homicides they found excusable seem to have been deserving of pardon, though in some cases it might not have been quite such a routine matter had they kept to the unvarnished truth. Other cases might be regarded as rather more serious and yet as affording the opportunity for the king to use his prerogative worthily. The evidence discussed does not suggest that murderers were being helped to obtain pardon by the complete falsification of the facts. Premeditated slaying can nearly always be ruled out; manslaughter not always when the killing was in a brawl.

The system of pardoning did not command the wholehearted co-operation of the jurors who had to swear to the circumstances when justification or excuse was alleged. Their sympathies were generally on the side of the supposedly excusable slayer, sometimes on that of the killer in extenuating circumstances. If they seldom perverted justice, their verdicts were weighted, and the habit of allowing their sympathies to affect them in this way was unhealthy. There was enough prejudice and corruption without this temptation to commit perjury on behalf of unintentional slayers, victims of an overstringent system. The authorities did not fully appreciate these dangers and far too often relied uncritically on the verdicts. Some doubts were felt, however, about the special inquisitions into alleged excuse, which could be regarded as hole-and-corner affairs and less reliable than verdicts given in court. Some people objected to them and a proposal to eliminate them was one of the reforms attempted under Edward I.

XI

ATTEMPTS AT REFORM

THE most valuable reform of the system of pardoning would have been to reduce it drastically by exempting slaying by mischance and in self-defence from the need for pardon and excluding clearly felonious homicide from its scope. Bracton would perhaps have approved the former course and certainly would have acclaimed the latter. The system was not to be reduced to its proper proportions in this way for centuries yet, but some attempts were made to exclude certain types of killing because they involved no guilt at all or too much. The tendency to require verdicts of excusable homicide to precede pardon was important under Henry III, but while it checked it by no means dammed the flow of pardons to criminals. Only under Edward I do further governmental attempts at reform emerge. At the same time criticism was openly voiced and may not have been without effect. But it came from different quarters and only spasmodically. It is difficult to establish any coherent programme either within or without governmental circles.

The magnates used their influence in individual cases but were unlikely to worry about the general treatment of excusable homicides. The exercise of the royal prerogative in favour of murderers might, on the other hand, incur their disapproval, and it is possible that a statute of 1278 which aimed at limiting the pardoning of homicides who did not appear in court was made at their instigation. Apart from this, the one occasion on which they promoted legislation on this topic reveals their concern for their own rights and, as incidental to these, the treatment of their servants. This was in 1293, when, in order to enhance the deterrents against poaching and other offences in forests, chaces, parks, and warrens, the king, at the instance of the magnates, granted that foresters, parkers, and warreners should not suffer any penalty for killing offenders who would not surrender when discovered and when hue and cry had been raised, but who forcibly resisted arrest. The king added a salutary warning against abuse of their new immunity by these officers to kill personal enemies on the pretext that they were committing these offences; if they were convicted of such slaying they were to be treated just as if they had killed anyone else in the king's peace. Killing whilst trying to attach malefactors in forests and so on was now to rank as justifiable homicide, equally with killing ordinary thieves who resisted arrest. The motives of the promoters of this statute may have been selfish, or at best mixed, but it was a sensible act and removed an anomaly which had occasioned much harsh treatment of officials of this kind, as well as depriving their lords of the services of those who fled and were outlawed. Notable among these lords were the king's brother, Edmund of Lancaster, and their brother-in-law, the duke of Brittany.[1]

Criticism of the system of pardoning came also from legal writers. Bracton himself did not criticize it openly and directly except when he complained of clemency being shown to felons. A close study of his borrowings from Roman and Canon Law would have revealed several points of disagreement as to the relative culpability of different types of homicide, but he did not himself point the contrasts with the practice of the English courts. His disapproval has to be inferred from his care to evade the issue. 'The man who commits homicide by misadventure or in self-defence deserves but needs a pardon. Bracton cannot conceal this from us.'[2] Thus Maitland deftly indicates his attitude. His reluctance to state the fact explicitly went so far that in his analysis of the types of homicide he managed to avoid mentioning that the slayer in self-defence who had not been outlawed needed pardon, although he admitted the accidental slayer's need of it. Only in the section on outlawry did he deal with the practice of pardoning in any detail. There he asserted that both types of excusable slayer should be accepted 'ad gratiam et ad pacem sine difficultate, gratia tamen principis comitante',[3] and a little later he

---

[1] Cf. below p. 286. The latter is particularly likely to have pressed for this change, since one of his foresters, Richard de Leghton, had been outlawed after the eyre of 1279–80 and was still unpardoned. He now surrendered and was in York gaol when the duke obtained pardon for him early in 1294, in time for him to produce it at the eyre which was already in session in Yorkshire. See pp. 237, n. 1, 288, n. 4.   [2] *Hist. Eng. Law*, ii. 479.

[3] *De Legibus*, f. 132[b].

remarked that the king 'tenetur etiam aliquando de gratia concedere ei [the outlaw] vitam, ut si per infortunium vel se defendendo hominem interfecerit'.[1] Thus he was not afraid to state categorically that the king was bound to pardon such homicides, even though he did so of grace. The king was under a moral obligation at least to act in this way. Bracton did not, in this section, discuss the grave problem of the nature of the king's duty and the possibility of his being compelled to discharge it, or of some control of the way he exercised his prerogative. But if he believed that the pardoning of such outlaws was, in some undefined sense, obligatory, he must have felt even more strongly about the pardoning of excusable slayers who were not fugitives or outlaws. They, surely, had an even more compelling right to pardon, though Bracton may well have doubted whether they should have stood in any need of it, especially if they had killed 'of necessity' in self-defence, or accidentally without any negligence.[2]

Some legal writers of the time of Edward I were more outspoken than Bracton. They had little use for the royal prerogative and especially that of clemency. Fleta did not deny that homicide by misadventure and in self-defence might be dealt with by the grant of pardon, but he made it a matter of right not of grace: 'Tenetur rex de iure quod suum fuerit perdonare.'[3] It was only to those responsible for road accidents that he took an altogether original and hostile line. Britton was even more inclined to regard acquittal as appropriate in cases of excusable homicide, though this emerges only in relation to appeals. Both writers introduced a novel procedure here and their theory may have been of practical significance. Earlier,

[1] Ibid., f. 134–134^b.

[2] In practice he seems to have acted as other justices did. Towards the end of his life he was commissioned to hold several inquisitions into alleged excusable homicide. On the first three occasions the verdict was self-defence and pardon followed (*Cal. Pat. Rolls, 1247–58*, 624; ibid., *1258–66*, 247, 287, 298). No pardons seem to have resulted after the next two (ibid. 384, 485), but this need not be attributed to any special severity on his part since it is probable that he did not in fact hold the inquisitions. Although he was commissioned in five more cases, in one of them twice over, he does not seem to have acted and other commissioners eventually held most of the inquisitions (ibid. 650, 676, 679; ibid., *1266–72*, 27, 127, 145, 162, 231; cf. C. 144/6, no. 6; *Cal. Inquisitions Misc.* i, no. 2127). Perhaps he was now getting too old and frail to travel about the west country in order to hold them, or was too busy about ecclesiastical duties.

[3] Lib. i, cap. 28. Gilbert de Thornton omitted Bracton's 'de gratia' here, but did not substitute 'de iure'. See Harvard MS. 77, f. 39.

it seems, no excuse could be put forward as an exception to the appeal or as a defence by the appellee. Bracton gave no hint that this could be done, and no other evidence has been found to suggest that a defence could be based on the nature of the killing unless it could be asserted to have been justifiable.[1] The *Summa* of about 1290 attributed to Gilbert de Thornton does not suggest any change on this point since Bracton's day, but both Fleta and Britton listed other defences.[2] Fleta considered that the justices ought not to order a judicial combat until they had examined whether the deed was felony, misfortune, or trespass, giving examples of accidental slaying and referring also to killing by lunatics and children in terms borrowed from Bracton,[3] although he did not state explicitly that the appellee could except to the appeal on all these grounds, apparently expecting the justices to take the initiative and satisfy themselves that the killing was one which could properly give rise to an appeal of felony. But in the next chapter he went on to say that an appeal abated if the victim had been killed as a nocturnal thief, or as a fleeing outlaw, or because for some other reason he could not have been spared without risk to the slayer, or in defence of the slayer's home. He seems, therefore, to have been trying here to enlarge the category of justifiable slaying, not to maintain that all types of excusable killing gave rise to exceptions to appeals. Britton, less cautiously, declared that the appellee might say that although he committed the deed, yet he did not do it of felony aforethought, but of necessity in self-defence, or in defending his wife or his household or his liegeman or his lord or lady from death, or he might say that he killed in defence of the king's peace, or by misadventure without felony aforethought. If these exceptions were upheld the appellees were to go quit by judgement.[4] These writers

---

[1] Since appellors seldom persisted in prosecuting people who could claim to have killed excusably it is difficult to state categorically that excuses could not be put forward. But there are enough instances to suggest that the normal procedure was for the appellee to except to the appeal on other grounds; once it had been abated in this way and he had been arraigned at the suit of the king he would put himself on the jury relying on a verdict of excusable homicide. For some examples of the jurors finding excusable slaying after the appeal had been quashed see K.B. 27/146, m. 19[d]; K.B. 27/163, m. 5[B]; J.I. 1/371, mm. 7, 22[d]; J.I. 1/1051, m. 12[d] (though here the appellee did not put himself on a jury at once).

[2] The *Mirror of Justices* included misadventure among the exceptions to an appeal of homicide; see *Selden Soc.* vii. 101.   [3] Lib. i, cap. 31.

[4] Lib. i, ch. 24.

held, then, that appeals ought not to be allowed to proceed against excusable slayers but there was some doubt or disagreement as to the manner in which the excuses should be brought to light and established.

No direct evidence for any modification of the justices' treatment of appeals in these cases has been found before 1302, but in that year an appeal *coram rege* against an excusable homicide was disposed of in an apparently novel way. The appellee did not except to the appeal, but put himself on the country as to his guilt or innocence; the appellor also put herself on the country. A jury came—the slaying had occurred in London—and found that the slaying had been in self-defence, the slayer having intervened when the victim and his man tried to take some apples from a poor costermonger against his will; both had attacked him with their swords; he had fled towards Fenchurch but had been cornered and then had defended himself only with his staff.[1] This was, of course, a particularly convincing verdict. The justices instructed the appellee to sue to the king for pardon, and he promptly secured it and produced his charter before them. A schedule attached to the roll gives it in full. The pardon was unusual in that it mentioned that it was based on an inquisition on which both appellee and appellor had put themselves.[2] This formula seems to have been quite new and it is significant that it was included in the enrolment of the pardon on the patent roll.[3] While it would be rash to suppose that this was the first occasion when a jury was allowed to give such a verdict and the justices recommended an appellee to the king's grace, it may well have been one of the first.[4] Thus it is doubtful whether this procedure was being employed at the time when Fleta and Britton wrote; possibly they were aware that verdicts on excuses were now in order in appeals; more likely they were anticipating a future development.

[1] K.B. 27/168, m. 24^d; K.B. 27/170, m. 56. [2] It omitted the proviso 'stet recto.'
[3] C. 66/123, m. 37. Unfortunately it is omitted in *Cal. Pat. Rolls, 1301–7*, 114.

[4] In 1294 Edward I pardoned a man on the record of the justices, appointed to hear an appeal brought against him by the victim's sister, that he killed him in self-defence. The same procedure may have been followed here, but this is very improbable, since the appellee would surely have excepted to the appeal for contravening Magna Carta, cl. 54. The likelihood is that this appeal was quashed for this reason and that a verdict was then taken after arraignment at the suit of the king. See ibid., *1292–1301*, 82; cf. ibid. 112. One or two other pardons came after appeals which may have been withdrawn or quashed.

The procedure in 1302 did not exactly follow either of those suggested by these writers. It reveals a less radical change and one less injurious to the rights of appellors, for it was only in cases in which there was very clear evidence of excuse that the jurors themselves were likely to mention it without prompting. In this case the coroner's roll is available and shows that the verdict given at his inquest had been self-defence and the details agreed with those described later.[1] Moreover, the appellor is said to have consented to accept the verdict to be given *coram rege* and this suggests that she was content to leave the issue of self-defence to the jurors. Probably, she actually agreed to this in court. This procedure did not give the appellee as much help as that first suggested by Fleta would have done, nor did it involve his excepting to the appeal on the grounds that the killing had been excusable, not felonious; it did not allow acquittal as Britton would have done, but still involved pardon.

Although this new treatment of appeals did not as yet allow the courts to acquit but only to remand appellees *ad gratiam*, there are other indications that opinion was shifting in favour of the acquittal of killers who up to now had needed pardon, besides foresters, parkers, and warreners. Britton may have been echoing such opinions when he wrote of acquittal when the excuse raised as an exception was verified. One very important and praiseworthy example of this kind has already been dealt with: the acquittal of infant killers up to and sometimes over the age of seven. There is no evidence that this practice was ordered by the king, though it may have been so and presumably had at least his tacit consent.[2] But at one point Edward I seems to have envisaged relaxing his prerogative hold on a much wider range of excusable killers, removing homicide by accident and perhaps even in self-defence from the excusable category altogether. There is no hint as to his motive in this. He may have been affected by the views of advanced legal theorists, Bracton's in particular. Or, independently of these, he may have had some inkling of the unfairness of a system which demanded pardon even for the man who was entirely guiltless of crime, who had himself been unlucky to become involved in a misadventure which proved fatal to

---

[1] *Cal. Coroners Rolls of the City of London*, ed. R. R. Sharpe, no. 14.

[2] Such acquittals occurred in the King's Bench, e.g. K.B. 27/126, m. 51 (1291). Unfortunately the age of this infant is not stated.

someone else. Or it may be that his justices' fussiness in consulting him over obvious cases of accidental slaying proved wearisome to him, although he was not prepared to relinquish the decision to exercise his prerogative to the Chancellor. Whether in a moment of impatience at the calls made on him or as a deliberate policy of reform, he repudiated the need for pardon in some cases. This move was precipitated by the reference to him of a case from the Yorkshire eyre of 1279, at which William, son of John de Bately, had been presented for the death of Alice, daughter of Adam de Schipker. He had pleaded not guilty and the jury had given the following account: William, who was the king's bailiff in the Wapentake of Morlay, came one day to Middleton in the course of his duties; en route he saw a target and wishing to take a shot at it he put an arrow in his bow and shot, but while the arrow was in flight Alice, by a quite unforeseen chance, came between him and the target and was struck so that she died. The justices remanded William *ad gratiam* but also decided to raise the matter with the king themselves. They subsequently did so and he instructed them not to proceed to judgement in such cases, since he entirely remitted this sort of misfortune. William was thereupon acquitted.[1]

Some other prisoners at this eyre seem also to have benefited from the king's ruling,[2] but two who had killed in self-defence may in fact have suffered from the justices' uncertainty whether it applied to all clearly excusable homicide or only to accidental. They had decided to consult the king about them, but seem to have done nothing further, so that the two prisoners were left in prison. In April 1282 they both obtained release on bail, and a few weeks afterwards pardon.[3] But two others who

[1] J.I. 1/1060, m. 13ᵈ. He had earlier been bailed; cf. *Cal. Close Rolls, 1272–9*, 213; C. 144/14, no. 41, which shows that Alice was 2½ years old 'et nullum bonum sciuit'.

[2] John Strikeleued had also shot by accident. He had shot wide of the target and lost his arrow. His father told him to shoot again while he stood nearby to see where the second arrow fell, so hoping to locate the first. The second arrow glanced off the bough of a tree and killed him. The justices decided to consult the king and meanwhile John was to be in custody, but later he was granted bail 'habendum ipsum ad voluntatem domini Regis' (J.I. 1/1060, m. 58ᵈ). His case was so similar to William's that the ruling would obviously apply to it, yet the justices appear to have been reluctant to acquit him outright. In a third shooting accident no further decision is recorded (ibid., m. 12ᵈ).

[3] Kirkeby and le Fevere, see ibid., mm. 12ᵈ, 59ᵈ; J.I. 1/1057, m. 60ᵈ; *Cal. Close Rolls, 1279–88*, 151; *Cal. Pat. Rolls, 1281–92*, 22; cf. C. 47/86/31, no. 837.

had killed in self-defence are not known ever to have obtained pardon despite the decision to consult the king about them, and they may have been allowed to go quit in accordance with his ruling in Bately's case.[1] It is not improbable that Edward was momentarily inclined to allow acquittal of slayers in self-defence, for he was prepared to remit his suit against fugitives who had killed in this way. The same justices in eyre in Yorkshire spoke to him about a case of this sort, 'per quod dominus Rex remisit sectam suam', and the justices announced that the fugitive need not be outlawed but might return if he wished.[2] It may be, however, that Edward expected still to be consulted in such cases and did not intend the justices to allow return entirely on their own authority or to acquit.

Whatever his intentions the more liberal policy had very little effect as regards either fugitives or those who appeared in court. Even on this occasion there was doubt how widely to apply the king's instructions and indecision or even inadvertency aggravated the situation of some when it should have been alleviated. Edward himself may have been at fault for not making his intentions clear. Moreover, it is evident that if he was really attempting a new policy he did not publish it widely enough and it had little if any effect beyond this particular Yorkshire eyre. Instructions of this kind to a particular group of justices tended not to be given wider currency, or at any rate to be generally disregarded. Thus an impulse towards reform, which, whatever the motives prompting it, would have liberalized and rationalized the treatment of excusable homicide was nullified by lack of precision, perseverance, and publicity, The weight of tradition was too heavy to be shifted so far by would-be reformers and Edward's own attempt was short-lived and almost entirely ineffective in substituting acquittal for pardon.

Even though the major reform of 1279 was abandoned, if indeed it had seriously been intended to apply it generally, there were lesser reforms which could have ameliorated the situation of many non-felonious slayers. There was great need

---

[1] J.I. 1/1060, mm. 24ᵈ, 25ᵈ. The first of these had earlier been bailed (*Cal. Close Rolls, 1272–9*, 34).

[2] J.I. 1/1057, m. 6 (Gilbert son of Ulketel who had killed William le Blomer). J.I. 1/1060, m. 4 reports the same case, but with no reference to consulting the king or his reply.

to define and in some areas to revise the criteria for recommending pardon. This really called for legislation, but this was put through only in the matter of slaying forest offenders. Instead of defining culpability more clearly reformers fell back on schemes which would discourage those with a guilty conscience from seeking pardon at all. Legislation to this end was brought in in 1278, when the Statute of Gloucester, cap. 9, as Maitland summarized it, required that 'No more writs for inquests were to be granted, but the accused was to appear before the justices and "put himself upon the country for good and ill".'[1] The wording was as follows:

Le Rey comaunde qe nul bref de la Chauncelerie seit graunte de mort de home, de enquere si home occie autre par mesaventure, ou sei defendaunt, ou en autre manere par felonie, mes *si tel seit en prison*, *e* devaunt Justices erraunz, ou Justices assignez a Ghaole deliverer, se met en pays de bien et de mal, e len trusse par pais, qil eit fet sei defendaunt, ou par mesaventure, dunqe par record des Justices, face le Rei sa grace si lui plest.[2]

One aim of this statute was to put a stop to the practice of pardoning those who were still fugitives on the grounds that they had slain excusably. If they hoped for pardon they must surrender and stand their trial along with prisoners who had submitted to arrest at once; on a verdict of excusable homicide by the trial jury the justices would remand *ad gratiam*. This requirement would, it was hoped, sort out the fugitives into the sheep who would surrender confident in their excuses, and the goats who would opt to remain at large. Moreover, the trial jury could be interrogated by the king's justices, more authoritative people than some of the commissioners, and the whole matter could be investigated and the degree of responsibility estimated in the light of their experience of such cases. Evidently, it was felt that fugitives were at an unfair advantage so long as their friends in their absence could procure the holding of special inquisitions which, if favourable, would lead to pardon, and if adverse would leave them in no worse position

[1] *Hist. Eng. Law*, ii. 481.
[2] The words italicized are absent from one version. The reference to felony here is an echo of the wording of the writs for inquisitions. The statute did not attempt to prohibit the pardoning of felonious homicide without any inquisition being held.

than their present one, whereas those who stood to right did
so at the risk of their lives. There was probably some feeling
also, that the special inquisitions were too likely to be favourable;
that they were too open to influence. Thus even prisoners
were not to secure pardons by their verdicts. A further consideration may have had some importance. Chapter 9 concludes
with the decree that appeals are not to be quashed for such
light cause as they have been and appellors are allowed a year
within which to appeal. This shows some recognition of the
fact that they were not getting a fair deal, and this may well
have extended to criticism of the pardoning of homicides
who had been outlawed on appeal. The requirement that
fugitives seeking inquisitions leading to pardon should surrender and appear in court would, if effective, at least ensure
that there was an immediate opportunity for an appeal to be
made or renewed.

For a time the statute had some effect on the treatment both
of fugitives and those already in gaol. One of its results was to
encourage prisoners to obtain special gaol deliveries instead of
inquisitions, though no doubt it required an exceptionally
clean conscience or a very cool nerve to precipitate trial in
this way, instead of waiting for the next general delivery of
their prisons. At the beginning of 1279 four justices were
appointed to deliver the gaol of Bridgnorth of Richard de
Middelhope taken for the death of Henry son of Hamo.[1] It
does not appear that they did so, but three years later he was
pardoned as other justices of gaol delivery had found that he
had killed him in self-defence.[2] In April 1279 William son of
Neyra was pardoned for the death of his mother, the justices
who had been appointed exactly a month before to deliver
Aylesbury gaol of him, having found that he had killed her by
accident.[3] No parallel cases have been found earlier in the
reign and it is fair to conclude that inquisitions into the circumstances would have been preferred to these special gaol deliveries
had it not been for the statute. But while pardons after remand
ad gratiam at general gaol deliveries continued throughout the
reign, and indeed became more and more numerous as the

[1] *Cal. Pat. Rolls, 1272–81*, 338.
[2] Ibid., *1281–92*, 9; cf. J.I. 1/739, m. 51^d.
[3] *Cal. Pat. Rolls, 1272–81*, 311, 344; cf. J.I. 1/65, m. 36^d. He did not appear at
the eyre in 1286, but the order to arrest him was rescinded as the slaying had been
presented as an accident when he had been shooting at dogs.

general eyre lapsed, special gaol deliveries in cases where excuses could be found do not feature prominently in the 1280s.[1] This result of the statute was short-lived; but another more lasting result may have been to encourage excusable slayers to surrender just before a general gaol delivery, counting on remand *ad gratiam* there.

Apart from its encouragement to obtain a special gaol delivery, the influence of the statute is not at first very obvious on the patent rolls. In November Edward pardoned a man on the testimony of the stewards of the household that the killing had been in self-defence;[2] probably they had held an inquest *ex officio* in place of the coroner. Entries of pardons at this period tend to be very brief and it is uncertain whether some followed a verdict of some sort or not.[3] One granted in April 1279 was based on the finding of a special inquisition that the killing had been in self-defence, but since the commissioners had been appointed well before the statute it may have been considered not to affect their proceedings, even though they had held the inquisition after it.[4] As late as mid 1280, some regard was being paid to the statute[5] but during the course of this year any

---

[1] A clerk, Richard de Slauston, was pardoned after justices of gaol delivery had found that he had killed in self-defence; see *Cal. Pat. Rolls, 1281-92*, 284, 478. But he had surrendered only after being placed in exigent at the eyre and thus cannot be said to have obtained a special delivery in lieu of an inquisition into the circumstances at the outset; cf. J.I. 1/65, m. 37ᵈ; C. 47/49/6, no. 196. Moreover, he secured bail on the verdict (see *Cal. Close Rolls, 1279-88*, 451) and pardon only after nearly five years. A large number of persons surrendered in this way after an eyre, many of them not having known that they were to be prosecuted there.

[2] *Cal. Pat. Rolls, 1272-81*, 282.

[3] The next entry, in December, ibid. 296, does not refer to any excuse, but J.I. 1/1004, m. 97 shows that the killing was justifiable; the statute did not, therefore, explicitly apply, since it referred only to killing in self-defence or by misadventure.

[4] *Cal. Pat. Rolls, 1272-81*, 308; *Cal. Inquisitions Misc.* i, no. 2213. The pardon was produced at the eyre (J.I. 1/65, m. 46ᵈ). Also in April, William de Saham was commissioned 'to enquire whether John de Mildeby, in York gaol for the death of Geoffrey son of Richard Sitling, killed him by misadventure or by felony' (*Cal. Pat. Rolls, 1272-81*, 313). However, it looks as though John got no more than bail as a result, since he appeared before the itinerant justices in the following year and was pardoned on their record that he had killed by accident (ibid. 364; J.I. 1/1060, m. 58). Another problematical case is that of a Welshman, pardoned in May on testimony before the king that he had killed by misadventure (*Cal. Pat. Rolls, 1272-81*, 315). What sort of inquisition, if any, had been held does not appear, but the presentment at the eyre much later on agreed that he had slain in this manner (J.I. 1/739, m. 90).

[5] Robert Fulconis and Robert Malet were appointed in April to inquire by a Berkshire jury whether Albert Morone, Guy his brother, and Donatus de Cremona,

attempt to observe it strictly was abandoned. On 15 May
Robert de Hadenhale was pardoned for the death of Richard
Tramel; neither the enrolment on the patent roll,[1] nor the
pardon as quoted at the eyre in 1292–3[2] refers to an inquisition
into the circumstances, but in fact the sheriff of Shropshire had
been instructed to inquire in full county court if he had slain
him in self-defence,[3] and there can be little doubt, that a
favourable verdict there was the ground for the pardon,
although it kept discreetly silent on this point. A particularly
significant case is that of Thomas Alein, whose pardon in
August for the accidental death of his brother seems to have
contained no reference to any inquisition although one had
just been held.[4] The pardon, stating baldly that the killing was
by mischance not felony, was quoted at the eyre, and the report
there continues: 'Et quia hoc idem compertum est per inquisitionem per vicecomitem staff. et Coronator. eiusdem
Comitatus per preceptum domini Regis inde factam', and no
one comes forward to speak against him, therefore he is granted
firm peace.[5] This reference by the justices to the inquisition is
noteworthy, and it may be that they felt happier about a
pardon based on an inquisition of the old type, not before
justices as required by the statute, than one which revealed no
grounds for clemency beyond the bare assertion of some excuse.
Certainly, they showed no hostility to the inquisition by sheriff
and coroners and by now probably regarded this part of the
statute as a dead letter. Nor is it easy to suppose that they would
ever have taken it upon themselves to repudiate pardons not
granted in compliance with it. While the Chancery clerks may
still have been trying to disguise the frequent departures from

prisoners in the Tower of London, had killed Leonard de Casal Motant at Reading,
or if he had killed himself, and if so whether by misadventure or otherwise. They
held the inquisition in May and it found that Guy had killed him in self-defence
(*Cal. Inquisitions Misc.* i, no. 2232). The return was endorsed: 'Quia posuit [se]
pro bono et malo etc. Fiat perdona per Regem.' This seems to indicate that the
commissioners had power to try the prisoners, even though they were not appointed
explicitly as justices of gaol delivery, but possibly the prisoners had already put
themselves on the country at a gaol delivery at the Tower. In either event, the
endorsement stresses the need for their doing this before pardon could be granted.
The enrolment of the pardon refers to none of these proceedings. See *Cal. Pat.
Rolls, 1272–81*, 370.   [1] Ibid. 369.

[2] J.I. 1/739, mm. 90, 95.
[3] *Cal. Inquisitions Misc.* i, no. 2231.
[4] *Cal. Pat. Rolls, 1271–81*, 394; *Cal. Inquisitions Misc.* i, no. 2235.
[5] J.I. 1/804, m. 76ᵈ; cf. m. 63ᵈ.

it, the justices made no bones about them, and soon the cat was out of the bag even in Chancery. By September 1280 a pardon was frankly granted 'as it appears by inquisition made by the sheriff and coroners . . . that he killed him by mis-adventure',[1] and another on sufficient testimony that the victim 'was killed by misfortune. And the like was found by inquisition which the king ordered to be made by the sheriff of York'.[2] From the Yorkshire eyre roll of 1293 it is evident that the slayer in this case had fled and his chattels had been con-fiscated at an earlier eyre, evidently that of 1279, so that it is quite likely that he was still a fugitive when the pardon was granted.[3] In October a man was pardoned after an inquisition taken by the constable of Dover Castle and the coroners of Kent had found slaying by misadventure,[4] and the commission in July to inquire into the slaying shows that the culprit was an outlaw.[5] Finally, in November, a man was pardoned a death and any consequent outlawry, 'as it appears by an inquisition taken by the sheriff. . . that he killed him by misadventure'.[6] Thus the requirement that the homicide must actually be on trial before a recommendation to mercy could be accepted was soon disregarded, and although orders for inquisitions by sheriffs, coroners, and others were now scarcely ever enrolled on the patent rolls,[7] their frequency is attested by the actual pardons which refer to them and also by surviving returns and a few Chancery warrants.[8] Pardon was still granted occasionally even on the verdict of an inquisition *de odio et atia*. Nor does this evidence suggest that at this time Edward hesitated to pardon fugitives and outlaws who had not yet surrendered to custody, but this part of the policy was of more lasting effect.

It will be noticed that it was precisely while this half-hearted attempt to enforce the statute was being made that Edward I himself showed greater leniency than ever before, instructing the justices in Yorkshire to acquit those who had killed by

[1] *Cal. Pat. Rolls, 1272–81*, 397. The inquisition is *Cal. Inquisitions Misc.* i, no. 2241.
[2] *Cal. Pat. Rolls, 1272–81*, 398.
[3] J.I. 1/1098, m. 11. Cf. above, p. 251.
[4] *Cal. Pat. Rolls, 1272–81*, 399.
[5] *Cal. Inquisitions Misc.* i, no. 2238.
[6] *Cal. Pat. Rolls, 1272–81*, 401; cf. J.I. 1/804, m. 56ᵈ.
[7] They appear sporadically, e.g. *Cal. Pat. Rolls, 1281–92*, 159, 286; ibid., *1292–1301*, 545, 552; ibid., *1301–7*, 344.
[8] But later on special inquisitions did become infrequent and pardons for excusable slaying were generally based on verdicts given at gaol deliveries.

accident. It is particularly significant that he even told them he remitted his suit against a fugitive who, they had informed him, had killed in self-defence.[1] This ran directly counter to the statute's requirement that pardon should not be granted on such grounds until the slayer had appeared in court in person. It looks as though the king was reacting against the statute, tacitly repudiating though not repealing it, and this suggests that it had not been made on his initiative but was, like the modification of the *quo warranto* procedure at the same Parliament of Gloucester, a concession on his part. The king's willingness to brush it aside may, however, have received less publicity than the statute itself had done. Persons who found themselves in need of pardon and their friends would not necessarily know much of either, but a general report that the procedure was to be made more difficult may have spread far enough to discourage a good many possible petitioners. Whatever the reason, the number of pardons in the next decade remained comparatively low. This may be partly explained by the tendency, already noticed, for those remanded *ad gratiam* not to sue out their pardons; but the failure of so many individuals to seek pardon before trial may not be unrelated to the doubts about the application of the statute, although it may also be due in part to growing confidence in the outcome of the trial itself.[2] The king's absence from England for much of the period was also, no doubt, a contributory factor. The author of *Fleta* summarized the statute and regarded it as being still in force in 1290,[3] but the only section of it which was of any significance then was the requirement that fugitives must surrender. Yet it was not forgotten and fourteenth-century reformers tried to revive its underlying principles.[4]

Edward was not always prepared to respect the rule as to fugitives, but he did so on certain occasions. There was an impressive example of this about 1283. Three foresters had killed a malefactor resisting arrest in 1282; they petitioned for a writ ordering an inquisition to be held as already promised to their lord, Edmund of Lancaster. The response to this was the king's order that they should be imprisoned and after that

---

[1]. See above, p. 280.
[2] There was a very large crop of pardons after the general eyre of 1292–3 for homicides who had awaited trial there.   [3] Lib. i, cap. 23.
[4] See below, p. 324.

the sheriff and coroner should hold the inquisition and send
its verdict to him.[1] Sometime after 1286 an outlaw's petition
for pardon met with the order to surrender at Dover Castle
ready to stand to right.[2] But later a rather different line was
taken. At this time outlawry was already being used as a
process to compel the appearance in court of persons sued for
trespass or for failing to render account.[3] The pardoning of
outlawry of this kind did not, of course, effect anything more;
the grantee was pardoned his contumacy and the resulting
outlawry, but still had to come before the justices. The practice
of limiting pardons for criminals to outlawry may have been
influenced by this form of pardon. It was particularly desirable
to insist on standing to right in cases of mayhem and theft in
which an appellor was not unlikely to come forward, and this
requirement was most effective if the pardon was limited to
outlawry and made conditional on immediate surrender.[4]
Towards the end of 1291 homicides were also beginning to
obtain pardons for outlawry stipulating this,[5] and a number
of men put in exigent at the eyre of 1292–3 and thereupon
outlawed received similar pardons. Some of them may have been
ready to stand trial, for many people who were placed in
exigent promptly surrendered, and it may be that some who
were outlawed did not hear in time that they were on the
wanted list. But still it was optimistic to expect surrender when
only the outlawry was pardoned. Edward weakened in his
demands. On 1 July 1293 he pardoned the outlawry of
Yorvorth de Forton, and in December, when the latter had
failed to surrender within the stipulated forty days, granted

---

[1] S.C. 8/296, no. 14776. The inquisition was held in 1283 (*Cal. Inquisitions Misc.* i, no. 2262) and pardon granted in 1284 (*Cal. Pat. Rolls, 1281–92*, 118).

[2] S.C. 8/274, no. 13685; he was charged with complicity in the slaying of William de Prene at Oxford; cf. *Cal. Pat. Rolls, 1281–92*, 258–9.

[3] e.g. ibid. 320, 344.

[4] e.g. ibid. 380 (an Irish case).

[5] In October one was pardoned 'provided that he surrender to Neugate gaol by the Purification to stand to right, and that the keeper of the City of London certify the king thereof; this pardon to be null if he have not surrendered' (ibid. 448), and another 'provided that he surrender to prison within a week after Easter to stand to right' (ibid.). Neither of them surrendered. The first, John de la Bataill, later fought in Flanders and was pardoned on this account for both the death and his outlawry (ibid., *1292–1301*, 336). J.I. 1/739, m. 56[d] shows that the other, Bartholomew de Preston, also defaulted. Probably, the pardons had been obtained by their friends whose faith in their innocence was not matched by their own consciences.

him another pardon in precisely the same terms.[1] Soon he seems to have been pardoning fugitives in the usual way.

The rather stricter attitude to outlaws is reflected in the decisions of the justices in eyre. Now that some pardons were intended to cover only outlawry, not the actual slaying, they sometimes took objection to those which were not sufficiently explicit. Thus in 1292 they were unwilling to accept a charter which omitted to state that the king pardoned the slaying, as the prisoner claimed, but declared only that he pardoned the outlawry promulgated against him for it: 'since there was no mention in the charter of the king's pardoning his suit of the peace for the death . . ., but only the outlawry', they remanded him to prison.[2] The king sent for the record, which was forwarded to him, but apparently without result. The omission cost the slayer dear; he was still in prison in 1294, and then obtained pardon only on condition of fighting in Gascony.[3] Conversely, in view of this new strictness it was now worth while for an outlaw to obtain a second charter, pardoning the outlawry specifically, if his first referred only to the homicide.[4]

The itinerant justices now also showed themselves particularly severe to persons who had already obtained pardon for homicide but failed to appear before them to have it proclaimed. Among the outlaws pardoned on condition of surrendering within a given time were some who had earlier been pardoned for homicide but outlawed when they defaulted at the eyre.[5] This severity towards people who neglected to

---

[1] *Cal. Pat. Rolls, 1292–1301*, 28, 58.

[2] J.I. 1/739, m. 47 (Richard de Acton). The pardon had been granted in 1279 and was for his outlawry for the death of Thomas del Esshe—a perfectly normal phrase at that date to cover both outlawry and the actual homicide. See *Cal. Pat. Rolls, 1272–81*, 300.

[3] *Rôles Gascons*, iii, no. 3836.

[4] Richard de Leghton, then in prison, obtained pardon on 4 April 1294 at the instance of the duke of Brittany, for the death of Adam de Wyghale; on the 20th he was pardoned, at the same instance, for his outlawry for it. For his case see above, pp. 237, n. 1, 274, n. 1.

[5] e.g. an inquisition in 1283 found that William Campyon had killed in self-defence; he was pardoned forthwith (*Cal. Pat. Rolls, 1281–92*, 79), but did not stand to right at the eyre in 1292, was there placed in exigent, and consequently outlawed (J.I. 1/739, m. 86). Early next year he got his second pardon, which was for the outlawry, and which required him to surrender within forty days to Shrewsbury gaol and to 'take his trial notwithstanding former letters patent of pardon to him for the said death' (*Cal. Pat. Rolls, 1292–1301*, 11). He duly surrendered and came before the justices of gaol delivery armed with the second

appear before the justices with their pardons suggests that there was now a more definite policy of enforcing appearance. The same hostility towards defaulters appears in the practice at the eyre of 1292-3 of outlawing accidental killers. It has been noticed that the justices revoked some decisions to allow them to return.[1] The pardons which stipulated surrender were evidently one result of this general policy. It looks as though there was a determined effort, in which Edward was now readier to play his part, to ensure that killers who sought pardon appeared in court. Judicial examination of their cases was emphasized. This was reasonable while a general eyre was being held, and would not necessarily hamper the use of the prerogative at other times. But there is a further significance in this policy, for this time it affected felonious as well as ostensibly excusable homicide, and thus contained a threat, however oblique, at the prerogative of mercy to the undeserving. It can scarcely have been expected that the immediate surrender of outlaws for trial without pardon of the king's suit for the slaying would always be stipulated. This would have meant the total elimination of pardons to the notoriously guilty, not only the decline of those to outlaws whose fate in court was unpredictable. But even if the number affected was limited, it was a promising move towards bringing the use of the prerogative under eventual control.

This attempt to secure that fugitives from justice surrendered before their crimes were pardoned, or at least before a provisional pardon became operative, met with only moderate success even in the early 1290s. The king could still be persuaded to grant full pardon to absentees. But while the eyre was in progress most pardons were based on verdicts of excusable homicide given there or at gaol deliveries dealing with those who surrendered after being placed in exigent by the itinerant justices. Outlaws who could not hope for such verdicts, or would not bank on them, stayed at a safe distance unless their friends could persuade the king to pardon them without stipulating surrender. The policy may have had the effect of

pardon, which, as recorded here, stressed that it would cease to be valid if he had not surrendered on time (J.I. 3/90, m. 3). The sheriff testified that he had given himself up within the forty days, and as the second charter itself contained the statement that the king had pardoned the homicide in an earlier charter, he was now given firm peace.

[1] Above, p. 138.

delaying the pardoning of some undesirable characters. In the next decade it was suspended. The king's aim now was to herd outlaws into his army, not his prisons, and to give prisoners themselves the opportunity to go free on enlistment. But it was not forgotten and at the end of his reign some fugitives were again pardoned only outlawry.[1]

This was the most important attempt at greater strictness under Edward I. There are, however, indications of some efforts, mainly on the part of Chancery officials not of the king himself, at stricter handling of the evidence supplied as grounds for pardon. It has been seen that there was some need to check this. More information was desirable in a good many cases. Deliberate and total falsification of the facts was probably rare, but they might be misrepresented to some extent and set in the most favourable light. The return from a special inquisition or the record of the justices' rolls might be too summary to substantiate the verdict of slaying by mischance or in self-defence, or allow the king to form his own judgement of the merits of the case. In fact, these documents were seldom considered inadequate because they were deficient in factual detail; it was defects in form that most often led to a second inquisition being ordered, and these defects sometimes appeared only in the returns sent to the king, not in the original verdicts. The review of these cases tended, then, to focus on formal irregularities rather than substantial error or obscurity.

When a prisoner put himself on the country and the verdict was that he had killed in self-defence or by mischance, the record sent to the king might not contain the whole of the requisite formula. For example, in January 1300 Robert Miller was accused before the Justice of Chester of killing Robert Seliman. The verdict was that he had killed him in self-defence and he was remanded *ad gratiam*. But on 31 March the king wrote complaining that the record was insufficient in that it did not mention that Miller could not otherwise have escaped death and had not acted through felony or malice aforethought; so he ordered the Justice to hold another inquisition.[2] The return which accompanies this writ is a record of the original inquisition, dated 26 January, including the statement that Robert Miller could not otherwise have escaped death and

---

[1] e.g. J.I. 1/966, m. 6; *Cal. Pat. Rolls, 1301–7*, 487, 533.
[2] C. 47/93/1, no. 13.

had not acted through felony or malice aforethought.[1] It looks
as though the Justice had not carried out the order to hold a
second inquisition, but had simply amplified the record of the
first; whether what he now sent was an exact record of its
verdict is, of course, open to doubt, but probably it had contained more than the first record, so that even this formal
defect occurred only in the transcript, not the actual proceedings.

The writ for a second inquisition went out in the king's
name, but it appears to have been the Chancery officials who
detected irregularities in the wording of the return, and indeed
they might go so far as to order a new one without consulting
him. Edward I, himself a legalist when it came to regalian
rights, was probably not much concerned with this kind of
formalism in returns which, after all, were the basis for the
exercise of his discretion in matters of grace not of right. He
and his immediate entourage treated the inquisitions with less
gravity than the Chancellor might have wished. He could even
take the line that they were held mainly to satisfy public
opinion that he was not abusing his prerogative. Thus a privy
seal writ of 7 August 1300 was expressed with unnecessary and
unseemly frankness:

> Come notre foial et loial Johan de Grey nos ei fait entendant,
> qe piecea un Roger le Gardyner par mescheance ferit Johan Cuddyng
> desouz Loye en la ville de Harewold, en contee de Bedeford, dont il
> receust la mort. Nous ia soit ce qe nos creoms bien au dit Johan,
> et a ses ditz, ne mie pur ce, pur la manere qe gentz ne peussent
> dire qe nous grantissiens trop legerement pardon de mort de homme,
> voillantz sur ce estre certefiez, vous mandoms qe par serment de
> bons et de loiaux hommes du dit Conte, par les queux la verite en
> porra mieuz estre sieue et enquise, faciez diligeaument enquerre
> la verite de ceste busoigne, et la manere coment elle est alee en
> touz pointz.[2]

The intention may have been to avoid offending John de Grey,
himself a royal justice, yet the writ to the sheriff ordering an
inquisition was hardly the place for these tactful disclaimers.
The very fact that Wardrobe clerks were now drawing up writs
of this kind was a threat to the due formality in the granting
of pardons, as seen in Chancery. At the same period as this writ

[1] Ibid., no. 14. Pardon was not granted until February 1301; see *Cal. Pat.
Rolls, 1292–1301*, 569. [2] C. 145/59, no. 46.

others were sent out under the privy seal which had unfortunate results.

The writs which issued from Chancery kept to the formula which had been established soon after the middle of the century, but those which were issued in 1300 under the privy seal were in French and were not an exact translation of the Latin formulas of their Chancery prototypes. They tended to resemble the *ex parte* type of writ, used hitherto mainly for inquisitions into justifiable homicide, and so gave more than an indication that the killing was alleged to be excusable. However, they did not go into details as the *ex parte* writs often did. The chief objection to them was that they omitted the questions whether the homicide had been by felony and malice aforethought, and if so by what sort of felony and malice. They also added a rather pointless question as to the killer's reputation, borrowed it would seem from the writs which inquired into the good or ill fame of clerks who had purged themselves in church courts and were seeking restitution of their chattels.[1] The earliest of these French writs varied in form. One of the first which have been noted, dated 22 July 1300, begins simply: 'Come nous soioms requis qe nous vousissiens pardoner...' and asks only 'coment et en queu maniere' the killing occurred, and 'ou et quant, et de quele fame' the killer is 'et ad este auaunt ces houres'.[2] In the following weeks more elaborate writs for inquisitions were sent out under privy seal. Some combined elements of both the writ *de odio et atia* and that ordering an inquisition into the circumstances thus:

Come nous eoms entendu qe T. par procurement de ses misours est indite de la mort W. qui grant pietea fut tuez... nous... voillantz estre certifiez coment et en queu manere le dit W. fut tuez, et ou, et quant, et de quele fame le dit T. est et ad este auant ces houres, et sil est coupables de cele mort ou noun...,

order inquisition into the matter.[3] But at the same time others

[1] e.g. C. 145/59, no. 53; cf. no. 51.

[2] Ibid., no. 45. On the same day a similar writ was issued on behalf of Adam de Strensale. The verdict which this evoked would appear from the *Calendar* to have been that Adam had killed in self-defence, that he was of good fame, but given to drink (*Cal. Inquisitions Misc.* i, no. 2366). This final unsolicited comment must, however, be rejected. What the return actually said was that he was of good fame 'e uncore est', not 'ebriose est' (C. 145/59, no. 44).

[3] C. 145/59, no. 52 (29 August); cf. no. 56 (1 September), where there is no reference to mischance and the verdict was not guilty.

omitted any suggestion of malicious prosecution, and these came to provide the favourite formula:

Come nos eoms entendu qe R. de S. tua grant pietea sei defendant T. B. en le conte auandit. Nous ala requeste de notre foial et loial P. de V. vueillants estre certefiez coment et en queu manere le dit T. fut tue, et ou, et quant, et de quele fame le dit R. est et ad este auant ces houres, vous mandons qe par serment de bons et de loiaux hommes . . . enquiergez diligeaument la certeinte de totes ces choses.

However, a few of the French writs were longer and much closer to the Chancery ones. Some of these were issued in August.[1] The shorter formula continued in use during September,[2] but by mid October the longer formula reappears.

By now some returns to the earlier mandates were probably coming in and were revealing the fact that the questions put to the jurors did not include all the matters that were strictly considered necessary. Some verdicts, it is true, were in accordance with the traditional type. Either the commissioners had not observed that certain familiar questions were now omitted, or they decided, rightly, that the omission was inadvertent and that it would be wise to deal with all the usual points. But these verdicts were in a minority. Some of those elicited by the faulty writs seem to have got by, even though they were confined to the points raised in the writs, but most of them, to judge by the documents in C. 145/59 and 60, were judged insufficient and by 7 October Chancery was sending out writs for second inquisitions to rectify them. If the killing was allegedly by mischance, the second writ ran:

Licet compertum sit per inquisitionem quam per vos nuper fieri fecimus quod B., indictatus de morte J. interfecit ipsum J. per infortunium, quia tamen in inquisitione illa nulla fit mencio utrum idem B. interfecit ipsum J. per infortunium vel per feloniam aut maliciam excogitatam nec ne, eam insufficientem reputamus. Et ideo vobis precipimus quod per sacramentum proborum et legaliorum hominum . . . inquiratis utrum idem B. interfecit ipsum J. per infortunium vel per feloniam aut maliciam excogitatam nec ne. Et si per infortunium tunc per quod infortunium, et si per feloniam

---

[1] e.g. C. 145/59, nos. 25, 26, 27 (4), all dated 30 August 1300.
[2] The latest short French writ noticed was issued on 9 October on behalf of Adam Kalveknave (C. 144/9, no. 22; cf. *Cal. Inquisitions Misc.* i, no. 2391).

aut maliciam excogitatam, tunc per quam feloniam et quam maliciam et qualiter et quo modo . . .[1]

If the killing was said to be in self-defence the writ was similar, inquiring if it had been by felony and malice aforethought, and if so by what felony or what malice, how and in what manner.[2] If necessary, it inquired also whether the killer could otherwise have escaped death,[3] but this had generally been mentioned in the first returns.

Apparently, it was the Chancery officials who took the first steps to rectify the situation in this way. The Chancellor was not prepared to execute the king's order to issue a pardon if it was based on verdicts he considered formally incorrect without further investigation; the warrants sent to him were accompanied by other documents, including the verdict, and if he found that this omitted the vital points he would order a second inquisition, though, as has been seen, the defects of a few inquisitions escaped his notice. The Chancellor ordered second inquisitions, by the writ *Licet*, on his own authority, for such writs went out so quickly that there can have been no prior consultation with the king, and in no case has a second warrant been found. Moreover, in three cases the pardon bore the date of the warrant which preceded the writ *Licet*,[4] which indicates that the king did not issue a second one after the satisfactory verdict had reached the Chancery. The Chancellor, then, ordered the second inquisitions and on receipt of their verdicts issued the pardons on the strength of the earlier instructions, so that the whole check-up was usually made without any reference to the king.

However, at one moment the king himself, or probably the officials of the Wardrobe who were responsible for drafting the privy seal writs, also tried to cope with the situation they had created. On 5 November a privy seal writ was addressed to the sheriff and coroners of Northumberland, who had evidently held an inquisition in accordance with the faulty type of writ.

[1] C. 145/59, nos. 28 (26 November), 69 (14 October).

[2] Ibid., nos. 55 (7 October), 70 (24 October), 71 (3 November); C. 145/60, nos. 21, 24, 25.

[3] e.g. C. 145/59, no. 29. This writ begins 'Quia inquisicio quam per vos nuper fieri fecimus . . . insufficiens est pro eo quod in inquisitione illa non fit mencio utrum . . .'

[4] C. 81/22, no. 2180; C. 81/23, no. 2259; *Cal. Inquisitions Misc.* i, nos. 2407, 2395; *Cal. Pat. Rolls, 1292–1301*, 541, 563.

They were now, most unfairly, reproached because 'vous sur ce nous auez returne vos lettres patentes hors de fourme de tote manere de enqueste, et rien nous auez certifie solonc les poinz des nos lettres auantdites, dunt nous auoms graunt meruaile'.[1] Accordingly, they were told to hold another inquisition but unfortunately even now no instructions were given as to the specific points to be dealt with, so the second inquisition, held on 12 November, also neglected them.[2] Thus after all it fell to Chancery to obtain a proper return; on 24 November a writ *Licet* ordered yet another inquisition; this was held on 3 December and duly found that the slaying had not been by felony or malice aforethought.[3] The warrant for pardon was dated 18 November, and the enrolled pardon 3 December.[4] This case is significant for the victim, a woman, had been struck 'per infortunium', the blow having been aimed at her husband. The king might well have had doubts about granting pardon in this case as in that of John Tubbe,[5] but that three inquisitions were required this time was evidently not due to doubts as to the substance of the verdicts and the merits of the case, but simply to the formal disqualification of the first two.

This was the only case, during these months in the autumn of 1300, in which there is any hint that the king himself may have shown any concern for the formal correctness of the verdicts. But in 1301, when the matter had caused considerable trouble, he hesitated to pardon in one case, sending the return to the Chancellor and instructing him to examine it with the justices and others of the council at London and advise him by letter as to what he should do.[6] A couple of years later he referred a verdict to the Chancellor, partly so that he might decide if it was formally correct, though there is no reason to think it had resulted from a faulty writ.[7] By now, no doubt, Edward had become aware of what the Chancellor had been doing when he received warrants for pardon accompanied by inadequate verdicts.

All returns seem to have been scrutinized carefully at this period, not only those which resulted from the short privy seal

---

[1] C. 81/22, no. 2216ᴮ; cf. *Cal. Chancery Warrants*, 122.
[2] C. 145/59, no. 76; cf. *Cal. Inquisitions Misc.* i, no. 2401.
[3] Ibid., no. 2403; C. 145/60, no. 23.
[4] *Cal. Pat. Rolls, 1292–1301*, 558.   [5] See above, p. 123.
[6] *Cal. Chancery Warrants*, 126; cf. *Cal. Inquisitions Misc.* i, no. 1830.
[7] *Cal. Chancery Warrants*, 169. For this case see below, pp. 308–9.

writs. For example, early in July 1300, a Chancery writ had appointed commissioners to inquire whether Nicholas le Bret had killed Hamo le Bret by misadventure or feloniously and of malice aforethought.[1] They found he had killed him in self-defence and on 13 October they were instructed by a writ *Licet* to hold another inquisition, as the first verdict was less than sufficient since it did not state whether he had killed him by felony or malice aforethought or not. The more substantial discrepancy between writ and return, the reference to misadventure in the one and self-defence in the other, seems to have passed unchallenged. The Chancellor's scruples in these cases would be more impressive were it not for the facts that most of the slayers concerned had served in the Scottish war and so could claim pardon quite apart from any excuse or mitigating circumstances, and that the whole exercise failed to bring to light a single case in which pardon was not thought merited, so far as the extant returns show.[2] Despite this, for the remainder of the reign Chancery continued to fault returns and records which did not include the whole of the correct formula.[3] The desire to show up the inefficiency of the Wardrobe clerks may have contributed something to the zeal with which the Chancery officials pounced on the returns to the privy seal writs for inquisitions, but this continued insistence that even the records of courts which had remanded *ad gratiam* must satisfy their standards shows that there was more than inter-departmental rivalry behind it. Still the motive seems to have been respect for administrative technicalities rather than fear that the king was being misled into granting unmerited pardons.

[1] C. 145/59, no. 67; cf. *Cal. Chancery Warrants*, 110, *Cal. Pat. Rolls, 1291–1301*, 552, 556.

[2] In two cases the return to an inadequate French writ is not known to have led to pardon, but no writ *Licet* or second inquisition has been found in either. In one (*Cal. Inquisitions Misc.* i, no. 2366), Adam de Strensale, trying to levy a distress, was attacked by William of York armed with a long knife; Adam killed him with his sword in self-defence. In the other (ibid., nos. 1844, 2405) an axe was used in self-defence. Pardon may have been refused in both cases because of the discrepancy in weapons. This factor emerged in the original inquisitions, so that even if second ones were held they were not needed to bring it to light.

[3] e.g. C. 47/76/3, no. 61, where a writ of 16 January 1304 complains that the record of a gaol delivery was altogether insufficient as it did not specify whether a killing in self-defence was in felony and malice aforethought or not. It was over a year before the homicide, Ellis Juckyns, obtained his pardon; see *Cal. Pat. Rolls, 1301–7*, 320. Cf. C. 47/50/6, no. 104; C. 47/70/4, no. 103.

The attempts at reform, unco-ordinated as they mostly were, show that the problems of the system of pardoning were not entirely overlooked. Changes were made, or at least mooted, and they were in the right directions, aiming at greater leniency where there was reasonable excuse and greater severity where there was not. The motives of those who promoted them were not all disinterested, but there was some concern for the suffering of the innocent, some sense of responsibility towards society whose peace might be threatened by the too-ready pardoning of the guilty. The king himself showed such inconsistency and lack of purpose that it is doubtful if he ever really gave serious and sustained attention to these problems. At times he had good intentions. Some of his reforms lasted, others were soon abandoned, and the chance to achieve a general and radical improvement in the treatment of excusable slaying was lost. The policy of strictness towards culpable homicide was little, if at all, forwarded by the efforts of Chancery officials, preoccupied with the form rather than the substance of the verdicts, whilst it was all too likely to be stultified entirely by the monumental blunder of debasing pardons into bait for recruits to Edward's armies. It was peculiarly unfortunate that military needs arose just when one reform, the requirement of surrender before pardon, had made some impact, but there are signs that Edward was losing interest even in this a year before the recruitment started.[1]

[1] See above, p. 287.

XII

LAW AND ORDER

'IF a man kill another by misfortune, yet he shall forfeit his goods in strictness of law, in respect of the great favour the law hath to the life of a man, and to the end that men should use all care, diligence and circumspection in all they do, that no such hurt ensue by their actions.'[1] Thus Sir Matthew Hale tried to justify, or at least explain, the treatment of such slayers, who, in his day, not only needed pardon but suffered forfeiture of chattels even though they had not fled. Whether it could be accounted for in this way or not, it might at least be pleaded in extenuation that the system of pardoning had some utility as a deterrent against negligence and the use of excessive force in self-defence or in handling criminals. There is no means of telling whether the prospect of having to obtain pardon if they accidentally killed someone had any influence on the way in which people acted when engaged in dangerous operations. Guarding against negligence was a matter of common sense and consideration for others. Those who acted impulsively and without due attention were not very likely to be induced to show greater diligence and circumspection by fear of this contingency. But those who were acting in self-defence might possibly be affected by it, and by the possibility of not getting pardon.

A very high standard indeed was necessary in the conduct of those who were assaulted or otherwise provoked if they were to run no risk of causing death. In the absence of medical skill the most trivial injuries could prove fatal, cuts becoming septic, for example, or complications setting in after a knock on the head. A great many people died as the result of bones being broken. It is true that some people survived very grave injury, especially to the head, in what seems an astonishing way, if the survivors' accounts when they appealed their assailants can be accepted. But while some men undoubtedly showed remarkable powers of recuperation, almost any sort of injury

[1] *Pleas of the Crown*, i. 491.

was potentially fatal. However little force a man had employed in defending himself, however careful he had been not to strike at a vital spot, he might find that he had given what proved to be a mortal blow,[1] perhaps only after his attacker had lingered for months. Again, inflicting punishment or even slapping someone who had been quarrelsome or insulting could prove fatal.

The verdicts of inquisitions before special commissioners and at the eyre or gaol delivery suggest that considerable restraint was often shown under the most severe provocation. Great emphasis was placed on the slayer's attempts to escape without defending himself. In many cases, however, he appears to have taken evasive action simply because he had no weapon with which to do so until he chanced upon some serviceable implement in the course of his flight. The jurors often gave a vivid account of this, piling on suspense and the desperate sense of being trapped, imparted to them presumably by the defendant himself. If such verdicts are trustworthy a great many innocent victims of attack were saved at the last moment by finding some utensil or even a broken paling. One may believe that it was sometimes the discovery of some object with which to defend himself that made a fugitive turn at bay. Yet this does not mean that he was not acting in self-defence, and when he may have been almost at his last gasp. The jurors need not always be suspected of deliberate misrepresentation, even in this small degree, since they often had to rely very largely on the survivor's own account of the matter, eye-witnesses not having been in at the kill. But stories of this kind show only that the need to prove that the slayer had been in the most dire straits before he struck back at his assailant was very well recognized. They do not prove that these particular slayers had earlier refrained from defending themselves from fear of the legal consequences.

There are many cases which are similar so far as evasive action is concerned, but in which the man who was eventually cornered in a room or cul-de-sac, against a churchyard wall, a hedge, a dyke or river, or who tripped and fell in his head-long flight, or was overtaken by his assailant and thrown to the ground, had all the time been armed at least with a knife. His failure to draw it earlier may suggest lively anxiety not to

[1] e.g. J.I. 1/1201, m. 22.

defend himself with an edged weapon. On the other hand it can be explained by the inadequacy of a general purposes knife as a lethal weapon, especially against an adversary armed with sword, axe, or even bludgeon. The knife was hardly ever used except for in-fighting. Knife-throwing was not a common skill, and in only one or two instances was one said to have been thrown in self-defence.[1] Generally it was a case of David against Goliath, but David with no missile. Pinned at last to the ground by an assailant who was fleeter, stronger, and better armed, his only salvation might indeed lie in a lucky knife thrust in the body; but, again, a well-merited verdict of self-defence would not mean that the slayer had shown any particular restraint by not rounding on his attacker earlier with this inferior weapon. However, there are a good many cases also in which both attacker and attacked were armed with knives, yet the latter was reluctant to use his and tried to get away; similarly, both might be carrying hatchets. The assailant might be known to be a formidable opponent and prudence dictate avoiding the engagement so long as possible. Nevertheless, it seems likely that in some at least of these cases self-restraint was shown under provocation, till a pacifist policy proved of no avail.

It is only when the well-armed victim of assault tried to dodge it or fled without using his weapon that it is safe to assume that he was acting with deliberate restraint. There are at least a dozen cases in which a man armed with a sword did not, according to the jury, draw it at all, or not until he had been persistently attacked and was unable to get away. Men who carried swords were not likely to get involved in village brawls and those of inferior status and having only inferior arms were not very likely to launch unprovoked attacks on them.[2] This number is, therefore, by no means negligible. It was particularly desirable that the verdict in these cases should show that the sword had not been used except of dire necessity; otherwise the superiority of his weapon over his assailant's would have weighed heavily against the defendant. Indeed, the jurors might go so far in helping him that they made the habit of carrying a sword appear to indicate

---

[1] e.g. J.I. 1/1098, m. 84, where the slayer, not being able to reach his assailant to strike him with his knife, threw it.

[2] Although townsmen carried them.

anything but a warlike disposition. For example, according to one verdict, Richard Faucun attacked Peter Wyth, striking him on the shoulder with a stick, which broke; Peter's own stick fell from his hand and Richard picked it up and chased him with it; Peter fled as far as he could to a certain dyke which he could not cross; turning back thence he fled to the muddy bed of a stream and went in up to the knees; Richard hit him again with his stick, which also broke, and then drew his knife and struck him through the arm, meaning to kill him. Peter repeatedly begged for mercy, but Richard would not spare him, but assaulted him more and more lethally. As Peter could not cross the stream without drowning nor escape elsewhere alive without defending himself, he drew his sword and struck Richard on the head.[1] Improbable as this account is, it is so derogatory to Peter's dignity that it can hardly have been invented by him; even if it contains some exaggeration it must be accepted as basically correct. Another man who had a sword was chased four or five times round a thornbush before he struck his assailant with it, though he had earlier used it to damage the latter's weapon.[2] In other cases while it was admitted that a cornered man drew his sword, he, so it was asserted, merely held it in front of him to warn his assailant off, but the latter ran on it and was killed by his own impetus.[3] These examples show that the use of a sword even in self-defence was known to require special justification,[4] and they at least suggest genuine reluctance to use one unless it was absolutely necessary.

There are similar cases of men who were attacked while carrying hatchets and who fled as far as they could without defending themselves, only wielding this formidable implement as a last resort against a less well-armed assailant.[5] Fugitives who turned at bay and shot their pursuers were said to have done so only when cornered.[6] This explanation is less plausible in their case because of the time and elbow-room needed to insert the arrow and draw the bow; again the jurors were apt to try to make it more convincing by recounting in detail the bowman's attempts at escape. One is said, like the swordsmen,

---

[1] J.I. 3/98, m. 6ᵈ.   [2] *Cal. Inquisitions Misc.* i, no. 2296.
[3] See above, pp. 125, 263. Cf. J.I. 1/323, mm. 52, 57ᵈ.
[4] Cf. the case of Robert de Caterale, quoted above, p. 113.
[5] e.g. J.I. 1/11, m. 27; J.I. 1/280, m. 18; J.I. 1/966, m. 9; *Cal. Inquisitions Misc.* i, nos. 2305, 2321, 2406.
[6] e.g. J.I. 1/486, m. 2; J.I. 1/409, mm. 4, 6; J.I. 3/102, m. 6ᵈ.

to have held his loaded bow in front of him, his assailant having no respect for the arrow in the bow, rushing on it and disembowelling himself.[1]

Whatever scepticism may be felt towards some of these accounts, they can hardly all be dismissed as the invention of biased jurors. Men were not all hot-headed and violent. Some were only too anxious to avoid a fight and may have realized that the use of excessive force, especially with edged weapons, would get them into trouble with the law. An injury inflicted with an edged weapon made one liable to be appealed of felony and breach of the king's peace. Death inflicted in this way, even through necessity, involved the anxious business of securing pardon, and made it more difficult to put up a convincing plea of self-defence. There was a distinct possibility that it would not be accepted. To some small extent, then, the rule that these cases must be referred to the king may have served as a deterrent. And however seldom, in the stress of the moment, the victim of assault paused to calculate and weigh the distant chances of failure to get pardon against the immediate danger of being killed or gravely injured, the system must have had some effect in disseminating the idea that self-defence did not justify any degree of violence whatever. The men who served on juries inquiring into this matter must have become familiar with the general rules. Even if they did sometimes concoct a favourable tale, or over-emphasize the favourable features in a mainly accurate verdict, this in itself only serves to show that they well understood what was needed. Sustained self-restraint may not have been shown in practice as often as they made out, but its desirability was widely known and the procedure for obtaining pardon helped to publicize it. A great many men served on the inquisitions held to determine whether the circumstances justified clemency. This service in itself was educational. It familiarized the jurors, and no doubt their families and neighbours as well, with the general criteria of justifiable and excusable use of force, and may have promoted self-discipline.

But this familiarity had its own dangers. Knowledge of the procedure for obtaining pardon, and awareness of the comparative ease with which it could be obtained by those who could afford it, could detract from the deterrent effect of the

[1] J.I. 3/18, iv, m. 5.

need for it. Again, it is impossible to form any general judgement on this contingency, but some individual cases may be
quoted to show that certain people may have taken it very much
for granted that they could escape the worst consequences of
over-readiness to engage in a fight. The Arnhales, Richer and
his son John, provide a good example. In 1257 Richer obtained
pardon for killing Alan de Waghene in self-defence.[1] In 1268
John obtained pardon for killing Alan le Fevre of Skeftling, an
inquisition having found him not guilty. He produced this
pardon the same year at the eyre in Yorkshire.[2] At this eyre
both he and his father were indicted for killing Nigel, lay
brother of Meaux. It was presented that the three men had met
and quarrelled, Nigel striking Richer on the head with a staff
and felling him to the ground; whereupon John had shot
Nigel in the head. The jury found that Richer had struck
Nigel in the stomach, but that he had not died from that blow,
but from the wound on the head inflicted by John. The latter
produced the king's pardon on grounds of self-defence.[3] The
pair were evidently prone to get into a quarrel and quick off
the mark when things looked serious. They well knew the
drill for getting pardon, and perhaps became over-confident.
Richer had been given firm peace in 1258 for the first slaying,
and seems to have become a little careless, for he lost his pardon,
but his involvement in the 1268 incident may have reminded
him of it as he then obtained its renewal.[4] In the end their
bellicosity brought its own punishment, for John was himself
killed, apparently in a brawl.[5]

At the eyre of 1267 Thomas de Carleton was charged with
two homicides and produced a pardon for each, one granted in
1263, the other in 1267 at the instance of Cardinal Ottobon.[6]
But in his case there is no reason to suspect that he was
encouraged by his first pardon to act with excessive force in
future. On the first occasion a man had assaulted him on the
highway because of contentions between them and had been

[1] *Cal. Pat. Rolls, 1247–58*, 547; J.I. 1/1109, m. 27ᵈ shows that he had fled.
[2] *Cal. Pat. Rolls, 1266–72*, 203; *Cal. Inquisitions Misc.* i, no. 2174; J.I. 1/1051,
m. 31ᵈ.
[3] Ibid., m. 32; *Cal. Pat. Rolls, 1266–72*, 212.
[4] Ibid. 228.
[5] J.I. 1/1070, m. 46ᵈ. Richer appealed a number of men of slaying him, but
then denied that he had brought the appeal. At the king's suit two were found
guilty and others to have been present at the fray.
[6] J.I. 1/569ᴬ, m. 23; *Cal. Pat. Rolls, 1258–66*, 228, 254; ibid., *1266–72*, 79.

killed by Thomas's servants; he himself had been found not guilty and had made concord with the widow. On the second, an inquisition had found that the deceased 'of his own temerity ... rushed upon the sword of the said Thomas who was then constable of the city of Norwich, when the said Thomas and the commonalty of the said city were assembled for a show of arms ... so that he wounded him by mischance'.[1] Hugh Galun was pardoned in 1269 for accidentally killing Margery Tyrwit and his lands and chattels were restored.[2] In 1270 he was in prison at Newcastle upon Tyne, charged with killing Walter, son of Leolfy, and secured release on bail.[3] But few recidivists have been noticed before 1294.[4] The majority of those who secured pardon seem to have managed to avoid being involved in later homicides, whether excusable or felonious.

Pardons became so common that there was a possibility of counterfeit ones coming into circulation, and this could have meant a serious gap in the defences against crime. Forgery of the king's charters had been reduced to a fine art in some quarters. Fugitives from justice whose life was at stake had the strongest motives for wanting forged pardons, but were in a poor position to secure their fabrication. On no occasion in the thirteenth century, so far as has been discovered, was a pardon for homicide challenged as a forgery, and it is not until 1301 that there is definite evidence that a forger of letters patent of pardon was in business. It was then revealed that a pardon for robbery had been obtained from a forger of the king's seal. It is characteristic of the indulgent attitude to criminals induced by military needs that this fact emerges from a pardon, by reason of service in Scotland, to the robber in question for obtaining the forged pardon for his robbery.[5] By 1305 another forgery had come to light and some of those suspected of helping to fabricate and publish it were tried in the King's Bench.[6] Other types of evidence do not suggest that counterfeit pardons

---

[1] *Cal. Pat. Rolls, 1266–72*, 79.

[2] Ibid. 332; cf. *Cal. Inquisitions Misc.* i, no. 3142; *Close Rolls, 1268–72*, 152, 185.

[3] Ibid. 313.

[4] For one clear case see J.I. 1/238, m. 48[d]; *Cal. Pat. Rolls, 1266–72*, 526.

[5] *Cal. Chancery Warrants*, 142; at the same time he was pardoned this robbery and other felonies, including homicide. See *Cal. Pat. Rolls, 1292–1301*, 615, 618. The pardon for the forged pardon was not, apparently, issued until eight months later; ibid., *1301–7*, 40.

[6] See K.B. 27/179, m. 71[d]; K.B. 27/182, m. 68[d]; *Select Cases in the Court of King's Bench*, Selden. Soc. lviii, no. 80.

for homicide had been obtainable in the thirteenth century and went undetected. All but a tiny fraction of the pardons produced before the king's justices can be identified on the patent or close rolls. Several of those which have not been found enrolled were almost certainly genuine as there is evidence for an inquisition having been appointed to inquire into the circumstances; in some cases the favourable verdict of such an inquisition has itself survived. Since some genuine grants are known not to have been enrolled, and since some of the patent rolls are wanting, it is not surprising that thirty pardons recorded on the eyre rolls remain unaccounted for, spread over the period from 1216 to 1307, and it is only in the last few years that forgery need be suspected.

There were other ways in which the system of pardoning might prove detrimental to the preservation of law and order. Its very severity might deter people from doing all they could to check breaches of the peace. The fact that killing in defence of someone else might need pardon may have made some men reluctant to come to the assistance of the hard-pressed victim of assault or the losing side in a scrap which had developed into mortal combat. It is very clear that onlookers were present on many occasions, whereas intervention was somewhat infrequent. No doubt it was a very good thing to limit the fight, discouraging large numbers from entering it on either side. But many spectators seem to have preferred to hold the ring for a prolonged bout between two unequally armed combatants, or to have followed the chase at a discreet distance when all that was necessary was to overpower a single assailant. Sometimes one of them handed a weapon to the losing party, or he seized one from them. They might even encourage him to greater efforts. One man was said to have killed in self-defence when the onlookers called out to him that he would be killed if he did not strike back.[1] But failure to participate more actively was likely to be based on short-term considerations; people did not wish to be hurt or to be involved in a quarrel. The severity of the law towards those who helped the victims of attack may have been a further deterrent, but probably only as part of the general background of rather unreasoning respect for order, not a conscious calculation of the possible legal consequences of intervention. This severity might, however,

[1] C. 47/86/31, no. 817.

hamper police work, which in thirteenth-century England was very largely dependent on the local inhabitants. Some strictness was necessary in controlling the activities of communal groups, still more those of their individual members. There was a real risk, for example, that the duty of watch and ward might be used as cover for an attack upon a personal enemy. A greater risk was that the members would lose their heads in a crisis, acting precipitately and with excessive violence. The liability of these people to be arrested and charged with slaying while discharging their duty as citizens was a perhaps unavoidable curb on efficiency. That permanent officials, especially gaolers, also needed pardon—and sometimes did not get it—was far more important. In their case the system was much to be commended.

On balance, the pardoning of homicide in self-defence and by mischance is likely to have promoted respect for the king's peace to a far greater extent than it discouraged attempts to maintain it. Unjust as it was to individuals, the system was of some educational value. Its very uncertainties encouraged a keen sense of responsibility and the exercise of self-control; the smallest degree of negligence, the uncontrollable reflex action when violence erupted might perhaps count against the unintentional slayer. Precautionary pardons and the flight of *meticulosi* show that many people were over-anxious, believing that the courts were even stricter than they really were. Yet this very anxiety could lead indirectly to innocent people eventually being driven to crime. Because of ignorance, panic, or mistrust of their neighbours' feelings towards them and so of the outcome of an inquisition, many excusable homicides fled, and many of the fugitives were outlawed. One would expect to find that most of them took to the forests and if they survived swelled the ranks of brigands, or tramped the countryside stealing what they could to keep alive. But the evidence by no means suggests that they were all reduced to such straits. Some, including of course many but not all of those who abjured the realm, went abroad. Some took sanctuary in places like Beverley and Ripon, where they could live in safety, even if confined within an area of a few square miles. Some did not go far from home; some may have become mendicant tramps, begging their way through the land.[1] But many seem

[1] Cf. J.I. 1/210, m. 38, where an outlaw was said to have returned to his

simply to have migrated to a part of the country where they were not likely to be recognized and to have found work there. They were not, after all, habitual criminals, and seem to have shrunk from turning now to a career of crime. This emerges from the pardons obtained by men who fought in the wars from 1294 on. At first these pardons listed the crimes committed by individual warriors, sometimes two or three. Later, general pardons were granted to cover all their crimes committed before a certain date, no doubt because these tended to be too many to enumerate in a small space, and some might have slipped the grantees' memory. But it is noticeable that service pardons for homicide granted on grounds of accident or self-defence scarcely ever included subsequent crimes as well. Yet there would have been no danger in admitting to these, since they would have been pardoned just as readily. Similarly, men who are known from other sources to have killed excusably do not appear to have obtained pardons covering crimes in general. As they now had an excellent opportunity to get pardon for any crimes committed since their flight for homicide and took no advantage of it, there is every reason to suppose that they had committed none, having conducted themselves as law-abiding citizens in the meantime.

If their harsh treatment turned few excusable homicides into professional criminals, there was a possibility that it would not seem harsh enough to the victim's relatives and provoke violence on their part. The pardoning of excusable homicide, if in fact it tended to deprive the relatives of the satisfaction of seeing capital punishment inflicted, might be expected to have caused some reaction. The evidence has suggested that in many cases there was ultimately no conflict between the king's view of excuse or extenuating circumstances and theirs. The pardon would seldom be granted until the circumstances had been ascertained on the oath of local jurors, and their verdict seems often to have satisfied the relatives also that the killing had not been intentional, in which event they seem to have had

district as a beggar. He had been outlawed apparently for felonious homicide. He was arrested and hanged. A fugitive placed in exigent at the eyre in 1279, where he was presented for accidental killing, promptly secured pardon on the strength of the record of the presentment. It seems clear that he had been in touch with his friends, or that they had gone ahead and obtained pardon for him, knowing that they could get it to him. See J.I. 1/371, m. 14; C. 47/64/8, no. 238; *Cal. Pat. Rolls, 1272–81*, 337. Cf. above, p. 140.

no wish to see the killer punished. Even if they were unable to extort compensation from him they would be content to let the matter rest. A few instances have been found of unwillingness by the appellor to accede to the position of the jury and the king, but in most of these he or she conformed eventually, yielding to the pressure of public opinion and official disapproval or even unofficial menaces. Since the continuation of the appeal after pardon tended to be frowned upon, the next of kin might be tempted to have recourse to more direct action. It is worth inquiring, therefore, whether vendettas tended to be carried on against pardoned killers.

There is a case in point on the Staffordshire eyre roll of 1272.[1] The jurors reported that Philip le Simple had killed Richard le Franceys. Later it was testified that Ralph le Franceys, Richard's brother, and Philip had been together in the forest and a dispute had arisen between them over Richard's death, with the result that Ralph had killed Philip. An inquisition had been held into the death of Richard le Franceys and had found that Philip le Simple killed him in self-defence. On the strength of this Philip had been pardoned.[2] Thus Ralph took vengeance on him despite the verdict of self-defence and the king's pardon. Yet the wording of the account on the eyre roll suggests that this vengeance was not premeditated, but occurred at a casual encounter. There is no hint that Ralph had secretly lured Philip into the forest. Two other men may have been present, though they were acquitted of complicity. It is explicitly stated in the all too familiar terms, *mota contentione*, that the quarrel blew up, not that it was deliberately provoked. A chance meeting between the original victim's brother and the man who had slain him, ostensibly in self-defence, would obviously give an opportunity for the former to show his discontent at the verdict and precipitate a fight, even though he had not, in cold blood, contemplated taking vengeance in preference to embarking on the frustrating business of appeal.

There is another possible example of vengeance being taken on a slayer who had just obtained pardon. William Gerberge son of Avelina de la Grove was pardoned on 12 May 1301 on condition of going to fight in Scotland, for the death of John

---

[1] J.I. 1/802, m. 43.
[2] *Cal. Pat. Rolls, 1266–72*, 304. Cf. above, p. 41.

son of Petronilla de Drayton.[1] William Pecche was pardoned
for the same death.[2] In 1302 Agnes widow of William Gerberge
appealed Stephen de Goseford, Robert and William de Drayton,
Petronilla de Drayton, and many others of her husband's
death, and it seems most likely that he was the Gerberge who
had been pardoned for killing Petronilla's son. An inquisition
found that the slaying had been in self-defence and Stephen
and others were pardoned.[3] This verdict, if true, rules out any
notion that it had been in revenge for the death of John son
of Petronilla. These particular slayings probably occurred in
faction fights. The pardons for John's may have annoyed the
Drayton–Goseford faction. There can be little doubt that they
acted with excessive force, and the memory of it was not absent
from their minds at the time of the fight.[4] On the other hand
it is unlikely that they deliberately sought out William in order
to be avenged for it. The motive of revenge was latent, not
dominant. Thus long-standing enmity between two families
sometimes erupted into a fatal fight and was perhaps exacer-
bated rather than alleviated by a pardon. A subsequent fatal
encounter, whilst not a case of direct vengeance on the pardoned
slayer, may be attributable in part, but only in small part, to
the pardon. Something of this kind may also have followed the
pardoning in 1292 of Alexander son of John de Pylkington for
the death of Adam de Wode, for Adam son of Alexander de
Pylkynton was slain in 1300 and eight of the Wode family
were appealed, together with others, of the slaying.[5]

---

[1] Ibid., *1292–1301*, 591; cf. ibid., *1301–7*, 10.

[2] Ibid. 25, 37.

[3] Ibid. 91, 135; cf. K.B. 27/172, m. 62. The Draytons seem to have preferred
punishment by judicial action to violence as the method of revenge, for Sir William
Gerberge was indicted, probably at their instigation, for procuring John's death.
He was convicted, but claimed benefit of clergy. Pecche had been put in exigent
by justices of oyer and terminer (C. 47/70/4, no. 110) and outlawed, but by the
time of Sir William's trial had been pardoned; accordingly no verdict should have
been taken against the latter on the charge of procuring the slaying. In 1305 he
took action in the King's Bench and recovered his chattels and former status, since
the court agreed that he could not lawfully be tried, until the principal, Pecche, was
proved guilty and outlawed, and while his outlawry stood, but his pardon had
completely extinguished it. See K.B. 27/182, m. 89.

[4] It is significant that their pardon was granted at the instance not only of the
Queen but also at that of the good men of Yarmouth, who had every reason to
try to put a stop to anything like a feud between these local families if one was in
fact going on.

[5] *Cal. Pat. Rolls, 1281–92*, 503; ibid., *1292–1301*, 550. Cf. J.I. 1/409, m. 28;
C. 144/27, no. 20. They got the appeal transferred *coram rege*, maliciously, so it

Pardoning does not, then, seem to have provoked the victims' kin into wreaking vengeance on the pardoned slayer himself or a member of his family at all often, but there are cases of vengeance on a slayer who had not yet been pardoned, and one at least of these may be attributed to the expectation that he would be. This shocking case was the 'execution' at Newcastle of a man who had killed in self-defence. There had been a quarrel in which Peter of Ypre and another man wounded Richard Hagge, who in self-defence struck back at Peter with a knife, so that he died at once. Richard himself was gravely wounded, but made his way to a house. John Jakes, a cousin of Peter's, came and raised the hue and fetched the coroners and bailiffs. Together they dragged Richard from the house to the place where the corpse lay and the coroners demanded of Richard whether he had killed him. He replied that if Peter was dead he had killed him, but in self-defence. The coroners willed to have him executed 'sub colore iudicii vindicando mortem', and ordered that Richard should be beheaded. John Jakes held his head by twisting a rod through his hair while forcing an unknown pauper to behead him. John was tried at the eyre and pleaded that he did this to avenge his cousin's death and to kill a felon. But since the jury confirmed that Richard had killed Peter in self-defence, and had not committed or confessed to any felony, John was sentenced to be hanged.[1] The border counties, of course, retained the custom of beheading felons taken in the act if sufficient evidence of guilt was forthcoming when officials arrived on the scene, and were more tenacious of family feuds. Action such as this would seem less atrocious here than in the south, yet even so the jurors' disapproval is apparent.[2]

Elsewhere, relatives seem seldom to have taken the law into their own hands, even against felonious slayers. There are a few instances of what looks like vengeance taken in hot blood immediately or soon after a slaying, but with nothing to suggest that the chances of a successful appeal had been calculated and found wanting.[3] On the whole it seems that extra-judicial

was said, in order to delay matters, and failing to appear there were put in exigent (K.B. 27/161, m. 50). See above, p. 271 for the death of Adam de Wode.

[1] J.I. 1/653, m. 26[d].

[2] Cf. above, p. 127 for a rather similar case at the same eyre of 1293.

[3] e.g. J.I. 1/1043, m. 12[d] (above, p. 135, n. 3). For another possible example see above, p. 259.

vengeance was most improbable and when it did occur was the result of hot-headedness, not of calculation and dissatisfaction with the treatment of appeals and the granting of pardons.

In making all homicides, except those who had slain justifiably, answerable to the king and depriving the victims' relatives of any legally enforceable right to compensation the penal system may slightly have over-reached itself. The procedure, which was meant to ensure that all criminals were brought to book, tended to drive some previously law-abiding persons towards a criminal career. But, so far as can be judged, this tendency did not have very serious results at this period. The chief threat to law and order lay in the king's failure to be severe enough towards homicides who deserved punishment. His indiscriminate use of his prerogative may have provoked a few people to take the law into their own hands and 'execute' the slayer of a kinsman. But a far more sinister possibility was that it might tend to derogate from the deterrent force of the penal law. To estimate the potential effect of pardoning on the prospects of punishment the number of pardons for felonious homicides should be set against the total committed, but this is unknown. However, it has been seen that until 1294 the number of pardons for demonstrably felonious homicide was small, and it is certain that only a minute fraction of the thousands of murders committed was pardoned. The tendency was to moderate the practice of pardoning felonious homicide and some efforts were made to check the abuse of inquisitions into claims that slayings had been accidental or in self-defence. The system was by no means a general invitation to commit murder; the hope of doing so with impunity was confined to certain classes and even so might prove illusory. In 1293 efforts were still going on, though losing impetus a little, to contain the unfortunate effects of the prerogative; Edward was ready for a certain degree of self-limitation; his justices were taking a strict line. Things were moving, however fitfully and slowly, in the right direction so far as the preservation of law and order was concerned. In 1294 they were abruptly put into reverse.

The first general proclamation that recruits for Edward's wars would receive pardon as soon as they found mainpernors to guarantee that they would serve and later stand to right was made on 12 June 1294 in order to raise troops for Gascony.[1] The outbreak in Wales soon after meant that some of the recruits had to be switched there from Gascony, and new pardons might now require service first in Wales and subsequently in Gascony.[2] Not all who enlisted at this time did so in response to the proclamation, which empowered Brabazon and Bereford to enrol criminals in this way. Some offenders were obtaining pardons as they were about to serve under individual lords as early as July. Guy de Shenefeld was pardoned a fine of 100s. for a forest offence at the instance of Hugh de Veer as he was about to go to Gascony with Hugh in the king's service; Guy's pledges were also pardoned the various sums in which they had been amerced for not producing him before the forest justices on the strength of his serving in this fashion.[3] In September Edward pardoned a more serious matter, the harbouring of a felon, as the harbourer was going to serve in Gascony under the earl of Lincoln.[4] Soon homicides were also enlisting, either because service offered them a livelihood or because they were becoming aware that it might turn out to be a means of securing pardon.[5] Thus pardons were granted retrospectively for service already done or being done, as well as for future service, and various lords and commanders recruited criminals sometimes knowing them to be such, as well as the specially appointed commissioners.

The next commission to recruit prisoners and outlaws was for the Scottish war in 1296.[6] In 1297–8 large numbers who had accompanied the king to Flanders were pardoned in view of their service there.[7] Evidently it was now widely known by the criminal classes that enlistment was an avenue to pardon and they were prepared to fight first in the expectation of attaining it. Edward acknowledged their claims when, in the late summer of 1298, a proclamation was made 'by the king at Carlisle that all persons coming to his presence by Martinmas to ask pardon for trespasses against the peace, who had done service in his wars or any of them before that date, should have pardon for homicides, robberies etc'.[8] Those who claimed

---

[1] See above, p. 248.
[2] e.g. *Cal. Pat. Rolls, 1292–1301*, 129. This particular recruit was later allowed off service altogether.   [3] Ibid. 80; cf. 82.   [4] Ibid. 87.
[5] Ibid. 96, 226.   [6] Ibid. 186.
[7] Ibid. 313, 323, 325, 327, 329–34, 336, 347. Warrants for pardons for others survive; see above, p. 219.   [8] Ibid. 393.

pardon in response to this proved a considerable number.[1] In 1300 many serving soldiers were pardoned, including, as has been seen, a number who had killed excusably. At the same time pardons were being granted on condition of future service, sometimes at the grantee's own cost, not at the king's wages as earlier.[2] Very large numbers were thus recruited for service in Scotland, especially for his campaign there in 1303. His luring men out of sanctuary in this way has already been mentioned.[3] He also took advantage of the fact that the liberty of the bishopric of Durham was in his hands, having been seized in accordance with the judgement given in Parliament, to recruit a prisoner in the gaol of Durham castle.[4] Other prisoners were enlisted, some in the Marshalsea,[5] but throughout most of the criminal recruits seem to have been at large.[6] The number of prisoners awaiting trial at any moment was far too small to account for more than a tiny proportion of the hosts of recruits. But they did not have to wait for a commissioner to visit their prisons. Friends were allowed to produce the mainpernors and get the commissioners' certificates when pardon was obtained for future service. They could act also for fugitives so that such grantees did not have to run the risk of coming before the commissioners in person, a risk which might put some of them off, although the proclamation promised them safe-conduct.

Recruitment soon became quite indiscriminate, but at first some attempt was made to exclude certain classes of criminal. There was an interesting limitation in the proclamation of 1294. The recruits were required to present the commissioners' certificates that they had found mainpernors to the Chancellor, who was then to give them letters patent of pardon of the king's suit for their crimes and also for outlawry if it had been promulgated against them *at his suit*.[7] This would imply that those who had been appealed and thereupon exacted and outlawed in the county court were not to be pardoned in this way. The

---

[1] Ibid., especially 358–74. [2] Ibid. 357. [3] Above, p. 248.
[4] *Cal. Pat. Rolls, 1301–7*, 137. Edward also appropriated the bishop's unique palatine authority to pardon homicide, pardoning men who had been appealed by an approver for homicide within the liberty and who had served in Scotland; see ibid. 148, 153, 165. [5] Ibid. 146.
[6] This was pointed out by F. M. Powicke, *The Thirteenth Century*, 648, for earlier campaigns.
[7] *Rôles Gascons*, iii, no. 3038. This section is omitted in some versions.

right of the victim or his next of kin to bring about outlawry was thus respected, in spite of the pressure of man-shortage in the war. However, by this date the proportion of criminals outlawed at the suit of an appellor had declined, and so the restriction, if in fact it was observed, can have affected comparatively few cases,[1] and Edward I's later proclamations and the resulting pardons no longer purported to affect only those outlawed at the king's suit.

When the king commissioned certain officers to enlist outlaws and others for a prospective campaign there was also some slight limitation of the type of criminals who could be raised in the requirement that they find mainprise both for their military service and for standing to right in court on their return. Usually six mainpernors were produced, and often they came from the same district or county, so that they would appear to have been reputable, established people, not fellow vagrants with perhaps an equally murky background; some were described as landholders of the county; one recruit had four knights and two squires as his mainpernors.[2] Their willingness to act as pledges suggests that the men they sponsored were not known to be criminals of the most vicious and hardened kind. But a great many pardons were soon being granted in the course of or after military service; once it became known that by serving in the wars subsequent pardon could be relied upon, with the condition of standing to right, indeed, but with no awkward demands for pledges, even this obstacle to the most heinous and

---

[1] It seems that some attention was actually paid to it. On the surviving certificates (chiefly in C. 202/D/1 and 2) that mainpernors have been found, most of the outlaws pardoned for homicide are simply described as such with no indication who had brought about their outlawry, but a fair number of them are said to have been indicted or *rettati* and outlawed, and these phrases imply that they had not been outlawed on appeal; they may have been used deliberately to indicate that the pardons complied with the strict requirement of the proclamation. Similarly, many of the pardons enrolled on the Gascon rolls state that the recruit had been *rettatus* and outlawed at the suit of the king; these statements, too, were presumably inserted in deference to it. For example, *Rôles Gascons*, iii, no. 3038, where the grantee is stated to have been outlawed 'ad sectam nostram pro morte Ranulphi Floce . . . unde rettatus est'. A similar rule applied to the recruitment of prisoners, and thus the Constable of Bristol Castle was ordered to accept mainpernors for three thieves, who were reported to be suitable, able-bodied recruits, provided that they had not been appealed of crimes, including homicide, by anyone other than an approver (ibid., no. 3399). Cf. K.B. 27/168, m. 24, where a prisoner was to be released to fight in Scotland since the court had testified that the appeals against him had been withdrawn, and K.B. 27/173, m. 40ᵈ.

[2] John Fitz Roger of Doversdale, C. 202/D/1.

habitual criminals profiting by enlistment was removed. There is nothing to suggest that the king would refuse to pardon a soldier on the grounds that his record was too frightful for clemency, or that the commissioners would turn down volunteers on these grounds. Service pardons often referred to assorted crimes committed by the grantees, or even to any felonies in the most general terms. Practically speaking, the opportunity to secure pardon by enlistment was unlimited.

It might be supposed that only able-bodied male criminals could benefit by the policy of recruitment. But this was not so, although there were very few exceptions. The king, of course, would require only fit men to be accepted for active service, but it was not necessary for the man who secured pardon for prospective service to serve in person. A few homicides were allowed to send substitutes; all they had to do themselves was to pay the substitutes' wages. Thus Henry le Filz Neel was pardoned for the death of two men and all his other trespasses on finding mainprise for the service of William le Filz Neel 'with a barded horse, as befits a man at arms, at the expense of the said Henry during the king's pleasure'.[1] Even an able-bodied homicide might be given the option of serving in person or by deputy. It might not prove easy to find anyone willing to take his place, and one at least who had been given this option in the end performed the service himself.[2] As in the case of the Filz Neels, a member of the slayer's family was the most likely substitute; one of the earliest volunteers for Gascony in 1294 was the son of Robert de Corbrigg, who was pardoned for homicide by reason of his son's offer to serve.[3] No case has been found of a member of her family enlisting in order to secure pardon for a woman alone, but one man secured pardon for himself and his wife by serving in Scotland.[4] Although few substitutes were sent to fight for him, there is no reason to think that Edward felt any hesitation in sanctioning such arrangements. His concern was to raise troops. The prospect of contributing to his military effort was of no value whatever as a

---

[1] *Cal. Pat. Rolls, 1301–7*, 140; cf. 430.

[2] Ibid. 139, 174.

[3] Ibid., *1292–1301*, 96. It appears from J.I. 1/653, m. 20ᵈ that his son had been involved in a squabble with the victim's son and it was this which led to Robert's beating up the victim so that he died three weeks later. His son may have volunteered because he felt that he had occasioned Robert's action.

[4] *Cal. Pat. Rolls, 1292–1301*, 360.

deterrent to men of some means if it involved no more than finding a proxy and paying his wages for a few months, but this aspect of the matter does not seem to have worried the king. Risking one's own life in combat was a more serious consideration, but most of the men concerned were all too used to danger and violence and recruitment went on apace.

It is not possible to estimate the total of troops raised by this means. The number of pardons for them was so large that they were sometimes entered on separate patent rolls. Some of these appear not to have survived. Most of the pardons on condition of service in Gascony were entered on the Gascon rolls, parts of which are lost or illegible.[1] Surviving writs containing the names of mainpernors for service show that a good many of the resulting pardons were not entered on the extant rolls. Some warrants sent to Chancery also have no corresponding enrolled pardons. The total of service pardons was undoubtedly higher than the numbers which can now be traced, even if these writs and warrants are included as evidence that pardons were granted. Among the enrolled pardons themselves are some granted at the instance of one or other of the well-known commanders in the wars; some of them refer to service, others do not, though it is likely that these were also granted in return for it.[2] However, as this is doubtful they cannot be counted in. The enrolment of one pardon below another was often abbreviated to 'consimiles litteras habet . . .', and it is not always clear whether this means that the second was also in return for service. Any figure even for the recorded service pardons granted by Edward I must therefore be approximate. The total for homicide in England[3] is around 1,700, nearly all of which were granted within a decade. In addition there were many pardons for other felonies. The grand total must

---

[1] This dispersal gave rise to some difficulty when it was desired to check an entry. In the next reign it was necessary to obtain a certificate from a former Keeper of the Wardrobe that Richard Grim had been pardoned by Edward I. See *Reg. Drokensford*, Somerset Record Soc. i. 164. The only other evidence for this seems to be the list of his mainpernors in C. 202/D/2.

[2] Some letters backing their recruits' applications for pardon or for a writ to the sheriff to proclaim it in the county court have survived. For example, S.C. 1/27, nos. 59, 179; S.C. 1/28, nos. 51, 52.

[3] An attempt has been made to exclude pardons for homicides in Gascony, Ireland, and the Channel Islands, but it is not always easy to distinguish them. Pardons to men who had committed homicide in both Ireland and England have been included.

have been well over 2,000. Pardoning on this scale could not fail to have deplorable results.

The figures alone show that enlistment was a welcome alternative to life-long outlawry. Some recruits may have found soldiering a congenial profession. John Hert, for example, was pardoned on testimony by John Segrave that 'he did good service in the last two wars of Scotland, and is going with him to Scotland again on the king's service',[1] and Michael Duraunt in 1303 'in consideration of his service in Flanders and Scotland, as testified to by William Martyn and Gilbert de Knovill, and of his having found manucaption before the king to go to Gascony at the king's wages during pleasure'.[2] For many men living precariously under aliases the army may have offered a refuge and a welcome means of livelihood. But for those who responded to Edward's proclamations with the sole object of earning pardon the period of service was likely to be quite short. A few months might see the end of the campaign; service in Flanders turned out to be neither very active nor prolonged. As it came to be widely known that pardon could be won in the wars homicides tended to enlist promptly. One pardon, obtained for service already being performed in Scotland, was granted within eight weeks of the actual slaying.[3] The whole business of serving in Scotland, getting pardon, and presenting it to the king's justices to proclaim firm peace might be completed within eighteen months of it.[4] Moreover, the period of service might be curtailed. It was possible to get demobilized early on grounds of physical unfitness. Michael Duraunt, for example, was permitted to return home from Gascony 'ob corporis sui debilitate', and was provided, in addition to his pardon, with letters under the privy seal testifying this and ordering that no one should molest or injure or interfere with him in any way on this account.[5] But this was his third campaign, and he at least had already done staunch service.

---

[1] *Cal. Pat. Rolls, 1301–7*, 48.

[2] Ibid. 105. A pardon for the same death had been enrolled for him in 1297 (C. 67/26, m. 4) but presumably had not reached him.

[3] That for William Moury, dated 28 June 1303, *Cal. Pat. Rolls, 1301–7*, 146; cf. J.I. 1/1108, m. 20, where the slaying was said to have occurred on 5 May 1303.

[4] Isaac del Hill killed a man after 20 November 1303; he performed his service and obtained pardon, dated 21 August 1304, producing it before justices of oyer and terminer appointed in April 1305. The same dates apply in the case of William de Bereford, except that his pardon was dated 22 August. See J.I. 1/1108, mm. 1ᵈ, 18; *Cal. Pat. Rolls, 1301–7*, 251, 252.   [5] J.I. 1/117, m. 74; cf. m. 43ᵈ.

At the end of a campaign hundreds of former outlaws and fugitives and some former prisoners would be let loose on the country. No detailed casualty lists for foot-soldiers are available to indicate to what extent enemy action had thinned their ranks. A great many charters of pardon were sealed in Chancery but remained there unclaimed until the order was given to destroy them.[1] Pointing this out, Maxwell-Lyte remarked: 'We may fairly assume that the beneficiaries died, or got killed, before being able to apply for delivery of them.'[2] But a few pardons escaped destruction and those which survive show that death was not the sole reason for failure to collect them. Indeed, in some cases it is likely that administrative muddle was responsible for the charters remaining in Chancery. The clerks there were capable of duplicating entries on the patent and other rolls. This may sometimes have implied equal confusion over the engrossed pardons. Thus it may be that Thomas de Chalkeleye, whose pardon, dated at Carlisle 15 September 1298, was twice entered on the patent roll, in fact walked off with a charter in his pocket, despite the fact that sealed letters patent for him of this date are still filed in the Public Record Office.[3] Several other surviving grantees are known to have failed to claim their charters.[4] William de Blaby seems to have served in two quite separate campaigns to obtain pardon, in Flanders for the first, unclaimed pardon, and in Scotland for the second, which it may be supposed he actually received;[5] both grants related to homicides, robberies, and larcenies, but the second added receiving felons; by the time

---

[1] See above, p. 58.

[2] *The Great Seal, 399.*

[3] *Cal. Pat. Rolls, 1292–1301*, 361, 363; C. 202/H/5, no. 17. Nicholas le Charetter's pardon was also entered twice on the patent roll (*Cal. Pat. Rolls, 1301–7*, 158, 164) and this evident confusion may have extended to the duplication of letters patent for him, so that his surviving pardon too does not necessarily imply his failure to claim and get possession of its duplicate (C. 202/H/5, no. 45). There is a slit for the tag but no sign that it was actually sealed. He was not a volunteer but a prisoner in Somerton gaol. See J.I. 3/104, m. 7.

[4] e.g. a pardon dated 2 May 1299 to Adam Freland de Bedehunte for theft and other trespasses in Middlesex and for his abjuration of the realm was unclaimed (C. 202/H/5, no. 22. It was enrolled; see *Cal. Pat. Rolls, 1292–1301*, 411). On 16 October 1301 pardon was granted, by reason of his service in Scotland, to Adam Frilond of Bedefonte, Middlesex, for robberies and other trespasses against the peace (ibid. 618). There can be little doubt that this was the same man, and that having failed to collect the pardon drawn up and sealed for him in 1299, he had had to resort to enlistment to secure that of 1301.

[5] C. 202/H/5, no. 1 (1298); *Cal. Pat. Rolls, 1292–1301*, 618 (1301).

he was able to collect his charter it seems that he had remembered this addition to his criminal record and so realized he needed a still more comprehensive one. Simon de Sandon certainly seems to have abandoned his engrossed pardon dated 14 September 1298 as inadequate to cover all his crimes.[1] It was for services overseas and related only to the death of William Dun. Within a month a second was enrolled for service in Flanders and Scotland which included prison-breaking also.[2]

There could also be a quite different reason for a service pardon never being claimed. The case of Ralph le Ercedekne of Cornwall raises an interesting possibility. Since Thomas le Ercedekne, evidently a relative, and Ralph de Arundell had become sureties for his proceeding to Scotland with a barded horse and staying there at his own cost, for the duration of the war, Edward I on 13 February 1303 pardoned him the death of Guy de Pultimor and also robberies, receiving felons, and other trespasses against the peace. The pardon is enrolled, and an unsealed letter patent, perhaps only a draft, survives.[3] It is evident that Ralph did not obtain another sealed charter, for in September he was in prison at Exeter, where he was indicted before justices of gaol delivery for the death of Guy and was found guilty, but as he claimed benefit of clergy was handed over to the bishop.[4] Plenty of clerks fought for Edward, and his career of crime does not suggest that Ralph was likely to shrink from becoming a soldier because of his clerkly character. But it looks as though his mainpernors had been too optimistic in thinking they had persuaded him to seek safety through enlisting, and that he defaulted without applying for the pardon drawn up through their good offices. Similar unwillingness to take advantage of a pardon on condition of serving in Flanders may explain why Robert le Vavasour's sealed pardon for robbery, etc., was never claimed.[5]

Yet the chances of coming through a campaign unscathed seem to have been good. A great many veterans appeared

---

[1] C. 202/H/5, no. 5; *Cal. Pat. Rolls, 1292–1301*, 359.

[2] Ibid. 370 (6 October).

[3] *Cal. Pat. Rolls, 1301–7*, 115; C. 202/H/5, no. 37; he was charged with killing another man as well, and there was some objection to his purgation in 1306; see *Reg. Winchelsey*, Canterbury and York Soc. 777.

[4] J.I. 3/104, m. 17.

[5] C. 202/H/5, no. 6. This may also account for the survival of a sealed pardon for John Russel, who had taken sanctuary at Beverley after slaying a man and was recruited by the king's commissioner along with nine others in 1303. His pardon

before the justices in these closing years of the reign armed with their charters and, where necessary, certificates of service.[1] There were so many of them that the entries concerning their appearance, the production and proclamation of their pardons were often grouped on the plea rolls almost as though they had stepped forward and been dealt with in squads. Nor had all of those who failed to appear punctually expiated their crimes by falling in battle. The general eyre had been discontinued during the wars, and the next judicial visitation, in many counties, took the form of a commission of oyer and terminer or trailbaston. The scope of these commissions seems not to have been sufficiently publicized,[2] and since many people did not realize that pardons were expected to be produced before them there were defaulters, a considerable number of whom seem to have thought they could safely wait for an eyre. They were disillusioned, sometimes by being arrested on the order of the justices if the jurors had chanced to mention that they had been pardoned, sometimes, more brutally, by learning that they had been placed in exigent and outlawed. In the latter event second pardons were needed, and the number of such pardons obtained shows that there were still more survivors to add to the long lists of those who came before the justices at

(C. 202/H/5, no. 35) is unusual in that a summary of it is written on the tag for the seal, which may suggest that it was one of a batch intended to be sent off together; and indeed all the ten pardons were enrolled together (*Cal. Pat. Rolls, 1301-7*, 142). It may have been the intention, therefore, to send the whole batch to the commissioner, and Russel's may have been omitted because by the time the others were dispatched he was known to have changed his mind. He cannot have served and been killed, unless he was unlucky enough to become a casualty within days of joining the army, for this company was required to present itself for service on 31 May, while the pardons were dated 27 May and should have been ready for dispatch very shortly after. It is probable, therefore, that on second thoughts he preferred the security, however confined, of Beverley, to the perils of war. If so, he probably miscalculated his chances, for at least seven of the other nine survived; six produced their pardons before justices of oyer and terminer in 1305 (J.I. 1/1108, mm. 11^d, 12^d, 14, 15, 19), and the seventh, Robert le Spenser, was put in exigent by them, but later obtained pardon for his outlawry (ibid., m. 19, *Cal. Pat. Rolls, 1301-7*, 500).

[1] It was useless to produce a pardon granted on condition of future service unless it was supported by evidence that the service had been duly performed. This evidence generally took the form of a certificate from the commanding officer, but failing this application could be made to the Wardrobe, which could certify the length of time spent in the army (cf. J.I. 1/884, m. 2^d); pay rolls might provide the information in many cases, but not, presumably, for the recruits who undertook to fight at their own expense.

[2] Prisoners remanded *ad gratiam* at gaol deliveries were not required to appear before them, and this may have aggravated the confusion about their powers.

the first opportunity. It is clear that a very large proportion of the recruits came back and were given firm peace with no guarantee that they would not later revert to a lawless way of life. Many of them, however, seem to have been anxious to remain henceforth in the king's peace and made protracted efforts to secure its proclamation for them.[1]

The service pardon's proviso of standing to right was enforced as strictly as was possible. Defaulters who obtained a second pardon were now normally required to surrender to gaol by a fixed date. Thus care was taken to ensure that there would be an opportunity for appellors to come forward, and since the vast majority of the pardons were granted for felonious slaying it might have been expected that many appeals for this would in fact be made. It was desirable that they should be, and that many should succeed, for this was now the only way to secure that well-deserved punishment was inflicted, and that the availability of pardon did not encourage future crime. But appellors did not come forward. One reason for this may have been that they, like many of the slayers, did not realize that the pardons would be proclaimed by the justices of oyer and terminer or trailbaston, but thought they would have to wait until the next general eyre. Another reason was that appeals were so very unlikely to succeed. The Statute of Gloucester may have given them some encouragement, and at this period a few appeals, mostly brought by the victims' widows, did lead to the conviction and execution of homicides, but the chances of success were small, even in a straightforward first appeal. Second appeals, after pardon, had come to be frowned upon.

---

[1] e.g. Simon, son of Ralph de Stowe obtained a service pardon in 1304 for the death of Alice Lucas, for felonies, etc., breaking the prison of Storteford, and any consequent outlawry (*Cal. Pat. Rolls, 1301–7*, 244). He paid the full fee to the Hanaper in 1305 (E. 101/211/1, m. 6), but failed to appear not only before justices of oyer and terminer in Cambridgeshire, but also before the king in the hustings of London, and was outlawed. In 1307 he was pardoned the outlawry on condition of surrendering to Newgate (*Cal. Pat. Rolls, 1301–7*, 513). A criminal like Simon was faced with something of a problem if he was to appear punctually with his pardon before the king or his justices in all the counties in which he had committed crimes. Cf. Miles Pichard who was pardoned in May 1301 'by reason of his long services, for the death of John Payn and for divers robberies' in Suffolk and Surrey, of which he was appealed by one approver and a robbery in Yorkshire of which he was appealed by another (*Cal. Pat. Rolls, 1292–1301*, 591); was pardoned for the death of William le Couk in 1302; got a pardon for homicides, etc., in 1304 and apparently paid for this one (E. 101/211/4, m. 5) but, failing to appear before justices of oyer and terminer in Oxfordshire, was outlawed, and was pardoned his outlawry in March 1307 (*Cal. Pat. Rolls, 1301–7*, 9, 245, 510).

The authorities' earlier rough handling of the rights of appellors had created a situation which could not be rectified so easily. Thus, just when these rights could have been most useful to society at large potential appellors had no mind to assert them. The proviso of standing to right on appeal was useless as a deterrent. Indeed, as will be seen in a moment, initial appeals themselves came to be still further discouraged by the fear that the returned outlaws would take vengeance on those who had brought about their outlawry.

The rights of the injured party and of the family did nothing now to redress the damage done to the penal system by this great spate of unwarranted pardons. However, the insistence on standing to right and the outlawing of those who failed to do so again show that Edward I was attempting to limit the damage as far as possible. He did not relax the rules for the pardoned recruits. They still had to go through the final stages of the usual procedure before they were received into his firm peace. Their chattels were judged forfeit for flight from justice. Only in remitting the Chancery fees in some individual cases did he show special favour to them. It was not his intention to let what he regarded as a temporary expedient affect the normal severity of the treatment of homicides, including excusable slayers. Even while relying on this expedient he showed little inclination to be more generous with pardons to civilians, though his resolution flagged a little, especially when his new queen, the French Margaret, interceded for them. His efforts proved futile. The damage done by the resort to recruitment by the promise of pardon could not be contained. Any able-bodied male criminal, amateur or professional, could now count on pardon if he chose to earn it in this way. In proclaiming his readiness to pardon criminals who undertook to enlist, Edward had professed to be prompted by sympathy not only with the fugitives from justice but also with the lawful people who were suffering from their depredations. His hope, so he claimed, was to promote the 'quiet of the people of our realm' by drawing off those who were afflicting them, but he did not explain just what was to become of the survivors at the end of the campaign and after they had appeared in court with their pardons; it might be hoped that they would adopt an honest mode of life, but there was no way of guaranteeing this. So far as outlaws who had become professional brigands were

concerned there would be some relief in their temporary
removal to foreign parts, and if on their return the survivors
reverted to this profession the situation might have become
no worse than it had been originally, but for the fact that they
would have had a good opportunity to get together and orga-
nize themselves in larger gangs. But when prisoners awaiting
trial were recruited their pardons could only increase the number
of undesirables let loose on the country. Edward's action was a
military expedient; it could not fail to have disastrous social
results. So long as the wars and this method of recruitment
continued able-bodied criminals had little to fear from the
courts and the dangers of campaigning were in no way comparable to capital punishment as a deterrent. The expedient
was damaging to punishment regarded either as prevention
or deterrent. Moreover, although Edward did not envisage
granting service pardons as a regular practice his handling
of Scottish affairs had inaugurated a long period of endemic
warfare with which the Hundred Years War was soon to be
associated. The temporary recourse was to become an addiction.
The veterans who returned after a campaign found difficulty
in settling down to civilian life; the fact that they included
many former outlaws and hardened criminals did not make
matters any easier.

One immediate danger was their seeking to revenge themselves on those who had brought charges against them. Complaint was made already in 1309, in the 'Stamford Articles',
cl. 9, that those indicted of larceny, robbery, homicide, and
other felonies 'trop legierement purchacent la Chartre le Roi
de sa pees', and that those who had indicted them were consequently terrified to remain in their districts. The reply was
striking: in future pardon for felony was not to be granted
except in the cases in which it had been customary in times
past , i.e. 'si hom tue autre par mesaventure, ou soy defendant,
ou en deverie, & ce soit trove par Record de Justices'.[1] If this
ruling gave undeserved credit to earlier kings for confining
pardons so strictly it was still more optimistic as to the possibility of future restraint. The Ordinances of 1311, however,
continued the attempt to impose it; cl. 28 ordained:

That no felon nor fugitive be from henceforth protected or
defended from any manner of felony, by the king's charter of his

[1] *Rot. Parl.* i. 444[b].

peace ... unless in a case where the King can give grace according to his oath, and that by process of law and the custom of the realm, and if any charter be from henceforth granted and made in any other manner to anyone, it shall avail nothing, and be holden for none.

In insisting on the record of a court and due process of law the Articles and the Ordinances were evidently harking back to the Statute of Gloucester of 1278, and reading more into it than it had actually contained. In 1328, when the king's youth and situation again facilitated criticism of the prerogative, the Statute of Northampton, cap. 2, made another attempt at limiting pardons to excusable homicide. It was also, apparently, laid down that they should be granted only in Parliament, for the Statute of Westminster of 1330, cap. 13, on the complaint that pardons for robbery and homicide had been granted out of Parliament, 'whereby such misdoers have been the more bold to offend', enacted that the earlier statute be fully observed on this point. Edward III, in fact, continued to pardon felons who served in his wars, but he did make some attempt to cope with the problems raised by their discharge.

In 1333 he wrote to his sheriffs as follows:

Because the king has been victorious in the late war against the Scots he has pardoned those who were in his service in the said war, the suit of the king's peace which belongs to him, for felonies ... and ... outlawries ...; and now the king has learned from the complaint of many that certain of those whom the king so pardoned are rendered more bold thereby to perpetrate evil deeds, and that they propose to band themselves together and avenge themselves on the king's lieges who informed against them previously, arrested, or otherwise molested them;

accordingly he ordered the sheriffs to cause them to

find sufficient mainpernors to answer for them that they will not harm the king's lieges aforesaid who have accused them, etc. and that they will conduct themselves well and faithfully to the king and his people, and also to cause proclamation to be made that none of the said men so pardoned, under pain of losing the said pardon and forfeiture of life, members and goods, shall make illicit gatherings in fairs, markets, or other public or private places, and shall use no armed force or do anything to disturb the peace; and to take all those who are found doing the contrary and keep them safely in prison, so that they may not be delivered thence without the king's special order.[1]

Another abuse was observed in this year. Men who had not actually served were obtaining pardons by pretending to have done so. The king ordered the justices *coram rege* to check that the service really had been performed before allowing the pardons.[2]

Despite the statutes, it was not only the service pardons which were now going to great numbers of undeserving and undesirable characters. The practice of pardoning non-combatant felons could not easily be kept within the old bounds when so many of their fellows were finding clemency. Another scandal was that many pardons were couched in general terms, referring to all felonies and trespasses and outlawries, instead of particularizing the individual crimes of which the grantees acknowledged they were suspect. In 1336, the statute of 1328, cap. 2, was re-enacted again, with the addition of the requirement that those who already had charters of pardon should come before the sheriffs and coroners and find mainpernors for their future good conduct.[3] In 1340 it was asserted that the statutes had been disregarded and it was accordingly decreed that any charter henceforth granted against the statutes should be null.[4] As it was thought that the king was acting irresponsibly when petitioned and yielded to improper pressures or was deceived, in 1353 Parliament attacked the people at whose instance improper pardons were conceded.[5] In 1369 Edward III actually revoked a pardon granted at the instance of William of Windsor when he learned that the slaying had been felonious 'ex malicia precogitata et ab antiquo maliciose machinata'.[6] But in 1390, in response to a Commons

---

[1] *Cal. Close Rolls, 1333–7*, 129. Cf. ibid. 173–4, where the sheriff of Yorkshire was instructed to inquire concerning such people and arrest them.

[2] Ibid. 158. In 1336 a pardon was queried in the King's Bench on the grounds that the grantee had not served, as it asserted, in Scotland, but had remained in England throughout. A jury confirmed this. The grantee was remanded to prison while the court considered his case further and died there. See K.B. 27/304, part ii, m. 21^d.

[3] 10 Ed. III, caps, 2 and 3.

[4] 14 Ed. III, stat. 1, cap. 15. A jury would now be sworn in to certify the justices of the validity of the excuse given in the pardon. See, e.g., J.I. 3/141^A, m. 20; cf. *Some Sessions of the Peace in Lincolnshire*, ed. R. Sillem, Lincoln Record Soc. xxx. 117.

[5] 27 Ed. III, stat. 1, cap. 2.

[6] K.B. 27/435, part ii, m. 7; *Cal. Pat. Rolls, 1367–70*, 292.

complaint, Richard II insisted on preserving his liberty and regality in the matter of pardoning treason, murder, and rape, conceding only that a charter should be disallowed in court 'pur murdre, mort de homme occys par agayt assaut, ou malice purpense, tresoun, ou rape de femme' unless the crime was specified in it, and laying down rules of procedure to ensure that no such pardon was issued without his authorization.[1]

Thus in the fourteenth century pardons for homicide and other felonies were believed to be having a seriously detrimental effect on law and order. Criminals were confident that they could secure them on the next campaign, and some of the campaigns in France especially afforded them a chance to live in very much the manner to which they were accustomed. A system which had been meant to allow penalties in general to be as severe as possible was perverted into the very large-scale commutation of punishment into military service, and even apart from the service pardons the king's clemency was thought to be too indiscriminate. The excessive number of pardons may have been only a minor factor amongst many others, but it undoubtedly contributed something to the prevalent lawlessness.

[1] 13 Ric. II, stat. 2, cap. 1.

XIII

CONCLUSION

THE system of pardoning the king's suit for homicide which has been examined here was not altogether irrational and vicious. It had not come into being entirely without design, and the motives which produced it were far from disreputable. It was intended to contribute, if only in a small way, to the campaign against violence which was seen to entail much more effective punishments for all culpable homicide than the old wites. If this campaign was to succeed the legal right to wergild had to be eliminated, yet the relatives of the slain were not all ready to forgo it voluntarily, and others besides the slayers may have thought punishment in life and limb too severe in some circumstances, such as killing in an honourable fight. The king's discretion to pardon was seen from the earliest times as a useful means of avoiding inequity and of reconciling public opinion to legislation extending such punishment.

Unfortunately, while there was no reason to extend it to excusable slaying, it would have been imprudent to allow wergild still to be obtainable in court even for this. Homicides of this type had to be subjected to very careful investigation before their character could be recognized. Remission by the king himself of his suit on the recommendation of his justices must have seemed the natural method of dealing with them, since not only was it the surest way of preventing laxity, but it also purported to conserve the claims of the victims' relatives to some sort of agreed compensation. It had the further advantage of recognizing and, indeed, emphasizing their right to prosecute a capital charge if they saw the killing in a more serious light. Thus royal pardons, as they developed in the twelfth century, had their place in a deliberate remoulding of the penal system. They were calculated to facilitate this remoulding. The claims of excusable slayers and also of bereaved relatives were subordinated, but not lost to sight, in the pursuit of a rational and constructive policy.

In practice things did not work out well. It is impossible to tell how far the business of pardoning went at this time. It may be that many excusable slayings were concealed from the king's justices. Even in the thirteenth century local sympathies were generally with the slayers, but concealment was becoming difficult. The business of obtaining pardon was, however, becoming more organized, if not particularly efficient. Those who sought pardon could find people in the king's service who could give advice and even approach the king on their behalf. If the excusable slayer appeared in court there was every likelihood that the justices would refer his case to the king, at first actually drawing his attention to it themselves, later generally remanding *ad gratiam* so that the prisoner had to obtain a writ of *certiorari* from him asking for their record. This greater formality added to the cost, and as the century went on fees piled up, so that by the next even the proclamation of peace at the eyre entailed considerable expenditure. Many slayers were too poor to meet these costs; still less could they afford the additional sums which would have to be paid for a special inquisition and the grant of pardon before trial. Many who deserved pardon fled without hope of obtaining it, either because the cost was prohibitive, or because they were too ignorant or mistrustful to rely on its being recommended and granted. Nor was the prospect of detention pending trial one to be faced with confidence. Several excusable slayers, children as well as adults, are known to have died in prison. Thus the need for pardon imposed great hardship, both mental, physical, and pecuniary, on large numbers of excusable slayers, and indirectly even on justifiable slayers and people who had not slain anyone at all, the *meticulosi*.

In some respects, however, the system was not, perhaps, quite as harsh as it might have been. In practice the treatment of individual adults who were acknowledged by all concerned to have killed with good excuse and who took the appropriate action was neither arbitrary nor invariably severe. Their claim to remission of the king's suit was a powerful one: it was ceded almost automatically, once the excuse was established, though not as a rule entirely free of charge. It certainly did not depend on the king's whim. It was described as a matter of grace, yet if it was the king's prerogative it was also his duty to grant it, and he himself could recognize that there was a category of homicides which 'we are accustomed to pardon'.[1] Unhappily, however, this category was not properly defined. It was inevitable that the intervention of his grace would retard definition and in fact he himself seems to have found it hard to make up his mind on some points or sustain a policy once it had been tentatively adopted. His justices were in doubt, or if some had definite views others took an opposing line, on a number of cases of not uncommon types. Their perplexity and disagreement were enough to give the impression that the treatment of all excusable homicides was unpredictable and so popular distrust and misunderstanding were not allayed for a long time. The notion that the king himself would react in an arbitrary way even when the justices recommended mercy, must have augmented the fears of these killers, and fear was contagious, spreading to those who were in no way responsible for deaths and causing many to flee in panic. Gradually some of the misunderstanding was dissipated, and some slayers felt more confident that their excuses would be accepted and were ready enough to stand trial, but still this confidence was far from universal in the time of Edward I, when many excusable slayers judged it safer to rely on military service to win his pardon.

Some rules emerged, although the justices tended to be less severe to certain types of slaying than consistency would have required. Thus, while there was some discrimination among accidental deaths, some of which were held to require pardon while others were not, it did not rest on very logical principles. Some emphasis was placed on the absence of intent but not enough on negligence. Riders and drivers were generally exonerated from all blame for fatal accidents, regardless of the possibility that they had been negligent in using faulty harness, leaving their beasts uncontrolled, or riding mounts they were incapable of controlling. Pardon was not thought necessary as a rule for this fairly common type of fatality, but it was needed for most other accidental homicides, apart, generally, from those which resulted from falling or dropping axes and so forth from trees. The criteria for accidental homicide were not, then, altogether overstrict; indeed, sometimes as in cases of transferred intent and the killing of strangers in chance encounters, they were too lenient. Yet the justices might well

[1] See above, p. 220.

have ventured to acquit much more often than they did, or they could safely have been authorized to do so. If some accidental killings needed no pardon there could have been no valid objection to acquittal for others in which there was no guilty intention and no negligence was proved. Edward I acknowledged this momentarily and many of the justices revealed their own view on the matter when they invited fugitives to return without stipulating that they should then obtain pardon.

The criteria for killing in self-defence as set forth in the writs ordering inquisitions were too stringent, but juries generally contrived to produce verdicts which complied with them well enough to be accepted by justices and commissioners, or got round them by finding mischance instead of self-defence. But not all juries wished to see the slayers pardoned and some were found guilty in court despite earlier favourable verdicts. Probably, the sentences were generally just, but in a few cases, at least, there is reason to prefer the earlier findings and to believe that men who merited pardon were executed.

The continuing severity of the treatment of excusable slayers would seem more tolerable if it were found to have redounded to the advantage of the victims' kinsmen. The pardons emphasized that slayers were answerable to them as well as to the king, stipulating that the grantees should make peace with them or stand to right on appeal. The second stipulation was of little value to them, although it might prove not altogether useless in counteracting the effects of excessive use of the prerogative. It was only the proviso of making peace with the family which could render the pardons themselves positively beneficial to the latter. If effective in preserving some sort of reparation the pardons would indeed have fulfilled a most useful function, especially as the only other approved way of securing it was the not very widely used licensed concord. This function would have gone far to balance the interests of the bereaved relatives and the claims of the slayers not to be treated as criminally liable. In practice the proviso turned out to be singularly ineffective. Not only did it give no legal right to damages, but soon it failed even to give countenance to a moral right to some agreed reparation. In the middle of the thirteenth century it was dropped altogether. Although settlements continued to be made out of court the evidence suggests that they were seldom reached in cases of excusable slaying. They may, indeed, have been most frequent when people who had no need of pardon were blackmailed by threats of appeal. No doubt, the original problem of preserving some form of legal redress was a formidable one, and that of establishing adequate penalties for crimes of violence was more urgent and remained more pressing. Yet the failure to find a better way of reconciling the two aims left a regrettable gap.

The stipulation of standing to right on appeal remained in the pardons, with very few and insignificant exceptions. But potential appellors seldom availed themselves of the opportunity it gave them to secure the punishment of pardoned killers. They appear to have been very properly reluctant to prosecute those who had been shown to have killed excusably. Although the system would have permitted this and did not avert capital punishment if the appeal succeeded, the chances of such an appeal being made were small and of its succeeding negligible. There was no risk to speak of that genuinely excusable slayers would be executed on appeal after pardon. But the relatives' reluctance to exploit their right extended also to cases of felonious killing and thus they did little to counteract the effects of the granting of pardon to those who did not merit it. However, a few, more persevering and perhaps more vindictive than most, did renew their appeals and a certain number of pardoned murderers were outlawed as a result; one or two may even have been hanged. To this very limited extent the formula of the pardons mitigated the dangers which their too liberal grant held for the suppression of violent crime.

Its suppression had been and should have continued to be the overriding aim. This alone could justify the treatment both of excusable slayers and the victims' relations, which involved real hardship, anxiety, and loss. Once this treatment could reasonably have been held necessary to the success of the policy of intensifying punishment. But by the thirteenth century this policy had so far succeeded that the original function of pardons of the king's suit was largely outdated. Wergild had completely disappeared. Capital punishment was the established penalty for serious crimes. There was no need now to fear that appellors would minimize their charges in the hopes of securing the award of compensation. However, it might be argued that the retention of a class of excusable

homicide—that which required though it deserved pardon—
was still of some use in suppressing violence. Thorough investigation of these cases was still necessary if intentional
slayers were not to escape punishment by passing off their
crimes as accidents or acts of self-defence. Moreover, the need
for pardon supplied something of a deterrent against resorting
to excessive force in genuine self-defence and in arresting and
guarding felons. So far as fatal accidents were concerned it is
unlikely that it did much to remind people of the duty to take
every possible care when engaged in potentially dangerous
occupations, but it may have had some small influence here,
despite the failure of justices and commissioners to go very
deeply into the problem of negligence when verdicts were
taken in these cases. While it was not very convincing to argue
that killing by mischance must still be treated as requiring
pardon if felonious slaying was to be dealt with effectively,
there was a rather better case for treating slaying in self-
defence in this way, but it was much less cogent than it had
been originally. The time had come when the class of excusable
homicide could safely be greatly curtailed though not entirely
eliminated. It would certainly not have been prudent to
encourage the acquittal of slayers who were mentally deranged;
some guarantee of their safe-keeping was necessary and in this
respect greater strictness in the conditions of pardon was
desirable. Some types of slaying which passed as self-defence
or mischance were culpable in some degree and for these the
system of pardoning was appropriate, though again it might
well have been administered with more discrimination.
Clemency in these cases should not have been a routine matter,
as it tended to be.

There was still some room for the king's discretion in determining the fate of slayers whose deeds lay near the borderline
of felony. Just because the only punishment now was capital
there was need for some means of averting its too summary
infliction in these cases. Appeal against sentence and subsequent pardon or commutation of the penalty were hardly
practicable given the state of the king's prisons and the uncertainty of communications. Unless gradations of punishment
were to be reintroduced, with the probable weakening of its
deterrent force, pardon before trial was, perhaps, as good a
way as any to deal with unpremeditated slaying in brawls

or under extreme provocation, slaying in what may be described as extenuating circumstances but without full justification or excuse. It even allowed the king to impose some act of expiation, such as going on crusade, if he saw fit. Finally, there were the individual, unforeseeable cases in which capital punishment would have been obviously inequitable or would have outraged public sentiment. For these the prerogative of mercy would always be proper. Confined within these limits, then, the king's pardons would have been a useful, indeed, in the conditions of the time, a necessary adjunct to the penal system.

These considerations help to explain why the continued use of the prerogative in so many cases was tolerated. Some of them, at least, influenced men's attitude to it. Contemporaries did not see the problem of pardoning as a whole or, so far as is known, attempt to draw up a balance sheet to discover whether the social gains warranted the social damage inflicted by it. Nevertheless, some did appreciate various aspects of the problem and suggested modifications of the system, especially restricting its application in very much this way. Nor was the plea for reform entirely impracticable and hopeless. The kings, both Henry III and Edward I, were not rigidly opposed to it. If they had no mind to abdicate any part of their prerogative they were at least aware, when other preoccupations did not make them oblivious, of their responsibility to use it to promote equity and yet in a manner consistent with their paramount role as guardians of law and order. Indeed, Henry III's anxiety to establish the truth of the excuses put forward by fugitives or prisoners who sought pardon before trial led to such frequent use of inquisitions that the pardoning of homicides without a verdict of justification or excuse came to be somewhat disreputable, unacceptable to Bracton and no doubt to others. It had been politic for Henry I and perhaps Henry II to show themselves ready to relax the policy of punishment in life or limb on occasion. The most appropriate occasion would be slaying in fair and open fight. Less appropriate but politically expedient would be some incidents in which powerful lords and their men were involved, cases in which resort to arms in defence of honour and property was still not widely regarded as a heinous crime. But the sooner this sort of behaviour could be regularly treated as felony the better. Henry III and Edward I were conscious of this. However, they were not unaffected by the same social and political motives, though probably they, especially Henry III, were more affected by religious and sentimental ones. Thus the king's grace could still be secured by influence, bought or earned. Yet, he was evidently somewhat inclined to restrict it to excusable homicide, and those who could not hope for a favourable verdict in court or at a special inquisition may have come to feel less and less hopeful of buying pardon. They needed an influential backer for their petitions, but only the most influential patrons may now have felt happy about seeking pardon for them merely on the strength of the king's friendship. Support was often obtained in demonstrable cases of self-defence, but it is particularly significant to find how often it was sought when the slaying might not quite have qualified as such, slaying *mota contentione*. In other words it was desirable when there were extenuating circumstances, and this fact points to some strictness in sifting excuses. The prominence of pardons *ad instantiam* does not imply that the king yielded very frequently to improper pressure. He did so sometimes, but it is doubtful whether, between 1226 and 1294, he did so often enough to do any great damage. Some felons were pardoned; a certain number of undesirable characters were let loose on the country. But such characters could not count on getting pardon. Many of those who secured it did so only after years of exile. Thus it is unlikely that their pardons tempted many others into a career of crime. Bracton was rightly apprehensive of this, but the evidence does not suggest that the abuse of the prerogative gave much encouragement to felons when he wrote. Probably the people most influenced by the notion that pardon would be forthcoming were the servants of great lords who were apt to act arrogantly and too forcibly, but even they might find themselves let down by their masters.

Except when subjected to some sort of pressure the king was, then, exercising self-restraint, concentrating his pardons more and more in the area of excusable homicide and slaying in extenuating circumstances, and as a rule he required to be convinced that the excuse was genuine and the circumstances truthfully related. He relied greatly on verdicts given at special inquisitions or before his own justices. This reliance was inevitably liable to abuse. Some verdicts were biased, others flagrantly corrupt. However, the great majority of those which can be checked by other evidence appear to have been correct in their main findings. There was a tendency to strain the truth, embroidering points favourable to the slayer, playing down those which might not be at all helpful. But the motive for doing this seems often to have been to make sure that the killer who deserved pardon secured it, rather than to pass off wilful killing as excusable. The formulas of the writs ordering inquisitions were rather too strict and invited this kind of distortion in the interests of equity. Thus verdicts which were not unimpeachable on certain points seem often to have been honest enough in finding there had been an excuse. There was some tendency to emphasize the features in an incident which were known to impress the authorities, but, so far as can be judged, the verdicts had not yet degenerated into common form. Some felonious slayers got pardon by means of perjured inquisitions, but there is little reason to think that the pardons which followed verdicts were misplaced often enough to undermine respect for law and order. The king himself was not indifferent to the danger here if his pardon could be obtained too easily. There are even some slight indications that Edward I took a rather more severe view of some types of homicide than did his justices. One or two cases of transferred intent and of slaying under compulsion were referred to him but are not known to have secured his pardon. However, if there was any plan to impose a stricter definition of excusable homicide it does not seem to have been pursued with any determination, or even communicated to the justices.

Certain further reforms were, however, attempted and some were successful. They tended to limit still more both the need for pardon and the murderer's hope of obtaining it. Although there was no open acknowledgement that felons ought not to receive it at all, measures were adopted at least to prevent their getting it by subterfuge. The special inquisitions themselves became the target for attack, being objectionable because the jurors were suspected of corruption or bias and because they were held on behalf of slayers who were not actually standing trial. The enactment of 1278 seems not to have had the king's good will, and certainly he soon ceased to pay any regard to it. But one element in this reform, the requirement that the slayers' excuses should not be investigated while they were still at large, did commend itself to him, and, although he did not go so far as to make this a general rule, he did himself later sometimes require surrender before inquisition or at least before his provisional pardon took effect. The statute indicates some mistrust of verdicts given at special inquisitions on behalf of prisoners as well as absentees. But after this attempt to eliminate special inquisitions into excuses as grounds for pardon had failed, little was done to improve the standard of the verdicts. Such checks as were made were likely to concentrate on matters of form rather than substance. Chancery officials were zealous in maintaining adhesion to formulas, some of which they seem originally to have borrowed unintelligently from writs of a different type and which set the jurors unnecessary problems. Returns which did not deal with all the points contained in the writs for inquisitions might be queried, but this was not done very often until the Wardrobe clerks with the king in Scotland or on the border in 1300 drafted French writs for this purpose to be dispatched under privy seal. These writs omitted questions which were considered essential in Chancery and another writ had to be issued there to order second inquisitions to supplement the first insufficient returns. Such vigilance was rarely shown when the initial returns were obscure on points of fact, or even found accident when the writs had asked about self-defence, or vice versa. A show of strictness may have been beneficial, but it would have been of greater value had it been directed at the factual statements. The king himself, or his counsellors, did occasionally demand more information, but no sustained effort was made to test the reliability of the verdicts.

Attempts to limit the need for pardon were more successful than attempts to exclude wilful homicide from its scope. The category of excusable slaying was narrowed. The justices, apparently with the king's approval or at least acquiescence, took to acquitting very young child killers instead of remanding them *ad gratiam*. This very important reform was vitiated to some extent by uncertainty for some years as to the age at which acquittal should be admitted, and then by its being fixed too low. Nevertheless, it was of real value and revealed concern for a small group of innocent persons who were quite powerless to voice their own grievance. Edward I's own gesture of remitting his suit against accidental slayers once for all and allowing them to be acquitted was unproductive of any lasting reform.

The spark of enlightenment shown by his order to the justices in Yorkshire in 1279 flickered out and the order fell into oblivion. Perhaps he had acted impulsively without considering the implications and possible repercussions of what could have been a notable reform. When one aspect of the problem was tackled by legislation, apparently inspired by some of the magnates, he showed himself all too much alive to possible abuses of a lenient policy. Converting into justifiable homicide the killing of offenders in forests and chaces who resisted arrest was a sensible move, but Parliament made no attempt to follow it up by alleviating the situation of other excusable slayers. These two reforms were valuable as far as they went, but unhappily they affected a comparatively tiny proportion of such slayers.

The failure of more radical reform was not due to total lack of perception or indifference to their plight. Both kings, or some of their advisers, and many of the justices recognized the need for some reform. Inertia and resistance to radical change no doubt contributed to the continued sacrifice of innocent individuals to the vague hope of preventing unintended leniency to guilty ones. Ironically, it was the intentional leniency to the latter which was really beyond control. The kings would not resign their prerogative. It was not altogether unassailable, as fourteenth-century legislation was to show, but even these later attempts to limit its abuse had little effect. Before 1294 it was not abused gravely enough to provoke any very powerful attack. Edward appeared to yield to some proposals for reform but soon ignored even statutory restrictions. He was in a strong enough position to pervert it at his pleasure when the moment came.

Whatever may be said in mitigation, it cannot be claimed that the system of pardoning down to 1294 was a sound one. It had had considerable merits, so far as its functions can be inferred, in the twelfth century, but in some respects it had proved inadequate to achieve the useful purposes it was intended to serve, or had outlived such usefulness as it had had. The prerogative was still needful in the case of homicidal maniacs, the occasional cases of condemnation in error being discovered in time—among which popular sentiment included surviving execution—and slaying in extenuating circumstances. But both incontrovertibly excusable and felonious homicide might by now have been excluded from it. Some of those in positions of authority were uneasily aware of this and made some improvements; more might have followed, but they did not face up squarely to the task of radical reform in time. The opportunity for this was lost in the first two decades of Edward's reign. Within a few years of his abortive decision to exclude accidental slaying a new attitude to excusable homicide was beginning to manifest itself; some people were arguing that to seek pardon was an admission of guilt. The act of pardoning was being taken to supply its own justification, just as a little later the indiscriminate forfeiture of chattels would be taken to imply that some offence, albeit slight, had been committed. Once views of this sort gained acceptance the inequity to excusable slayers was masked and there was little hope of their need of pardon being dispensed with. So far as felonious homicide was concerned the tendency down to 1294 was towards greater caution and restraint in the exercise of the prerogative of mercy, but it had not gone far enough to render pardon unobtainable through influence. Edward I's expedient of that year, repeated throughout the rest of his reign and for long afterwards, shattered any hope of its being extended to them more sparingly, let alone withheld altogether.

APPENDIX I

The Writ de Odio et Atia

THE writ *de odio et atia* impinged so often on the history of inquisitions into excusable slaying that it has to be considered in any examination of them. Conversely, its connections with these inquisitions complicate its own history, which is tangled enough even without them, and have led to several misunderstandings. It is desirable, therefore, to append some study of this writ and the resulting inquisitions, dealing especially with those aspects which overlap with the other type of inquisition or may provide instructive comparisons with it.

McKechnie held that the writ was invented by Henry II,[1] but the evidence for this view is inconclusive. In 1178 an appellor was convicted of bringing an appeal 'pro odio' and his amercement is recorded on the pipe roll.[2] The entry does not state how his conviction was secured, but it is very probable that it was indeed by the verdict of a jury sworn in to answer whether the appeal was made by hatred. In 1185 the pipe roll records a payment of 2 marks 'pro inquirenda veritate de appellatione'.[3] This time the use of an inquisition is more clearly indicated, though it is not stated to have been concerning hatred or malice.[4] Still, taking the two entries together, the inference that the inquisition *de odio et atia* or something very like it was held under Henry II is likely enough. Certainly it was familiar under Richard I, for in 1191 William Wischard owed 10 marks for having an inquisition of the neighbourhood as to whether he was appealed of malice or not.[5] In 1195[6] and 1196[7] there are two similar entries on the pipe rolls, the second mentioning *invidia et atia*, and there are some half-dozen cases on the few surviving plea rolls of this reign in which the defendant denies the charge and asks for the verdict of a jury whether the appeal is malicious. While some defendants offered as much as 10

---

[1] *Magna Carta*, 2nd ed. 361.   [2] p. 104.   [3] p. 89.
[4] But it should be noticed that inquiries of this kind were apparently sometimes made without statements being taken on oath. An inquisition was ordered in an appeal of robbery in 1212 and one appellee gave six palfreys for it and 40s. 'per sic quod per sacramentum fiat'. Another gave 20s. 'pro habenda inquisicione per sacramentum'. See *Curia Regis Rolls*, vi. 237; cf. 210 and 270 which records that the appeal was withdrawn.   [5] *Pipe Rolls, 3–4 Ric. I*, 110.
[6] Ibid., *7 Ric. I*, 214–15.   [7] *Chancellor's Roll, 8 Ric. I*, 186.

marks one such proffer was for a jury drawn from two counties.[1] In other cases the sums proffered were smaller: £5, 5 marks, or even only £1 or 1 mark.[2]

From the start the evidence suggests a bewildering variety in the uses of the inquisition. Its ostensible purpose was to establish the fact that an accusation was not made bona fide. But there could be different grounds for challenging it in this way. The accused might hope to establish that no felony had been committed, or, if one had been, that it was not he who perpetrated it. The first aim is of some significance at this period. While every appeal, not only appeals of homicide, had to allege that the crime had been committed *nequiter*, in felony, the action *quare vi et armis* was not yet available as a means of obtaining damages for trespass. If the injured parties wished to obtain a hearing in the king's court rather than some local one, there was, for a time, little they could do save bring an appeal there of felony and breach of the king's peace. Thus there was a standing temptation to magnify the seriousness of assaults which had not amounted to mayhem and to allege robbery in cases, for example, of levying distress or eviction from tenements. The inquisition *de odio et atia* afforded a means of investigating the circumstances of incidents which were the subject of exaggerated appeals. For example, when, in 1198 William of Evesham appealed Ralph Giffard of breaking into his lord's house and wounding him in the thigh with a lance, Ralph offered 20s. for a writ *de odio et atia*. This was one of a number of appeals and counter-appeals and Ralph could hardly hope it would be found that he had taken no part in the affair. But he probably hoped that the appeal would be quashed because it exaggerated William's injuries, since 'duo milites qui debuerunt videre locum plagi dixerunt quod nullum plagum nec locum plagi invenerunt'.[3] In several early cases an appeal was brought against a landlord or his men who had taken possession of a tenement when the lease ran out, or in the course of some dispute over tenure. While the appellor alleged felonious assault and, perhaps, robbery, the appellee might obtain an inquisition *de odio et atia* hoping that it would find that he had not resorted to criminal violence but had exercised no more force than was necessary to assert his right.[4] In most of these cases,

---

[1] *Pipe Rolls, 3–4 Ric. I*, 110; *Rot. Curiae Regis*, i. 57–8.

[2] *Chancellor's Roll, 8 Ric. I*, 186; *Pipe Roll, 7 Ric. I*, 214; *Curia Regis Rolls*, i. 39.

[3] Ibid. 63; cf. 39.

[4] e.g. Henry Engaine's appeal of robbery and assault against Robert de Walterville which dragged on from 1203 to 1208. At first Robert obtained, for 1 mark, an inquisition *de odio et atia*, but this apparently found that the appeal was not malicious and it was allowed to continue (*Select Pleas of the Crown*, Selden Soc. i, nos. 91, 92, 93; *Curia Regis Rolls*, iii. 62, 202, 299; iv. 37, 56–7, 83, 183, 226). In 1207 when the judicial combat was at last imminent he gave 10 marks for another

if the decision is recorded, the appeal was quashed. A verdict that the appeal was malicious, and often that the appellee was not guilty, meant that he was deemed to have committed no felony. Thus the king would not be concerned to see that he was punished as a felon. None the less, the appellee might have inflicted some damage on the appellor and the latter's claim to compensation was not always disregarded. Indeed, the appellee's object in obtaining the writ was probably sometimes simply to get licence for a concord with the appellor. Already in the time of Richard I, two men owed over 30 shillings each for licence to make concord in appeals made 'per atiam'.[1] Concord might be the aim when the appellor's good faith was challenged on different grounds. For example, the appellee might not have been directly involved in the crime or the appellor himself might not be entitled to appeal.[2]

There is no evidence that the writ *de odio et atia* was used under John to get a capital charge reduced to the dimensions of excusable homicide and so bring about a settlement. An accidental death was investigated in 1206 and the three appellees seem, indeed, to have gone quit after obtaining an inquisition *de odio et atia*, but the jury held the death to have been entirely accidental, not homicide by mischance; the appellees were absolved from all responsibility whatever for the deceased's fall from a boat and drowning.[3] It cannot therefore provide proof that the writ *de odio et atia* was being used in cases of excusable homicide in the same way as it was used where an appeal of assault was exaggerated. In fact, this type of inquisition was not brought most frequently, as McKechnie thought, in cases of homicide before 1215. Its use in cases of robbery, rape, arson, assault, breach of the peace together greatly outnumbered them on the early plea rolls.

inquisition (*Rot. de Oblatis*, 411). This one seems to have been more favourable to him and in the following year a concord was achieved (*Curia Regis Rolls*, v. 254). Henry had brought an assize of novel disseisin against him over the same episode (ibid. iv. 57; cf. *Earliest Northamptonshire Assize Rolls*, ed. D. M. Stenton, no. 919).

[1] *Pipe Roll, 7 Ric. I*, 214, 215. Cf. *Curia Regis Rolls*, iii. 13–14, where several men appealed of robbery offered ½ mark for a jury; later the parties were given licence to make a concord 'quia athia credebatur esse'.

[2] e.g. an appeal of homicide was probably compromised after an inquisition *de odio et atia* which concerned Robert de Bosco's appeal of Walter de Grantcurt for the death of Ralph Fitz Thorold. A concord was said to have been mooted between *Ralph* de Bosco and Walter, but there can be little doubt that this was a scribal error for Robert, and that he and Walter were considering terms, 'per gratum domini regis' (ibid. vi. 152, 166, 200, 265). Now in this case details are available and it emerges that Walter was charged with instigating the death, although he had been absent from the district at the time. He could also challenge Robert's standing in the case, denying that he was related to Fitz Thorold or a member of his mainpast.

[3] *Lincs. Assize Rolls, 1202–9*, ed. D. M. Stenton, no. 1508.

One of the multifarious uses of the early inquisition *de odio et
atia* was, then, to draw attention to circumstances which discounted
the charge of felonious assault. Quite often, by doing this it seems to
have persuaded the appellor to withdraw.[1] More often the appeal
was quashed. A favourable verdict could thus have the effect of
acquittal. And, indeed, writs *de odio et atia* were no doubt obtained
by some appellees, and perhaps even some indicted persons, simply
in the hope of acquittal. Quite early the writ was sometimes worded
in such a way that the jurors were required to pronounce, even
if indirectly, on the issue of guilt or innocence. They were asked
whether the charge had been brought *de odio et atia* or because the
accused was guilty,[2] and later this was the normal form of the writ.
In early cases at the eyre the appellee might pay for an inquisition
'utrum ipse appellet eum iusta causa, an odio et attia'.[3] In such
cases the purpose might be to have what amounted almost to trial
by jury, and this was certainly a significant function of these inquisitions.

It has been thought that the writ was obtained as a means of
dodging the dreaded judicial combat, but in fact it was often obtained
by female appellees or against female appellors: in these cases there
was no danger of trial by battle, for although a woman occasionally
produced a champion to fight to prove her charge, the justices
frowned on this. Down to 1215, however, there was some possibility
that ordeal would be involved instead of combat, and this was an
even more daunting prospect and could equally well induce the
appellee to seek to get the appeal quashed. But still there were cases
in which the appellee would not himself have to go to the ordeal;
according to Glanvill, if the appellor was a woman the appellee
could choose whether he or she should go to it,[4] and the early plea
rolls show that the justices often permitted the appellee to choose
whether he or the appellor should go even if both were men.[5] Thus
the use of the writ *de odio et atia* cannot be entirely explained by
the urge to escape undergoing a painful and dangerous test. The
very nature of the test, whether combat or ordeal, was objection-
able, as well as participation in it. The irrationality and unreli-
ability of such proofs were leading appellees to seek something like
trial by jury instead. At the same time, indeed, defendants who had
been indicted, not appealed, were buying permission for it, putting
themselves on the country as to guilt or innocence. Thus trial by
jury was already used in many cases where prosecution followed

---

[1] e.g. *Curia Regis Rolls*, i. 230–1; 469; ii. 6, 88; 50; iv. 216.
[2] e.g. *Lincs. Assize Rolls, 1202–9*, no. 1508.
[3] Ibid., no. 607.   [4] *De Legibus*, Lib. xiv, caps. 3, 6.
[5] e.g. *Lincs. Assize Rolls, 1202–9*, nos. 595, 843, 851. In each case the appellee
chose that the appellor should make the proof, whereupon the latter withdrew.

presentment even before the abolition of ordeal, which was in theory the normal method of proof in such cases. Ordeal was almost as unpopular with the justices as it was with those required to undergo it, and when an indicted person wished for trial by jury instead it was a simple matter, provided he could proffer a mark or so, to get permission to put himself on the country. But it was less simple for the appellee, who would generally have to show good reason why proof should not be by battle or ordeal. The writ *de odio et atia* provided an additional means of doing this. Moreover, it had the advantage that an adverse verdict was not final. The appellee's life was not yet at stake. If the jurors found, as they occasionally did, that he was appealed not out of malice but because he was in fact guilty, he would still have the opportunity of defending himself by combat or ordeal, should this prove necessary. But it might not: in one case an appellor withdrew in spite of the verdict that the appellee was guilty of robbery, as the jurors believed.[1] Thus the appellee who secured this type of preliminary inquisition stood to lose nothing from an unfavourable and might gain everything from a favourable verdict, though he could not be sure of this.

If the inquisition was held by itinerant justices the chances of a final decision were good. If the appeal was found to be made *de odio et atia* they might not only quash it but state specifically that the appellee should go quit. Often, even if they did not state this, no arraignment at the suit of the king followed. For example, in the Lincolnshire eyre of 1202 there were four cases in which jurors found the appeal was made out of spite. In one the appellees were definitely acquitted; in the other three the appeals were considered null, and there was no prosecution at the suit of the king.[2] Although a favourable verdict was not necessarily the end of the whole matter, it often was so in the time of John. In straightforward cases at the eyre, then, verdicts that appeals were malicious and the appellees not guilty generally meant that the latter were acquitted forthwith and the appellors amerced. But when an inquisition *de odio et atia* was sought and held elsewhere the result might be less tidy and conclusive. It was often difficult to make the writ effective. The appellee might obtain it but only to find there was delay in holding the inquisition;[3] it might never be held. The *Curia Regis* itself sometimes hesitated to acquit on a verdict taken locally and adjourned the case to the eyre.[4] A request made in the court for an inquisition was also likely to lead to similar adjournment, especially if an eyre was in progress.[5] It was thus a lengthy business in many

---

[1] *Curia Regis Rolls*, ii. 15, 66.
[2] *Lincs. Assize Rolls*, nos. 539, 607, 616, 841.
[3] e.g. *Pipe Roll, 13 John*, 1; *Curia Regis Rolls*, vi. 206.
[4] e.g. ibid. iv. 275.   [5] e.g. ibid. 147–8, 211; 163–4.

cases and in some application for the inquisition may have been little more than delaying tactics.

There are only a few cases in the reign of John in which persons accused of homicide are known to have obtained the writ in order to secure release from prison. In 1205 Agnes de Clive, Adam Fitz Peter, and Turold Fitz Geoffrey gave 3 marks, according to the pipe roll, for an inquisition whether Elyas de Bridehal appealed them 'per atiam an eo quod sint culpabiles', and, if they were not guilty, for being handed over to the custody of lawful men.[1] The corresponding entry on the roll de Oblatis shows that the charge was one of homicide.[2] Then in 1214 William Esturmy gave 5 marks for an inquisition whether he was appealed of the death of Thomas Bugsall 'eo quod inde sit culpabilis an per odium et atyam'.[3] The sheriff who held the inquisition reported its verdict of not guilty, and was thereupon ordered to let him be bailed.[4] There are other cases in which men who were said to be not guilty were subsequently bailed although this does not appear to have been their objective in securing the writ.[5] There are also instances of bail being sought or granted after inquisitions which may have been de odio et atio, though this is not stated.[6] If the writ was used for this purpose it was naturally secured some time before the trial of the appellee, but nearly all of John's known writs de odio et atia were produced in court in the course of the trial; the plea rolls reveal only two or three cases in which the writ had been obtained earlier and led to special inquisitions as a result of which appellees may have been released on bail. One or two entries on the pipe rolls show that the writ was secured by someone who had been indicted, not appealed, and one of these may have aimed at bail.[7] This, was not, then, an important function of the writ in the time of John though it was a minor one.

Only one case has been found in which an inquisition de odio et atia may perhaps have been the prelude to John's pardoning an offence. The pipe roll of 1204 (p. 183) records John de Chedinton's debt of 20 marks and one palfrey for the king's peace for an alleged forest offence 'unde ipse rettatus fuit odio Willelmi de Cahain et pro quo ipse Johannes utlagatus fuit'. It would appear that William had procured his being indicted, but whether his malice had actually been established by an inquisition remains uncertain.

A request for an inquisition de odio et atia might be turned down.

---

[1] *Pipe Roll, 7 John*, 57. [2] *Rot. de Oblatis*, 244.
[3] Ibid. 543; *Pipe Roll, 16 John*, 175. [4] *Rot. Litt. Claus*, i. 206.
[5] e.g. *Earliest Northants Assize Rolls*, no. 676; *Pipe Roll, 6 John*, 188.
[6] e.g. *Rot. de Oblatis*, 343. Cf. *Pipe Roll, 10 John*, 44. The order for William Esturmy's release gives no indication that the inquisition which had found him not guilty was, as other evidence shows, one *de odio et atia*. [7] Ibid., *6 John*, 102.

In 1201 Adam de Beston appealed William Gramaticus of robbing
him when he tried to secure the release of his forester whom William
had imprisoned, and then of imprisoning Adam also.[1] William had
earlier proffered 100 marks and a palfrey for an inquisition whether
the appeal was 'per vetus odium et per atiam an non', but had not
actually received the writ, so his debt was later cancelled.[2] He
now, in the king's court, offered 100*s*., stating that the appeal was
made through malice and hatred, in particular over a certain wood;
later he raised his proffer to 10 marks, on behalf of his men as well
as himself. But the proffer was rejected and judicial combat ordered.
William then obtained licence for concord at the cost of £100.[3]

The diverse uses of the inquisition *de odio et atia* and its affinity
with the trial jury create difficulties in the interpretation of Magna
Carta, clause 36, and these have been aggravated by the fact that
later on the writ *de odio et atia* came to be confined almost entirely to
obtaining bail. Dealing with it in this connection, Bracton referred
to the free issue of the writ.[4] The second statute of Westminster,
cap. 29, did so too mentioning Magna Carta, and from these statements the writ *de odio et atia* has been identified with the writ of
inquisition of life and limb, which, according to clause 36, was to be
freely granted and not denied.[5] It does not, of course, follow that
this clause had been concerned mainly, or even at all, with the
function of the writ to obtain bail, a function which had vastly
expanded in the meantime. Moreover, even the complete identity
of the writ of life and limb and that *de odio et atia* is open to doubt.
The first no doubt included the second, but there were other types
of inquisition in cases involving life and limb, the most obvious
being that obtained by persons who were indicted and wished to
put themselves on the country. The writ obtained with this object
secured trial by jury in a straightforward manner, whereas that *de
odio et atia* sometimes achieved it by a roundabout route, circum-
venting but not running directly counter to the rights of appellors
to fight in proof of their charges. The framers of the Charter were
presumably concerned to see that both types of inquisition were
freely available: it would be hard to say which was uppermost in

---

[1] *Curia Regis Rolls*, i. 379.   [2] *Rot. de Oblatis*, 106.

[3] *Pipe Roll, 3 John*, 160. Litigation over the wood continued however. See
Curia Regis Rolls, iv. 8; v. 53, 241.   [4] *De Legibus*, f. 123.

[5] In support of the identification McKechnie quoted a case from 1231 in which
a private court was asserted to have made 'sacramentum . . . de vita et membris'
when it took a verdict on an appeal which the appellee said was malicious (*Magna
Carta*, 361, n. 2). But this was not a verdict *de odio et atia*. The jury was a trial jury
and the steward of the lord of the court, the abbot of St. Edmund's, defended his
franchise by showing that while the ordeal was in order he had used it, and now
it was replaced by jury he used that instead. See Bracton's *Note Book*, no. 592;
Curia Regis Rolls, xiv. no. 1737.

their minds. They wanted trial by jury to be the right of everyone charged with felony. This clause would have been momentous indeed had not the Lateran Council of the same year given the death-blow to ordeal in England and accelerated the already strong trend to rely on trial by jury. As it is, those who drew it up deserve credit for their rational and far-sighted policy. One of their aims in clause 36 was, then, to make the writ *de odio et atia* freely available for this purpose, but whether they had any of its other uses in mind cannot be determined. Probably they valued also its testing of the bona fides of dubious appeals, even if this did not lead to immediate acquittal. Bail is more problematical. They may have been aware that it could lead to this, but it is unlikely that this was a major consideration.[1] It seems unlikely that they connected the writ of inquisition of life and limb with pardon; it is doubtful whether it had begun to be used for this purpose even in the form *de odio et atia*, and unlikely that they would be aware of this even if it had so been used once or twice. That it was worth while insisting that the writ should not be denied is shown by the case of William Gramaticus.

The year 1215 was a turning-point in the history of the writ, but not because of Magna Carta. As a result of the decree of the Lateran Council trial by jury practically ceased to be a privilege which might have to be bought. The courts were now only too anxious for the accused to consent to be tried in this way. However, appellors still had to offer to fight to prove their charges and for certain appellees the problem of evading this kind of proof persisted, and they might assert that the appeal was made *odio et atia* as a means of getting trial by jury substituted.[2] Occasionally an appellee still proffered payment for a jury, sometimes for a jury *de odio et atia*, in the course of the trial,[3] but even apart from Magna Carta's insistence that this should be free, such proffers were generally quite unnecessary. Some appellees could put themselves on the country without more ado. Others could except to the appeals and abate them on various grounds. Without seeking a special verdict *de odio et atia* they often claimed incidentally to have been charged from these motives and sought to have this point put to the trial jury. Thus men appealed of robbery in 1232 put themselves on the country 'quod non sunt culpabiles et quod ipsi eos appellant per odium et atiam'.[4] It was advantageous if appellees could draw attention to the reasons why a malicious charge might have been brought, especially if they could show that the motive was to hamper

---

[1] Cl. 36 was not taken to prohibit payment for the writ when it was used for this purpose. But then, as will be seen, payments also continued to be made occasionally for the inquisition in court.   [2] e.g. J.I. 1/1043, m. 8ᵈ.

[3] e.g. *Curia Regis Rolls*, x. 156 (1221).   [4] Ibid. xiv, no. 2133.

them from proceeding with an appeal or an action already pending against the appellors. It might be worth while to pay for a special inquisition for this purpose, but it was not essential to do so. On the other hand, the appellor himself might ask for an inquisition to clear him of the charge of having appealed *odio et atia*.[1] Thus the plea rolls show that the allegation of hatred and malice was constantly bandied about and that a jury was sometimes sworn in just to deal with it, but normally it formed only one element among the issues with which the trial jury might have to deal. Nor was it only the accused who made the allegation. Although they were not obliged to do so juries often, when bringing in a verdict of not guilty, asserted that the appeal had been malicious and they, too, sometimes described the motive prompting it in some detail. Now and again the plea rolls reveal that the justices interrogated them on this point;[2] generally they appear to have volunteered the information, but it may be that the clerks omitted any reference to judicial concern with it.[3] The malicious accuser and his abettors would be amerced. Juries continued to mention malice throughout the reign of Henry III and in 1285 the second statute of Westminster, cap. 12, laid down punishment for unsuccessful appellors and payment of damages to the appellees.

As the use of the writ in court declined its use to obtain bail spread. Frequently under Henry III and Edward I it was obtained by indicted prisoners as well as those arrested on appeal. Its wording was adjusted accordingly, asking whether the prisoner was *rettatus* instead of *appellatus odio et atia*. Bracton[4] and registers of writs quote it with these alternatives, and the distinction was generally scrupulously observed. This is particularly well shown by an entry on the close roll of 30 Henry III. Three men who were detained for the death of Thomas Gladewin obtained an order for bail 'quia idem Ricardus rettatus est et predicti Robertus et Johannes appellati sunt de morte illa odio et atia etc.'.[5] However, on one occasion at least, probably through the ignorance of the applicants, the writ referred to their being *rettati* when they were appealed.[6] Sometimes, of course, the prisoner might be both *rettatus* and *appellatus*. Although indictments might indeed have been maliciously procured they must

---

[1] e.g. J.I. 1/954, m. 56.
[2] e.g. J.I. 1/235, m. 2ᵈ, where the jury had just stated that the supposed victims were still alive; J.I. 1/701, m. 23.
[3] In some cases the defendant had earlier obtained bail after an inquisition *de odio et atia* and the statement in court may have been based on its findings.
[4] *De Legibus*, f. 123.
[5] *Close Rolls, 1242–7*, 411.
[6] C. 144/3, no. 2. Cf. *Close Rolls, 1242–7*, 261, 379. The order for bail used the term *rettati* and a second was needed; this one used *appellati*, but seems to have substituted the appellor's name for that of the victim.

often have been made in all good faith against those the inquisitions found not guilty. The fact that the writ was constantly used by indicted prisoners indicates that this formula was not taken over-seriously. The writ was regarded as the normal means of securing bail; the allegation of malice and hatred might or might not be significant. The released prisoner had to stand trial in court, despite the verdict, and could be arraigned at the suit of the king if, as generally happened, an earlier appeal was not now prosecuted. There was, of course, no guarantee that the juries of presentment and trial would uphold the earlier verdict when the released prisoners surrendered to bail. In 1235 a man was hanged at the eyre in Essex despite the finding that he had been maliciously appealed and the jurors of the inquisition *de odio et atia* were amerced.[1] As the writ became the normal means of securing bail for those detained for homicide the chances of final conviction were far from negligible.

Although the inquiry as to hatred and malice was not always appropriate when bail was the objective the writ continued to emphasize it, a new formula being added, requiring the inquisition not only to answer the question whether the accusation was made *odio et atia* or because the accused was guilty, but also 'si odio et atia, quo odio et qua atia?' This occurs in what seems to be the earliest surviving writ, one from 1236.[2] Bracton emphasized its importance.[3] Within a few years an important additional question was introduced: if the prisoner had not slain the victim, who had done so? This appears in surviving writs from the 1240s and is also indicated by enrolments of orders for bail, starting in 1241, which state that the prisoners were accused *odio et atia* and go on to give the names of the actual slayers.[4] It looks as though this was a new departure at this moment, for in the next two years the enrolments give much prominence to this part of the return, so much so that many of them omit any explicit mention of *odium et atia*, but order release on bail because some other named person is guilty.[5] A verdict which substituted another suspect was obviously of the greatest value to the prisoner who, even if released now, would still have to stand trial later. It would be interesting to know whether this question was suggested by prisoners who were aware that someone else was guilty, perhaps, indeed, had already fled or been

[1] J.I. 1/230, m. 8.   [2] C. 144/3, no. 1.   [3] *De Legibus*, f. 123.
[4] e.g. C. 144/3, nos. 2, sqq. (1244); *Close Rolls, 1237–42*, 294, 372, 382.
[5] Ibid. 482; ibid., *1242–47*, 75, 76, 82, 86, 91, 92, 96, 102, 103, 104. It seems evident that these orders were in fact based on inquisitions *de odio et atia*, since they clearly indicate the new wording of the writ; all but one of these entries say that the prisoners were 'appellati etc.' or 'rettati etc.', and the *etc.* probably indicated the finding that they were accused *odio et atia*.

convicted,¹ or whether it was formulated by officials with the idea of using these inquisitions to gain information leading to further and better warranted arrests.

While the use of the writ to obtain bail was officially recognized it was seen that it might be carried too far. Accordingly its wording was modified in 1249 so as to prevent its use by those imprisoned on the order of the king's justices. The formula was now as follows: 'Rex vicecomiti salutem. Precipimus tibi quod per sacramentum proborum et legalium hominum de comitatu tuo per quos rei veritas melius sciri poterit diligenter inquiras si J. captus et detentus in prisona nostra . . . pro morte R. unde appellatus [*or* rettatus] est, appellatus [*or* rettatus] sit de morte illa odio et atia, an eo quod inde culpabilis sit, et si odio et atia, quo odio et qua atia, et si inde culpabilis non sit, quis inde culpabilis sit. Et inquisicionem inde factam sub sigillo tuo et sigillis eorum per quos facta fuerit nobis mittas et hoc breue, nisi indictatus fuerit vel appellatus coram Justiciariis nostris ultimo itinerantibus in partibus illis et propter hoc captus et imprisonatus.' According to some of the registers of writs the final clause was added by John de Lexington in the time of Henry III.² This statement appears to be quite correct. Lexington was Chancellor only from September 1247 to August 1248 and again for a few months from 15 October 1249. The clause appears in an enrolment on 3 December 1249 though by the 13th it was being shortened to 'nisi etc.'³ By May 1250 even this brief reference was dropped. Nevertheless, the documents in C. 144 show that from now on it was regularly included in the order to hold the inquisition.⁴ The reason for the alteration appears from a writ of 1 December 1249 ordering the recapture of Geoffrey de Childingwod, who had been appealed, had failed to appear at the eyre, where an inquisition had found him guilty, but had later been arrested. On the false suggestion of certain persons the king had then had an inquisition held by means of which he had been delivered from prison, as was said. If he was still in prison, the sheriff was on no account to release him. If he was not, he was to be retaken.⁵ It seems evident that an inquisition *de odio et atia* was involved and was considered utterly improper in the circumstances. The new

¹ In one case an outlaw was named; ibid. 96, and in others fugitives, ibid., *1237–42*, 372, 382.

² See E. de Haas, *Antiquities of Bail*, 98, n. 1.

³ *Close Rolls, 1247–51*, 243–4, 246, 248, 255, 257, 265, 266, 270–4, 276. One enrolment, ibid. 247, states that the writ was 'sine clausula', and another, ibid. 259, was 'sine Nisi'.

⁴ C. 144/3, nos. 38, 40, 42, 43, sqq. are the early examples. The clause is included in C. 144/3, nos. 14 and 16 which are filed among the writs of 29–30 Henry III, but they are dated the 39th and 34th, not the 30th year of his reign.

⁵ *Close Rolls, 1247–51*, 243.

formula guarded against such abuse in future. It might, perhaps, also be taken to prohibit the purchase of the writ during trial to test the good faith of appellor or presenting jury or avert trial by battle, though it is unlikely that the king or Lexington had this in mind. Indeed, the practice of so doing had now pretty well ceased. If the new clause discouraged it at all there can have been very few prisoners likely to be affected by it.

By the time Bracton was writing *De Legibus Anglie* the writ was used almost, though not quite exclusively, to secure release on bail. Dealing with it in this connection he asserted that inquisitions could be held only for those actually in prison.[1] Returns to inquisitions show that this rule was acknowledged and no verdict might be given if the jurors stated that those concerned were at large.[2] This change in the main use of the writ *de odio et atia* after 1215 is now well recognized, but its history in the later thirteenth century is still obscure and misunderstood in several ways. First, its relationship to the writ ordering inquisition whether a slaying was excusable or felonious has led to very understandable confusion. Secondly, the prevalence of the writ has been gravely underestimated.

Sir J. F. Stephen believed that the writ could be employed by those appealed of homicide when there was excuse or extenuating circumstances. Speaking of the Statute of Gloucester of 1278, which he mistakenly took to have abolished this writ, he said: 'It would seem from this statute that the commonest cases of accusations "de odio et atia" were cases of misadventure or self-defence. The survivors of the deceased in such cases were likely to accuse of wilful homicide those whose negligence or violence had caused their relation's death; and the statute provides that these cases are no longer to be bailable, and that when the trial comes on, the jury, if they think that the case was one of self-defence or misadventure, are neither to convict nor acquit, but to find specially to that effect, upon which the king, if he pleases, may, upon the record or report of the justices, pardon the party.'[3] It has been seen that the aim of the statute, cap. 9, was to stop inquisitions whether killings were excusable or felonious being held except when the suspect appeared before the king's justices.[4] They were no longer to be held, as they had so often been, on behalf of fugitives from justice and outlaws. It had nothing whatever to do with the question whether bail should be granted. If it had already been granted it was implicit that former prisoners would have to surrender for trial if they

---

[1] *De Legibus*, f. 123. Elsewhere, f. 141, he mentioned *odium et atia* as an exception to an appeal.

[2] e.g. C. 144/5, no. 25.

[3] *History of the Criminal Law of England*, iii. 37. [4] Above, p. 281.

wanted an inquisition of this type, but otherwise there was no connection with bail. The rule incidentally constituted an attack on the practice of granting pardon after inquisitions *de odio et atia* held by the sheriffs but this was not sufficiently common in itself to have provoked the statute. Any type of inquisition leading to pardon except when the accused was on trial was equally objection-able. As it turned out the statute was disregarded and even in-quisitions *de odio et atia* continued to supply the grounds for pardon. Thus, where it may have been intended to do away with an excep-tional use of this type of inquisition the statute was ineffective. Stephen's belief that it abolished the writ was entirely without foundation. There was no attack whatever on its now normal and proper function of securing bail.

McKechnie also associated the writ with excusable homicide. He was right in thinking that once it had come to be used chiefly for bail it was obtained mainly on behalf of homicides. Prisoners detained on other charges could more easily be released on finding pledges or mainpernors, but homicides could not in theory be released without the king's own authorization. However, he went further. 'The man accused of murder had no right to be released on bail ... This was hard where the accused was the victim of malice, or guilty only of justifiable homicide. Prisoners, in such a plight, might purchase royal writs that would save them from languishing for months or years in gaol. The writ best suited for this purpose was that *de odio et atia* ... Before Bracton's day this change had taken place: the writ had come to be viewed primarily as an expedient for releasing upon bail homicides *per infortunium* or *se defendendo*.'[1] But this writ was not best suited to their case, nor for that matter was bail the most sensible objective. Excusable slayers appear sometimes to have been allowed bail on the strength of unsworn statements of the circumstances of the killing, though even in these cases the possibility that an inquisition had been held should not be ruled out.[2] But as early as 1226 a sheriff was ordered to hold an inquisition to ascertain whether a woman had killed her child through madness or maliciously and wilfully, and to release her on bail if the verdict was that she had been mad.[3] In the fol-lowing year the king ordered the release on bail of a man who had been found by an inquisition to have killed his son by accident not 'per odium vel athiam', but it is possible that this had been an inquisition *de odio et atia* which gave a twisted verdict.[4] However that may be, inquisitions into the circumstances of the slaying were soon obtainable by any excusable slayers who sought bail,[5] and by

---

[1] *Magna Carta*, 362–3.
[2] e.g. *Rot. Litt. Claus.* ii. 194.
[3] Ibid. 158.
[4] Ibid. 198.
[5] e.g. *Close Rolls, 1242–7*, 50, 53, 145, 210, 491.

1230 they were obtaining them with a view to pardon also. This was obviously the type of inquisition best suited to their case, and pardon rather than bail was the most satisfactory and definitive outcome. None the less, a fair number opted for the latter, probably because it was cheaper, and a good many of these did get the writ *de odio et atia*, perhaps through ignorance that it was not altogether appropriate, as it was not, for example, when they had been indicted. But the number of excusable killers who obtained this type of inquisition, as an avenue either to bail or pardon, was small compared with the great numbers of prisoners who claimed to be in no way responsible for the slaying on account of which they were detained and who were accused, according to the verdicts, entirely out of malice. The writ could be used by excusable slayers, but it was certainly not viewed primarily as an expedient for their benefit. Indeed, it is probably just because the use of it by them was at first somewhat anomalous that this is recorded while the grant of bail to others as a result of this type of inquisition was so common-place that the orders for release ceased to refer to it. This is the simple explanation of any apparent preponderance of excusable slayers among those for whom the writ *de odio et atia* was issued.

It is, of course, also the explanation of the supposed decline of the writ from mid thirteenth century. 'The use of the writ', says Dr. de Haas, 'proved to be merely transitory.'[1] Although she quotes incidental references to it 'as late as 1314–15', she considers that it was 'largely inactive' after the statute of Gloucester, 1278, c. 9,[2] and is at some pains to account for its decline. One reason she suggests was the growth of other types of inquisition. She mentions reasons for thinking that the writ was *de cursu* by 1259, but although she remarks that this might explain why it ceased to be recorded on the close rolls, she asserts that a study of the *Calendar* 'for succeeding years impresses one with the fact that the *odio et atia* claim is superseded by the broader investigation of the jury of inquisition into the nature of the charges. When this substitution occurs, an important reason for the decline of the writ of spite and hate has been found'.[3] She, like Stephen and McKechnie, associates the history of this writ with excusable homicide, but whereas McKechnie thought that it was to the last mainly employed by excusable homicides, she thinks it declined because they were now obtaining bail after a different type of inquisition. In fact the writ did not decline as early as she supposes, and her view of the damage done to it by other types of inquisition is exaggerated.

Dr. de Haas remarks on a sudden decrease in 1248–9 and says that '*odio et atia* claims practically cease to be reported in the Close

---

[1] Op. cit. 126.   [2] Ibid. 127.   [3] Ibid. 121–3.

Rolls' after 1249.[1] This remark requires some qualification. References there to inquisitions *de odio et atia* might occur either in the orders for bail, or incidentally in other types of enrolment. So far as orders for bail for those detained for homicide were concerned, the references disappeared almost completely for the rest of the reign.[2] But an incidental reference may reveal that an inquisition had been held. For example, in 1258, the enrolment of a writ to the sheriff of Yorkshire to release on bail William son of John de Langefeld gives no hint of one, but a second writ to him three months later ordering restitution of William's lands and chattels shows that he had been granted bail because an inquisition held by the sheriff had found he had been indicted *de odio et atia*.[3] In 1269 a prisoner from Essex in Newgate was found to have been maliciously appealed; this was mentioned in a writ to the sheriff of Essex telling him to send the names of his mainpernors. The subsequent writ to the keeper and bailiffs of London ordering his release omitted it.[4] In a couple of cases where the enrolled order for bail did refer to the inquisition the prisoners were detained for theft and appropriating treasure trove.[5] The fact that these were very unusual crimes to involve this type of inquisition would suggest the reason why it was mentioned when it was normally being omitted. It would be very strange if it was employed for prisoners such as these and not for homicides. Considerations such as these might in themselves raise doubts as to the decline of the writ at this time. Its very normality is the obvious explanation of its failure to feature in most of the enrolments. But there is no need to rely on inferences to show that it was in common use. The actual writs ordering inquisitions *de odio et atia* and/or the returns to them have survived in considerable numbers in the Chancery files known as C. 144. Some of these are in very poor condition and it is not possible to say precisely how many of them resulted in enrolled orders for bail. Enough of them can be identified among the enrolments to show that getting on for 140 of the orders for bail entered on Henry III's close rolls without any reference to an inquisition in fact followed one, and

---

[1] Op. cit. 120.

[2] One reference was in an order to the mayor and sheriffs of London to release a monk of Bermondsey who had been found to have been charged maliciously with homicide. A note follows the enrolment: 'Et sciendum quod breve istud concessum fuit extra formam communem pro liberacione predicti Arnaldi, qui monachus est, eo quod in foro laicali respondere non potest' (*Close Rolls, 1261–4,* 10–11). The inquisition had been held, exceptionally, by one of the king's justices and the abnormal circumstances explain why it was mentioned. For another order see ibid., *1264–8,* 472.   [3] Ibid., *1256–9,* 191, 210.   [4] Ibid., *1268–72,* 80, 82.

[5] Ibid., *1259–61,* 359; cf. 434 (where a fugitive maliciously charged with robbery was to be bailed if he surrendered); ibid., *1268–72,* 20. In the last cases special commissions including justices had been appointed to hold the inquisitions.

all but a handful of these come from the years after 1248. Not many writs and returns have survived from earlier years, but some 20 of them are matched by entries on the rolls which do refer to *odio et atia*. Thus it is quite clear that the change in the years 1248 and 1249 was simply in the form of enrolment; until then it had been usual to refer to the inquisition when enrolling the order for bail. For the rest of the reign it was taken for granted and not mentioned. It is fair to conclude that inquisitions of this type normally supplied the grounds for granting bail; but there were some cases in which other types had been held. A few enrolments referred to inquisitions having established innocence, justification, or excuse. It is significant, however, that the files show that some of these also had been held on the strength of writs *de odio et atia*. The total number of orders for bail fluctuated. They tended to drop when an eyre was being held and also in periods of crisis and civil war. But they were increasing not decreasing after 1249, and the great majority were probably secured by inquisitions *de odio et atia*.

The picture under Edward I is more complicated. Far more of the orders for and returns from inquisitions *de odio et atia* have survived for this reign, though there are gaps, especially from 1294 to 1299.[1] Down to 1278 just over half the enrolments which do not mention inquisitions can be shown to have followed them. Then for nine years, though the totals were small, the great majority of orders evidently followed inquisitions of some kind, while in each of the years 1288, 1289, and 1290 all or all but one did so. The evidence from these years shows that it is safe to assume that the failure of the writs to mention them is of no significance—except as proof of their being altogether normal. But whilst the enrolled order almost always resulted from some type of inquisition even though it did not state this, it must not be taken for granted that it was nearly always *de odio et atia*. The suggestion that inquisitions into slaying by self-defence or mischance were ousting those *de odio et atia* is based on a certain amount of evidence from the close rolls. For 1279 there are very few and for 1280 and 1281 practically no entries concerning bail. From then until 1286, and again from 1293 to 1297, they are comparatively few, and among them orders based on other types of inquisition appear to be almost as frequent, sometimes indeed, preponderant. But here again it is necessary to distinguish. A good many prisoners, as has been seen earlier, remanded *ad gratiam* at gaol deliveries or even by justices of oyer and terminer secured bail not pardon. Many of the orders for bail accordingly

---

[1] A few orders for bail on grounds of *odium* and *atia* are to be found in C. 202/ C/1, 2, 4. One order for bail in 1299 (that for William in the Walles, *Cal. Close Rolls, 1296–1302*, 235) is known from quite a different source, J.I. 1/1108, m. 1ᵈ, to have been based on a writ *de odio et atia*.

followed verdicts of justifiable or excusable slaying given in court
not at special inquisitions held by the sheriff or commissioners
appointed *ad hoc*. Naturally there was no need for a writ *de odio et
atia* in these cases. Justices of gaol delivery required to be authorized
to try persons charged with homicide by a writ *de bono et malo*,
showing that the prisoners accepted trial by jury, but this of course
was not concerned particularly with those who could put forward
some excuse. Only occasionally were they specially instructed to
inquire into alleged excuses. Thus the orders for bail following
verdicts before them do not imply that any other type of writ was
replacing that *de odio et atia*, only that the frequency of gaol deliveries and the tendency to opt for bail instead of pardon did mean
that a good many prisoners got bail without having to secure the
holding of special inquisitions. The numbers were, in fact, greater
than the close rolls indicate, for it can be shown from extant returns
in the C. 47 files that the clerks who enrolled the orders were casual
about mentioning that the inquisition had been held in court, omitting this factor in a third of the cases checked against these returns.
Gaol delivery rolls themselves reveal it in several additional cases.

However, there remain a number of entries on the close rolls
showing that bail was allowed because inquisitions, not apparently
before justices, had found the prisoners not guilty, or to have slain
justifiably or excusably or when mad. It is natural enough to suppose that these latter were inquisitions into the alleged circumstances. Such inquisitions were still sometimes followed by bail
rather than pardon, as the *Calendar of Miscellaneous Inquisitions*
reveals. But the C. 144 files show that this was not the normal
procedure. Under Henry III an occasional inquisition *de odio et
atia* found the killing excusable and led to bail. Under Edward I
such cases were quite numerous. The documents in C. 144 show
that in this reign seventy orders for bail enrolled on the close rolls
as implying only that some kind of inquisition had established
excuse, justification, or exoneration in fact followed inquisitions
de odio et atia, while in over thirty other cases although the enrolment
gave no hint of any kind of inquisition verdicts of excusable slaying
had in fact been given by them. It must be concluded that far from
reducing the use of this writ, the tendency of imprisoned excusable
slayers to seek bail instead of pardon actually extended its usefulness at a time when it was rather less often obtained by other
prisoners. In the years from 1282 to 1297 when inquisitions at gaol
deliveries were often mentioned the number of enrolments which
are not known to have resulted from one or other type of inquisition
is so small that they could make little difference to the general
picture. Probably most of them should be assigned to inquisitions
de odio et atia, if any, since the enrolments were freer with references

to the verdicts at gaol deliveries. In the closing years of the reign
they became more reticent, but the other evidence still suggests
a much higher proportion of inquisitions elsewhere.

It would, then, be altogether incorrect to say that the writ *de
odio et atia* was losing ground to the writs ordering inquisitions into
excuses. On the contrary, it was frequently used when they would
have been more appropriate as a means of getting bail. Moreover, it
was even used, as has been seen, to obtain pardon, thus encroaching
on their sphere far more blatantly. But only some eight cases of
this kind have been found among the C. 144 files. When prisoners
charged with homicide wanted to obtain bail without waiting for a
gaol delivery they still used the writ almost as a matter of course;
only a handful even among the justifiable and excusable killers now
preferred an inquisition of another type. On the other hand, for
much of the reign, this sort of impatience was seldom shown, and
the total number of homicides who obtained bail was smaller than
of old. The explanation of this lies partly, as has often been suggested, in the frequency of gaol deliveries. A general eyre, of course,
had an effect on them, particularly in 1293, when there were
apparently scarcely any grants of bail. But it is very noticeable that
the falling off occurred chiefly in time of war, first during the Welsh
wars, in the first of which they virtually disappeared so far as the
available evidence shows, and then from 1294 onwards, when
enlistment may have offered an acceptable alternative to some of
the more indigent prisoners, and the business of applying for the
writs was complicated by the movements of the king and the administration.

The writs and returns in C. 144 go down to the time of Henry
VI, but among them those *de odio et atia* continue only into the
reign of Edward III. There are a fair number from that of Edward
II and down to 1352 the number per annum is much the same as
from the last years of Edward I. Then they disappear. The chance
of survival of these small slips of parchment relating to matters
which were not of lasting concern was not high. It is remarkable
that so many have in fact survived from the thirteenth century.
Their absence does not in itself prove that the writ ceased to be
used before the middle of the fourteenth. As Holdsworth said 'both
Coke and Hale treat it as an existing writ. But Hale says it was
disused in his day, and points out that, by reason of the greater
frequency of gaol deliveries, the prisoner was tried more quickly
than he could get provisionally released by this writ'.[1]

---

[1] *Hist. Eng. Law*, ix. 108. Coke's belief that it had been abolished by statute in
1354 and then reinstated in 1369, when all acts contrary to Magna Carta were
repealed (*Second Institute*, cap. 26), is unfounded. 28 Edward III, cap. 9 did not
prohibit inquisitions *de odio et atia*, but inquisitions by sheriffs as to those suspected

There was, then, a slower decline in the use of the writ than has been thought. No attack seems to have been made on it by the government. But there were some efforts to prevent its abuse. The danger of the sheriffs' holding the inquisitions on their own was recognized. Soon after Lexington's addition to its wording, the writ *de odio et atia* was modified again with a view to tightening up the procedure. The sheriff was ordered to hold the inquisition together with the coroners in full county court. This requirement appeared in the summer of 1255.[1] At the same time the writ insisted that the inquisition must be such that the sheriff would guarantee its accuracy: 'Et inquisicionem inde factam quam pro te et heredibus tuis Warantizare volueris sub sigillo tuo et sigillis eorum per quos facta fuerit nobis mittas. . . .' But this was soon altered to include the jurors instead of the sheriff's heirs: 'Et inquisicionem qualem tu et ipsi Warantizare volueritis . . . mittas.'[2] The returns gave the names of the jurors and were sealed with their seals. But later the juries were suspected of including persons who were open to influence, and in 1275 the first statute of Westminster, cap. 11, complaining that many who were guilty of homicide were being replevied by favourable inquisitions *de odio et atia*, held by the sheriff, provided that in future they should be taken by lawful men, of whom two at least should be knights, having no affinity with the prisoners.

The writ *de odio et atia* was nearly always addressed to the sheriff of the county in which the prisoner was detained, and the inquisition held by him, after 1255 in the presence also of the coroners. It was exceptional—as were the times—when in 1263 the keeper of the peace in Buckinghamshire was ordered to hold the inquisition,[3] the barons having appointed these officials to administer the shires alongside the sheriffs. In November 1261 Gilbert de Preston had been appointed to hold an inquisition by men of the neighbourhood of Midilton whether Hugh Child charged with killing William son of Agnes Specy was charged *odio et atia* or because he was guilty. The writ was endorsed 'Per dominum Regem pro fratre Johannis de Midelton', so it may be that this very unusual departure was due to the latter's efforts on his behalf. The verdict, duly recording that it was taken before Preston, found that Hugh was in no way guilty, and he was pardoned on the strength of it in January 1262.[4]

of felony and the arrest of the latter thereupon, which might be followed by their paying ransoms to obtain release.
    [1] C. 144/1, 15, where the return mentions that the inquisition was held in full county court before sheriff and coroners; C. 144/4, nos. 29, 31 sqq.
    [2] C. 144/4, nos. 31, 35, 37 sqq.
    [3] C. 144/5, no. 39. In 1258 a return had been sent to the council (C. 144/4, no. 46) which suggests that the baronial party was interested to some extent in supervising the use of the writ. For an exception in 1256 see *Close Rolls, 1254–6*, 263–4.
    [4] C. 144/5, no. 24; *Cal. Pat. Rolls, 1258–66*, 229, 197.

This seems to have been an officially authorized experiment in using this type of inquisition as a basis for granting pardon, but making it more reliable by having a royal justice hold it. Possibly, the baronial party which, minus Simon de Montfort, was having discussions with the king at this juncture, had proposed such a modification of the usual procedure. There are a few other examples of justices being commissioned in this way.[1]

Boroughs and lordships which enjoyed the liberty of return of writs might hold the inquisition, but it looks as though some sheriffs doubted their right to do this. In 1271 the sheriff of Oxfordshire was ordered to hold an inquisition, but he returned the verdict with the note that it had not been taken in full county court before himself and the coroners as the king's writ ordered, but the bailiffs of the liberty of Oxford had held the inquisition and brought it into the full county court as was customary, so they said, asking that the writ be attached to the verdict and returned to the king. The sheriff had refused to do this as it had not been held in full county court. The knights and others present there, however, had said that they were accustomed to use this liberty, so on their testimony the sheriff directed the finding of the inquisition to the king with the caveat 'Valeat illa penes vos quantum valere debeat'. So anxious was he to draw attention to what had occurred that the whole of this statement was copied out also on the dorse of the king's writ.[2] He may have thought the verdict likely to be challenged for it found that a malicious accusation had been made against the prisoner by a man with whom he often played at dice over which they had squabbled, a not very convincing motive. Similarly, the sheriff of Hertfordshire sent in a verdict with the note that the return to the writ had been made by the bailiffs of the liberty of Berkhamsted 'et si ullus defectus in inquisicione predicta inueniatur michi non reputetur, set balliuis libertatis predicte'.[3] The sheriff of Devon once held inquisition in the full county court and returned both its verdict and that of a second held in Exeter, where the death had occurred,[4] but on another occasion he was content to leave the matter in the hands of the bailiffs of the city.[5] The sheriff of Lincolnshire took the coroners with him into the hall of pleas in the city of Lincoln where he held an inquisition which belonged within the liberty.[6] The sheriff of Northamptonshire declined to hold one in the county court because the prisoners concerned were not in his custody but in that of the abbot of Peterborough

[1] Cf. above, p. 353, n. 5; C. 144/15, no. 32; *Cal. Pat. Rolls, 1266–72*, 599.
[2] C. 144/2, no. 17.   [3] C. 144/30, no. 36.
[4] C. 144/33, no. 12.   [5] C. 144/32, no. 20.
[6] C. 144/33, no. 7.

until the abbot had been before the king and council with proof of
his franchise and the king had repeated his order.[1]

These examples suggest that the holding of the inquisition was
regarded as a serious matter and that the sheriffs expected the
returns to undergo close examination. Some took the trouble to
inspect them before they were sent off. One sheriff himself added
an answer to the question as to whether the prisoners were indicted or appealed before the itinerant justices, the verdict having
omitted this.[2] The sheriff might decline to execute the writ if he
had doubts as to it being right to do so in special circumstances, as,
for example, when a jury at a gaol delivery had failed to reach
agreement and the justices had remanded the prisoner to gaol
until the king gave orders about him. This sheriff did, however,
hold the inquisition when a second writ came.[3] There is evidence
to show that sheriffs did not always carry out their orders scrupulously, but the evidence in itself reveals that their failure to do
so might be brought to the attention of the central government.
Sometimes it was merely the failure to hold the inquisition which led
to a repetition of the order.[4] But this failure might be due to corruption not merely to inefficiency. Edward I had to write to the
coroners of Shropshire telling them to hold an inquisition *de odio
et atia*, since some of the enemies of the prisoner, Hugh de Walle
of Wenlock, had persuaded the sheriff to hold up the writ sent to
him and prevent the holding of the inquisition; they were also
to attach the sheriff to appear before the king to answer for this
contempt of his mandate.[5]

Irregularities are also sometimes revealed by the eyre rolls. For
example, the sheriff of Yorkshire put himself on the country when
accused of having extorted money before he would execute the
writ, and was found guilty of refusing to hold the inquisition *de
odio et atia* until he was paid 7 marks, and also of taking a further
40s. from the prisoner before he would release him in accordance
with the king's order following the verdict.[6] A scandalous inquisition
de odio et atia was reported at the Sussex eyre of 1279. Geoffrey son of
Mathew Knolle had killed a man and had been appealed but the
appellor did not now come to prosecute. Geoffrey had fled to

---

[1] *Chronicon Petroburgense*, Camden Soc. 107–8.   [2] C. 144/32, no. 18.
[3] J.I. 1/784, m. 25.   [4] e.g. C. 144/6, no. 19.
[5] C. 144/30, no. 19. The coroners' inquisition found that Hugh had been
accused *odio et atia* because he had brought an action by writ in the county court
against lord Roger Aleyn and others, including Mabel of Wenlok. No doubt
Aleyn's influence accounts for the sheriff's dereliction of duty. The charge against
Hugh was exaggerated, but not wholly spiteful. He had lodged with Mabel and
had struck her, breaking a rib. She appealed him of causing her to miscarry and
so slaying the child in her womb, but the jury at the eyre asserted that she had not
been pregnant. See J.I. 1/739, m. 81.   [6] J.I. 1/1060, m. 16.

Winchelsea to the house of Robert Paulin, who had gone to the king's court and obtained a writ *de odio et atia* addressed to the sheriff. Together with William Cokesbrain the sheriff held the inquisition *in camera*, when he should have held it in full county court; he returned the findings to the king's court and it was testified that Geoffrey was in prison when he was not, and afterwards he was mainperned in his absence. The sheriff could not deny all this so he was committed to custody.[1] Another sheriff took 2 marks to allow three prisoners out of gaol during the period when the writ was being obtained and the inquisition held, and they were then 'traditi in ballium' although they were already at large.[2]

It has been seen that the writ had for long been in theory available only to prisoners. Usually this rule was respected and if it was obtained on behalf of someone who was not in prison the inquisition would probably not be held. Some of those concerned might be there, some not. The latter would not be dealt with. Thus one sheriff sent off a return showing that a prisoner was not guilty, but explained that others 'contenti in breui non fuerunt in prisona ideo nichil actum est'.[3] Once the return had been examined and approved Chancery sent a second writ to the sheriff ordering him to release the prisoner if he could find mainpernors.[4] The sheriff had to keep it and a list of the latter ready to produce before the itinerant justices should they fail to bring him to court punctually.[5] In special circumstances the sheriff was ordered to send the list to the king, but this does not appear to have been a normal requirement.[6]

The returns in C. 144 make it possible to study the way in which the writ was used and still more the response of the jurors to it and, if their verdicts are to be accepted, the situation which rendered it so necessary. But their veracity is, of course, open to doubt. Verdicts *de odio et atia* in cases of excusable slaying have already been compared with the accounts given on the plea rolls when the cases have been identified there. It has been found that they tended to

---

[1] J.I. 1/915, m. 4ᵈ; C. 144/16, no. 40.

[2] J.I. 1/802, m. 46, where they were acquitted.

[3] C. 144/12, no. 8. Cf. C. 144/5, no. 25.

[4] No further payment was required for this, according to registers of writs.

[5] Failure to do so got several officials into trouble. Eyre rolls reveal that they were brought to task for releasing prisoners without warrant in cases in which the order for bail is in fact enrolled. For example, J.I. 1/872, m. 35ᵈ (Robert Atteheth), *Close Rolls, 1251–3*, 54; J.I. 1/695, m. 26 (Nicholas of Gloucester), *Close Rolls, 1234–7*, 144; J.I. 1/117, m. 60ᵈ (Walter de Tregavene), *Cal. Close Rolls, 1296–1302*, 352.

[6] As already seen the list was required when the inquisition was held in a county other than that in which the grantee was in gaol; cf. C. 144/23, no. 10; C. 144/29, no. 6. A writ apparently returned to Chancery is attached to the close roll for 1279 (C. 54/96, m. 4) and asks for the name of the mainpernors. But this also was an exceptional case in that the king himself had recently ordered the arrest.

be more lenient in finding excuses where trial juries thought the
killer had slain culpably, but that they sometimes asserted the
excuses with less corroborative detail than the subsequent verdicts
included. When the inquisition was held in cases where there was no
suggestion of excusable slaying, but the aim was solely to get bail on
a verdict that the prisoner was not responsible in any way whatever,
there is equal reason to feel scepticism. Some of the verdicts were
demonstrably false since in some cases where more than one suspect
obtained an inquisition the findings were mutually inconsistent.
A distinction must, of course, be made between the replies to the
questions as to whether the prisoner was guilty or maliciously
accused and, secondly, if he was not guilty, who was. Answers to
the latter were not mere *obiter dicta* but an essential part of the
inquisition. However, the jurors could not be expected to engage
in prolonged detective work and may often have dealt with it
perfunctorily, repeating rumours of precisely the type to which
they often attributed the prisoner's own situation. Sometimes, more
candidly, they admitted that they could not name the actual
slayer. Again, while the verdict might be correct in the main, it
could include details which were at variance with those described
elsewhere. Finally, while it might rightly exonerate the prisoner, it
might err in stating that he had been accused out of malice and the
motives attributed to his accusers could be pure guesswork.

The reliability of the verdicts in so far as they absolved the prisoner of guilt or confirmed the charge can be tested, very roughly,
by comparison with the findings in court in a considerable number
of cases. The difficulties of identification and comparison have
already been indicated in the discussion of excusable homicide.
In dealing with verdicts *de odio et atia* these difficulties are enhanced.
Many of the released prisoners were charged only with minor
complicity. Some do not even appear among those indicted at
the eyre, or at least have not been noticed. An exhaustive search
would undoubtedly yield many more identifications. Some hundreds
have been made and these should provide a fair sample, but even
so interpretation of the evidence is often uncertain. For example, if
the man who had obtained bail did not surrender to it at the eyre
this raised—and still raises—the presumption of guilt, but it does
not fully establish it. No doubt his mainpernors would be anxious
to keep track of his movements but still they might not succeed;
if he had died in distant parts they might be unaware of this and
so unable to see to it that his death was reported to the justices.
On the other hand, if his death was reported the question of his
guilt would not now be fully investigated. Accordingly, cases of
this last kind may provide no clue and have been disregarded here.
Another problem in attempting to get some idea of the proportion

of verdicts in court which conflicted with those *de odio et atia* is that several persons were often dealt with together in the inquisition but at the eyre some might be found guilty and others not. When only one inquisition was held, even though it dealt with several prisoners, it has been counted only once for the purpose of judging its reliability, so that disagreement on the guilt of one has been counted and agreement on the innocence of others disregarded. In this respect the count underestimates the numbers of prisoners who were properly released.

Excluding cases in which the verdict was excusable killing, or there is other evidence for this, enough information has been found to make some comparison feasible in nearly 250 of the cases in the C. 144 files, though there is still an element of doubt in some forty of them. In just on 20 per cent evidence from the eyre rolls appears to conflict seriously with the verdicts *de odio et atia*, prisoners who had secured bail now being found guilty and sentenced or being regarded as guilty *in absentia*. This figure accords closely with that obtained by a similar comparison with 50 odd verdicts *de odio et atia* known only from the close rolls: 21·4 per cent.[1] It suggests that the number of felonious slayers released as a result of apparently perjured or mistaken verdicts *de odio et atia* was not enormous, though if these are fair samples the total must have been considerable, approaching 200 under Henry III and almost as many under Edward I. Most of those whose fate is known from the eyre rolls were eventually punished by outlawry, but by no means all. Verdicts in their favour at the inquisitions might induce such a feeling of confidence that the guilty slayers risked standing trial and a number who had been bailed were in fact sentenced to death. Others appeared in court and claimed benefit of clergy. Thus the results of false verdicts *de odio et atia* were not quite as detrimental to order as they might seem at first sight, though undoubtedly many

[1] The same sort of comparison has been made for some 170 grants of bail recorded on the close rolls with no indication there or in the other evidence that an inquisition of any type had been held. It has been suggested that most of these grants also followed inquisitions *de odio et atia*. But the results vary noticeably between the reigns of Henry III and Edward I, and bear out this suggestion much better for the former than for the latter period. Under Henry disagreement appears in only 17·6 per cent of the cases. This suggests equal if not greater strictness in granting bail. But for the time of Edward just on 33 per cent of the grants were made to prisoners who later were thought guilty, and this points to some laxity, either the failure to require the verdict of an inquisition, or the acceptance of unfounded verdicts. Whatever the explanation, it seems clear that it was not more difficult to obtain bail now, and the falling off in the number of grants in the latter part of the reign cannot be ascribed to a stricter policy. The C. 144 figures also show a similar discrepancy, nearly all the verdicts from the time of Henry III which have been checked appearing to be confirmed; but there are so few of them that they cannot be taken as representative.

scoundrels saved their skins by this means. Possibly a few innocent men saved theirs too, for it may sometimes have been the jurors at the eyre who erred, not those at the inquisitions.

While some verdicts were too charitable to the guilty others were unjust to the innocent. Their answers to the question who was really guilty were unreliable. There were cases in which the prisoner exonerated by the jury *de odio et atia* obtained on his behalf was stated to be guilty by one obtained for someone else.[1] In others where more than one inquisition was held the blame might be laid on the same person, or on different persons but without diametrical contradiction. But the general reliability of the answers to this part of the inquiry can be tested more effectively by comparison with the eyre rolls, though this presents even graver problems of identification, and guilt or innocence was not always clearly established even there. Over 120 inquisitions have been compared on this point with entries on the rolls. This check suggests that there was general agreement in just over two-thirds, disagreement in nearly one-third. But this is an extremely rough estimate. There are cases in which the verdicts overlap, but are very far from coinciding, agreeing perhaps only on one name among several suspects mentioned by the two sets of jurors. When one member of a family was found not guilty by one jury and another member by a different one, agreement on the guilt of the rest of the family is not very significant. Again, when someone else had already confessed, been convicted or outlawed, the reliability of the jury *de odio et atia* on this issue was not seriously put to the test. Yet even a statement that someone else had already been executed for the slaying might be untrue, for one jury at least was later found to have invented a fictitious character and asserted that he had confessed and been beheaded in order to exonerate the guilty.[2] Other juries were quite

---

[1] C. 144/8, no. 2; C. 144/10, no. 5; C. 144/13, nos. 9, 15.

[2] This was in the case of Paulinus de Weteleye and his deceased brother, Thomas. The jury *de odio et atia* found that Hugh de Hale had killed Thomas, had confessed and been beheaded, and that Hugh's concubine had accused Paulinus out of malice (C. 144/17, no. 22). The presenting jury at the eyre disagreed with this and gave an unusually circumstantial account: the brothers, they said, fought each other through drunkenness as they came from the inn in Deneby; Paulinus struck Thomas in the chest with a knife and he died at once. This tallied with the verdict at the coroner's inquest. Paulinus had withdrawn but he now appeared and put himself on the country. The trial jury said that a certain Hugh la Ley drank with them in the inn at Deneby on a Sunday, and quarrelled with Thomas over some arrows made of poor wood which Hugh had sold him. Paulinus and Thomas beat Hugh, who went away but lay in wait for them as they journeyed home. The brothers parted, and as Thomas came along alone at dusk Hugh emerged from a ditch and slew him. The justices put this verdict down to corruption among the jurors, and had sixteen knights sworn in instead. Paulinus agreed to put himself on their verdict and the twelve trial jurors said they did not wish to challenge any

capable of finding scapegoats among the local people and asserting their guilt in order to give more weight to their exculpation of prisoners. Their answers to the question who is guilty were much more often proved erroneous than their assertions of the prisoners' innocence.

Most inquisitions *de odio et atia* which found the prisoners not guilty declared that they had been charged out of malice and hatred, but this was not a necessary corollary. It has been seen that some 80 per cent of these verdicts may probably be accepted as reliable so far as guilt or innocence was concerned, but it must not be assumed that 80 per cent or more of those who obtained inquisitions were altogether wrongfully detained. A good many who were eventually found not guilty of homicide were said at the eyre to have been implicated in some minor way, and some of these, though acquitted of homicide, now fined for their offences. The arrest of such persons was justified. Thus endorsement in court of the inquisition's finding of not guilty does not necessarily imply that the original charge was malicious. Jurors at inquisitions might themselves admit this. Their verdicts were not indiscriminately hostile to the accusers even when they favoured the accused. A few accusations were put down to the honest but mistaken convictions of appellors or presenting jurors. One charge was found not to have been made 'per aliquod odium vel atyam nisi per ignoranciam patrie', and another not 'per aliquod odium vel aliquam atyam set per quandam communem famam que laborauit in villa'.[1] Evidently it was not generally held that spreading rumour or failure to investigate it more thoroughly amounted to malice. Again, an innocent man might have been arrested owing to confusion with a guilty one who bore the same name; this, naturally, was found not to be due to malice.[2] Several verdicts stated that the accuser had relied on some circumstantial evidence and expressly excluded it. Though this evidence as summarized in some verdicts seems very slight,[3] it may have been enough to throw suspicion on the accused and the accusers may indeed have acted in good faith. This is more credible in some other cases in which the prisoner had

of them. The knights and jurors from the four neighbouring vills stated that the two brothers quarrelled on their way home from the inn at Deneby and Paulinus struck Thomas in the chest with a knife which penetrated almost through his body; he withdrew for a long time. They never knew Hugh de la Leye in those parts, nor had heard of any such person staying there. So Paulinus was hanged (J.I. 1/1060, m. 5).

[1] C. 144/18, no. 34; C. 144/30, no. 23.
[2] C. 144/18, no. 17.
[3] e.g. C. 144/4, nos. 25, 45; C. 144/34, no. 26; C. 144/9, no. 10 where three people were accused though not maliciously, merely because the killing occurred outside the hospice where they were staying.

been involved in a fatal brawl.[1] In such circumstances an appeal
might well not be malicious and presentment was proper, since the
jurors were required to name all the participants. Their arrest was a
wise precaution; equally, their release on bail was right when an
inquisition had absolved them from guilt. Some participants may
be thought lucky to have been treated in this way, but then, as has
been seen, those who had not themselves struck a mortal blow
were always treated leniently; they would probably be acquitted
of homicide if brought to trial and could easily secure pardon
beforehand from the king. But while the detention of those who had
taken an active part in the brawl was the correct procedure it was
less justifiable to detain persons who had been present but had taken
no part. However, juries sometimes considered charges against
them not malicious. It was found, for example, that a prisoner 'pro
alico hodio vel athia non fuit appellatus, solum eo quod interfuit
loco quo predictus Willelmus interfectus fuit'.[2] It accorded with the
severity of the courts in similar circumstances when a charge was
found not malicious against a man who had been sleeping in his
chamber at the time when someone was slain in the hall.[3] A similar
accusation against a woman who had failed to raise the hue and
cry when a man was killed in the house where she was present could
not be considered reasonable since she had herself been severely
wounded, and the jurors refrained from ruling out malice.[4] Circumstantial evidence was taken to exclude malice in the case of the
wearer of a burel surcoat who had been detained because someone
in a surcoat resembling his had been noticed at the scene of the
slaying.[5]

But even when there were some suspicious circumstances the
charge could have been prompted mainly by malice, and in several
cases where they acknowledged grounds for suspicion the jurors still
took the line that spite rather than reliance on too flimsy evidence
was responsible for the charge being made. Sometimes, perhaps,
they were influenced by knowledge of actual or possible motives.
In some cases of the detention of people who had been present the
reason for the jurors finding malice does not emerge.[6] This finding
was probably correct when the prisoner had responded to the hue
and cry or had been trying to stop the fight.[7] Yet even in such cases
the victim's associates might possibly have misunderstood attempts
at pacification. Again, it is difficult to judge whether accusations
against other members of the actual slayer's household and friends
as well as himself were spiteful, though juries were apt so to regard

---

[1] e.g. C. 144/7, no. 16.
[2] C. 144/3, no. 41; cf. C. 144/16, no. 17.
[3] C. 144/4, no. 15.   [4] C. 144/4, no. 23.   [5] C. 144/17, no. 43.
[6] e.g. C. 144/13, no. 57.   [7] e.g. C. 144/14, no. 62; C. 144/26, no. 3.

them.[1] Perhaps in some cases all the jurors really intended was to emphasize that the accusation was misguided.

In many cases where there was some sort of evidence against the prisoners the jurors ignored the question of malice;[2] others took refuge in an ambiguous reply,[3] but they were not always allowed to evade the issue; the sheriff might press for an answer.[4] In many of these rather dubious cases, then, the juries managed to refrain from pronouncing on the accusers' motives one way or the other. Perhaps they should still be given the benefit of the doubt. Yet very often the evidence against the prisoners was no more than some association with the actual killer or was too flimsy to give rise to genuine suspicion unless there was already some animus against them. About 100 of the C. 144 inquisitions found that there was some sort of evidence; the jurors were divided on the question of malice, finding it in a good many cases, sometimes keeping silence on it, denying it quite often. Their views on it, when stated, are not always convincing. The most that can be said is that in a fair proportion of these cases the charge may not have been malicious, and very often the jurors recognized this either tacitly or expressly.

In considering the juries' views on malice it is worth turning again to the returns which found justification or excuse. In these cases, the accusations presented a special problem. The writ *de odio et atia* was not really appropriate to them. The prisoners should have obtained an inquisition into the circumstances of the slaying and this could then have given a straightforward answer. But since the authorities did nothing to prevent their use of this writ to obtain bail many juries were faced with the question of malice when, especially if the prisoner had been indicted, it was beside the point. Nor were all appeals in these cases malicious or vindictive. Even an appeal against a justifiable slayer could be made in an honest attempt to clear the victim's good name. Thus a jury *de odio et atia* might have to give a negative or twisted answer even when they described the slaying as justifiable, or nearly so.[5] In the case of homicidal maniacs detention was most necessary and was not regarded as malicious.[6] Accusations in other types of excusable

---

[1] e.g. C. 144/12, no. 31; C. 144/14, no. 72, where neighbours were accused; C. 144/18, no. 28 (in this case the slaying had been in self-defence so there was reason to suspect malice); C. 144/24, no. 2; C. 144/26, no. 24 where killing by a servant of one of the accused had been in self-defence; C. 144/28, no. 7 where a brother and cousin of the slayer were accused, and no. 26 where among others a special friend of a slayer in self-defence was accused.

[2] e.g. C. 144/11, no. 6; C. 144/16, no. 26.   [3] e.g. C. 144/14, no. 49.

[4] e.g. C. 144/29, no. 15.

[5] e.g. C. 144/26, no. 27, where the question was taken to apply to the slayer's motives, not his accusers'.

[6] See C. 144/17, no. 53; C. 144/28, no. 27; C. 144/29, no. 46.

killing were more difficult to judge, as were those made when the
death had been completely accidental. Juries were nearly always
severe towards those who brought charges against people concerned
in fatal road accidents, as they took the usual lenient attitude to
riders and drivers who could not control their horses.[1] But apart
from these rather special cases, jurors were generally ready to
acknowledge that accusers could honestly have taken a different
view of an accidental slaying. Indeed, even if the prisoner had been
involved only in a very minor way and it completely exonerated
him from responsibility, the inquisition might find that the charge
was not malicious.[2] No malice was found in a number of cases of
accidental slaying of the types which usually required pardon.[3]
Rather surprisingly the appeal against 7-year-old Robert Parleben
was not considered malicious but to have been made 'eo quod
culpabilis'.[4] This verdict was probably too kind to the appellor,
but the good faith of those who secured the detention of the prisoner
was often recognized with better cause. There was even more reason
to acknowledge the accuser's good faith if the killing had been in
self-defence, and juries often did so explicitly.[5] On the other hand
they sometimes hesitated to be so definite and gave an ambiguous
answer, refrained from answering this question at all, or gave it
a twisted meaning.

Often, as has been seen, the jurors took the question about
odium and *atia* to relate to the prisoner's state of mind, not that of
his accusers. He had killed, they said, 'nullo odio seu atya' but in
self-defence,[6] or by mischance.[7] Occasionally, to be on the safe side
they denied that either the killing or the accusation had been *odio
et atia*.[8] Sometimes they made it very clear that they interpreted the
writ as ordering inquisition whether the slaying was excusable or
felonious. One verdict of slaying in self-defence concluded that the
victim had been killed 'sine aliqua alia atya precogitata vel aliquo
odio precogitato'.[9] Even a verdict which found death from natural
causes might take the question in this way and declare that the

---

[1] e.g. C. 144/4, no. 39; C. 144/16, no. 18.

[2] e.g. C. 144/11, no. 4; cf. C. 144/30, no. 31.

[3] e.g. C. 144/25, no. 10; C. 144/27, no. 31; C. 144/28, no. 4 (where the victim
had accidentally run on the prisoner's knife); C. 144/29, no. 26; C. 144/30, no. 1;
C. 144/34, no. 5 (for this case see above, p. 105, n. 2).

[4] C. 144/18, no. 16; cf. above, p. 154.

[5] e.g. C. 144/8, nos. 11, 21.

[6] C. 144/8, no. 7; C. 144/23, no. 16; C. 144/25, no. 4; C. 144/27, nos. 5, 20, 26;
C. 144/28, nos. 6, 9; C. 144/29, nos. 34, 42, 47, 49; C. 144/30, no. 33; C. 144/31,
nos. 1, 8 and 11.

[7] C. 144/27, no. 32; C. 144/28, no. 8; C. 144/29, no. 30; C. 144/31, no. 4.

[8] C. 144/25, no. 10.

[9] C. 144/31, no. 6.

prisoner 'nec odio nec atia est culpabilis'.[1] Giving this twist to the question obviated the difficulty of assessing the motives of those who had secured the detention of the prisoner concerned.

Juries seem, then, to have been at some pains to be fair to both the prisoners and those who had accused them. Anxious as they were to ensure that excusable slayers were released they showed some ingenuity in avoiding the conclusion that the charges against them were malicious. Most indictments and many appeals were not considered so although the slayings had been either justifiable or excusable in their view. If these cases are added to those in which there was some circumstantial evidence to explain the charge, quite a respectable number of the verdicts indicate that the prisoners had not been detained merely through malice. They led to the grant of bail to people who deserved it, yet whose arrest had been proper or at least not altogether uncalled for. Still the great majority of the verdicts found hatred and malice and there can be no doubt that a great many people were arrested and kept in prison for no other reason than spiteful accusation, or malicious innuendos creating false suspicions in the minds of presenting jurors.

When the inquisition found *odium et atia* it was required to account for them in detail. This the jurors were generally prepared to do, although the motives they attributed to the accusers were often preposterously trivial. In a few cases—under twenty—they found that the charge was malicious but professed themselves unable to suggest the reason for the malice. In a few others, they simply omitted to mention any cause for it. But the 'don't knows' were in a tiny minority. Those who served on the inquisitions would not easily admit defeat on this point. Often they produced not merely one but several grounds for spite. Sometimes they simply mentioned that there was bad feeling without going into more detail. But usually when they found the charges malicious they contrived to produce specific grounds for the malice, even though this involved scraping the bottom of the barrel of local gossip, rumour, and conjecture. Resourceful and ingenious as they were, they could not always discover any pre-existing enmity directly between accuser and accused and had quite often to fall back on motives attributed to a third party, or hostility towards a third party, such as a member of the accused's family, or his lord. Malice might be attributed to the appellor himself, to one of his relatives, his lord or lady, an acquaintance who procured the appeal by bribery or intimidation, or by promoting a joint venture in blackmail. In a great many cases the charge had been brought by a jury, whether at the coroner's inquest, the sheriff's tourn, or in a local court. The whole presenting

[1] C. 144/24, no. 13.

jury might be found to have acted from malice or to have been influenced by one malicious juror, or to have acted on the strength of information given to it or rumours put about by enemies of the prisoner.

In a good many cases the person who made or procured the charge had at some earlier date been beaten up by the prisoner. When this is stated baldly it is hard to judge whether it had generated enough lasting ill feeling to account for a capital charge being brought. Sometimes this may have been given as the motive in default of any other means of explaining the charge away. Still, it is a plausible enough motive—very plausible compared with some that were put forward—and probably was often the correct explanation. Nearly seventy accusations were found to have been made in the hope of extorting money or in pique because demands for it had been refused. Generally they were made by the widows of the deceased, either on their own initiative or at the instigation of a third party. Liability to malicious charges of homicide appears to have been an occupational hazard of local and especially manorial officials. Over sixty cases of malicious charges against officials occur in these files. The jurors *de odio et atia* seldom bothered to look for any motive beyond the desire for revenge for officiousness and petty tyranny, yet it may be assumed that most of these prisoners were indeed innocent since the jurors were most unlikely to be biased in their favour. The other most frequent reasons put forward to explain malicious accusations were disputes over land, rights of common, nuisances, debts, litigation resulting from these and other matters, criminal charges, spiritual ones in court Christian, quarrels and enmity between neighbouring villages or the men of different lords, trade rivalry, especially between innkeepers, attempts to divert suspicion from those actually guilty or even other innocent suspects. Finally, there were several cases in which the jurors found that the local bad character had been charged out of malice. He might be a drunkard who made a frequent nuisance of himself.[1] Other falsely accused prisoners owed their plight to unpopularity because they picked quarrels and were apt to fight.[2] These look like cases of giving a dog a bad name and the accusations may have been hasty and prejudiced rather than consciously malicious.

Although it is possible to fit the majority of the alleged motives for malice into these general categories there is plenty of variation in the details supplied and many of these stories are too circumstantial to be dismissed as mere copies of well-known models. The stories, or a great many of them, ring true. Whether they were in fact the true explanation of malicious charges is another matter. In some

[1] As in C. 144/32, no. 9.   [2] C. 144/13, no. 70; cf. no. 68.

cases, especially when there had been public threats of retaliation, the jurors may have leapt to the conclusion that the threats had been carried out in this way and looked no further for possible sources of suspicion against the prisoners. More often, probably, having decided that the prisoner was innocent, they looked around for anyone with a grudge against him and attributed perhaps to the first they found the circulation of malicious rumours. But it is significant that juries *de odio et atia* often found not one but several motives, attributing them either to one and the same accuser or to various accusers. This suggests that they recalled any occasions when the prisoner had given offence or any quarrels that he had had and held all those concerned responsible for putting them about, either individually or in concert. In such cases it seems that they can seldom have had any knowledge of the origin of the rumours, but could hope that one at least of their conjectures coincided with the truth. In many cases, however, an actual appeal had been made or it was known who had given the information on which the indictment was based, and, if they dissented from the charge, the jurors may have been hard put to it to dig up any grounds for malice. Even so, it may be that they did not invent so much as give undue credence and perhaps some touching up to such petty and common squabbles as they could unearth between accuser and accused or their associates. Thus the family likeness between these stories does not mean that they were generally baseless, although the jurors may quite often have erred in attributing malicious charges to them.

Some of the alleged motives were extremely trivial, yet very petty grievances, mortifications, and grudges may conceivably have led to charges which, perhaps, were not expected to be taken very seriously and the jurors need not be suspected of error in putting all of them forward. Even motives which now seem hardly credible were convincing enough to the thirteenth-century justices. It has been remarked that the motives for malicious charges were sometimes stated at the eyre, where the jurors or the appellee himself might declare an accusation to have been made *odio et atia*. Unfortunately, they were seldom recorded on the eyre rolls. One notes tantalizingly that the defendant had been defamed 'per athiam quam Juratores manifeste ostendunt'.[1] In the few cases which have been noticed the alleged malice was of one or other of the types found in the inquisitions *de odio et atia*, such as the wish to extort blackmail, spite over the impounding of beasts, an attempt to extinguish the appeal of wounding which the defendant had been bringing against the present appellor.[2] The justices seem to have been quite happy to accept such explanations of the motives for

[1] J.I. 1/358, m. 25.   [2] J.I. 1/497, m. 28ᵈ; J.I. 1/954, m. 50; J.I. 1/62, m. 2.

false charges and there is little reason to think that verdicts of this kind surprised anyone or raised doubts. A number of the inquisitions *de odio et atia* attributed false accusations to lords who hoped to secure the escheat of their tenants' lands on their conviction for homicide; this motive seems far-fetched, yet Bracton actually quotes it as a typical ground of malicious accusation.[1] Again, while it is unbelievable that the canons of Dodnash procured a charge of homicide against a donor of land and his wife because they wanted to be free of the allowance payable to the couple in respect of the land during their lifetime,[2] it is relevant to note that presenting jurors in 1285 indicted an abbot for killing a corrodian in order to save payment of the corrody.[3] The jurors *de odio et atia* may have been honestly mistaken, even though they were probably subconsciously biased against their secular and ecclesiastical superiors.

The cases in which prisoners released on bail as the result of an inquisition were later found guilty or placed in exigent at the eyre provide some clues as to the honesty of the findings on malice. It so happens that these particular verdicts tended to deny it or to ignore the question.[4] Many of them acknowledged that there were some grounds for suspicion, thus disagreeing with the juries at the eyre only in the weight they attached to the evidence against the prisoners. Moreover, several of those which did find malice supplied no explanation of it. Thus there seems to have been reluctance to invent motives for charges with which the jurors disagreed but which were plausible and were later to be upheld. A few of these verdicts found familiar motives which may have been borrowed, others more distinctive but not remarkably far-fetched ones. There is no obvious reason, so far as the content goes, to condemn them as the inventions of partisan jurors.

Nor does the evidence suggest that even the most outrageous and far-fetched verdicts at special inquisitions *de odio et atia* failed to convince the authorities. Not that all the verdicts were immediately accepted and followed by orders for release on bail. The returns were sometimes scrutinized with some care although it was impossible to insist always on an answer on all the issues, and gradually the attitude to them seems to have become laxer. In March 1250 a second writ went to the sheriff of Yorkshire complaining that the inquisition into the slaying of Thomas Dropedeuel and his son by four men had not been held adequately since he

---

[1] *De Legibus*, f. 143ᵇ. Yet even he would surely have rejected the verdict that three lords, the prior of Guisborough, the abbot of Byland, and Richard de Malebys all secured an accusation from this motive against one man for the death of a woman who had died from natural causes (C. 144/29, no. 41).

[2] C. 144/3, no. 22. [3] J.I. 1/619, m. 60.

[4] e.g. C. 144/30, no. 3; J.I. 1/409, m. 14.

had not informed the king 'quo odio et qua atia appellati sunt', and ordering him to hold another and more diligent one.[1] The date of this display of strictness may be significant. Lexington had just made his addition to the formula of the writ and evidently he was interested in it and determined to tighten up the procedure.[2] No doubt he was directly responsible for this second inquisition being required. His policy was continued, if not by his immediate successor as Chancellor, at any rate by Wengham, in whose first year of office at least three returns were found inadequate. One was endorsed 'set non videtur factum odio et atya quod per istam inquisitionem declaratur'.[3] In another case the Chancellor's dissatisfaction was expressed with some force: 'Quia inquisicio quam per te fieri fecimus . . . ob multas causas insufficienter facta est, tibi precipimus quod . . . diligenter inquiras. . . .'[4] In 1255 one inquisition was found 'insufficiens et male concepta',[5] and on 1 December no fewer than five writs went out demanding new inquisitions into the slaying of Alan le Pestur, with which a large number of Norfolk men had been found to have been charged maliciously, since the first inquisitions were deemed insufficient.[6] In the following year a return was rejected because it did not state either who was guilty or by what hatred and what malice the prisoners had been arrested,[7] but after this the first inquisitions appear nearly always to have passed muster, perhaps because the jurors came to have fewer scruples about putting forward conjectural explanations of the alleged malice.

Although the authorities sometimes demanded a more adequate reply to the question about the grounds for malice they do not seem to have hesitated to accept a verdict that the charge was malicious just because the malice was explained in an improbable way. And so far as can be seen, verdicts were seldom rejected or held to need to be supplemented. A considerable number of the inquisitions in C. 144—something like a fifth for the reign of Henry III—are not known to have resulted either in bail or pardon. But difficulties of identification probably account for some of these, and it certainly cannot be assumed that anything like this proportion failed to secure one or the other. Neither pardons nor orders for bail were invariably enrolled. Some of the defendants who appeared late or not at all before itinerant justices were stated to have been bailed on the king's order—in one case the sheriff actually produced the king's writ ordering bail[8]—although the writs were not apparently enrolled.[9] It cannot be said, therefore, that there is evidence for

[1] C. 144/3, no. 34.   [2] See above, p. 349.   [3] C. 144/4, no. 26.
[4] C. 144/4, no. 27.   [5] C. 144/1, no. 16.   [6] C. 144/4, no. 31.
[7] C. 144/4, no. 37.   [8] J.I. 1/1108, m. 9.
[9] e.g. J.I. 1/210, m. 28ᵈ; J.I. 1/238, m. 51; J.I. 1/302, m. 54; J.I. 1/323, mm. 44ᵈ, 54; J.I. 1/619, m. 62; J.I. 1/786, m. 15ᵈ; J.I. 1/1060, m. 2. The return of the

bail being refused in a great number of cases, but it is doubtful if it always followed automatically, even when the verdict was an unambiguous not guilty. Occasionally there is a note to show that the prisoners found it needful to apply for a transcript of the inquisition.[1] But applications of this kind seem to have been most exceptional, the order for bail normally being drawn up without any action by the prisoners once the return had been sent by the sheriff to the king or his Chancellor or his council; probably it was examined fairly perfunctorily and passed without difficulty except when there was confusion as to whether bail or pardon was sought. Even then it might be approved without much attention being paid to this point. One return is endorsed simply 'Rex concedit'; it showed that the victim had tried to stop a fight and had fatally wounded himself on an arrow held by a great friend of his.[2] The friend was pardoned on the strength of this return, though there is nothing on it to show that he was seeking pardon rather than bail.[3] The cases in which bail is not known to have been granted do not reveal a preponderance of unsatisfactory returns. In most there were firm assertions of innocence; indeed, there is a rather surprisingly high proportion of verdicts that the supposed victim was in fact still alive or had died a natural death.[4] Very few of these verdicts are obviously faulty, and where there are defects which may account for bail being denied they are generally points of form rather than substance, or minor omissions, such as failure to identify those who spread malicious rumours or to account for their malice.[5]

Some of the verdicts *de odio et atia* were deemed insufficient; some were contrary to later findings at the eyre. Some of the findings as to malice are frankly incredible. Yet there is evidence to show that many jurors took their duties seriously, struggling to be fair both to the accused and his accusers in spite of the difficulties presented by the actual formula of the writ. No doubt a good many

inquisition *de odio et atia* which found that Robert de Kinton had killed in self-defence is endorsed 'Ponatur per pleuinam', and a similar one concerning Henry del Parlur bears the order: 'Tradatur in Ballium corpus pro corpore usque aduentum Justiciarum', but no enrolments of these orders have been found. See C. 144/23, no. 15 (1283); C. 144/8, no. 7 (1293). Later Henry was pardoned on condition of serving in Gascony; see *Rôles gascons*, iii, no. 3057.

[1] e.g. C. 144/29, nos. 10, 34; cf. *Cal. Close Rolls, 1288–96*, 21; J.I. 1/1098, m. 73ᵈ; C. 47/86/26, no. 668; *Cal. Pat. Rolls, 1292–1301*, 40.

[2] C. 144/30, no. 1 (John de Fulewode).

[3] *Cal. Pat. Rolls, 1281–92*, 395. The inquisition had been held by the bailiffs of Tyndale and later at the eyre in Tyndale he produced his pardon. See J.I. 1/657, m. 8ᵈ.

[4] e.g. C. 144/10, no. 12; C. 144/18, no. 15; C. 144/27, no. 13; C. 144/28, no. 33; C. 144/29, no. 2; C. 144/30, no. 21.

[5] e.g. C. 144/5, nos. 18, 38; C. 144/7, no. 47.

favoured prisoners who were guilty, more, perhaps, than the evidence of the eyre rolls suggests. Some verdicts were flagrantly corrupt, such as that for Paulinus de Weteleye, yet it is worth remembering that he was found out in the end despite his procuring not one but two verdicts in his favour.[1] It should not be assumed that it was always easy to suborn all the jurors. On the whole verdicts as to the guilt or innocence of the prisoners compare favourably with those which found the slaying excusable. Answers to the question who else was guilty were less reliable. Answers to the questions about malice cannot be tested. Yet it is apparent that many juries were reluctant to ascribe it to accusers even when they disagreed with them. It cannot be doubted, therefore, that a great many of the attributions were made in good faith, and the motives often correctly assessed, unlikely as many were. Even allowing for much guess-work, gullibility, over-readiness to discover familiar grounds for malice, some deliberate inventions, it must be concluded that a great many findings and explanations of malice were true, An appalling number of charges were made not only from vindictiveness over substantial wrongs but also from petty spite arising from minor annoyances and humiliations. Thus the inquisitions *de odio et atia* did invaluable work in freeing on bail prisoners who should never have been detained, as well as some whose detention pending further investigation was not unwarranted. Their verdicts in so far as they influenced decisions taken subsequently in court, helped to save the falsely accused from conviction. Biased as many of them may have been, the guilty profited from them far less often than the innocent.

[1] See above, p. 363, n. 2.

APPENDIX II

Clerical Excusable Homicides

CLERKS who had slain excusably were in a strong position since they could seek either pardon or trial in an ecclesiastical court, where the worst penalty would be degradation, even if they failed to purge themselves. But the very fact that these alternatives were open to them was confusing. To be on the safe side many of them pursued both concurrently or by turns and thus the obscurity as to the correct procedure is intensified in these cases.

Clerks were likely to be better informed and better off than lay homicides. Accordingly, many obtained pardon before trial. Those who appeared before the king's justices already furnished with pardons were likely to claim benefit of clergy before producing the latter.[1] Probably this was in deference to the ecclesiastical rule against answering to charges of felony in secular courts, rather than to any fear that the pardons would be disallowed. The justices, ignoring the claim to benefit, would proclaim them in the ordinary way and pronounce firm peace. Some of the clerks who obtained favourable inquisitions before trial were content with bail. A fair number did not get any inquisition, perhaps because detention in the bishop's prison was not stringently enforced.

Some sixty cases before 1307 have been noted of clerks who had slain excusably, or had some claim to have done so, appearing in court without yet having secured pardon. Most of them claimed benefit of clergy, but two seem to have abandoned this claim and accepted trial by jury.[2] If the clerk persisted in his claim and this was backed by the bishop's representative, a verdict was taken to discover in what capacity he should be handed over, whether as guilty, not guilty, or excusable. Once this had been established he was delivered to him 'pro tali'.[3] A few who had been found by earlier inquisitions to have killed with excuse were now found guilty and handed over 'pro convicto'.[4] There might be some

[1] e.g. J.I. 1/1108, m. 4ᵈ.
[2] See C. 47/70/4, no. 103; C. 47/68/9, no. 224. Both had slain in self-defence.
[3] Those found not guilty might be handed over 'absque imprisonamento faciendo et purgatione capienda' (J.I. 1/664, m. 51), but generally they were acquitted. Those who would not agree to the jury were handed over as undefended. See J.I. 1/409, m. 12.
[4] e.g. John de Fulford, C. 144/28, no. 11, *Cal. Close Rolls, 1279–88*, 507, J.I.

difficulty over accepting the claim to benefit of clergy, either because
the bishop was not represented or because his agent, though present,
could not produce sufficient warrant to act for him in the case.
Possibly this apparent negligence was sometimes calculated absten-
tion. For example, Geoffrey son of Reginald claimed benefit at
the eyre but as no ordinary sought his delivery the justices ordered
that the truth should be inquired by the country; the jury found
that the victim, a woman, had found him sleeping with her daughter
and had seized him and raised the hue, asserting that he was a
thief; in the mêlée which followed her husband's servant wounded
him with intent to kill, but he knifed her and escaped. This was
regarded as self-defence; he was remanded and pardoned.[1] But
it is easy to see why the ecclesiastical authorities might prefer not
to become involved on his behalf. In more reputable cases their
representatives might be present and willing to claim the prisoner
but not be able to exhibit a proper warrant. This occurred in the
case of Richard de Slauston; a special delivery of Aylesbury gaol
had been appointed to try him and this may have meant that the
bishop of Lincoln had insufficient notice. The justices decided not to
hand him to the bishop's representative, though he was present,
but remanded him *ad gratiam*, as he was found to have killed 'per
infortunium et fugiendo'.[2] William Brun, who was found to have
killed in self-defence, was also remanded *ad gratiam* because the
bishop's representative had not got sufficent warrant.[3]

   Taken by themselves, these cases would suggest that it was normal
for the clerical excusable slayer to be handed over to purge himself
in court Christian and it was only when there was some hitch over
claiming him that he would be remanded to await the king's grace.
But other evidence does not bear out this inference. Many remands
ad gratiam followed verdicts of excusable slaying regardless of the
fact that the prisoners were properly claimed for the Church. There
seems to be no evidence on which to decide whether the prisoner
himself had any choice between this and remand. However, if he
wanted pardon his delivery to the bishop would be no obstacle to
obtaining it. Indeed, the decision on the plea roll to hand the clerk
over might be followed by the note that the king had sent for the

---

1/1098, m. 48[d]; Laurence le Broc, C. 144/17, no. 10, *Cal. Close Rolls, 1272–9*, 398,
J.I. 1/181, m. 6; William Shyrewald, C. 144/29, no. 24, *Cal. Close Rolls, 1288–96*,
18, J.I. 1/302, m. 77.

   [1] J.I. 1/302, m. 69[d]; *Cal. Pat. Rolls, 1292–1301*, 4. Another prisoner was remanded
quousque because no one claimed him but he seems to have killed with adequate
excuse; see J.I. 1/1256, m. 17[d].

   [2] C. 47/49/6, no. 196. He had surrendered after being placed in exigent at the
eyre. He was now granted bail, and pardoned a few years later; see above,
p. 283, n. 1.

   [3] J.I. 3/103, m. 4[d]. He also obtained bail; see *Cal. Close Rolls, 1296–1302*, 561.

record.[1] Half a dozen clerks got pardon after being handed over, apparently with a view to purgation; some did so at once,[2] others after considerable delay. John de Charwelton waited three years for his,[3] and John Huscarl a year. The tendency to vacillate between pardon and purgation is nowhere better illustrated than in his case. He had slain his brother Ralph in self-defence, according to the verdict at Somerton gaol delivery, and was handed to the custody of the bishop of Bath and Wells at the latter's peril.[4] He applied immediately to the king, who sent for the record on 23 January 1289. This record seems not to have produced any result and another was sent. It was over a year before his pardon was issued, dated to 16 February 1290. But meanwhile he purged his innocence before the bishop and a writ ordering the restitution of his lands, goods, and chattels was drawn up and enrolled under the date of 10 February; it was cancelled as he did not have it, no doubt because his pardon was at last ready and this in itself secured their restitution.

Confusion may sometimes have been engendered by the fact that clerical prisoners were entitled to be in ecclesiastical custody even after remand *ad gratiam*, though most seem to have been remitted to the king's gaol. Justices of gaol delivery at Warwick decided that one prisoner should be handed to those acting for the bishop to be kept in custody 'sub pena qua decet, ad expectandam gratiam Regis'.[5] This may well have left him wondering what action he was expected to take; he applied for pardon in the following year but it was not granted till three years after that.[6] Conversely, a clerk who was expected to make his purgation might in fact be detained in the royal prison because the bishop borrowed it; this again might well mystify the detainee.[7]

As with lay killers, uncertainty as to the justices' decision meant that some clerks were left in suspense. John Fairfax, for example, had responded to the hue and cry when several men broke into a house and beat up the occupants; the ringleader, Adam de Righton,

---

[1] e.g. J.I. 1/804, m. 76.

[2] John Dansy, J.I. 1/619, m. 59[d], *Cal. Pat. Rolls, 1281–92*, 216; Robert Artureth, C. 47/53/2, no. 42, *Cal. Pat. Rolls, 1281–92*, 138; Henry de Vernay, J.I. 1/65, m. 46[d], *Cal. Pat. Rolls, 1281–92*, 223 (he had earlier been bailed after an inquisition; see *Inquisitions Misc.* i, no. 2271); Roger de Midford, J.I. 1/497, m. 51, *Cal. Pat. Rolls, 1281–92*, 18.

[3] C. 47/71/5, no. 175; *Cal. Pat. Rolls, 1281–92*, 192.

[4] C. 47/77/6, no. 229; *Cal. Pat. Rolls, 1281–92*, 345; *Cal. Close Rolls, 1288–96*, 69.

[5] J.I. 3/101, m. 3[d].

[6] *Cal. Pat. Rolls, 1301–7*, 390. The statement here that he was in Warwick gaol was probably due to a misunderstanding.

[7] See C. 47/77/6, no. 214. This prisoner is not known to have taken any further action.

had refused to surrender and assaulted John with drawn sword; John had struck him with his sword and felled him to the ground, but Adam had got up and later been mortally wounded by someone else. At the county court it was found that Adam had not died of the blow John had given him, but at the eyre in 1293 the jury said that he would have died of this blow even if he had not been struck again. John claimed benefit of clergy, but the eyre roll concludes with 'ad iudicium', so it is possible that no decision was actually reached.[1] He might well have been recommended to mercy since he had killed, if at all, in self-defence and trying to arrest a criminal. He appears eventually to have been released, for he fought in the Scottish wars and in return for this service was pardoned, at last, in 1303.[2]

There is no discernible principle determining the justices' choice between remand and delivery to the bishop. The majority of the prisoners were expressly remanded *ad gratiam* even though they had duly been claimed for the church. Most of these eventually got pardon, but not all did so at once. All but two of those who were remanded at general eyres or sessions of oyer and terminer do seem to have applied for and obtained it forthwith, but fewer than half of those remanded at gaol deliveries did so. Several preferred immediate release on bail, less than half of these got pardon later on. There remain six cases in which the clerks remanded *ad gratiam* seem to have obtained neither bail nor pardon, though one of them must have taken some, probably abortive, action, since the king sent for the record of the gaol delivery.[3] One of the others was mad.[4] The numbers involved are, of course, very small and it is dangerous to generalize from them, but it looks as though some clerks were in no great hurry to seek pardon, some were content with bail for a time, others indefinitely, while a very few may not even have bothered to seek formal release in this way.

It is harder to discover the fate of those—twenty-three of them— delivered to the bishop, apparently with the intention that they should be dealt with in court Christian and who did not subsequently get pardon. The printed bishops' registers of this period contain a small number of letters relating to the purgation of criminous clerks, but unfortunately none has been found relating to clerks known from the plea rolls to have killed excusably. There is, however, another source of information: the close rolls. When an excusable slayer was delivered to the bishop the king would normally retain his free tenements and chattels in his hand until he was notified by the bishop that the clerk had successfully made his purgation.[5] The

---

[1] J.I. 1/1098, m. 59.   [2] *Cal. Pat. Rolls, 1301–7*, 181.   [3] J.I. 3/105, m. 6.
[4] J.I. 3/96, m. 10^d.   [5] See J.I. 1/361, m. 39; J.I. 1/1060, m. 24^d.

consequential order to those who had charge of land and goods to restore them or some other writ concerning them might be enrolled. Three entries of this sort have been found showing that John de Fynham, Geoffrey Segrave, and John Huscarl purged their innocence. All three had slain in self-defence.[1] Huscarl, as already noted, was pardoned as well. It should be observed that this type of evidence would not be available in some cases even though the clerk purged his innocence. One handed over fined at once with the king's justices to recover his chattels,[2] another for his land.[3] Others incurred forfeiture anyhow because they had fled. Moreover, orders for restoration might not be enrolled. Thus the paucity of evidence for purgation does not necessarily imply that only a tiny proportion of these excusable slayers made it. It is most unlikely that any appreciable number of them were unable to secure compurgators, though it has already been seen (p. 167) that in 1312 a mad clerk failed in his purgation. There is better reason to suppose that several could not or did not bother to attempt it. One handed over in 1279 was a lunatic.[4] Another was a monk.[5] At least six others had earlier been released on bail, and just as this seems to have convinced some laymen that there was no need to secure pardon after remand *ad gratiam*, so it may have persuaded clerks that there was no need to make purgation after delivery to the bishop; it is unlikely that he took the order to keep them in custody seriously; the accompanying threat 'at his peril' or *sub poena* suggests that the justices expected laxity on his part. This course would not, presumably, do for any beneficed clerk or one who aimed at a career in the church, but most of those concerned were probably in minor orders and had no such ambition. One was described as a tanner, another as under age.[6]

The information as to compurgation is so exiguous that it is impossible to establish the procedure in cases of excusable homicide. The three references to it use the expression 'purged himself' or 'purged his innocence', just as do entries relating to clerks who had been handed over 'pro convicto'. This seems to suggest that the excusable slayers found compurgators to swear to their innocence rather than to the validity of their excuses. This might raise difficulties among scrupulous clerks and seems, on the face of it, an improbable procedure. The earliest case observed of an actual commission to investigate an excusable slaying with a view to purgation, that from 1312, ordered inquiry both as to guilt and as to the clerk's mental condition at the time of the slaying. It appears

[1] *Cal. Close Rolls, 1272–88*, 479, J.I. 1/956, m. 46; *Cal. Close Rolls, 1279–88*, 382, J.I. 3/35ᴬ, m. 5ᵈ; *Cal. Close Rolls, 1288–96*, 69, C. 47/77/6, no. 229.
[2] J.I. 1/409, m. 4.   [3] J.I. 1/1060, m. 51.   [4] J.I. 1/1060, m. 1ᵈ.
[5] J.I. 1/1188, m. 23.   [6] J.I. 3/91, m. 4ᵈ; J.I. 1/736, m. 45.

that the excuse was an important factor, and it seems likely to have been taken into account in other cases, including the far commoner ones of self-defence and mischance, but possibly it was established in the investigation into the clerk's good fame and so on which was a preliminary to purgation, rather than being included in the actual formula of the oath.

Purgation was not in itself enough to satisfy the ecclesiastical authorities that the slaying had not rendered the clerk irregular. This was a point which needed an independent investigation, although the latter might take account of both the verdict in the secular court and successful purgation.[1] A meticulous clerk would take the initiative in getting the matter cleared up. Thus in 1296 one approached Archbishop Winchelsey, who instructed his commissary to hold an inquisition by clerks and trustworthy laymen into the death of a boy who had run up behind a chaplain and fatally injured himself on the sharp iron edge of a spade which he was carrying over his shoulder. The chaplain had been arrested but found innocent in the secular court 'quantum ad laicos pertinet'.[2] Later on, a deacon, who had struck and whose brother had killed one of a large gang of armed men as they attacked them and their father, even thought it prudent to go to the Pope at Avignon to obtain his decision whether this involved his irregularity.[3] Bishops were, however, competent to decide this issue, as the bishop of Exeter did in 1409 in a case of killing in self-defence.[4] In each case the circumstances described were held not to entail irregularity. Sometimes it was left to the bishop to initiate proceedings. Even a priest might refrain from getting him to pronounce on the matter, and it is of some interest to find an earlier bishop of Exeter refusing to admit the king's presentee to a benefice because he had notoriously committed homicide and the bishop did not know whether he had acted, as he claimed, in self-defence.[5] However, he ordered an investigation. An archdeacon took action against a vicar who had killed in self-defence, but this was beyond his competence and the bishop ordered an inquiry.[6] All but one of these cases come from a later period and they provide too scanty material for comparison of the definition of justifiable and excusable homicide in secular and ecclesiastical legal practice down to 1307.

[1] See *Reg. Lacy*, Canterbury and York Soc. ii. 21 (1436).

[2] *Reg. Winchelsey*, ibid. i. 137–8.

[3] *Reg. Greenfield*, Surtees Soc. cliii, no. 2868 (1317).

[4] *Reg. Stafford, Episcopal Registers of the Diocese of Exeter*, ed. F. C. Hingeston-Randolph, 77.

[5] *Reg. Brantyngham*, ibid. i. 165 (1385).

[6] *Reg. Grandisson*, ibid. i. 336 (1327–8).

BIBLIOGRAPHY

THIS is not an exhaustive bibliography of the later works used, though it has been necessary to rely mainly on original sources. There is no general study of the king's pardon in the Middle Ages, although it is discussed in passing in the general histories of English Law. Some aspects of his pardons for homicide and the related topics dealt with here have received special treatment in some of the other works listed below. These also include short accounts of pardoning in Ireland and Scotland. Mr. T. A. Green is completing a study of legal and social concepts of criminal liability in the fourteenth and fifteenth centuries which deals with homicides committed in self-defence, through accident and by the insane.

BENNETT, J. W., 'The Mediaeval Loveday', *Speculum*, xxxiii.

BLACKSTONE, W., *Commentaries on the Laws of England* (1773).

CAM, H. M., *The Hundred and the Hundred Rolls* (London, 1930).

CHRIMES, S. B., *Introduction to the Administrative History of Medieval England* (Oxford, 1952).

COOPER, LORD, *Select Scottish Cases of the Thirteenth Century* (Edinburgh, 1944).

DE HAAS, E., *Antiquities of Bail* (Columbia University Press, 1940).

GABEL, L. C., *Benefit of Clergy in England in the Later Middle Ages* (Northampton, Mass., 1929).

GALBRAITH, V. H., *Studies in the Public Records* (London, 1948).

GOEBEL, J., *Felony and Misdemeanor* (New York, 1937).

HALE, MATTHEW, *The History of the Pleas of the Crown.*

HAND, G. J., *English Law in Ireland, 1290–1324* (Cambridge University Press, 1967).

HAVARD, J. D. J., *Detection of Secret Homicide* (London, 1960).

HEWITT, H. J., *The Organization of War under Edward III* (Manchester University Press, 1966).

HOLDSWORTH, W. S., *A History of English Law* (London, 1923).

HUNNISETT, R. F., 'The Origins of the Office of Coroner', *Transactions of the Royal Historical Society*, 5th Series, viii.

—— *The Medieval Coroner* (Cambridge University Press, 1961).

HURNARD, N. D., 'The Jury of Presentment and the Assize of Clarendon', *English Historical Review*, lvi.

KAYE, J. M., 'The Early History of Murder and Manslaughter', *Law Quarterly Review*, lxxxiii.

KEAN, A. W. G., 'The History of the Criminal Liability of Children', *Law Quarterly Review*, liii.

KEEN, M. H., *The Outlaws of Medieval Legend* (London, 1961).

Kenny's Outlines of Criminal Law, 19th edition (1966).

LAPSLEY, G. T., 'The County Palatine of Durham', *Harvard Historical Studies*, viii.

McKECHNIE, W. S., *Magna Carta*, 2nd edition (Glasgow, 1914).

MAITLAND, F. W., *The Early History of Malice Aforethought*, Collected Papers, i.

—— *Bracton and Azo*, Selden Society, viii.

MAXWELL-LYTE, H. C., *Historical Notes on the Great Seal* (Stationery Office, 1926).

MOREY, A., Bartholomew of Exeter (Cambridge University Press, 1937).

OAKLEY, T. P., *English Penitential Discipline*, Columbia University studies in History, no. cvii (1923).

PERKINS, R. M., 'A Rationale of Mens Rea', *Harvard Law Review*, lii.

PHILLPOTTS, B. S., *Kindred and Clan* (Cambridge University Press, 1913).

PLUCKNETT, T. F. T., *A Concise History of the Common Law*, 5th edition (London, 1956).

—— *Edward I and Criminal Law* (Cambridge University Press, 1960).

POLLOCK, F., and MAITLAND, F. W., *The History of English Law before the Time of Edward I*, 2nd edition (Cambridge University Press, 1898).

POWICKE, F. M., *King Henry III and the Lord Edward* (Oxford University Press, 1947).

—— *The Thirteenth Century* (Oxford University Press, 1953).

PUGH, R. B., *Imprisonment in Medieval England* (Cambridge University Press, 1968).

RICHARDSON, H. G., *Bracton, the Problem of his Text*, Selden Society Supplementary Series, ii (1965).

—— and SAYLES, G. O., *Governance of Medieval England* (Edinburgh University Press, 1963).

—— *Law and Legislation from Æthelberht to Magna Carta* (Edinburgh University Press, 1966).

SAYRE, F. B., 'Mens Rea', *Harvard Law Review*, xlv.

SCHULZ, F., 'Bracton and Raymond de Peñafort', *Law Quarterly Review*, lxi.

STEPHEN, J. F., *History of the Criminal Law of England* (London, 1883).

TOUT, T. F., *Chapters in the Administrative History of Mediaeval England* (Manchester University Press, 1920).

WALKER, N. D., *Crime and Insanity in England* (Edinburgh University Press, 1968).

WINFIELD, P. H., 'The Myth of Absolute Liability', *Law Quarterly Review*, xlii.

—— *The History of Conspiracy and Abuse of Legal Procedure* (Cambridge University Press, 1921).

INDEX

PRINTED IN GREAT BRITAIN
AT THE UNIVERSITY PRESS, OXFORD
BY VIVIAN RIDLER
PRINTER TO THE UNIVERSITY